3006

SOCIAL WORK AND SOCIAL WELFARE
An Introduction

SOCIAL WORK AND SOCIAL WELFARE
An Introduction

Joseph Heffernan
University of Texas—Austin

Guy Shuttlesworth
University of Texas—Austin

Rosalie Ambrosino
University of Texas—Austin

WEST PUBLISHING COMPANY
St. Paul/New York/Los Angeles/San Francisco

Cover Image   Robert Rauschenberg, *Painting with Red Letter S,* 1957, oil and collage on canvas, 51″ x 52″, Albright-Knox Art Gallery, Buffalo, New York, Gift of Seymour H. Knox, 1959

Cover Design   David Farr, Imagesmythe, Inc.

Design   Merle Sanderson

Copyediting   Gnomi Schrift Gouldin

Artwork   Alice Thiede

Typesetting   West Publishing Company

Composition   Rolin Graphics, Inc.

Photos

I Frank Keillor/Jeroboam, Inc., 12 Kit Hedman/Jeroboam, Inc., 29 The Bettmann Archive, 46 Board of Education—City of New York, II Ed Buryn/Jeroboam, Inc., 69 Jane Scherr/Jeroboam, Inc., 100 James L. Shaffer Photography, 124 James Coit/Jeroboam, Inc., 151 James Motlow/Jeroboam, Inc., 161 courtesy of the National Committee on the Prevention of Child Abuse, 174 Jane Scherr/Jeroboam, Inc., 199 Peeter Vilms/Jeroboam, Inc., 218 Frank Smith/Jeroboam, Inc., 237 Billy Barnes/Jeroboam, Inc., 252 Bill Powers—Frost Publishing Group, Ltd., III Kit Hedman/Jeroboam, Inc., 278 Peeter Vilms/Jeroboam, Inc., 301 Bill Powers—Frost Publishing Group, Ltd., 314 Bill Powers—Frost Publishing Group, Ltd., 325 Jane Scherr/Jeroboam, Inc., IV Frost Publishing Group, Ltd., 349 United Nations, 353 cartoon courtesy of Ben Sargent copyright 1983 *The Austin American Statesman,* 363 Olaf Källstrom/Jeroboam, Inc., 371 Philip Jon Bailey/Jeroboam, Inc., 380 Bruce Kliewe/Jeroboam, Inc.

COPYRIGHT © 1988 By WEST PUBLISHING COMPANY
50 W. Kellogg Boulevard
P.O. Box 64526
St. Paul, MN 55164–1003

Library of Congress Cataloging-in-Publication Data

Heffernan, Joseph.
   Social work and social welfare.

   Bibliography: p.
   Includes index.
   1. Social service—United States.   2. Social workers—United States.   I. Shuttlesworth, Guy.   II. Ambrosino, Rosalie.   III. Title.
HV91.H424   1988   361.3′2   87–34505
ISBN 0–314–93185–6

to our students

CONTENTS

Chapter **12**   Old Age: Issues, Problems, and Services   **245**

Part **III**   Social Work: Its Practice and
Methodology   270

Chapter **13**   Direct Practice: Social Work with Individuals
and Families   273

Part **IV**   Special Issues   334

Preface

The approaches to social welfare have changed over the decades, but the problems to which the social work profession respond have remained. This does not occur because the profession has been ineffective, but because as society advances, so do the standards of what are called solutions. Thomas Merton has suggested that in a community of saints, sin needs to be redefined. So, too, with social problems and social responses. There is a rhythm of social responses to social welfare problems. At this time, poverty, child welfare, and the care of the dependent and neglected stand high on the social agenda. At other times, these problems are barely perceived while other problems demand public attention. It is our intent that this work will help the student develop a frame of reference for understanding social welfare and an approach to addressing social issues which will serve them well in times of commitment and retrenchment.

This is a collaborative work and we have all reviewed the chapters that were the responsibility of our co-authors. Where consensus was possible we sought it; where it was not possible we sought to identify, in their best light, the diverse views that exist about the established wisdom of social work. Each of us contributed the perspectives of our own education: sociology and psychology in the case of Ambrosino, sociology and history in the case of Shuttlesworth, political science and economics in the case of Heffernan, and social work for all three authors. The text is inter-disciplinary in that sense, but it is disciplined by the continuity and the certainty of unresolved social problems to which social work skills are relevant.

Four "referent groups" played an important role in improving this book: our families, our students, our colleagues in Austin, and our colleagues in the profession. We do not know exactly how Bob, Megan, Will, Jean, and Linda felt about supporting this project; we only know that they supported it. We have a better idea about how the clerical staff at the University of Texas School of Social Work, particularly Teri Carter, Kelly Larson and Emma Drozdowski, felt about keeping up with the various drafts of these chapters. They did more than type; they also served as first-line editors. We are especially indebted to Maria Swall-Varrington for her valuable input.

We also personally thank the diverse group of reviewers whose comments significantly contributed to the quality of this publication: Arthur Berliner, Texas Christian University; Richard Enos, North Texas State University; John Erlich, California State University—Sacramento; Bruce Hall, Colorado State University; Mark Lusk, Utah State University; Susan Robbins, University of Texas—Houston; Mona Schatz, Colorado State University; Carl Wilks, University of Tennessee—Memphis. Their input was greatly appreciated.

The referent group of greatest relevance has been our students. Their comments in classes over our collective sixty years of teaching helped us to shape our views of what they wanted and needed to know to become better social workers and citizens in our complex society.

Last but not least, we express our gratitude to our acquisitions editor, Thomas LaMarre, for his persistence and encouragement in the book preparation and publication. Also, many thanks to the production guidance and abilities of Mary Garvey Verrill of West Publishing Company and to all those who helped with this publication along the way. We hope this book itself contributes to the profession of social work.

SOCIAL WORK AND SOCIAL WELFARE
An Introduction

I

Introduction

This beginning section introduces the reader to the nature of social welfare and social work: what social welfare encompasses and what social workers who function in social welfare settings do. Historical and theoretical contexts also are provided that can be used as a framework for understanding subsequent chapters in the book.

Chapter 1, "Social Work: A Helping Profession," examines social welfare as a broad system intended to maintain the well being of individuals within a society. The roles and functions of social work professionals who work within the social welfare system also are explored. This chapter portrays the social welfare system and the profession of social work as challenging and dynamic arenas for those interested in careers in one of the helping professions.

Chapter 2, "Social Welfare: Past and Present," discusses the historical context of social welfare and social work. Selected historical welfare policies that have influenced the structure and format of our contemporary social welfare institutions are examined, and the evolution of social work as a profession is explored.

Chapter 3, "A Systems Approach to Understanding Social Work and Social Welfare," provides a theoretical framework for subsequent chapters. The social work profession's use of systems theory and an ecological perspective for viewing individuals within the broader context of their environment is explained. This framework is discussed from a broad societal perspective, a family perspective, and an individual perspective to help the reader see how this framework can be used at all levels by social work practitioners. An introduction to the problem-solving approach, a generalist social work approach that incorporates systems theory, also is explained.

These chapters lay the groundwork for content addressed in the remaining chapters of the book. A systems perspective and problem-solving approach serve as a framework for understanding the functions that social workers play in intervening in all settings and with all populations discussed in Section II. The methods of social work presented in Section III incorporate systems theory and the problem-solving approach. Finally, the special issues faced by the social welfare system and social work practitioners discussed in Section IV can be understood from a systems perspective and addressed using the problem solving approach.

1 Social Work: A Helping Profession

In a neighborhood community drug-abuse treatment center, social worker Tony Morales is leading a group of teenage boys who are residents of the center, helping them to develop skills in countering peer pressure from friends who are still using drugs. On the other side of town, Eloise Black, social worker at the adult activity center, oversees a group of volunteers preparing lunches for the meals on wheels program, which they will deliver to shut-in and elderly residents. The volunteers also provide companionship and monitor to ensure that the shut-ins and elderly are in stable health. At the downtown family service center, Grace Boyle, social worker, works with a small group of pregnant teenagers, assisting them in decisions regarding the management of their pregnancies. Across the hall, social worker Jan Smith counsels a young married couple experiencing marital conflict. South of town, Greg Jones, social worker with the adult probation service, assists a client in securing employment. Meanwhile, at the local office of the Department of Human Services, social workers Ida Green and Florence Nevil are meeting with local law enforcement officials to develop a cooperative relationship that will lead to a more efficient and helpful approach to handling problems of child abuse and neglect.

The situations just described represent only a few of the broad and diverse activities that encompass social work practice. Social workers are employed by a wide variety of local, state, and federal agencies as professionals who engage clients in seeking solutions to problems. The aim of this book is to provide the reader with an understanding of the goals and objectives of professional social work practice, the nature of the profession, and the types of problems that social workers assist their clients in resolving. Social work practice demands from its practitioners the utmost in intellect, creativity, skill, and knowledge. It is an exciting, challenging profession. Students who have the aptitude and desire to prepare for a career in the helping professions may find social work well suited to their needs and interests.

In this chapter, we will examine the professional culture, activities, knowledge base, and skills incorporated into social work practice. The broader field of social welfare, of which professional social work practice is the major discipline, also will be reviewed. But first, we will examine why people have unresolved problems and why they need professional assistance in seeking solutions to them.

WHY DO PEOPLE HAVE PROBLEMS?

No one is free from problems, and what may be a problem for one person is not necessarily viewed that way by another. For example, some people are very meticulous in their dress and spend hours putting their hair, clothing, and adornments in order so that their public appearance will reflect a state of perfection in personal grooming. Others appear to place little emphasis upon personal appearance. Decision making for some individuals comes only with great difficulty, while others seem to be little troubled with making choices.

Social workers deal with problems that inhibit optimal functioning for individuals and groups, or those that result in dysfunctional behavior. Poverty, marital conflict, parent-child relationship problems, delinquency, abuse and neglect, substance abuse, and mental/emotional stress are among the many problems brought to professional social workers for assistance.

Why do individuals develop problems of such magnitude that they need outside assistance for their resolution? That question may not be answered simply! It is obvious that no rational person plans to have debilitating problems. No child plans to spend a life in poverty, nor does an adolescent choose a life of mental illness. What newly married couple, much in love and looking forward to the future together, plans for marital disharmony, family violence, or divorce? Why, then, do these problems emerge? Why do some individuals experience happy, satisfying marriages, while others move from marriage to marriage without finding satisfaction? Why are some people prosperous and readily move up the occupational and income ladders, while others remain deeply enmeshed in poverty? A matter of personal choice? Of course not! Problems of social functioning result from an intermix of many factors. Briefly, we will examine the factors that contribute to adaptation.

Genetics and Heredity

From the biological standpoint, people are born with many of the physiological characteristics of their ancestors. Some people have a tendency to be tall, others short; some lean, others heavy; some physically attractive, others less attractive; and so on. Undoubtedly, many people have greater intellectual potential than others, some are more agile, others less so. To a certain degree these characteristics effect their adaptation and, indeed, opportunities throughout life. For example, regardless of skill or ability, it is virtually impossible for a 5'6" young man to become a professional basketball player, or for a somewhat obese young woman to be selected Miss America. Regardless of the desire or skill, opportunity is affected by physical characteristics. The reader is encouraged to think of other examples where genetic and/or hereditary factors might impose limitations on social behavior or opportunities.

Socialization

Whatever limits may be imposed by heredity, individuals develop as social beings through the process of **socialization**. Social behavior is learned behavior acquired through interacting with other human beings. Parents are the primary source of early socialization experiences. Family culture has a significant impact on the development of values, priorities, and role prescriptions. Families, of course, are not the only source of our social development. Neighbors, playmates, and those met at school and other community institutions also play a part. Children born to lower-income parents are socialized in a manner vastly different than those born to wealthy parents. Resources vary, and problem-solving opportunities are vastly different. Thus, the consequent development of behavioral repertoires varies greatly with learning opportunities afforded the individuals as they develop. The thoughts people have, and the mental attitudes they develop are as much a product of learning as are the skills they develop. Children who grow up in dysfunctional families often learn inappropriate techniques of problem solving!

Environmental

Geography, climate, and resources all effect quality of life and opportunities available for satisfactory growth and development. These factors vary throughout the land. Added to this are the economic and political forces that largely determine the availability of opportunities and resources around which people seek to organize their lives. Smog infested, polluted areas contribute to a variety of health problems. Unpredictable economic trends may result in hundreds and thousands of workers losing their jobs. Discrimination imposes limits upon opportunities for career development and securing adequate employment. The environment is a major element in the opportunity structure. It can serve as a stimulus for producing life's satisfactions or become a major source of the problems people experience.

SOCIAL WORK DEFINED

Social workers are actively involved in wide-ranging tasks, which makes a specific all-inclusive definition of social work difficult. For example, Box 1–1 lists some of the roles played by social workers today. Unfortunately, this has resulted in definitions that are so general that they fail to relate appropriately all of the activities that are encompassed by the profession. In an attempt to define the field of social work, Pincus and Minahan (1973) offer the following:

Social work is concerned with the interactions between people and their social environment which affect the ability of people to accomplish their life tasks, alleviate distress, and realize their aspirations and values. (p. 9)

Pincus and Minahan's definition is clear with regard to the goals of the profession. Perhaps, a more widely accepted definition is the one offered by the **National Association of Social Workers (NASW)**. This definition states that social work is

The professional activity of helping individuals, groups or communities enhance or restore their capacity for social functioning and creating societal conditions favorable to that goal. (NASW 1973, 4)

Broadly interpreted, both of these definitions are similar. Social work is viewed as an activity that seeks to remediate human problems by assisting individuals, groups, or communities to engage resources that will alleviate those problems. In addition, social work is concerned with enabling clients to develop capacities and strengths that will improve their social functioning. As these definitions indicate, social work is an active, "doing" profession that brings about positive change in problem situations through problem solving or prevention.

Box 1–1
Roles For
Social
Workers

Outreach worker: A social worker who identifies and detects individuals, groups or communities who are having difficulty (in crisis) or are in danger of becoming vulnerable (at risk) works as an outreach worker.

Broker: The social worker who steers people toward existing services that may be of service to them is called a broker in the same way that a stockbroker steers prospective buyers toward stocks which may be useful to them.

Advocate: A social worker who fights for the rights and dignity of people in need of help advocates their cause.

Evaluator: A social worker who gathers information, assesses problems and makes decisions for action is, among other things, an evaluator.

Mobilizer: A social worker who assembles, energizes and organizes existing or new groups takes the role of mobilizer. This is most often a community organization role, although not always.

Teacher: A social worker whose main task is to convey and impart information and knowledge and to develop skills is a teacher. This role may or may not be played in a formal classroom situation.

Behavior changer: A social worker who works to bring about change in behavior patterns, habits and perception of individuals or groups is a behavior changer.

Consultant: A social worker who works with other workers or other agencies to help them increase their skills and solve client's problems is a consultant.

Community planner: A social worker who works with neighborhood groups, agencies, community agents or government in the development of community programs is called a community planner.

Data manager: A social worker who collects, classifies and analyzes data generated within the welfare environment is a data manager. This role may be performed by a supervisor, administrator, or it may be carried out by a clerical person with the necessary skills.

Administrator: A social worker who manages an agency, a facility, or a small unit is operating in the role of administrator.

Care giver: A social worker who provides ongoing care—physical, custodial, financial—for whatever reason is acting as a care giver.

Betty J. Piccard. *An Introduction to Social Work: A Primer,* fourth edition, pp. 27–28. Homewood, IL: The Dorsey Press, 1988.

THE EARLY YEARS

Professional social work developed slowly over the years as a result of efforts to refine and improve its knowledge and skill base. As will be discussed further in Chapter 2, the early administration of relief to the needy was accomplished by a wide variety of individuals: overseers of the poor, friends and neighbors, church members, the clergy, philanthropists, and friendly visitors, among others. As early as 1814, the Reverend Thomas Chalmers expressed concern over wasteful and inefficient approaches used by relief programs and sought to encourage the development of a more humane and effective system for providing services and support. Chalmers emphasized the need for a more personalized involvement with the needy. He devised a system wherein his parish was divided into districts, with a deacon assigned to investigate each case in order to determine the causes of problems. If the resultant analysis indicated that self-sufficiency was not possible, an attempt was made to engage family, friends, neighbors, or wealthy citizens to provide the necessary assistance for the needy. As a last resort, the congregation was asked to provide assistance (Pumphrey & Pumphrey 1961).

Later, in the United States, the Association for Improving the Conditions of the Poor (New York City) and the Charity Organization Society (Buffalo, New York City, and Philadelphia) used similar approaches when organizing activities to help the poor. The **Charity Organization Society (COS)** had a profound effect on establishing social work as a specialized practice. The COS promoted "scientific philanthropy," emphasizing that charity was more than alms giving and had as its "long-run goal . . . to restore the recipient of charity to the dignity of as much self-sufficiency and responsibility as he could manage" (Leiby 1978, 111–112). Furthermore, the COS stressed the importance of individual assessment and a coordinated plan of service. The COS was the first relief organization to pay personnel to investigate requests for assistance and to refer eligible applicants to one or more existing agencies for intensive aid and supervision. Special emphasis was given to "following up" on the recipients of assistance, and efforts were made to secure someone to establish friendly relationships with them (Leiby 1978, 112–135).

Just as "friendly visiting" was encouraged, attention also was given to data collection and assessment. It was believed that a more structured, informed and skillful approach would increase efficiency, discourage dependence upon charity, lead to personal development and self-sufficiency, and reduce the practice of providing relief for chronic beggars.

This structured approach to managing charitable efforts quickly resulted in the need for trained workers. Mary Richmond, a major contributor to the COS movement (and considered by many to be the founder of the professional social work movement), inaugurated the first training program for social workers at the New York School of Applied Philanthropy, the forerunner of schools of social work. Richmond also formulated the concept and base for **social casework,** a practice method designed to "develop personality through adjustments consciously effected, individual by individual, between men and their environment" (Richmond 1922, 9). She also maintained a keen interest in personality and family development and stressed the environmental influence within which interpersonal interactions transpired. Believing that environmental factors were significant contributors to personal as well as family dysfunctions, she maintained a strong interest in social reform that would promote a better quality of life for individuals (Leiby 1978, 124). Richmond was convinced that this task should be included in the social worker's sphere of responsibility. In her classic work, *Social Diagnosis* (1917), she laid the framework for social casework practice. Under the impetus provided by Richmond, Jane Addams, and other early social work pioneers, a profession was born.

Schools of social work began to emerge along the Eastern seaboard and in larger cities of the Midwest, emphasizing direct social work practice (casework). Many were influenced by newly developing psychological perspectives, most notably those of Sigmund Freud and Otto Rank. Schools adopting Freudian psychology were more prevalent and became identified as "diagnostic" schools. Schools incorporating Rankian theory were known as "functional" schools. Shaping of curriculum around psychological theories increased the scientific knowledge base for social work practice.

By the late 1920s, **social group work** had gained visibility as a method of social intervention. Although not identified as a "treatment" modality, learning and social development were believed to be enhanced through structured group interactions. This technique soon found popularity in settlement houses and in work with street gangs, organized recreational clubs, and residents of institutions. Social group work became well entrenched as a viable helping method and later was adopted as a social work method.

Community organization had its roots in the New York Society for the Prevention of Pauperism, the Association for Improving Conditions of the

Poor, and the Charity Organization Society. It became prominent as a resource development method by the late 1930s. Dealing largely with community development and stressing the importance of citizen participation and environmental change, community organizers plied their skills in identifying unmet human needs and working toward the development of community resources to meet those needs. Skills in needs assessment, planning, public relations, organizing, influencing, and resource development were among the prerequisites for community organizers.

By the 1950s, social casework, group work, and community organization were all considered to be methods of social work practice. In 1955, the various associations established to promote and develop each separate method merged and became known as the National Association of Social Workers (NASW). NASW continues to serve as the main professional organization for social workers today, with a membership in excess of 100,000. NASW seeks to promote quality in practice, stimulates political participation and social action, maintains standards of eligibility for membership in the association, and publishes several journals, including *Social Work*. Each state has an NASW chapter with a designated headquarters, and local membership units are active in all major cities.

UNDERPINNINGS OF THE PROFESSION

Social work practice is based upon values, knowledge of human behavior, practice skills and planned change. Each of these attributes will be briefly described.

Values

Social workers are committed to the dignity, worth, and value of all human beings, regardless of social class, race, color, creed, gender, or age. The value of human life transcends all other values, and the best interest of human beings merits a humane and helpful response from society. People with problems, regardless of the nature of those problems, are not to be judged, condemned or demeaned. Social workers emphasize that nonjudgmental attitudes are essential for maintaining the client's dignity and privacy, and that clients must be accepted as they are with no strings attached. Furthermore, clients (or the **client system**, which may include more than one individual, such as a family or a group of retarded adults) have the right to autonomy, to determine courses of action that will affect their lives. Likewise, groups and communities hold these fundamental rights.

Knowledge

Social work practice is derived from theories of human behavior as well as experimental knowledge related to practice. Research is an integrally important contributor to understanding individual, group, and community behavior.

Research also is a method of identifying more effective interventive techniques. Students of social work are expected to have an understanding of the life cycle, personality development, social dysfunctioning, developmental processes, group dynamics, the effects of discrimination, social policy formulation, research methods, and community environments. Schools of social work encourage students to become familiar with a wide range of social and behavioral science theories that serve as a basis for understanding how client systems adapt and cope with problems and how theory guides planned social intervention. This knowledge undergirds the social worker's practice competence.

Practice Skills

Social workers are familiar with techniques related to direct practice with individuals (casework) and groups (group work), as well as communities (community organization). Organizing, planning, and administration also are included as areas of specialization for many social work practitioners. Research skills are essential for practice competence, too.

Planned Change

Professional social work intervention is based on a process of planned change. Change is indicated when client systems present dysfunctional problems that go unresolved. Planned change is an orderly approach to problem solving and is based on problem assessment, knowledge of the client system's capacity for change, and focused intervention. The social worker functions as a change agent in this process. Planned change is characterized by purpose and a greater likelihood of predictable outcomes derived from the change effort. Box 1–2 presents a statement of the purpose of social work formulated by social workers.

SOCIAL WORK METHODS

Social workers are committed to the process of planned change. In their role, they become agents of change, who focus on improving the conditions that adversely effect the functioning of clients (or client systems). Change efforts may be geared toward assisting individuals, groups, or communities (or all three), and appropriate methods of intervention for achieving problem solutions are engaged. Practice methods incorporate social work values, principles, and techniques in

1. helping people obtain tangible resources;
2. counseling and psychotherapy with individuals or groups;
3. helping communities or groups provide or improve social and health services and
4. participating in relevant legislative processes that effect the quality of life for all citizens.

Box 1–2
Working
Statement on
the Purpose of
Social Work

The purpose of social work is to promote or restore a mutually beneficial interaction between individuals and society in order to improve the quality of life for everyone. Social workers hold the following beliefs:

The environment (social, physical, organizational) should provide the opportunity and resources for the maximum realization of the potential and aspirations of all individuals, and should provide for their common human needs and for the alleviation of distress and suffering.

Individuals should contribute as effectively as they can to their own well-being and to the social welfare of others in their immediate environment as well as to the collective society.

Transactions between individuals and others in their environment should enhance the dignity, individuality, and self-determination of everyone. People should be treated humanely and with justice.

Clients of social workers may be an individual, a family, a group, a community, or an organization.

OBJECTIVES

Social workers focus on person-and-environment in interaction. To carry out their purpose, they work with people to achieve the following objectives:

Help people enlarge their competence and increase their problem-solving and coping abilities.

Help people obtain resources.

Make organizations responsive to people.

Facilitate interaction between individuals and others in their environment.

Influence social and environmental policy.

To achieve these objectives, social workers work with other people. At different times, the target of change varies—it may be the client, others in the environment, or both.

Developed by participants at the second meeting on conceptual frameworks hosted by the National Association of Social Workers.

Direct Practice with Individuals, Families, and Groups

When the social worker's effort is focused on working directly with individuals, families, or groups, the process is called **direct practice** with individuals (casework). This type of method is geared toward helping individuals, families, and groups identify solutions to personal or other problems related to difficulty in social functioning. In many instances, problems related to social inadequacy, emotional conflict, interpersonal loss, social stress, or the lack of familiarity with resources create dysfunction for individuals. Practitioners are skilled in assessment and know how to intervene strategically in providing assistance for those problems. Direct practice is often considered to be therapeutic in nature.

Direct Practice with Groups (Group Work)

Group work techniques seek to enrich the lives of individuals through planned group experiences. Group work stresses the value of self-development through structured interaction with other group members. This process is based upon theories of group dynamics and encourages personal growth through active participation as a group member. Groups may be natural (already formed), such as street gangs, or formed purposefully at the group work setting, such as support groups. In either instance, the value of participation, democratic goal setting, freedom of expression, acceptance, and the development of positive attitudes through sharing is stressed. Group work generally is not considered to be therapeutic nor should it be confused with group therapy, which also utilizes group processes. Group therapy is designed to be therapeutic in that it seeks to alter or diminish dysfunctional behavior through the dynamic use of group interaction. Members of therapeutic groups often share common emotionally distressing experiences (e.g., a group of recent divorcees) and through focused discussion develop options for more adaptive behaviors.

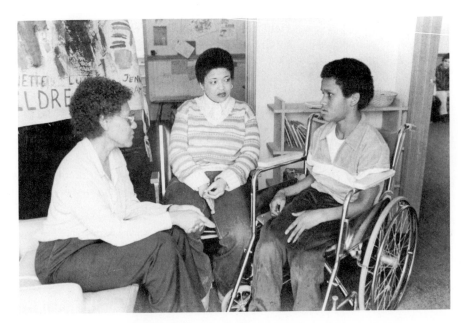

Social workers take on many roles in working with people. Here, a single mother and her disabled son receive counseling about family problems.

Community Organization

Social workers who practice at the community level utilize techniques of community organization to promote change. Recognizing that citizen awareness and support are vital to the development of resources in generating a more healthy and constructive environment for all citizens, community organizers work with established organizations within the community such as Lions and Kiwanis clubs, city governments, welfare organizations, the Junior League, political groups, social action groups, and other citizens' organizations in order to gain support for needed services and to secure funding for their maintenance. Social workers who intervene at this level may be employed by city governments, planning agencies, councils of social agencies, or related community agencies.

Social Work Research

While all social workers are involved in using research, many social workers specialize in social work research. This serves to increase both the knowledge base of practice and the effectiveness of intervention. Research also provides an empirical base upon which more focused policy formulation may be designed. Social research is essential in the process of establishing a scientific framework for problem solving and refining social work practice methods. Evaluative research enables agencies as well as practitioners to gain a better understanding of the effectiveness of efforts designed to meet goals and objectives around which practice efforts are focused. Competent social work practitioners keep abreast of the professional research and utilize research findings in their practice.

Social Work Administration and Planning

Administration and planning is a social work method that seeks to maximize the effective use of agency resources in problem solving. Administrators must be skilled in organizing, planning, and management techniques, as well as having knowledge about social work practice. Many social agency administrators begin their careers as direct practitioners, subsequently become supervisors, and then move into administrative roles. Social planning also is seen as a social work role, which is discussed in Chapter 15.

SOCIAL WORK: PROFESSIONAL ISSUES

Social workers are all too often identified as "welfare" workers, which, in the minds of many, links them primarily to public assistance. Obviously, this is a false premise, since social workers engage in practice in a wide range of service areas. **Social welfare** is the provision of institutional programs for the needy. **Social work,** on the other hand, is one of the professions that is instrumental in administering planned change activities prescribed by our social welfare institutions. Social work, like professional fields such as nursing and public administration, has experienced resistance in being acknowledged as a profession. To the extent that this is an important question, one really needs to ask, what are the characteristics of a profession?

Ernest Greenwood (1957) suggests that a profession is identified by the following characteristics:

1. a systematic body of theory;
2. professional authority;
3. sanction of the community;
4. a regulative code of ethics;
5. a professional culture.

Does social work possess these attributes? There is sufficient evidence that these characteristics are embodied in the social work profession. Education for social work practice is predicated on the foundations of social and behavioral sciences, as well as theory and knowledge produced by social work research and years of experimental practice. The social worker's authority is acknowledged by the community and clients who are involved with the profession. Authority presumes the social worker's expertise, including assessment capabilities as well as knowledge about appropriate interventions designed to alleviate problems. Community sanction for social work practice has become more evident within recent years through state laws requiring registration, certification, or licensing of social workers. The National Association of Social Workers has established a code of ethics (Box 1–3) for its members, and a strong professional culture has developed and is expressed through the conduit of state and national associations (such as NASW) of social work practitioners. The increasing number of social workers engaged in private practice also contributes to the recognition of social work's professional status. All evidence suggests that social work meets the standards identified by Greenwald for professional status.

Box 1–3
Code of Ethics
National
Association of
Social
Workers

This code is intended to serve as a guide to the everyday conduct of members of the social work profession and as a basis for the adjudication of issues in ethics when the conduct of social workers is alleged to deviate from the standards expressed or implied in this code. It represents standards of ethical behavior for social workers in professional relationships with those served, with colleagues, with employers, with other individuals and professions, and with the community and society as a whole. It also embodies standards of ethical behavior governing individual conduct to the extent that such conduct is associated with an individual's status and identity as a social worker.

See Appendix A for the entire *Code of Ethics*.

THE SOCIAL AGENCY

The majority of social workers perform their professional functions through the auspices of a social agency. **Social agencies** are organizations that have been formed by communities to address social problems experienced by a significant number of citizens. Agencies may be *public* (funded by taxes), *voluntary* (funded through contributions), or in increasing numbers, proprietary (profit-oriented). The typical social agency is headed by a board of directors of local citizens. It meets regularly to review the agency's activities and to establish policy that governs agency services. Many larger agencies have an administrator who has sole responsibility for supervising the agency's activities. In many smaller agencies, the administrator also may be involved in assisting clients with their problems.

Agencies are community resources that stand ready to assist in resolving problems that make day-by-day functioning difficult. Social workers are employed to carry out the mission of the agency. Many agencies do not charge fees for the services they provide. In some instances, however, agencies employ a "sliding fee scale" and adjust the fee to the client's ability to pay. All clients, regardless of ability to pay, are afforded the same quality of service.

Typically, agencies cooperate in meeting human need. Referrals are often made when clients have problems that can be resolved more effectively by another agency. Interagency coordination is a helpful process, maximizing community resources to bring about problem resolution.

EDUCATION AND LEVELS OF SOCIAL WORK PRACTICE

Professional social workers are involved in assisting clients with a large variety of problems. As a consequence, the nature and degree of skills necessary to effectively achieve problem resolution vary with the complexities of the problems encountered. Recognizing that professional competence is a right clients have in seeking assistance, regardless of how difficult their problems might be, the social work profession has established three differing levels of practice for meeting these divergent needs. The profession has also established the **Council on Social Work Education (CSWE).**

Bachelor of Social Work

The entry level for professional social work practice is the baccalaureate (BSW) degree. Social work practitioners entering practice at this level must complete the educational requirements of an undergraduate social work program accredited by the Council on Social Work Education. Currently, in the United States, there are 348 (CSWE 1986) accredited BSW programs. While professional social work educational programs offered by colleges and universities may vary, CSWE mandates that each must provide basic education in human growth and behavior, social policy, research, practice methods, and culturally divergent groups as a minimum requirement for meeting accreditation standards. All students who graduate from an accredited BSW program must complete 480 clock hours of field experience in a social work or related setting under the supervision of a social work practitioner. Students are placed in settings such as senior citizens centers, battered women's shelters, child welfare agencies, residential treatment centers, juvenile and adult probation programs, public schools, health clinics, hospitals, industry, and mental health agencies.

Educational curriculum for baccalaureate level practice is developed around the generalist method of practice. Typically, the generalist practitioner is knowledgeable about the systems approach to practice and is skillful in problem assessment, interviewing, resource development, case management, the use of community resources, in engaging clients in establishing intervention objectives, and problem solving. Baer and Federico (1978) have outlined **competencies** that undergird social work practice at the BSW level:

1. *Identify and assess situations where the relationship between people and social institutions needs to be initiated, enhanced, restored, protected, or terminated.*

2. *Develop and implement a plan for improving the well-being of people based on problem assessment and the exploration of obtainable goals and available options.*

3. *Enhance the problem-solving, coping and developmental capacities of people.*

4. *Link people with systems that provide them with resources, services, and opportunities.*

5. *Intervene effectively on behalf of populations most vulnerable and discriminated against.*

6. *Promote the effective and humane operation of the systems that provide people with services, resources and opportunities.*

7. *Actively participate with others in creating new, modified, or improved service, resource, opportunity systems that are more equitable, just, and responsive to consumers of services, and work with others to eliminate those systems that are unjust.*

8. *Evaluate the extent to which the objectives of intervention were achieved.*

9. *Continually evaluate one's own professional growth and development through assessment of practice behaviors and skills.*

10. *Contribute to the improvement of service delivery by adding to the knowledge base of the profession as appropriate and by supporting and upholding the standards and ethics of the profession. (pp. 86–89)*

Entry-level social workers are employed by agencies offering a wide spectrum of services. As direct practice workers, they may perform professional activities as eligibility workers for state human resources departments; work with children and families as protective services (protecting children from abuse and neglect) workers; serve as youth or adult probation workers; work in institutional care agencies that provide services for children, adults, or the aged; engage in school social work; be employed as program workers or planners for areawide agencies on aging; serve in mental health outreach centers or institutions; be employed as family assistance workers by industry; or perform their professional tasks in many other agencies providing human services. It is not uncommon for baccalaureate level professionals with experience and demonstrated competence to be promoted to supervisory and administrative positions.

Social work professionals at the BSW level of practice are eligible for full membership in the National Association of Social Workers. The professional activities they perform in helping clients resolve problems are challenging and rewarding. Many social workers desire to practice at this level throughout their careers. For others, an advanced degree in social work is desirable and opens up areas of practice that are not typically in the domain of the baccalaureate (BSW) practitioner. For those who have completed their undergraduate social work education from an accredited college or university, advanced standing may be granted by the school of social work to which they apply. Although not all graduate schools accept advanced standing students, the Council on Social Work Education provides a listing of those that do. Advanced standing students, when admitted to a graduate program, are able to shorten the time required to secure the Masters Degree without diluting the quality of their educational experience. Advanced practice in social work is predicated upon the Masters Degree in Social Work (MSW).

Master of Social Work (Advanced Practice)

Approximately ninety-one (CSWE 1986) colleges and universities have accredited graduate schools of social work. Students in these programs are engaged in an educational curriculum that is more specialized than the BSW curriculum. Students may specialize in direct services (casework or group work), community organization, administration, planning, or research. All students master a common core of basic knowledge, including human growth and behavior, social policy, research, and practice methods related to their area of specialization. Many graduate programs also offer fields of specialization, such as social work with the aged, child welfare, medical social work, industrial social work, mental health, or social work with the developmentally disabled. The two-year MSW program is balanced between classroom learning and clinical (field) practice. Graduates seek employment in such specialized settings as Veterans Administration hospitals, family and children's service agencies, counseling centers, and related settings that require specialized professional education.

Doctorate in Social Work

Professional social workers interested in social work education, highly advanced clinical practice, research, planning, or administration often seek advanced study in programs offering the Doctorate in Social Work (DSW) or the Doctor of Philosophy in Social Work (PhD). A number of graduate schools of social work offer education at this level. Students admitted tend to be seasoned social work practitioners, although this is not a prerequisite for admission to all schools. Education at this level stresses research, advanced clinical practice, advanced theory, administration, and social policy. Graduates usually seek employment on the faculties of schools of social work or in the administration of social welfare agencies, or with increasing frequency, in private clinical practice.

SOCIAL WORK CAREERS

The number of employed social service workers grew from 95,000 in 1960 to 385,000 in 1979 (U.S. Department of Labor 1982, 120). However, federal funding reductions have reduced the rate of growth of new jobs in social work. Based on current funding trends and federal priorities, it is unlikely that a similar growth pattern will be forthcoming. This should not discourage the student interested in the human helping professions. While some areas of practice currently are experiencing a zero growth rate, others are beginning to emerge with a vast potential for creative jobs for new workers. The field of aging is a good example. As more members of our population grow older, the need for additional support services is increased.

Social work is an ideal profession for individuals interested in working with people and in problem solving. That, in essence, is the heart of the social work profession. Positions in a wide variety of areas continue to attract social workers at all levels of practice, such as child welfare, health, corrections, mental retardation, family counseling, substance abuse, minority relations, and public assistance programs.

Wages in social work usually are adequate and increases are based on skill and experience. Baccalaureate level workers typically earn less income than the more specialized master's degreed workers. Entrance salaries may range from $15,000 to $25,000 per year depending upon experience, degree, location, and agency sponsorship. A few social workers earn upwards of $75,000 after extensive experience. Mobility often is a valuable asset to the worker looking for an initial social work job. Rural areas often experience shortages of workers while some metropolitan areas have a tighter employment market. Employment vacancies often are listed with college placement services, state employment commissions, professional associations, state agencies, or local newspapers.

SUMMARY

In this chapter, we have reviewed briefly the history of the development of social work, examined the practice base of the profession, identified the practice methods employed by social workers, discussed the professional attributes of the profession, and defined social work. When we move to specific social problem areas, the activities of social workers who work in those problem areas will be presented in greater detail. First, however, a brief review of the development of the social welfare institution will be presented.

KEY TERMS

Charity Organization Society
    (COS)
client system
community organization
competencies
Council on Social Work
    Education (CSWE)
direct practice
National Association of Social
    Workers (NASW)

social agencies
social casework
social group work
social welfare
social work
social worker
socialization

DISCUSSION QUESTIONS

1. What factors contribute to the problems that people experience?
2. Define *social work*. What are the goals of social work practice?
3. Trace the development of social work as a profession. What events do you feel were the most consequential in the development of the profession?
4. Differentiate among the various methods of social work practice. How are the methods similar? Different?
5. What are the underpinnings of the profession? How do they relate to social work practice?
6. Identify the levels of professional social work practice. How do these practice levels relate to professional education for social work practice?
7. Describe the competencies that undergird baccalaureate social work practice.

REFERENCES

Baer, Betty L., and Ronald Federico. 1978. *Educating the Baccalaureate Social Worker.* Cambridge: Ballinger Publishing Company.

Council on Social Work Education. 1986. *Colleges and Universities With Accredited Social Work Degree Programs.* Washington, D.C.: Author.

Greenwood, Ernest. 1957. "Attributes of a Profession," *Social Work* 2 no. 3 (July): 44–45.

Leiby, James. 1978. *A History of Social Welfare and Social Work in the United States.* New York: Columbia University Press.

National Association of Social Workers. 1973. "Standards for Social Service Manpower." New York: National Association of Social Workers; Itasca, Ill.: F. E. Peacock Publishers, Inc.

Piccard, Betty J. 1988. *An Introduction to Social Work: A Primer.* Homewood, Ill.: The Dorsey Press.

Pincus, Allen, and Anne Minihan. 1973. *Social Work Practice: Model and Method*. Itasca, Ill.: F. E. Peacock Publishers, Inc.

Pumphrey, Ralph E., and Muriel W. Pumphrey. 1961. *The Heritage of American Social Work*. New York: Columbia University Press.

Richmond, Mary. 1917. *Social Diagnosis*. New York: Russell Sage Foundation.

Richmond, Mary. 1922. *What is Social Casework?* New York: Russell Sage Foundation.

U.S. Department of Labor. 1982. *Occupational Outlook Handbook; 1982–83 Edition*. Washington, D.C.: U.S. Government Printing Office.

Zastrow, Charles. 1986. *Introduction to Social Welfare Institutions*. 3d ed. Chicago: The Dorsey Press.

SELECTED FURTHER READINGS

Compton, Beulah R., and Burt Galaway. 1975. *Social Work Processes*. Homewood, Ill.: The Dorsey Press.

Epstein, Laura. 1980. *Helping People: The Task-Centered Approach*. St. Louis: The C. V. Mosby Company.

Howell, Joseph J. 1972. *Hard Living on Clay Streets*. New York: Association Press.

Klein, Alan F. 1972. *Effective Groupwork*. New York: Association Press.

National Association of Social Workers. 1981. *NASW Standards for the Classification of Social Work Practice: Policy Statement 4*. Silver Springs, Md.: NASW Task Force on Sector Classification.

Slavin, Simon. 1978. *Social Administration*. New York: Haworth Press.

Tripodi, Tony, Phillip Fellin, Irwin Epstein, and Lind Roger. 1972. *Social Workers at Work*. Itasca, Ill.: F.E. Peacock.

2 Social Welfare, Past and Present

Social Workers of this period [the late 1800s] were outraged at the impossible living and working conditions of the poor and immigrant city dwellers who were crammed into slum housing, working long hours seven days a week.

. . . In 1889 Jane Addams founded Hull House in Chicago to serve this population. Similar organizations soon followed in New York and other urban areas. Settlement houses provided a center for neighborhood activity—places where people were able to become acquainted, form relationships in small interest groups, share in recreational and cultural offerings, and begin to learn how to live in the cities of America. At the settlements, neighbors met each other through dances, clubs, and recreational activities, and found much needed services such as health clinics, legal and housing counseling and nurseries. Citizenship classes were a particularly prominent part of these early settlement programs. Here, many adults for the first time gained some understanding of their rights under a democratic form of government; in addition, immigrants learned English and prepared for citizenship tests. (Fink 1974, 244–45)

What is social welfare? Who gets it? Who pays for it? Does it create dependency? Why is our social welfare system organized as it is? Social welfare in our society long has been a matter of dispute and controversy. Often the controversy surrounding the topic of social welfare results from a misunderstanding of the policies that govern social welfare as well as misinformation about people who are entitled to receive benefits. Welfare clients often are viewed as ne'er-do-wells or idlers, who are too lazy to work and are willing to live off the labor of others. Others identify them as victims of a rapidly changing society who lack necessary employment skills. Some view poverty, mental illness, unemployment, broken homes, lack of income in old age, and related problems as matters of personal failure or personal neglect. It is understandable, then, that people who hold divergent views would have different opinions about the nature of social welfare programs and the people served by them.

Determining who is in need has always been a problem in our society. This is particularly true in relation to providing assistance for those who are poor but appear to be able to work. This concern has resulted in analyses that are often incorrect and ill-founded. Does it seem reasonable to assume that individuals who are poor purposefully elect a life of poverty? Why, then, does the problem persist? Assessments which conclude that the poor have elected such a lifestyle, are lazy, or lack motivation often fail to consider how changing social systems contribute to outcomes that result in poverty for a substantial portion of the population. A frequent distinction is made between the needy poor and the undeserving poor. Many individuals are more accepting of the needs of the aged, disabled, and chronically ill. In this chapter, we will examine selected historical welfare policies that have influenced the structure and format of our contemporary social welfare institutions.

A DEFINITION OF SOCIAL WELFARE

What is social welfare? Definitions invariably reflect the definer's knowledge and value base. A broad definition of what constitutes social welfare may well include all organized societal responses that promote the social well being of its population. This definition would include, at least, education, health, rehabilitation, protective services for adults and children, public assistance, social insurance, bilingual education, services for the physically and mentally disabled, job training programs, marriage counseling, psychotherapy, pregnancy counseling, adoption, and a myriad of related activities designed to promote social well being. Perhaps the most widely accepted definition of social welfare is provided in the *Encyclopedia of Social Work,* which states that

> *Social welfare is an organized effort to insure a basic standard of decency in relation to the physical and mental well-being of the citizenry . . . [it] is characterized by a large complex of interlocking preventive and protective laws and organizations designed to provide at the least, universal access to the mainstream of society . . . [it involves] the everpresent, active assistance to individuals and groups to facilitate their attaining and maintaining a respectable lifestyle. (p. 1503)*

Social welfare denotes the full range of organized activities of public and voluntary agencies that seek to prevent, alleviate, or contribute to the solution of a selected set of social problems. The length and breadth of that list of social welfare problems are dependent on one's taste for specificity. By convention, social welfare problems are those problems associated with the attainment of a socially accepted minimum standard of living. Social welfare programs are designed, presumably, to ensure that the specified standard, in fact, is available to selected populations within a nation. In some instances, the standard is provided directly by the agency to the client, while in others the agency is structured to assist recipients to achieve the standard by their own effort. The standards sought are by no means uniform throughout the land; for example, those applied to the widowed mother and child are not the same as those applied to the unmarried mother and child. In some instances, the difference reflects a conscious social choice, while in others, the differences reflect accidents of history and/or geography. There is no one social welfare program in this country but, in fact, thousands.

As Wilensky and Lebeaux point out, social welfare programs may be of an institutional or residual nature (1965). **Institutional programs** are traditional, first-line efforts that, along with the market place and the family, are designed to meet the expected needs of individuals and families. For example, it is well established that people grow old and leave the work force. Their need for income, however, remains constant. Social insurance is designed to provide minimal incomes for eligible older adults, thus making the transition into retirement less traumatic and more secure. By contrast, **residual programs** come into play only when the normal structures of society have failed to meet the expected needs of individuals and families. Thus, residual programs are reactive and are expected to withdraw as soon as the institutional programs again are able to meet these needs. Depression relief programs are examples of residual social welfare programs. In fact, many residual programs, such as public assistance, which have been needed over protracted periods of time, have become institutional in nature.

THE VALUE BASE OF SOCIAL WELFARE

Any discussion of social welfare, its development, and social welfare organizations would be incomplete without identifying the value context within which they occur. **Values** are assumptions, convictions, or beliefs about the manner in which people should behave and the principles that should govern behavior. In as much as values are beliefs, they may vary with socialization experiences. Many values are dominant and are supported by the majority of the population. For example, life is viewed as sacred and taking another's life is viewed as a criminal offense by rich and poor alike. On the other hand, support of capital punishment is a value around which our society is divided.

The history of the development of social welfare reflects differences in values as they relate to social responsibility for making provisions for the needy. Values, however, are not the sole determinant of social policy. Availability of resources, coupled with economic, religious, and political influences, results in an evolving policy of social responsibility for the disadvantaged. One dominant value that has guided our social welfare system development is humanitarianism, which is derived from our Judeo-Christian background. The social application of humanitarianism, however, often is obscured by the resolve to find the most efficient and effective way to help the needy.

Our society also is influenced largely by the economic doctrine of **laissez faire**, which stresses limited government involvement, individualism, and motivation. Government welfare programs are viewed as a threat to those cherished and desirable ends. Problems of the poor and the disenfranchised are perceived as a matter of personal failure that only would be perpetuated by government welfare programs. Social responsibility for the needy, from the laissez faire point of view, would be carried out through volunteerism aimed at encouraging the needy to become self-sufficient. Work is considered the only justifiable means of self-maintenance, since it contributes to the productive effort of society.

Other values maintain that we all are members of society and, by virtue of that membership, are entitled to share in its productive effort. This belief argues that people become poor or needy as a result of inefficient social institutions. For example, the continually changing economic system results in layoffs, unemployment, obsolescent jobs, and transiency. Individuals do not cause these conditions—rather, they are victimized by them. Minority group members may suffer from inferior educational resources, limited (and usually menial) job opportunities, poor housing, and less than adequate health resources. No thoughtful analysis would lay blame for these conditions upon minority group members but would clearly identify institutional discrimination as the causal factor.

When considering these two value positions, the reader can readily understand that there are wide variations regarding societal responsibility for the needy. In our discussion of the historical influences that have converged to shape our present social welfare structure, the reader should look for value positions which have contributed to social policy formulation.

OUR ENGLISH HERITAGE

In England, prior to the period that has become known as Mercantilism, care for the poor was primarily a function of the Church. By extending themselves through charitable efforts to those in need, parishioners fulfilled a required sacred function. The resources of the Church usually were sufficient to provide the relief that was made available to the poor. The feudal system itself provided a structure that met the needs of most of the population. With the breakdown of the feudal system and the division of the Church during the Reformation, organized religious efforts no longer could provide for the increasing numbers of poor. Without the Church or the feudal manor to rely upon in times of need, the poor were left to their own means of survival. This often meant malnutrition, transiency, poor health, broken families, and even death.

Many of the poor found their way into cities where they were unwanted. Employment was always a problem, since most of the poor were illiterate and their skills generally were related to agricultural backgrounds. Many turned to begging. Local officials were pressed to find suitable solutions for the problem. As Europe struggled with the transition from an agricultural society to an industrial one, the numbers of dislodged persons increased. National practices differed but, in England, legislation originated in parishes throughout the country to deal with problems of the homeless, the poor, and dependent children.

Overseers were appointed by magistrates to assume responsibility for the poor residing in the various parishes. The overseer assessed the needs of the poor and made judicious responses to those needs. The role played by overseers was important, since it usually was their judgment alone that determined the fate of the poor.

Analyses of the situation invariably led to the conclusion that problems were of an individual nature and likely resulted from the economic transition. Unfortunately, legislation often had punitive overtones, which added to the burden of the poor and left them hopelessly entwined in impoverished conditions with little opportunity to find a way out. In response to these alarming conditions, the Elizabethan Poor Law [Liz 43] was passed in 1601. This legislation is significant in that it attempted to codify earlier legislation and establish a national policy for the poor. The **Poor Law** established "categories" of assistance, a practice found in our current social welfare legislation.

The first of two categories was designed for individuals considered to be "worthy," since there was little doubt that their impoverishment was not a fraudulent attempt to secure assistance. These included the aged, the chronically ill, the disabled, and orphaned children. Those eligible typically were placed in almshouses (poorhouses), where the physically able assisted the ill and disabled. This practice was referred to as **indoor relief,** since it provided services to the poor by placing them in institutions. In some instances, children were placed with families and often were required to work for their keep.

The second category included the able-bodied poor. Here, programs were less humane. Some of the able bodied were placed in prisons, others were sent to workhouses, and many were indentured to local factories or farms as slave laborers. Unlike the worthy poor, the able-bodied poor were assumed to be malingerers or ne'er-do-wells, who lacked the motivation to secure employment. The treatment they received was designed to serve as a deterrent to others, as well as to punish them for their transiency and idleness.

This act was to be of crucial significance in that it established the guiding philosophy of public assistance legislation in England until 1834 and in the United States until 1935. The important aspects of the law (Axinn & Levin, 1975, 10) that should be established in this connection are the establishment of

1. clear government responsibility for those in need;
2. government authority to force people to work;
3. government enforcement of family responsibility;
4. responsibility to be exercised at the local level;
5. residence requirements.

The Elizabethan Poor Law was enacted less out of altruism and concern for the poor than as an orderly process of standardizing the way in which they were to be managed. It established a precedent for subsequent social legislation in the United Kingdom as well as the United States.

SPEENHAMLAND

Although the Poor Law remained the dominant legislation under which services to the poor were administered, attempts were made to create labor laws that would serve as an incentive for the poor to engage in employment. One such effort took the form of "minimum wage" legislation and was enacted in Speenhamland in 1795. Motivated by a desire to induce large numbers of the poor into the labor market, the Speenhamland Act provided for the payment of minimum wages to workers and their families. Wages were adjusted according to family size, thereby assuring minimally adequate income even for the largest of families. Employers were encouraged to pay minimum wages and, where this was not possible, the government made up the difference. It was anticipated that business would be stimulated to produce more commodities through the added incentives provided by the government subsidy that, in turn, would create a need for more workers. Unfortunately, the effect of the subsidy program was to drive wages down, and employers then turned to the government to make up the difference.

The Speenhamland Act was not designed specifically to be a social welfare reform measure, although it did have implications for the working poor, the unemployed, and the impoverished. In effect, it was a work incentive program. While important symbolically, the overall impact of the Speenhamland Act was nominal. It ultimately was rejected by employers, expensive for the government, and never applied uniformly. It did establish the principle of government subsidy for private employers, a practice that is relatively widespread in our society today.

SOCIAL WELFARE IN COLONIAL AMERICA

Early American settlers brought a religious heritage that emphasized charity and the brotherhood of mankind. They also brought with them the heritage of the English Poor Laws. America, in the early days, was a land of vast natural resources, and settlers found it essential to work hard in order to survive. When neighbors became needy through illness or death, church members usually were quick to respond. No formal government network for providing assistance existed on any significant basis. Later, as the population increased, many colonies passed laws requiring that immigrants demonstrate their ability to sustain themselves or, in the absence of such ability, sponsors were required to pledge support for the new arrivals. Transients were "warned out" and often returned to their place of residence (Federico 1983, 98). In some instances, the homeless and unemployed were returned to England. Times were difficult, the Puritan work ethic embedded deeply, and with little surplus to redistribute to those in need, assistance often was inadequate. The practice of posting names of habitual paupers at the town house was a routine procedure in many towns and villages.

It is difficult to obtain reliable estimates of the magnitude of public welfare in colonial America. One important fact was that the presence of an indentured servant system rekindled in this country a replica of feudal welfare. In the indentured system of the Middle Colonies and the slavery system of the Southern Colonies, there was a clear lack of freedom for the pauper class. Often overlooked, however, was the existence of a set of harsh laws—reasonably enforced up until the time of Independence—which required masters to meet the basic survival needs of servants and slaves. (Almost half of all colonists came to the country as indentured servants.) Ironically, as the economy matured from plantation to artisan and became preindustrial in character, there also was an increase in its uncertainty. The result was that public relief was the largest expenditure in the public budgets of most major cities at the time of the Revolution.

Concomitantly, the rigid restraint of the Poor Law philosophy was thoroughly consistent with the fact that the colonial economy was one of extreme scarcity. Colonial law stressed the provision of indoor relief, that is, relief given within an almshouse, where paupers could be conveniently segregated and put to tasks that at least paid for their meager keep. The apprenticeship of children reflected a belief in family controls for children and stressed work and training for productive employment. Also, the deification of the work ethic and the belief that pauperism was a visible symbol of sin permitted a harsh response to those in need, as a means of saving their souls.

CHANGING PATTERNS AFTER THE REVOLUTION

Between the American Revolution and the Civil War, several broad patterns of welfare emerged, all of which were thoroughly consistent with the basic tenets of the Elizabethan Poor Laws. The American separation of church and state forced a severance of the connection between parish and local welfare office. Nevertheless, many states—most, in fact—retained a religious connection with the requirement that at least one member of the welfare board must be a "licensed preacher." Local governments accepted grudgingly the role of welfare caretaker and adopted rigid residency requirements.

The most important shift in this period was from indoor to **outdoor relief**. Outdoor aid, with its reliance on aid in-kind and work-relief projects, was most adaptable to the volatile economics of the first half of the nineteenth century. This led some to see early American welfare as principally an instrument for the regulation of the supply of labor. The contrary evidence, that it essentially is a fiscal choice, stems from the observation that the shift to outdoor relief occurred within places of both labor shortage and labor surplus.

Another significant movement before the Civil War was the shift away from public sector to private sector welfare, or voluntary welfare. The responsibility for welfare therefore was left to charitable institutions rather than remaining a public concern.

CARING FOR THE URBAN POOR

As the new nation grew, cities began to appear on the Eastern seaboard. With immigrants arriving regularly, jobs often were difficult to find and a large population of displaced poor began to emerge. Persons interested in those less fortunate sought avenues for meeting the needs of the poor. Although attaching the poor to subsistence level employment usually was the goal, there was concern over assuring that basic needs were met until income could be derived through employment. Although almshouses often were used to care for the chronic poor, outdoor relief found increased acceptance as a suitable way of caring for the poor. Outdoor relief was a practice of providing cash assistance to persons who remained in their own homes. Differing segments of the population found cause for alarm in both the practices of indoor and outdoor relief.

One of the earlier major organizations to seek solutions to problems of poverty was the New York Society for the Prevention of Pauperism, established in 1817. This society sought to find the causes of poverty and to remedy them. Following the precedent established by Thomas Chalmers in England, the society divided the city into districts and assigned "friendly visitors" to each district to assess and respond to the needs of the poor (Friedlander & Apte 1974, 21). Later, in 1843, the Association for Improving the Condition of the Poor was established in New York City to coordinate relief efforts for the unemployed. One significant technique introduced by the association was the requirement that relief could not be disbursed until the individual's needs were assessed so that agencies providing relief could do so more effectively.

Perhaps the most effective relief organization for the poor was Buffalo's Charity Organization Society. A private organization modeled after London's COS, it was founded by wealthy citizens who embraced the work ethic yet had compassion for the deserving poor. The COS sought to add efficiency and economy to programs serving the poor, as well as to organize charities in an effort to prevent duplication of services and reduce dependency upon charitable efforts. Like the Association for Improving Conditions of the Poor, which preceded it, the COS emphasized the necessity for assessing the conditions of the poor and added the dimension of engaging "friendly visitors" with clients in an effort to provide guidance, rehabilitation, and assistance in preparing for self-sufficiency. The COS had little sympathy for chronic beggars and viewed them essentially as hopeless derelicts.

CARING FOR SPECIFIC POPULATIONS

During these early years, many other private charities emerged to address special problem areas, such as the Orphan's Home Movement, which provided institutional care for children left alone as the result of the death of their parents. Other institutional services began to appear throughout the country to provide care for the deaf, blind, and mentally ill. These services largely were sponsored by state or local governments. There was often grave concern regarding the treatment received by inmates. Dorthea Dix, a philanthropist and social reformer, traveled the United States observing the care provided for the "insane" and was appalled by horrid conditions and inhumane care (Axinn & Levin 1975). Dix sought to convince President Franklin Pierce to allocate federal land grant monies for the purpose of establishing federal institutions to care for the mentally ill. Her plea was blocked by Congress, who believed such matters to be the states' responsibility. Resources allocated for institutional care by states were limited. The results were poor conditions and limited treatment.

Toward the latter part of the nineteenth century, a number of states developed centralized agencies following the precedent established by state boards of charities, agencies that had been organized in several states to oversee the activities of charitable institutions. State charity agencies sought to ensure a better quality of care for institutional inmates, as well as to seek greater efficiency and economy in the provision of poor relief. With the federal government assuming only limited responsibility for selected groups (veterans, for example), state agencies became the primary public resource for addressing the problems of the poor and debilitated (Leiby 1978, 130–131).

A new wave of immigrants from southern Europe entering this country in the late 1800s and early 1900s further added to the burden of unemployment, the homeless, and the poor. Reacting to the problems experienced by immigrants in coping with the new culture, Jane Addams, a social worker, was instrumental in anchoring the settlement house movement as a resource for dealing with problems of assimilation and in preparing immigrants to live in a new society. Education was emphasized for adults and children alike. In Chicago, Hull House, established by Addams in 1861, sparked the initiative for similar movements in other cities. It also sought needed social reforms to improve the quality of life and opportunity structure for all new citizens. By addressing the problems of poor housing, low wages, child labor, and disease, Hull House and other settlement houses became major social action agencies.

Following World War I, the nation entered a period of great social change and prosperity. The economy was improving and the nation experienced a sense of euphoria. In 1929, this euphoria ended with the economic downturn that led to the Great Depression. In short order, conditions were grave. Businesses considered to be stable ceased their production, banks declared bankruptcy, and thousands of workers lost their jobs. Although this nation had experienced recessions and depressions before, none was quite as devastating to the economic security of Americans as the Great Depression.

Many social workers in the early 1900s worked with poor immigrants in urban areas like this slum in New York City.

THE NEW DEAL

Today, it is difficult for us to comprehend the effects the Great Depression had on Americans. Savings were lost as banks collapsed, and many were left penniless, homeless, and without resources as unemployment increased. Jobs became scarce, and the unemployed had nowhere to turn. Organized charities quickly exhausted their limited resources. Pessimism and despair were rampant, and many experienced a sense of hopelessness. Unemployment insurance was nonexistent, and no federal guarantees existed for monies lost in bank failures. The economic disaster produced a state of chaos never experienced before on American soil. As conditions worsened, homes were lost through foreclosed mortgages.

State and local governments responded to the extent that resources permitted; however, many of the poor states lacked resources to provide relief even of a temporary nature. In the state of New York, an Emergency Relief Act was passed providing public employment, in-kind relief (food, clothing, and shelter), and limited cash benefits. This act later served as a model for federal relief programs.

Following the earlier constitutional interpretation by President Pierce, the Hoover Administration reinforced the position that federal involvement in relief programs was not mandatory but rather a matter that should be delegated to the states. Although sympathetic with those victimized by the Depression, President Hoover was convinced that the most effective solution to the Depression and its consequences was to provide incentives for business to regain its footing, expand, and provide jobs for the jobless.

The critical nature of the Depression was manifested in starvation, deprivation, and the suffering of millions of Americans and required an immediate response. Under these conditions, Franklin Delano Roosevelt, the former governor of New York, was elected President in 1932.

One of President Roosevelt's initial actions was to institute emergency legislation that provided assistance for the jobless and poor. Not only did this legislation mark the first time the federal government engaged itself directly in providing relief, it also invoked an interpretation of the health and welfare provisions of the constitution that established a historical precedent. The result mandated the federal government to assume health and welfare responsibility for its citizens. The statement was clear. Citizens were first and foremost citizens of the United States and second residents of specific states. This policy opened the door for later federal legislation in the areas of civil rights, fair employment practices, school busing, public assistance, and a variety of other social programs.

One of the first attempts to provide relief for depression victims was the Federal Emergency Relief Act. Modeled after the New York Emergency Relief Act, it provided food, clothing and shelter allowances for the homeless and displaced. In a cooperative relationship with states, the federal government made monies available to states to administer the relief programs. States were responsible for establishing agencies for that purpose and also were required to contribute state funds, where possible, for the purpose of broadening the resource base available to those in need. This established the precedent for "matching grants," which later became an integral requirement for public assistance programs.

Additional federal emergency legislation was enacted to provide public employment for the unemployed. In 1935, the Works Projects Administration (WPA) was created to provide public service jobs. Although resisted by private contractors, the WPA ultimately employed approximately 8 million workers over the duration of the Depression. States and local governments identified needed projects and supplied necessary materials for laborers, who were paid by the WPA. Many public schools, streets, parks, post office buildings, state college buildings, and related public projects were constructed under the auspices of WPA. It was anticipated that as the private business sector expanded, WPA workers would secure employment in the private sector.

Youth programs also were established. Perhaps the most noteworthy was the Civilian Conservation Corps, which was designed to protect natural resources and to improve and develop public recreational areas. Primarily a forest camp activity, the CCC provided young men between the ages of 17 and 23 with jobs, food, clothing, and shelter. Wages were nominal (around $25 per month), and the major portion of the wages ($20 per month) was conscripted and sent home to help support families. Many national parks were improved and developed by CCC labor. The National Youth Administration was also established under the WPA and provided work-study assistance to high school and college youth, as an incentive to remain in school. In addition, the NYA provided part-time jobs for out-of-school students to learn job skills and increase their employability (Friedlander & Apte 1974, 113).

Low-interest loans to farmers and small business operators also were extended through FERA programs as a means of enabling those activities to survive and become sources of employment for the unemployed.

In retrospect, it is clear that the Depression legislation was designed to be temporary in nature and had as its main focus the creation of work activities making it possible for individuals to earn their income rather than become objects of charity. It also was anticipated that the private economic business sector would prosper and emergency relief employment would no longer be needed.

The Depression legislation offered a temporary solution to the crisis generated by the Great Depression. The jobless found jobs, the hungry were fed, and the homeless were given shelter. Perhaps of more importance, the nation felt the full impact of system changes. The issue of blaming poverty on idleness and laziness was put to rest at least temporarily.

THE SOCIAL SECURITY ACT

The **Social Security Act** was passed by Congress and signed into law by President Roosevelt on August 14, 1935. This act is the most significant piece of social legislation enacted in the United States. It also paved the way for greater federal involvement in health and welfare. The act was a reflection that our economic system was subject to vacillations that would invariably leave many people without resources due to unemployment in an ever-shifting economic market place. It also acknowledged that older adults needed income security as an incentive to retire. This act was designed to be a permanent resource system administered by the federal government. The provisions of the act were outlined under three major categories. Chapter 4 will discuss these categories in greater depth. Briefly, the provisions of the act were social insurance, public assistance, and health and welfare services.

Social Insurance

Social insurance, commonly referred to as Social Security, was based on taxes deducted from employees' wages and matched by employer contributions. It was used to fund three insurance categories: Old Age Insurance, Survivors, and Disability Benefits. Eligibility was based on participation earned through employment. This established the concept of a governmentally administered insurance program. Benefits derived from the insurance program were considered to be a matter of right in that recipients had paid "premiums" from wages.

Public Assistance

Public assistance was based on "need" and was not established as a right earned through employment. This program was administered by states with monies made available by states and matched by the federal government (matching grants). Public assistance consisted of three categories: Old Age Assistance, Aid to Dependent Children, and Aid to the Blind. In 1955, the category of Aid to the Permanently and Totally Disabled was added. Benefits under each of these categories were invariably low and varied among the states according to each state's willingness to "match" federal funds. Eligibility requirements were rigid and rigorously enforced. Participation further was based on a "means" test, a test that required applicants to demonstrate that they were hopelessly without resources. The private lives of recipients were opened to the scrutiny of welfare workers in an attempt to minimize fraud and to assure that benefit levels did not exceed budgeted needs. Perhaps, the most controversial assistance program was Aid to Dependent Children. This program made limited funds available to mothers with dependent children where no man was present in the home. Since benefit levels were adjusted for family size (to a maximum of four children), there was concern that promiscuity and illegitimacy would be rewarded by increasing benefits as the family size increased. Rigid cohabitation policies were instituted mandating that mothers guilty of cohabitation would lose their grant funds entirely. Since most ADC recipients were able-bodied, there was also concern that welfare payments provided a disincentive for meeting their needs through gainful employment. In many ways, ADC recipients were treated as the "unworthy" poor and, as a consequence, were often dealt with in a punitive manner.

Public Assistance generally is referred to as *welfare* by the public. Since benefits are based upon impoverishment and not earned through employment, participation in the program carries with it a stigma of personal imprudence, ineptness, or failure.

Health and Welfare Services

Programs authorized under **health and welfare services** provided for maternal and child care services, vocational rehabilitation, public health, and services for physically impaired children. The provision of services was emphasized. Services authorized under this title are discussed more fully in subsequent chapters.

In the ensuing years, amendments to the Social Security Act extended each of these titles and included more people in their coverage. Social insurance later added health insurance (Medicare), and a health assistance program (Medicaid) was instituted for public assistance recipients. The ADC assistance category was redefined as Aid to Families with Dependent Children (AFDC) to allow states to provide assistance to families under limited circumstances when an employable-unemployed man was in the home (AFDCU). Only a few states adopted the AFDCU provisions. As requirements for participation in these programs became less stringent in the 1960s and 1970s, welfare rolls increased dramatically.

THE GREAT SOCIETY IN THE JOHNSON YEARS

Attempts to broaden the activities of government in securing the rights of citizens and providing for personal, social, and economic development were introduced through social reform measures enacted during the Lyndon Johnson Administration (1963–1968). The **Great Society** legislation extended benefits of many existing programs and services designed to help the poor, the disabled, and the aged. The Social Security Act was amended to provide for health care benefits to the aged under the Health Insurance Program (Medicare) and to public assistance recipients through the Health Assistance Program (Medicaid). New legislation also was designed to meet needs not specifically addressed through existing resources. The Older Americans Act (1965) established a legal base for developing senior luncheon programs, health screening, transportation, meals on wheels, and recreational activities. The Civil Rights Act (1964) sought to put an end to discrimination in employment and in the use of public business facilities. It also was targeted toward nondiscriminatory extension of credit. Education bills were passed that sought to rectify many of the educational disadvantages experienced by children of the poor.

Perhaps the most significant—and controversial—effort to achieve social reform came through the Economic Opportunities Act (1964). Dubbed the War on Poverty, the objective of this act was to "eliminate poverty" through institutional change. Poverty was viewed traditionally as an individual matter, and its causes generally were thought to be the result of personal failure and the lack of motivation or personal choice. Poverty program designers came to a different conclusion. Poverty was considered to be the result of inadequate social institutions that failed to provide opportunities for all citizens. Traditional approaches to solving the problems of poverty were considered unsuccessful. Changing the status of the poor would come not through working with them on an individual basis but rather through the modification of institutions producing the problems in the first place. Hence, Economic Opportunities Act programs were structured to assure the poor a greater likelihood of success by creating opportunities for decision making and participation. Educational programs such as Head Start, Enable, and Catch-up sought to extend relevant learning experiences to educationally disadvantaged children. Community Action Agencies encouraged the poor to become more vocal in community affairs and to organize efforts for community betterment. Special employment incentives were generated to teach the poor job skills. Youth job corps programs provided public service jobs contingent upon remaining in school, thus assuring greater potential for employment upon graduation. Job Corps centers taught teenage dropouts employment skills. Small business loans were made to individuals with potential for developing businesses. Rural programs extended health and social services for the poor in rural areas.

In a nation that boasted the highest standard of living in the world, it was believed that the scourge of poverty could be eliminated forever. The euphemism of War on Poverty was selected to rally the population to a full-scale commitment to assure that the enemy, poverty, would be overcome and silenced. Social action advocates found the climate produced by the Economic Opportunities Act favorable for their efforts. It was a heyday for the expansion of social programs, with spending often outstripping planning. The War on Poverty was short-lived as federal spending efforts were channeled to the war in Vietnam. Social legislation is invariably effected by the political climate. As government resources and attention were diverted to the Vietnam War, the domestic "war" was soon neglected and ultimately terminated during the Nixon Administration.

THE NIXON YEARS

Under the leadership of President Nixon, an effort was made to dismantle many of the social programs enacted during the New Deal and subsequent progressive social legislation. A fiscal and political conservative, President Nixon viewed the social welfare establishment as costly, ineffective, and a contributor to the poor's dependency. As a traditionalist, he was committed to the position that federal government was much too large and cumbersome and that many functions, including social welfare, could be assumed by the states. Notwithstanding that federal involvement in welfare had emerged largely because states lacked sufficient resources to provide supports, President Nixon was convinced that states and localities were better suited to determine policies and administer social programs. Upon entering office, he immediately authorized the reorganization of the federal poverty program. This resulted in its subsequent termination. Several popular programs, such as Head Start and job-training programs, were transferred to other government agencies. Under the Nixon Administration, a major welfare reform measure, the Family Assistance Program (FAP), was submitted for congressional approval as House Bill 1. Although never enacted into law, the reform would have eliminated the public assistance program and substituted in its place a proposal that was designed to provide incentives for recipients to work without losing all of their government benefits. The level of defined need, $1600 per year for a family of four, was far below benefit levels already in existence in the higher paying states but higher than the benefits in over half the states.

The Family Assistance Act failed but, on a more positive note, public assistance programs for the aged, disabled, and blind were combined by the enactment of the Supplemental Security Income (SSI) Act in 1974. SSI increased benefit levels for millions of recipients. Since the AFDC category, which would have been abolished by the Family Assistance Act, failed to pass, AFDC continues to be funded and implemented under the federal-state arrangements already in effect. Thus, AFDC benefits continue to vary appreciably from state to state. Table 2–1 illustrates the differences in the average monthly AFDC payments per person in the various states.

Table 2–1

Average Monthly AFDC Payment per Person

State	Amount	State	Amount
Alaska	$227	Oklahoma	$98
California	$164	Maryland	$98
Minnesota	$153	Illinois	$94
Connecticut	$153	Idaho	$93
Wisconsin	$153	Delaware	$91
Washington	$150	Ohio	$91
New York	$147	South Dakota	$87
Vermont	$136	Virginia	$86
Massachusetts	$136	Missouri	$85
Hawaii	$129	New Mexico	$81
North Dakota	$122	Indiana	$78
Michigan	$119	Florida	$77
Oregon	$117	Arizona	$76
Rhode Island	$117	North Carolina	$72
Iowa	$116	Kentucky	$70
Maine	$114	Nevada	$66
Utah	$111	Georgia	$65
New Jersey	$111	West Virginia	$62
Montana	$110	Louisiana	$56
Nebraska	$110	Arkansas	$54
Wyoming	$109	Texas	$53
New Hampshire	$108	South Carolina	$48
Pennsylvania	$104	Tennessee	$45
Colorado	$103	Alabama	$40
Kansas	$100	Mississippi	$31

Average = $109

Source: "Annual Report on AFDC Expenditures," Texas Department of Human Resources, Austin, Texas, 1985.

THE CARTER YEARS

The Carter Administration inherited a welfare system that had no positive constituency. Recipients, social workers, public officials, and tax-conscious groups agreed only on the inadequacy of the current system. Each of the four constituencies had in the immediate past initiated a welfare reform effort, and each constituency had failed to achieve its reform, largely because of the opposition of the others. Because of the political costs that had come to be associated with welfare reform efforts, no knights errant were ready to champion a new welfare reform effort. The problems to which previous knights errant had responded, however, were still very present. The rapidly expanding welfare costs in the Nixon/Ford years, in juxtaposition to the intractability of poverty, made welfare reform an urgent but unpleasant necessity.

Thus welfare reform again became an issue. The Carter Administration proposed that $8.8 billion be appropriated to create up to 1.4 million public service jobs. It was expected that 2 million persons would hold such jobs in a given year, as they were processed through these jobs on their way to regular employment in the public or private sector. Most of these jobs would pay a minimum wage (projected to be $3.30 in 1980) and be full-time, full-year jobs. The job income thus would be $6600.

In addition, a family would receive an income supplement from the second part of the program. The size of the supplement would be geared to family size. The jobs would not be eligible for the earned income tax credit of the fourth part of the program; a worker would always have an income incentive to move from the public job to regular employment in the public or private sector. Those eligible for such jobs would be adults—one per family—in the "expected to work" category of the second part of the program but could not find employment in the regular economy. Care was to be taken to assure that these jobs would not replace ordinary public jobs, thus removing the objections to the plan from the labor unions. However, Carter's proposal was not adopted, and debate about the most effective way to overhaul the welfare system continued.

THE REAGAN YEARS

Sensing a public mandate to reduce domestic spending, President Reagan began a relentless pursuit of reducing and eliminating social entitlement programs. Reagan viewed public expenditures for welfare as antithetical to economic progress. In his estimation, mounting inflation primarily was the result of federal domestic spending. He attributed the "sad state of our economy" to social progressives who had engineered welfare expansionism and, as a result, had caused the economy to falter. Many social support programs were reduced dramatically or eliminated. Funds supporting Title XX of the Social Security Act—which provided a wide range of benefits, up-graded the quality of the social service delivery system, and provided services to the aged, children and other populations at risk—were reduced drastically. Many transportation and job-training programs were discontinued.

The Reagan Administration promoted a policy of social and income assistance programs to be administered by states through block grants. The effect of this program would be to decentralize government and to return it to the pre-New Deal era, when states assumed responsibility for their own social problems. An unlikely coalition of conservative governors and liberal mayors joined efforts to defeat the Reagan initiative of welfare reform.

As part of his State of the Union message in 1982, President Reagan proposed his version of welfare reform. It went under the title *New Federalism*. The centerpiece was a plan whereby the states would assume financial and administrative responsibility for food stamps and AFDC, while the federal government would assume responsibility for the medicaid program. Figure 2–1 shows the projected federal expenditures for social programs as compared with real expenditures of the Carter Administration. The program was dubbed "The Welfare Swap." The plan went through a number of variations before it was dropped by the administration as politically not feasible. The problem was that neither conservative governors nor liberal mayors liked the idea. Following his reelection in 1984, President Reagan began again to push for reshaping welfare responsibilities among the various layers of government. A presidential task force was appointed, and it was to issue its report after the congressional elections in 1986. That election resulted in a Democratic landslide, and the responsibility for welfare reform has now shifted from the White House to Capitol Hill. The House of Representatives passed a welfare reform package in December of 1987 which, if adopted, will give the states more freedom in shaping their own program(s).

SOCIAL WELFARE IN THE FUTURE

A series of welfare reform proposals has briefly surfaced, each of which has been consigned to political oblivion because

1. it was crowded off the legislative calendar by other issues;
2. the cost estimates were hopelessly optimistic, and even ardent supporters withdrew their support when realistic cost estimates were reported;
3. proposals were offered with broadly sketched features, and the fine-tune planning efforts tended to turn away both liberals and conservatives.
4. most significantly, no plan so far proposed has been able to generate the consistent constituent support that would energize a member of Congress to take up the cudgel, fight the good fight, and make the necessary compromises. To the contrary, those who advocate specific welfare reform proposals risk the ire of the many others who have slightly and sometimes significantly different agendas of welfare reform. Unless and until circumstances or value orientations are modified sharply, welfare reform will remain dimly perceived. No one likes the current welfare system, but numerically and in terms of political resources, too many believe current offerings are better than specific proposed alternatives.

Speculation regarding the future structure, organization, and focus of social welfare is at best tenuous. As we have noted in this chapter, societal response to the needs of its socially and economically deprived is contingent upon many factors: available resources; values, and attitudes; an acceptance of the interdependence of its people; and a willingness to commit resources to those lacking them. Need levels may be defined stringently to include only those

Figure 2–1
**The Poor Lose,
Who Wins?**

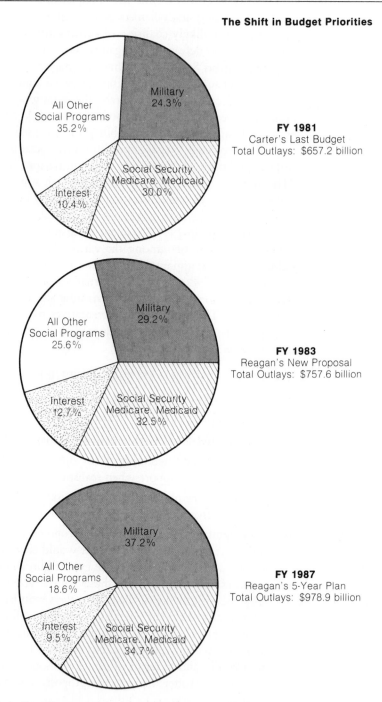

The Shift in Budget Priorities

FY 1981
Carter's Last Budget
Total Outlays: $657.2 billion

FY 1983
Reagan's New Proposal
Total Outlays: $757.6 billion

FY 1987
Reagan's 5-Year Plan
Total Outlays: $978.9 billion

Source: Coalition for a New Foreign and Military Policy, Washington, D.C. Reprinted by permission.

lacking food, clothing and shelter, or more broadly to include supports such as student loans for higher education. The more restrictively that the level of need is defined, the fewer societal resources will be allocated to meet needs.

The federal government's present policy of social welfare retrenchment will continue for some time. Definitions of need will become more specific and limited with the consequence that benefits will no longer be available through federal auspices. The result will be that persons with marginal incomes now eligible for limited supports will lose them, many prospective college students will be denied the privilege of attending college, individuals needing health care will not receive the necessary treatment and children with special learning problems will be denied access to special educational programs. These are but a few of the implications and realities of major federal welfare reductions.

In all likelihood, there will be a resurgence of initiative by private and philanthropic agencies to provide care for the casualties of federal reductions. Unfortunately, resources will not be adequate to meet present need levels. Volunteerism, a worthwhile and helpful activity, cannot replace the skills of professional workers. State and local governments will attempt to be responsive. Those with greater resources should be able to compensate for some of the lost federal resources. Poorer states, however, will be unable to bear the burden.

The challenge of finding alternative resources to support the poor will culminate in innovative programs and techniques to meet the need; however, funding will continue to be a problem at all levels. It may take many generations to restore the gains that have been made through the past fifty years. In a humane society, we have no other alternative.

SUMMARY

In this chapter a brief review of the historical contributions to our present day social welfare structure has been presented. Values and their influence on social policy have been identified and definitions of social welfare examined.

KEY TERMS

Great Society	Poor Laws
health and welfare services	public assistance
indoor relief	residual programs
institutional programs	social insurance
laissez faire	Social Security Act
outdoor relief	values

DISCUSSION QUESTIONS

1. Of what significance was the Elizabethan Poor Law to the subsequent development of public welfare in the U.S.?

2. How did the Speenhamland Act of 1795 differ from the Elizabethan Poor Law? What effect did the Speenhamland Act have on resolving the problem of the poor?

3. Argue the case that the Social Security Act has been the most significant social legislation passed in the United States.

4. What were the goals of the Economic Opportunities Act? How successful was this act in reducing poverty? Why was it discontinued?

5. Contrast President Johnson's Great Society programs with President Nixon's position on social welfare.

6. Discuss President Reagan's views on social welfare and his administration's plan to provide assistance for the poor.

REFERENCES

Axinn, June, and Herman Levin. *Social Welfare: A History of the American Response to Need.* New York: Dodd, Mead & Company, 1975.

Encyclopedia of Social Work. New York: National Association of Social Workers, 1977.

Federico, Ronald D. *The Social Welfare Institution.* 4th ed. Lexington, Mass.: D. C. Heath & Company, 1983.

Fink, Arthur E. 1974. *The Field of Social Work.* 6th ed. New York: Holt Rinehart and Winston.

Friedlander, Walter, and Robert Z. Apte. *Introduction to Social Welfare.* 4th ed. Englewood Cliffs, N.J.: Prentice–Hall, 1974.

Klein, Phillip. *From Philanthropy to Social Welfare.* San Francisco: Jossey–Bass, 1968.

Leiby, James. *A History of Social Welfare and Social Work in the United States.* New York: Columbia University Press, 1978.

Piven, Frances Fox, and Richard A. Cloward. *Regulating Labor.* New York: Pantheon Books, 1971.

Wilensky, Harold L., and Charles N. Lebeaux. *Industrial Society and Social Welfare.* rev. ed. New York: The Free Press, 1965.

SELECTED FURTHER READINGS

Compton, Beulah R. 1980. *Introduction to Social Welfare and Social Work.* Homewood, Ill.: The Dorsey Press.

Danziger, Sheldon H., and Daniel H. Weisberg, eds. 1986. *Fighting Poverty.* Cambridge, Mass.: Harvard University Press.

Fine, Sidney. 1964. *Laissez Faire and the General Welfare State.* Ann Arbor: The University of Michigan Press.

Howell, Joseph T. 1973. *Hard Living on Clay Streets.* Garden City, N.J.: Anchor Books.

Janson, Bruce S. 1988. *The Reluctant Welfare State.* Belmont, Calif.: Wadsworth Publishing Company.

Louchheim, Katie, ed. 1983. *The Making of the New Deal: The Insiders Speak.* Cambridge, Mass.: Harvard University Press.

Piven, Frances F., and Richard A. Cloward. 1971. *Regulating the Poor.* New York: Random House.

Ryan, William. 1971. *Blaming the Victim.* New York: Vintage Books.

3 A Systems/Ecological Perspective

Lisa, a 7–year–old Hispanic girl, is in second grade in a rural school in Texas. Her teacher noticed that she was withdrawn and depressed in school, and on occasion had bruises on her arms and legs. When asked about the bruises, Lisa became anxious and said she fell off her bicycle. Her teacher made a referral to the local child protective services agency for suspected child abuse. The social worker from the agency could not verify that abuse; however, she found Lisa's mother to be under a great deal of stress and referred both mother and daughter to the mental health center.

Lisa has an older sister in high school and a younger brother who is 5. Six months ago, Lisa's parents were divorced, and her father moved to an urban area, 200 miles away. Lisa always had a fairly close relationship with both her parents. Although she knew that they fought a lot and that her father drank and lost his job, she was taken by surprise when her parents told her that they were getting a divorce.

Since Lisa's father has moved out, her mother has spent much of her time crying or sleeping. Lisa's sister has been gone a lot with her friends. Lisa has tried hard to be supportive of her mother, cooking meals, cleaning the house, and taking care of her brother. However, she is only 7, and at times doesn't cook or clean exactly the way her mother wants her to. When her brother gets noisy, Lisa gets in trouble for not keeping him quiet. Lately, her mother has begun hitting her when this happens or when she doesn't do the housework correctly. Lisa feels abandoned by everyone since the divorce. Her mother is usually angry at her, and her friends, who come from two-parent families, seem less friendly to her.

Lisa's family lives in a small community in which there are few Hispanics or single-parent families. The few Hispanics are strong Catholics who do not believe in divorce. Lisa's mother does not get along with her relatives, who abused her when she was a child. She tried to enroll in a job-training program to get a job that pays more money, but none was available. She also tried to join a support group for abusive parents or divorced parents, but was told that only counseling at the mental health center is available. She feels lonely and isolated, and is increasingly frustrated about her life.

Lisa's case illustrates the many factors that influence how people react to what is going on in their lives. Lisa's present situation is affected by her relationships with her mother, father, siblings, friends, and teacher; her father's alcoholism and unemployment; her parents' divorce; the fact that her mother was abused as a child; her family's economic situation; the lack of social support available at the workplace, the school, the church, and the neighborhood to the members of Lisa's family; the lack of programs available to abusive parents and divorced parents; the lack of employment training programs; Lisa's cultural and ethnic background; and community and societal attitudes about divorce, female-headed households, and intervening in family matters. From Lisa's perspective, the family system, the economic system, the political system, the religious system, the educational system, and the social welfare system have not been there to meet her needs. Yet she continually interacts with all of these individuals, groups, and social structures, and also depends on all of them in some way.

This chapter will explore the systems/ecological framework, which can be used to understand social problems and issues faced by individuals and families in today's world. This framework also provides the broad base for the problem-solving approach, an intervention strategy used by generalist social work practitioners with Bachelor of Social Work (BSW) degrees. The problem-solving approach will also be discussed in relation to its applicability to addressing both social welfare problems and individual problems.

THE IMPACT OF WORLD VIEWS ON INTERVENTION IN SOCIAL PROBLEMS

All individuals perceive what is going on in their lives and in the world somewhat differently. All college students know that an argument between a parent and a teen-ager over almost any topic usually is perceived quite differently by the parent and the teenager. People view their environments and the forces that shape them differently depending on many things: their own heredity and intelligence; personal life experiences, including their childhoods; ethnicity and culture; and level and type of education. How people perceive their world determines to a large extent how involved they are in it and how they interact with it. Women who perceive themselves as unimportant and powerless may continue to let their husbands beat them and may not be successful at stopping the abuse or getting a job. On the other hand, women who perceive that they have some control over their lives and feel better about themselves may get into a counseling program and get a job at which they can be successful.

As with individuals, professionals from different disciplines also view their worlds somewhat differently. A physicist, for example, is likely to have a different explanation about how the world began than a philosopher or an Episcopal minister. A law enforcement officer may have different ideas about handling young teens from poverty areas who join gangs and harass the elderly than a social worker. A physician may treat a patient who complains of headaches by meeting the patient's physical needs, while a psychologist may treat the person's emotional needs through individual counseling to ascertain how the individual can better cope. The way professionals who work with people perceive their worlds largely determines the type of intervention they use in helping people.

The Difference Between Cause/Effect and Association

In the past, many professionals who dealt with human problems have had a tendency to look at those problems from a **cause/effect** or, causal relationship, or take a fairly singular approach to a problem. This approach lends itself well to narrow intervention; however, it not realistic when addressing social welfare problems. A cause/effect relationship suggests that if x causes y, then by eliminating x, we also eliminate y. For example, if we say that smoking causes lung cancer, then if we eliminate smoking, we will have eliminated lung cancer. This limited world view presents problems for many reasons. First, even in relation to smoking, we know that it does not always cause lung cancer and sometimes people who do not smoke get lung cancer. The relationship between smoking and lung cancer is also not always unidimensional. Other intervening variables or factors, such as living in a city with heavy smog, also increase a person's chances of getting lung cancer. The chances of getting lung cancer are more than twice as great if a person smokes and lives in a city with heavy smog. Lisa's case definitely cannot be discussed from a cause/effect relationship. Is the abuse Lisa suffers caused by the abuse her mother suffered as a child, by the divorce, by her father's drinking problem, by her mother's worries about money, or by the limited social support system available? It is unlikely that one of these factors caused the abuse of Lisa; however, they all likely contributed to the abuse in some way. In looking at factors related to social welfare problems, it is more appropriate to view them in **association** with the problem, or contributing to the problem, than to say that one isolated factor, or even several factors, directly causes a social problem.

The Need for a Broad Theory or Framework to Understand Social Welfare Problems

The fact that there are obviously many factors associated with or that contribute to social welfare problems suggests the need for a broad **theory** or framework to understand them. First, it is useful to discuss why theories are important at all.

All of us use theories in our daily lives. We are continually taking in facts, or information, from our environment and trying to order them in some way to make sense about what is going on around us. Although some of our theories may be relatively unimportant to everyone except ourselves, they are useful to us in being able to describe, understand, and even predict our environment. For example, a college student has a roommate who always turns up the stereo to full volume whenever the student gets a telephone call. Over the year that they shared a room, the student has gathered a great deal of information about when this happens. He is now able to articulate a theory he has based on this information to describe the situation, to understand why it happens, and to be able to predict when his roommate will exhibit this behavior. Making sense of the facts in this situation has made it easier for him to deal with this trying situation. A theory can be relatively insignificant, such as the one just described, or it can have major importance to many people, such as Robert Merton's theory about manifest and latent functions of organizations or Durkheim's theory about the occurrence of suicide.

A theory is a way of organizing a set of facts in an understandable way. A theory can be used to explain something, such as Lisa's family situation, to understand something, such as why a family in crisis would exhibit some of the behaviors of Lisa's family, or to predict something, such as what behaviors another family in a similar situation might experience. The same set of facts can be ordered in different ways, depending on who is doing the ordering and the world view of that person or group. If you think of facts as individual bricks, and a theory as a way of ordering the bricks so that they make sense, you can visualize several different theories from the same set of facts, just as you can visualize a number of different structures built from the same set of bricks.

A good theory must have three attributes, if it is to be widely used. First, it must be **inclusive,** or able to consistently explain the same event in the same way. The more inclusive a theory is, the better able it is to explain facts in exactly the same way each time an event occurs. For example, if the person in the roommate situation could describe, explain, or predict the roommate's behavior exactly the same way every single time the telephone rang, he would have a highly inclusive theory.

A good theory must also be **generalizable.** This means that one must be able to generalize what happens in one situation to other similar situations. Even though the person may be able to explain the facts about his roommate in a highly inclusive way, it is not likely that exactly the same situation would occur with all roommates in the same university, or the same city, or the United States, or the world. The more a theory can be generalized beyond the single situation it is describing or explaining, the better it is as theory.

Finally, a good theory must be **testable.** This means that we must be able to measure it in some way to ensure that it is accurate and valid. This is the major reason why we have very limited theory in understanding and predicting social welfare problems and human behavior. Only limited measures have been developed relating to what goes on inside people's minds, their attitudes, and their behaviors. How do we measure, for example, behavior change such as child abuse, particularly when it most often happens behind closed doors? Can we give psychological tests to measure attitudes that would lead to abuse, or can we measure community factors such as unemployment to predict child abuse? Any time we try to measure human behavior or environmental influences, we have difficulty doing so. This does not mean that we should stop doing research or trying to develop higher level theories. In fact, this is an exciting area of social work and the problems merely point out the need to develop skilled social work practitioners and researchers who can devote more attention to the development of good social work theory.

Because social work draws its knowledge base from many disciplines, many theories are applicable to social work. These include psychological theories such as Freud's theory of psychoanalysis and its derivatives, economic and political theories, social theories such as Merton's and Durkheim's, educational theories such as Dewey's problem-solving framework, and developmental theories such as Piaget's. While all of these theoretical perspectives are relevant to social work and understanding social welfare problems, looking at only one limits one's understanding and, in turn, one's intervention. Thus, it is important to focus on a framework or perspective that allows one to view social problems and appropriate responses that incorporate a multitude of factors and a multitude of possible responses, yet one that does not eliminate or prohibit the rich array of theories available from other disciplines, such as those just delineated.

THE SYSTEMS/ECOLOGICAL FRAMEWORK

Social workers, more than any other group of professionals, have focused both on the individual and beyond the individual to the broader environment. Consider the definitions of social work discussed in Chapter 1. All focus on enhancing social functioning of the individual or in some way addressing the relationships, the interactions, and the interdependence between persons and their environments. This is exemplified by the many roles social workers play within the social welfare system—true generalists, they advocate for changing living conditions of the mentally ill and obtaining welfare reform legislation that enables the poor to better succeed in obtaining employment and economic self-sufficiency; lead groups of children who have experienced divorce; educate the community about parenting, AIDS, and child abuse; and provide individual, family, and group counseling to clients. A broad framework is needed that allows for identifying all of the diverse, complex factors associated with a social welfare problem or an individual problem; understanding how all of the factors interact to contribute to the situation; and determining an intervention strategy or strategies, which can range from intervention with a single individual to an entire society and incorporate a variety of roles. Such a framework must account for individual differences, cultural diversity, and growth and change at the individual, organizational and societal levels.

The generalist foundation of social work is based on a systems framework, which also incorporates an ecological perspective. The authors choose to use the term *systems framework* rather than *theory* because the systems perspective is much broader and more loosely constructed than a theory. It is most useful in understanding social welfare problems and situations and determining specific theories that are appropriate for intervention. Additionally, whereas a systems approach has been written about in the literature extensively, it has not been tested or delineated with enough specificity to be considered theory. A number of advocates of the systems framework, in fact, refer to it as a *megatheory,* or an umbrella framework or perspective that can be used as a base for additional theories. A general systems framework has been discussed in the literature of many disciplines—medicine, psychology, economics, political science, sociology, and education—for many years, and has been used somewhat differently in each discipline. Its principles have been incorporated into the social work literature since the beginning of social work, and many social work proponents, such as Pincus and Minahan, Perlman, Germain and Getterman, and Bartlett, have developed specific approaches or explored varying aspects of social work from within the boundaries of this framework. More recently, social work has incorporated the systems framework with an ecological perspective, which is a variation on the original framework. Although the following discussion will clarify the differences and relationships between the two, many readings in social work will use both terms almost interchangeably and refer to both *systems theory* and *ecological theory.* Rather than get confused over semantics, it is suggested that readers pay attention to the broad definitions and principles of the **systems/ecological frameworks** and their commonalities rather than their differences. These important points in understanding a systems/ecological perspective and its significant contribution to social work will be highlighted.

   Systems theory was first used to explain the functioning of the human body, which was seen as a major system that incorporated a number of smaller

A systems/
ecological
perspective focuses
on interaction
between individuals
and environment.
With children,
social workers assess
strengths, needs, and
relationships with
family, friends and
classmates.

systems: the skeletal system, the muscular system, the endocrine system, the circulatory system, etc. Medical practitioners, as early as classic Greek times, realized that when one aspect of the human body failed to function effectively, it also affected the way that other systems within the body functioned and, in turn, affected the way the human body as a whole functioned. This led to further exploration of the relationships between subparts of living organisms. Thomas' *The Life of a Cell* clearly articulates the intricate interrelations among the many complex parts of a single cell that enable the cell to maintain itself and to reproduce. The contribution from biology to systems theory is the emphasis on the fact that the whole is greater than the sum of its parts, or that when all of the smaller systems or subsystems of an organism function in tandem they produce a larger system that is far more grand and significant than the combination of those smaller systems would be if they worked independent of each other. The larger system, when it functions optimally, is said to achieve **synergy** or the combined energy from the smaller parts that is greater than the total if those parts functioned separately. Imagine for a moment that your instructor for this course has given you an exam on the chapters you have covered thus far in this text. Each student takes the exam separately and scores of each student are listed. The lowest score is 50; the highest is 85. Now, suppose that your instructor decides to let the entire class take the exam together. Each individual in the class now functions as part of the total group, together solving each exam question. As a class, your score on the exam is 100. Your class has demonstrated the concept of the whole being greater than the sum of its parts, or the synergy achieved when smaller systems work together interdependently to form a larger system.

Von Bertalanffy (1968, 38) defines a system as "a set of units with relationships among them"; Compton and Galaway describe a system as "a whole consisting of interdependent and interacting parts" (1984, 112). An important aspect of a system is the concept of **boundary.** A system can be almost anything but, by its definition, it usually is given some sort of boundary or point when one system ends and another begins. The human body can be seen as a system, as discussed earlier, with the skin as a boundary and the various body subsystems as smaller components of the larger system. From a different perspective, the human mind can be seen as a system, with Freud's id, ego, and super ego as components within that system that interact together to form a whole greater than any of the three components alone: the human mind. An individual can also be part of a larger system, for example, a family system, which might include one or two parents, a child, and the family dog. One might wish to expand the boundaries of the family system and include the grandparents and the aunts and uncles. We can establish larger systems, such as school systems, communities or cities, states, or nations and focus on their interactions and interdependence with each other. We can also look at a political system, an economic system, a religious system, and a social welfare system and the ways that those broader systems interact with each other. The important thing to remember when using a systems perspective is that the systems that we define and the boundaries that we give those systems are conceptual; that is, we can define them in whatever ways make the most sense in looking at the broad social welfare or the more narrow individual problem that we are addressing. For example, when focusing on Lisa's family, if we were to define it as a system we would include within its boundaries her mother, father (even though he is out of the home, he is still involved and a part of Lisa's life), her brother, and her sister; but we would not include grandparents or other extended family members because they are not actively involved either physically or emotionally in any way with the family (see Figure 3–1). If we were looking at another family system, however, we might well include a large number of other members. The systems framework is a useful way to organize data to help understand a situation, and its flexibility allows us to define systems and their boundaries in a number of ways.

While we can draw boundaries wherever it seems appropriate when using a systems framework, it is important that we be able to ascertain how permeable those boundaries are. Some systems have boundaries that are easily permeated; we call those systems **open systems.** Some families exemplify open systems.

Figure 3–1   **Using an Eco-Map to Understand Lisa's Family Situation**

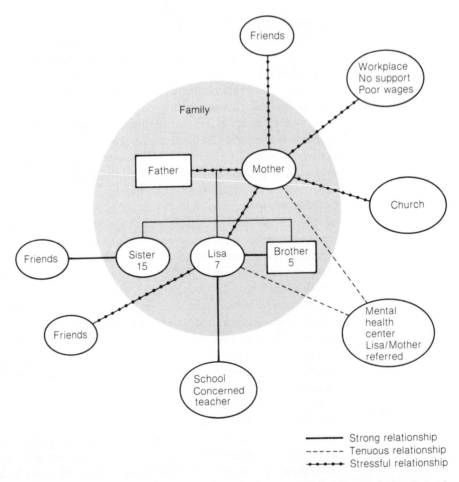

——— Strong relationship
- - - - - Tenuous relationship
•••••• Stressful relationship

Source: Adapted from Ann Hartman, "Diagrammatic Assessment of Family Relationships," *Social Casework* (October 1978).

Those are the families that readily incorporate others; when someone rings the door bell at dinnertime, a plate is always added. A cousin or a friend is often living there for a short or a long time period, and it is often difficult to tell exactly who is a family member and who isn't. Sometimes boundaries in systems are too open, as in the family where incest is going on, and the teenage daughters who go to school during the day and the father who works at night share the same bed. Unclear boundaries within systems can lead to family problems, such as incest.

On the other hand, systems can have extremely closed boundaries. Some families are very tightly knit. Although they get along well with each other, they are isolated and rarely incorporate other individuals into their system. They may have special family nights and traditions where they make it clear that the activities are for family members only. Organizations also may be open or **closed systems**. Some organizations welcome new members and readily expand their activities to meet new interests. Others are very closed and do not encourage new members, making those that try to enter the organization feel unwelcome, and are not receptive to new ideas. Usually, the more closed a system is, the less able it is to derive positive energy from other systems. Over time, closed systems tend to use up their own energy and to develop **entropy** (as opposed to synergy, which open systems are more likely to achieve because of their willingness to accept new energy), which means that they tend to lose their ability to function and can eventually stagnate and die.

An additional feature of the systems framework is its emphasis on the interactions and interrelations between units rather than on the systems or subsystems themselves. This lends itself well to the need for focusing on associations among large numbers of factors rather than on cause/effect relationships between two factors. The interactions and interrelatedness between systems suggest constant motion and fluidity as opposed to the stasis of those systems that stand still and do not move or change. The relatedness and interactions also incorporate the concept that a change or movement in one part of the system, or in one system, will have an impact on the larger system, or other systems, as well. Imagine a room full of constantly moving ping pong balls, each representing a system or a subsystem of a larger system. Hitting one ping pong ball across the room will change the movement of the other balls. Similarly, a change in the economic system (for example, inflation) will result in changes in other systems: the educational system could be affected because fewer students can afford to go to college; the social welfare system could be affected because more people will have financial difficulties and need public assistance and social services; the criminal justice system will be affected because more persons will turn to crime; and the political system will be affected because the party not in office is more likely to be elected because people are dissatisfied with what is going with the economy.

There are usually constant flows of energy within systems and across systems. This creates natural tensions, which are viewed as healthy if communication is open, because the energy flow creates growth and change. Feedback among systems is an important part of the systems perspective, which emphasizes communication. It is important that social workers and others who work within and across various systems understand the goals of those systems and their communication patterns. In unhealthy systems, for example, the various members of the system may be communicating in certain ways and may have certain unspoken goals that maintain the system because its members are afraid to change the system or the system is in some way productive for them. In a family where a father is an alcoholic, a mother may perpetuate his alcoholism and try to keep the family system as it is because her role is to keep the family together and protect the children from his alcoholism. If the family system changes, she will no longer be able to maintain that role; thus, she perpetuates the system as it is. In a social service agency that began a new program to get women off welfare, the workers became fearful that they would not get good evaluations if they didn't get large numbers of women into jobs. Thus, the goal of the agency became placing women in "dead end" jobs, which were easy for them to get, rather than getting them into training programs or more challenging, better paying jobs, which required more time from the workers and gave them fewer job entries to report.

The final concept of a systems framework is that of **homeostasis** or **steady state,** in which systems are not static but are steadily moving, as we have already suggested. The concept of steady state or homeostasis means that the system is constantly adjusting to move toward its goal while maintaining a certain amount of order and stability. A healthy system, then, may be viewed as one that is not in upheaval with massive amounts of turmoil but always ebbing and flowing to achieve stability and growth at the same time.

One criticism of the systems framework in social work is that it encompasses the broad environment yet ignores the psychosocial and the intrapsychic aspects of the individual. Proponents of the systems framework argue that the individual is perceived as a highly valued system itself, and that intrapsychic aspects and psychosocial aspects, which incorporate the individual's capacity and motivation for change, are part of any system involving individuals that cannot and should not be ignored.

Another criticism of the systems framework is that, because it incorporates everything, it is too complicated and it is easy to miss important aspects of a situation when you are looking at an entire forest. The ecological perspective, as articulated by Bronfenbrenner and Garbarino and expanded upon by social workers Germain and Gitterman, attempts to address this concern. Bronfenbrenner and Garbarino incorporate individual developmental aspects into the systems perspective of the broader environment but break the system into different levels. They describe their levels of the environment as you would imagine a series of Russian eggs, with a large egg cut in half that opens to reveal a smaller egg, that also opens to reveal a still smaller egg, that opens to reveal a still smaller egg (see Figure 3–2 and Table 3–1). They suggest that one consider the tiniest egg to be the **microsystem level,** which includes the individual and all persons and groups that incorporate the individual's day-to-day environment. The focus at this level would incorporate the individual's level of functioning, intellectual and emotional capacities, motivation, impact of past life experiences, and the interactions and connections between that individual and others in the immediate environment; also, if the relationships are positive or negative, if the messages and regard for the individual are consistent across individuals and groups, and if the individual is valued and respected.

Figure 3–2   **The Levels of the Ecological System**

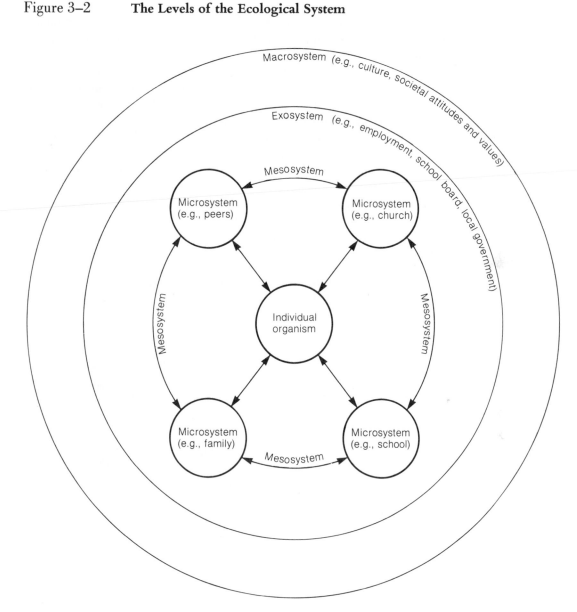

Source: Adapted from James Garbarino, *Children and Families in the Social Environment* (New York: Aldine, 1982).

The next level is termed the **mesosystem level.** This level incorporates the interactions of the individuals and groups within the individual's microsystem and the ways that those individuals and groups relate to each other but not to the individual upon whose microsystem we are focusing. This would mean, for example, relationships between a child's mother and father, or a child's teacher and her parents, or a child's friends and her family. If they are not getting along, even though the child is not directly involved in the interactions, it has an impact on the child.

The third level is the **exosystem level.** This level includes community level factors that may not relate directly to the individual but have an impact on the way the individual functions. This includes factors such as the workplace policies of the parents (if they cannot take sick leave when the child is sick, for example, it has an impact on the child), school board and community policies, community attitudes and values, and economic and social factors that exist within the neighborhood and community.

The final level is the **macrosystem level.** This level includes societal factors such as the cultural attitudes and values of the society (for example, attitudes toward women, minorities, the poor, violence); the role of the media in addressing or promoting social problems (some suggest, for example, that the media promotes violence and teen pregnancy); and federal legislation and

Table 3–1   **A Summary of the Ecology of Sociocultural Risk and Opportunity to Individuals as They Interact with Their Environments**

Ecological Level	Definition	Examples	Issues Affecting Children
Microsystem	Situations in which the child has face-to-face contact with influential others	Family, school, peer group, church	Is the child regarded positively? Is the child accepted? Is the child reinforced for competent behavior? Is the child exposed to enough diversity in roles and relationships? Is the child given an active role in reciprocal relationships?
Mesosystem	Relationships between microsystems; the connections between situations	Home–school, home–church, school–neighborhood	Do settings respect each other? Do settings present basic consistency in values?
Exosystem	Settings in which the child does not participate but in which significant decisions are made affecting the child or adults who do interact directly with the child	Parents' place of employment, school board, local government, parents' peer group	Are decisions made with the interests of parents and children in mind? How well do supports for families balance stresses for parents?
Macrosystem	"Blueprints" for defining and organizing the institutional life of the society	Ideology, social policy, shared assumptions about human nature, the "social contract"	Are some groups valued at the expense of others (e.g., sexism, racism)? Is there an individualistic or a collectivistic orientation? Is violence a norm?

Source: James Garbarino. *Children and Families in the Social Environment* (New York: Aldine, 1982), p. 28.

other social policies that have an impact on the individual whose systems we are examining. Advocates of the ecological framework agree that it is a derivation of systems theory and another way of defining boundaries of systems. They suggest that it is advantageous to use because it allows one to see the interdependence and interaction across levels from the microsystem level to the macrosystem level and also allows us to target intervention at a variety of levels to address social problems and individual needs. For example, we could provide individual counseling to a child who has a drug problem, counsel his family, help him develop a new network of friends, advocate for the establishment of a community program to treat teens with drug problems, and lobby for legislation to develop national media programs that educate the public about drugs.

Germain and Gitterman incorporate the ecological perspective somewhat differently in their approach. They stress the need to incorporate individual transitions and developmental stages when defining systems. They suggest that all individuals go through life transitions—marriage, the birth of a first child, moving into middle age, children moving out of the family, and so forth— and that as one moves from one life stage to another, transitional problems and needs develop that may need social work intervention. They reinforce the need to incorporate the unique needs and diversity of the individual at the core of any systems perspective taken.

In summary, a systems perspective emphasizes the fact that our lives are shaped by the choices we make, and that the environment shapes our choices, while our choices shape the way we interact with our environment. This continual interaction and cyclical perspective suggest that we cannot discuss the individual without focusing on the environment nor the environment without the strong forces that individuals play in its formulation. The individual and the environment are continually adapting to each other. The primary role of the social worker is to ensure that this adaptation is mutually supportive to both the individual and the environment.

The Utility of the Systems/Ecological Framework

The systems/ecological framework is intended to be used as a mechanism to order facts about social welfare problems or individual problems in such a way that appropriate theories can be identified to further explore the problems or to determine interventions. Box 3–1 examines some ways the framework aids social workers. It is useful to think of this framework as a way to "map the territory" or gather and fit together pieces of a puzzle to understand a situation. When dealing with a problem such as poverty, for example, which is addressed in the next chapter, many individuals may have unidimensional ways of explaining the problem—it is because people are lazy, for example, or the victims of their own circumstance. A systems perspective would identify many additional factors—a large, complex territory and a puzzle with many pieces. Individual factors, community factors, societal factors, the impact of the economic system and unemployment, racism, sexism, and so forth—all contribute to poverty in some way. Table 3–2 lists just some of the factors in the interaction between the individual and the environment. However, once the territory is mapped out or all of the puzzle pieces (or as many as possible)

Box 3–1
Value of
Systems
Ecological
Perspective to
Social Welfare
Problems and
Social Work
Practice

The systems/ecological perspective makes a number of valuable contributions as an organizing framework for social work practice.

1. The systems/ecological perspective allows one to deal with far more data than other models and to bring order to these large amounts of data from a variety of different disciplines.

2. The concepts relating to systems are equally applicable to the wide range of clients served by social workers, including individuals, families, groups, organizations, communities, and society.

3. The systems/ecological framework allows for identifying the wide range of factors that have an impact on social welfare problems and their interrelationships.

4. The systems/ecological framework shifts attention from characteristics of individuals or the environment to the relationships between systems and their communication patterns.

5. The systems/ecological framework views persons as actively involved with their environments, capable of adaptation and change.

6. The systems/ecological framework views systems as goal-oriented, supporting client self-determination and the client's participation in the change process.

7. If systems require constant transactions with each other to survive, the purpose of the social worker is to provide and maintain such opportunities for transactions for all populations and to work to reduce isolation of individuals and systems.

8. Social workers need to work to ensure that change and tension are not resisted in systems and to remove the notions that change and conflict are pathological.

9. Social workers need to be aware of the systems within which they work and how change within those systems affects the whole. This means that social workers must choose points of intervention with care.

10. Social workers are a social system and components of a social systems network.

Adapted from: B. Compton and B. Galaway, *Social Work Processes* (Homewood, Ill.: Dorsey Press, 1984), pp. 124–25.

are obtained, then the systems framework allows for further exploration of certain factors, parts of the terrain, or pieces of the puzzle. Once the "big picture" is obtained, we can better ascertain where to "hone in" and if more information is needed, in what areas, and if intervention is required, at what level and within which system or systems. One or more specific theories or frameworks can then be used to obtain more information or as a basis for

Table 3–2   **Factors that Shape Individual Functioning and Relationship with the Environment**

Personal Factors:
  Level of prenatal care received
  Intellectual capacity/ability
  Emotional capacity/mental health
  Level of social functioning
  Physical health
  Age
  Ethnicity/culture
  Motivation
  Life stage/transitional period
  Crisis level

Family Factors:
  Support systems/availability of significant others
  Family patterns/structure/values
  Economic level/employment
  Level of functioning/family crisis

Community Factors:
  Social class compared to rest of community
  Ethnic/cultural/class diversity/attitudes and values
  Social roles available within community
  Community support
  Economic conditions
  Employment opportunities
  Educational opportunities
  Environmental stress

Societal Factors:
  Societal attitudes and values
  Racism, sexism, poverty levels
  Supportive or lack of supportive legislation/programs/policies
  Media role

intervention. The advantage of the systems perspective is that we are less likely to miss a major aspect of a situation or intervene inappropriately. This perspective also allows for individualization and diversity, which also means that cultural and gender differences are readily accounted for.

THE SOCIAL WELFARE SYSTEM: A SYSTEMS PERSPECTIVE

The social welfare system in place at any given moment is the product of historical, economic, and political forces. It is constantly reshaped by changes in societal values and events. The scope of social welfare systems in the United States is not as broad, comprehensive, and integrated as most social workers would like nor is it as constrained and limited as some others would like to draw it. In a sense, it is not a formal system at all, but rather a collection of ad hoc programs developed in diverse and special political circumstances. Thus, we have programs for the aged, disabled, blind, and so forth, but each program has its own political history and its own political constituency.

Objectively speaking, an overview of the American social welfare institutions and social work practice would reveal an incredible range of public and voluntary agencies seeking to respond to social problems. For some problem areas, the response is thought through and generous, for others the response is niggardly and ad hoc, whereas still other social problems invoke no response at all. Seldom is attention given to how the response to problem *A* is related to its impact on problem *B*. As a matter of practice, if not of principle, the target populations of social agencies are those subgroups in our society that do not fare well and that are not adequately served by the primary social systems.

Typically, the social welfare system functions as a result of family breakdown, problems in income distribution, failure of the market systems, and institutional failure in church, school, hospital, or factory. While each person might give a somewhat different statement of mission, it is probably a minimum statement that the social welfare system *should* guarantee to each person a socially defined minimum standard of well being. In so doing the social welfare system interacts with the primary systems: the family system, the economic system, and the political system. Each of these primary systems, in its turn, has a principal function as illustrated in Table 3–3. The social welfare system is most frequently perceived as a residual social system which comes into play when there is a failure in the primary system or the primary system generates undesirable consequences. (Wilensky & Lebeaux, 1975).

As stated earlier the organized system of social services and institutions is designed to aid individuals and groups to attain satisfying standards of life and health. This view implies recurrent failure in other institutions. It assumes that individuals sometimes need outside help in coping with a complex social order. Social welfare institutions assist in time of crisis of the individual but, since recurrent and random crisis is the ordinary condition of social life, a structured set of social agencies needs to stand ready to respond to crises and failures—to overcome the crisis and enhance problem-solving and coping skills of communities, groups, and individuals, so that crisis is less frequent.

In this view, the social welfare system is seen as the structured set of responses developed to deal with systems dysfunction or systems failure. As an example of a social welfare response to a primary system *failure,* we have a set of child welfare functions to assist and replace the family in its child care roles. As an example of a response to a primary system *dysfunction,* we know that the market system distributes income unevenly, leaving some people poor, thus we have generated an income security system to provide various income guarantees to specific classes of persons in need.

Table 3–3
Social Systems

Systems	Functions
Primary:	
Economic System	The allocation and distribution of scarce resources to competing ends
Political System	The authoritative allocation of public social goals and values
Family System	The primary personal care and mutual assistance system between child and parent, between adults and care of the aged
Secondary:	
Other Goal Specific Systems	The list and function of "other" systems is dependent on taste for specificity; i.e., health system, defense system, environmental protection system, etc.
Social Welfare System	To respond to failure and/or dysfunction in primary and secondary systems

FROM A SYSTEMS FRAMEWORK TO A
PROBLEM–SOLVING APPROACH

The generalist model of social work practice taught at the BSW level suggests a problem-solving approach in working with clients at the individual, family, group, organizational, community, or societal level. The problem-solving approach begins with gathering data from a systems framework. Once data are gathered, or enough data to begin the problem-solving process, the type of intervention most appropriate to the problem can be considered.

Choices about how to help an individual or group necessarily are clouded in uncertainty. There is always the possibility that the intervention itself will fail to help, and perhaps even make matters worse. There is no absolute defense against this danger except inaction—and even inaction can make some matters worse. Systematic analysis of the problem, its component parts, contemplated strategies of intervention, and the probable consequences of faulty interventions—has been described as follows:

1. The social worker and client are faced with a given problem or set of problems;

2. The worker and client together explore the nature of the problem(s), gathering as much information as possible to ensure that problems identified are appropriate and clearly defined;

3. The worker and client identify goals and objectives to address the identified problem(s), which are ranked or otherwise organized;

4. Then, the possible strategies of intervention are listed to address each goal/objective;

5. The important consequences likely to follow from each intervention are identified with as much precision as is possible;

6. The worker and client select and implement a strategy, which may include the strategy of doing nothing, or involve individual and community resources;

7. The results of the action, or inaction, are monitored and evaluated with modifications made as necessary.

This approach is also evaluated for potential use by the client when future problems occur. The steps in the problem-solving process provide a guide to use when considering an intervention. These considerations apply when helping a troubled person or in providing congressional testimony. The determinations of what is the real problem and when, where, and how to intervene are always risks taken to promote desired change. Table 3–4 is a guide in the analysis of problem(s) addressed.

None of these steps guarantees that the best alternative will be identified, much less selected. No formula can be precisely identified that will substitute for creative imagination, but creative imagination is both fostered and controlled by a willingness to think hard about the real nature of the problem and the kind of solutions available. Social work is an art based upon a scientific understanding of a number of theoretical perspectives and approaches.

Table 3–4 Problem Analysis	*Establish the Context:*
	What is the underlying problem that must be dealt with?
	Why did the problem emerge at this time?
	How can the specific objectives to be pursued be identified?
	Isolate the Alternatives:
	What options are obvious immediately?
	What possibilities are there for gathering information that will generate nonobvious options?
	Predicting the Consequences:
	For each option, what consequences are expected?
	For each "expected" consequence, how predictable is its occurrence?
	What techniques are available that would reveal the consequences and their probability?
	Place Values on Alternative Outcomes:
	How can overarching criteria be defined by which different outcomes can be worked?
	How might these criteria be quantified?
	What other nonquantitative criteria are available to rank choices of differing magnitude?
	Identify the Decisional Mode:
	Who is going to decide, and in what time frame is a decision going to be reached?
	How can the decision, once made, be implemented?
	What techniques are available to monitor the decisions?

In the idealized version the social work professional is seen as a "problem solver" with generic responsibilities regardless of specific agency affiliation or the clients presenting a problem. The central precepts of integrative practice as identified in Pincus and Minahan (1973) are these:

1. individuals and groups typically need help in all aspects of their social functioning though the presenting problem may well be dysfunction or failure in one social system;

2. the social welfare service ought to serve to solve problems and provide problem solutions rather than treatment;

3. the social welfare system ought to be pragmatic, eclectic, and parsimonious;

4. the service to the individual should be individually structured so that the clients are met "where they are" and the service is continued until all aspects of the problem are identified and dealt with.

A major implication of the idealized conception of social welfare is that it requires the social worker at all organizational levels to be able to deal with the micro, meso, exo, and macro aspects of the problem. The problem of the individual needs to be perceived in terms that range from individual intrapsychic problems to problems of social role performance and role interaction to broad community or total social system problems. Intervention can take place anywhere throughout the social system. The social welfare system, as an ideal, is perceived to encompass the family, political, medical, educational, and economic needs of its clients and to integrate these needs into the solution of the client's present problem.

SUMMARY

Social welfare problems involve many complex and interrelated factors. These factors may be ordered in a number of ways to describe social welfare problems, to understand them, and to predict when they will occur and under what conditions. Because the problems are so complex and involve human behaviors and environmental influences that are difficult to measure, as well as a variety of disciplines, there is no theory that can be used to address all social welfare or human problems. However, the systems/ecological framework, which incorporates the concept that an individual may be seen as part of a larger environment with whom he or she continually interacts and is an interdependent part of that environment, is useful in organizing information to determine what else is needed and to develop an appropriate intervention strategy. This framework incorporates factors at the individual, family, organizational, community, and societal levels and allows for a variety of interventions at one or more levels.

KEY TERMS

association	macrosystem level
boundary	mesosystem level
cause/effect	microsystem level
closed system	open system
entropy	synergy
exosystem level	systems/ecological framework
generalizable	testable
homeostasis/steady state	theory
inclusive	

DISCUSSION QUESTIONS

1. Why is it difficult to develop good theory to address social welfare problems?

2. Briefly identify the key components of the systems/ecological perspective. Compare and contrast open and closed systems, and static and steady state systems.

3. Using a systems/ecological perspective, identify the systems that have an impact on Lisa's life at the present time.

4. Using the ecological perspective as delineated by Bronfenbrenner and Garbarino, identify at least one strategy you might use if you were a social worker to help Lisa and her family at each of the four levels of the ecological framework: the microsystem, the mesosystem, the exosystem, and the macrosystem.

5. Identify at least four advantages of using the systems/ecological perspective to understand social welfare problems.

6. Briefly describe the problem solving approach and its advantages to social workers within social welfare institutions.

REFERENCES

Compton, B., and B. Galaway, 1984. *Social Work Processes.* Homewood, Ill.: Dorsey Press, 1984.

Garbarino, James. *Children and Families in the Social Environment.* New York: Aldine, 1982.

Hartman, Ann. "Diagrammatic Assessment of Family Relationships." *Social Casework* (October 1978).

Pincus, A., and A. Minahan. *Social Work Practice: Model and Method.* Itasca, Ill.: Peacock Press, 1973.

Von Bertalanffy, L. *General System Theory.* New York: Braziller, 1968.

Wilensky, H., and C. Lebeaux. *Industrial Society and Social Welfare.* New York: Free Press, 1965.

SELECTED FURTHER READINGS

Anderson, R., and I. Carter. *Human Behavior in the Social Environment: A Social Systems Approach.* New York: Aldine, 1984.

Buckley, W. ed. *Modern Systems Research for the Behavioral Scientist.* Hawthorne, N.Y.: Aldine, 1968.

Council on Social Work Education. *Curriculum Policy for the Master's Degree and Baccalaureate Degree Programs in Social Work Education.* New York: Author, 1982.

Germain, C. *Social Work Practice: People and Environments.* New York: Columbia University Press, 1979.

Zastrow, C., and K. Kirst–Ashman. *Understanding Human Behavior in the Social Environment.* Chicago: Nelson–Hall, 1987.

II

Fields of Practice and Populations Served

This section explores the settings in which social workers practice and the special populations they serve. While not all settings and special populations can be presented in the limited space in this text, this section provides an overview of the major social problems and populations that are the domain of the social welfare system and social work practitioners. Each chapter presents a broad systems perspective to help the reader understand the issues social work practitioners face in addressing the specific social problem or special population. The specific roles and functions that social workers play in dealing with each field of practice and population served also are explored, so that the reader will have an idea of what types of social work jobs are available in that field of practice and what the nature of those jobs entails.

Chapter 4, "The Fight Against Poverty," focuses on how poverty is defined, why people are poor, who is poor in the United States, and what types of policies and programs exist to help reduce poverty levels in the United States. The roles social workers play in the fight against poverty also are discussed.

Chapter 5, "Mental Health and Developmental Disabilities," explores definitional issues concerning mental health, mental illness, and developmental disabilities. Critical incidents are addressed that have shaped the way mental health problems are viewed and the types of mental health services available. The many functions that social workers, who constitute the majority of mental health professionals in the United States, provide also are explored.

Chapter 6, "Health and the Role of the Social Worker in Health Settings," provides an explanation of the present health care system in the United States, the problems it faces, and the types of health care policies and programs available. Health care is the fastest growing area of employment for social workers today, and career opportunities for social workers in this setting also are explored.

Chapter 7, "The Needs of Children, Youth, and Families," provides an overview of the many problems facing families today. Divorce, alcoholism and drug abuse, child abuse and neglect, and teenage pregnancy are among the problem areas discussed. Factors that place families more at risk to experience these problems also are identified.

Chapter 8, "Services to Children, Youth, and Families," focuses on current policies and programs that prevent or alleviate the problems discussed in Chapter 7. The activities that social workers provide in serving children, youth, and families are described.

Chapter 9, "Criminal Justice," discusses the nature of crime and the criminal justice system, including the roles of law enforcement, the courts, and the prison system. A special section focuses on the juvenile justice system and differences in treatment of adult and juvenile offenders. Roles of social workers, including probation and parole officers, also are explored.

Chapter 10, "Social Work Services at the Workplace," explores a field of social work that is resurging and gaining popularity today. The importance of considering both the impact of the family setting and the work setting in understanding individual functioning and needs, and what social workers in the workplace do to help employees function better both in the workplace and beyond, are discussed.

Chapter 11, "Social Work in Rural Settings," focuses on an important segment of social work often not addressed. This chapter distinguishes important differences between rural and urban life and the implications for social workers who choose to practice in rural settings.

Chapter 12, "Old Age: Issues, Problems, and Services," discusses a special population that increasingly needs attention from the social welfare system and social work practitioners. This chapter examines issues and problems that an older population creates for society and identifies resources developed to provide physical and social support systems to meet their needs. Social work for the aged is a rapidly growing field, as more people fit this age category. The types of activities in which social workers who assist this population are engaged also are explored.

These nine chapters demonstrate the need for social services for individuals from birth through death in a variety of settings. They suggest that some individuals, by the nature of their age, ethnicity, and social class, are more at risk to need social services than others. They also demonstrate that social workers are employed in many settings—government poverty programs, mental health clinics, hospitals, prisons, schools, churches, rural areas, and nursing homes—and that opportunities for social work practitioners in terms of setting and population are almost limitless.

4 The Fight Against Poverty

aria and Joe Saldana live in an inner-city area in a large northern city. Both in their early thirties, they have five children, ranging in age from 2 to 14. Joe works on construction jobs when he can, and Maria works as a maid at a local hotel when she can find child care for her younger children. Joe and Maria have a combined income of $11,000, well below the poverty level for a family of seven. The rent for their two-bedroom house is $300 a month. Money for bus fare, utilities, and other necessities often leaves the Saldanas with no money for food at the end of the month, and last year the children often had to miss school during the cold winter because they didn't have any warm clothes to wear. Neither of the Saldanas works at a job that provides health insurance, which means that the family usually goes without medical care when someone is sick. Both of the Saldanas grew up living in poverty, and both quit school in junior high school to earn money to help their parents to provide for their brothers and sisters. Although they have a strong value system and are hard workers, they find it difficult to find jobs with adequate pay and benefits due to their limited education. Maria became sick after the birth of their last child, and shortly after that, Joe lost his job. When his unemployment benefits ran out and he couldn't find another job, Joe briefly left his family so that Maria could receive AFDC and Medicaid. However, several months later, Joe found a construction job, moved back with Maria, and the family no longer qualified for AFDC. Although the family still qualifies for food stamps, Joe and Maria have not applied for them because they have a great deal of pride and only want to turn to "welfare" when they are really desperate.

Both the Saldanas have hopes and dreams for themselves and their children. They would like to find more stable, better paying jobs so that they can buy a home in a better environment, and their children can have a better diet, better health care, and attend better schools. They want their children to finish high school and, perhaps, attend college so that they, too, do not grow up in poverty.

INTRODUCTION

In the United States, poverty is a recurrent policy issue: it surfaces as a hot topic, then gradually recedes from overt political consciousness, only to re-emerge. The circumstances underlying the process are not fully understood (Romanyshyn 1971). As the 1988 presidential election draws closer, it appears certain that the related issues of poverty and social welfare will remain a dilemma in American politics. Although there is frustration with the number of Americans who are poor (13.6 percent, in 1986, according to the Bureau of the Census), almost no one is satisfied with current public efforts to respond to poverty. Twenty-five years of academic research and political debate have left the issue unresolved if not undefined. Charles Murray's controversial book, *Losing Ground* (1984), argues that the increases we now are seeing in the poverty rate are a *consequence* of the programs designed to reduce poverty. He asserts that we have generated a new dependency by a misguided effort to be generous.

The mixed results in reducing poverty in the United States are a reflection of the highly categorical and pragmatic structure of U.S. antipoverty policy and programs. Chapter 2 reviewed the political history of providing assistance categorically; e.g., aid to children, the blind, and the elderly. In order to gain a perspective on actual practice, it is useful to focus attention on how poverty is defined, who are the poor in the United States, and a general perspective on poverty policy. This chapter also will include a detailed examination of those poverty-related programs for which social workers have primary responsibility.

THE CONCEPT OF POVERTY

Between 1960 and 1981, participation in Aid to Families with Dependent Children (AFDC) rose from 803,000 to 3.8 million, then leveled off to 3.7 million in 1987. The conservative position on the growth of welfare dependency rests on two arguments. One of these is that if the tax dollars used to pay for program expansion were left in the private economy, they would result in investment and job creation, which, in turn, would have a more beneficial impact on the poor than the poverty programs. The second conservative argument is that the structure of the poverty programs makes welfare payments, food stamps, and subsidized housing economically more favorable than many entry level jobs. This factor, along with the loss of stigma for many of being "on welfare," has destroyed the "natural" incentives for working and thus created a self-perpetuating welfare class (Gilder 1980). In an interview, conservative economist George Gilder, a proponent of many of the Reagan Administration's domestic policies, asserted, "In order to succeed the poor need most of all the spur of their poverty" (Editorial Research 1984, 14). While avoiding such a politically unpalatable suggestion himself, in a radio speech in December 1983, President Reagan said, "There is no question that many well-intentioned Great Society–type programs contributed to family breakups, welfare dependency and a large increase in births out of wedlock." (Editorial Research 1984, 14).

On the other hand, Michael Harrington (1984) sees the problem in a totally different light. His position is that the last quarter century of debate over poverty has been more hype than reality. In an earlier book, *The Other America,* Harrington ushered in the acute political awareness of poverty. Now, he says that the "apparently expensive" efforts to deal with poverty as a side issue diverted attention from the real issues of wage discrimination, structural unemployment, and very rigid class structures. To both the left and the right, poverty is a very practical problem, and it is inordinately difficult to accurately track or chronicle the results in the war against poverty.

No small part of the political and intellectual confusion stems from the simple fact that poverty is a surprisingly elusive concept. Poverty, at root, is the notion that a household's income is inadequate as judged by a specific standard. The translation of this concept into practical terms produces technical as well as ideological debates. Even to define *household* for purposes of a census count is not as simple a notion as once was thought. Is the unit composed only of the nuclear family, or do we count elders, boarders, roommates, etc., who share the dwelling? Similarly, at first such concepts as income appear to be hard concepts, but should income include goods given or traded outside the regular economy: for example, should it include employer or government benefits given in kind? What should be the time frame: a year or a month? Clearly, as each subelement in the concept comes up for definition, there is ample room for ambiguity.

In a very general sense, the approach to the specification of the poverty among us can be approached graphically, as in Figure 4–1. The curve expresses the frequency distribution of "incomes" among "households." Were all incomes equal, the distribution would be represented by a thin vertical line at the mean (average income). As it actually occurs, the distribution is unevenly grouped around the median (middle of range from low to high incomes). Far to the right are the "rich," and far to the left are the "poor." Over the past fifty years, primary distribution of income has been static; it has not shifted between rich and poor. It is true now, and has been true, that if we cut the median in half, we find roughly 20 percent of the households below that income. This means that roughly 20 percent of U.S. households make incomes that are less than half of what the typical "middle-income" (not very rich not very poor) family makes.

Similarly, if we multiply the median by roughly 2½ times, we would find 95 percent of all households below that point. This means that only 5 percent of all U.S. households make incomes at least 2½ times what the typical middle-income family makes. Thus, with simple lines we could classify households

Figure 4–1
**Household
Income, 1983**

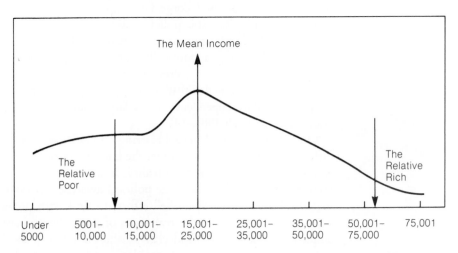

Source: Based on information from *Current Population Survey—P60*, various years, compiled by
J. Heffernan.

as 20 percent poor, 5 percent rich, and 75 percent in the middle. (This is
roughly how people would class themselves.) However, those points on the
horizontal axis are extremely arbitrary. Although this curve may have a
conceptual "elegance," it forces comparison of households of very diverse sizes
and circumstances. A more practical, yet less elegant, approach is to rank
households by size in relation to some priced market basket of goods and services. This is the "official" measure of poverty or **official poverty.** It provides a set of income thresholds adjusted for household size, age of the
household head, and number of children under 18. The specific thresholds for

Table 4–1
**Weighted
Average
Poverty
Threshold
in 1986**

Size of Family Unit	Threshold
One person (unrelated individual)	$ 5,572
□ 15–64 years	5,701
□ 65 years and over	5,255
Two persons	7,138
□ Household head 15–64 years	7,372
□ Household head 65 years and over	6,630
Three persons	8,737
Four persons	11,203
Five persons	13,259
Six persons	14,986
Seven persons	17,049
Eight persons	18,791
Nine person or more	22,497

Source: *Current Population Survey—P60, 1987.* Washington, D.C.: U.S. Bureau of the Census.

a working-age household head with a spouse and minor children are given in Table 4–1.

The figures in Table 4–1 are adjusted annually to account for inflation. This official income-line concept includes calendar-year income from all money sources: wages, salary, bonuses, private and social insurance, money payments for welfare, net child support, and net alimony. It does not include the value of in-kind welfare benefits, such as food stamps, medicaid, medicare, and public housing subsidy not given in cash, or employer-provided noncash benefits. The most serious reservation to the official concept of poverty is that it fails to reflect nearly 40 billion dollars of expenditures on such in-kind benefits. The numbers thus overstate the proportion of the population that is poor.

Three additional important points need to be made: (1) there is no one "right" or correct measure of poverty; (2) the progress against poverty has been unsteady over time; and (3) the progress against poverty has been uneven among the various groups that constitute the poverty population. Before examining the social worker's role in the reduction of poverty rates, it is necessary to look at these three confounding problems.

MEASUREMENT OF POVERTY

The first problem in measuring poverty has to do with a debate over the standard itself. According to some observers, a poverty standard should reflect how well those at the bottom of the income distribution fare relative to all others. Poverty lines thus should reflect the proportion of households that fall below a threshold expressed as a fixed fraction or percentage (such as half or 50 percent) of median income. Such a perspective views poverty as a problem

A meal is served at a shelter for the homeless. Increasing numbers of men, women and children have neither food nor shelter.

that would disappear only when the distribution of income became significantly more equal. Other observers suggest that the poverty threshold instead should be fixed by the total cost of some precise market basket of goods and services. In the United States, there has been very little shift in the distribution of income throughout this century. As suggested earlier in this chapter, about one-fifth (or 20 percent) of U.S. households have real incomes below one-half of the median income.

For practical purposes, the debate surrounding poverty in America has focused on an "absolute" definition of poverty, which tracks the threshold for poverty at the cost of a specified set of goods and services. (For a more complete discussion on the absolutes relative debate see D. P. Moynihan, *On Understanding Poverty*.) Even if there is agreement to use an absolute concept of poverty, the problem of measurement still is not resolved.

According to David Stockman, Reagan's first Director of the Office of Management and Budget, the U.S. Census Bureau's estimates of the number of people below the cash-income threshold fail to reflect poverty accurately. "In the mid 1960's when we began to measure poverty, such programs as Medicaid, food stamps, housing subsidies, and the like were only an insignificant share of government's direct aid to the poor. By 1973, over half of all aid was in-kind rather than in cash. Today, roughly 70 out of every 100 dollars of direct aid is given in-kind. Much of this aid goes to people who are lifted out of poverty by virtue of these programs" (Stockman 1984).

Many of the poverty measures are akin to hat tricks. The best measure available of how many really are considered poor has been provided by Sheldon Danzinger, Director of the University of Wisconsin's Institute for Research on Poverty. Danzinger distinguished among four definitions of income. First, there is pretransfer income or market income. This concept includes all income from wages, rents, interests, dividends, pensions, alimony, and child support to the family who receives it and, at the same time, subtracts each amount from the household paying it. This figure reflects a snapshot of poverty if there were no social insurance or welfare programs. The second definition includes prewelfare income. In addition to the first figure, this includes any money received from social income benefits, such as Old Age, Survivors, and Disability Insurance (OASDI), unemployment, railroad and federal retirements, and military service benefits. The third definition, which is related roughly to the official count presently used, adds payments from AFDC, SSI, and general assistance. The fourth definition also uses an adjustment for the money equivalent value of the various in-kind payments (housing subsidies, Medicaid, Medicare, etc.) to the poor (see Table 4–2).

Viewed in this light, the progress against poverty is considerable. Against a picture of no significant change, in which nearly a quarter of all Americans would be poor, is a contrasting "total" picture, in which the numbers have been reduced to less than one in ten in that condition.

POVERTY RATES OVER TIME

The march against poverty is by no means steady in the short run. Thinking in terms of many generations, there is enormous progress in reducing poverty,

Table 4–2 Percentage of Poor by Various Definitions of Poverty	Year	Official measure (1)	Adjusted for in-kind transfers underreporting, and taxes (2)	Adjusted for in-kind transfers only (3)	Pretransfer poverty (4)	Prewelfare poverty (5)	Relative poverty (6)
	1964	19.0	—	—	—	—	—
	1965	17.3	13.4	16.8	21.3	16.3[a]	—
	1966	14.7	—	—	—	—	—
	1967	14.2	—	—	19.4	15.0	—
	1968	12.8	9.9	—	18.2	13.6	14.6
	1969	12.1	—	—	17.7	13.3	—
	1970	12.6	9.3	—	18.8	13.9	—
	1971	12.5	—	—	19.6	13.8	—
	1972	11.9	6.2	—	19.2	13.1	15.7
	1973	11.1	—	—	19.0	12.4	—
	1974	11.2	7.2	—	20.3	13.1	14.9
	1975	12.3	—	—	22.0	13.7	—
	1976	11.8	6.7	—	21.0	13.1	15.4
	1977	11.6	—	—	21.0	13.0	—
	1978	11.4	—	—	20.2	12.6	15.5
	1979	11.7	6.1	9.0	20.5	12.9	15.7
	1980	13.0	—	10.4	21.9	14.2	16.0
	1981	14.0	—	11.7	23.1	15.1	16.9
	1982	15.0	—	12.7	24.0	15.9	17.8
	1983	15.2	—	13.1	24.2	16.1	18.6
	1984	14.4	—	12.2	22.9	15.3	18.7
	1985	14.0	—	11.8	22.4	14.9	18.0
	1986[b]	13.9	—	—	—	—	—

Sources: Column 1: for 1964, U.S. Bureau of the Census (1969); for 1965–1985, U.S. Bureau of the Census (1986a); for 1986, Danziger and Gottschalk (1985).

Column 2: for 1968–1979, Smeeding (1982), recipient value. for 1965 Smeeding shows 12.1 percent in contrast to an official level of 15.6 percent. That official level was computed from the survey of Economic Opportunity (SEO), which obtained more complete income reporting than the corresponding Current Population Survey (CPS); the latter produced the estimate of 17.3 percent in column 1. To maintain consistency with column 1, we reduced 17.3 percent by the ratio of 12.1/15.6 to derive the 13.4-percent value. In-kind transfers include food stamps, school lunch, public housing, Medicare, and Medicaid.

Column 3: for 1979–1985, U.S. Bureau of the Census (1986b), recipient value. For 1965, when food stamps, public housing, and medical assistance cost less than $1 billion, we roughly estimated that they would reduce the official poverty rate by only 3 percent.

Columns 4, 5, and 6: for 1965, computations from 1966 SEO data tape. For 1967–1985, computations from annual March CPS data tapes.

a. Note that this figure is *less than* the official measure in column 1 and the adjusted one in column 3, even though prewelfare poverty excludes welfare and in-kind income in determining poverty status. This anomaly reflects the fact that for 1965, column 5 is derived from the SEO whereas columns 1 and 3 are derived from the CPS.

b. Projected.

Source: Danziger, S., and D. Weinberg. *Fighting Poverty.* Harvard Press Cambridge, Mass.: 1986. p. 54.

and it is unthinkable that this country would ever return to the conditions of 1900. However, in the short term of a single generation, progress against poverty varies; not only is it uneven, but the poverty rate is on the rise in some periods (see Table 4–3, Figure 4–2).

Table 4 –3
**Poverty Rate
for All Persons
Officially
Counted as
Poor,
Definition 2, in
United States,
1959–1984
(percent)**

1960	22.2
1965	17.3
1970	12.6
1971	12.5
1972	11.9
1973	11.1
1974	11.2
1975	12.3
1976	11.8
1977	11.6
1978	11.4
1979	11.7
1980	13.0
1981	14.0
1982	15.0
1983	15.3
1984	14.4
1985	14.0
1986	13.6

Source: U.S. Census Bureau. *Population Reports, Series P–60*, 1986.

Figure 4 –2
**Poverty Rate in
the United
States,
1959–1984**

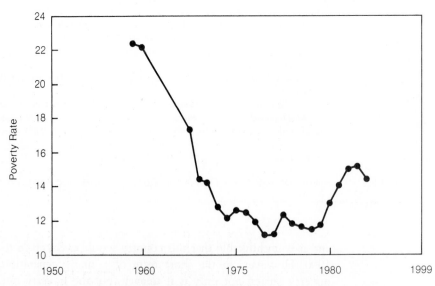

Source: Data from U.S. Congress, House Ways and Means Committee Paper 100–4–P626, March 1987.

As Table 4–3 and Figure 4–2 clearly show, the progress against poverty fluctuates over time. Many factors interact to produce short-run shifts downward and upward. Basically, however, four factors predominate in causing these shifts: (1) shifts in the overall performance of the economy; (2) shifts in the composition of households within the nation (for example, more single-parent households headed by women); (3) shifts in level of expenditure on social programs; and (4) shifts in the effectiveness of social programs. There is little doubt that the most profound influence is the performance of the overall economy. Except for the elderly, who largely have left the labor market, shifts in the performance of the economy almost perfectly track the performance of the poverty rate. In John Kennedy's famous metaphor, "the rising tides reach all ships, dingy and yacht alike." When an economy is strong, the rich get richer and the poor get less poor, with some raised above the poverty line. When the economy performs poorly, the rich get less rich and the poor get more poor, with some sinking below the poverty line. The data in Figure 4–3 reflect shifts in the overall economy and the poverty rate. Using median family income as an indicator we see that the overall economy closely tracks the poverty rate. It is clear that the best defense against poverty is a vigorous economy.

Figure 4 –3   **Poverty Rate Among Nonelderly and Poverty Line as Fraction of Median Family Income**

Source: David Elwood and Lawrence Summers, "Poverty in America: Is Welfare the Answer or the Problem?" Paper read at the Institute for Research on Poverty Conference, "Poverty and Policy: Retrospect and Prospects," December 1984.

SHIFTS IN THE POPULATION COMPOSITION OF THE POOR

A second factor to be evaluated in discussing poverty is the shift in the composition of the nation's population. Most dramatic in this regard is what is happening to the black population. The shift to a much lower marriage rate, a much higher divorce rate, a much higher birth rate among unmarried women, and a larger proportion of single black women not marrying or remarrying—all these have resulted in revolutionary changes in the composition of black families. The number of black families headed by a single woman increased by 97.5 percent between 1969 and 1982. The proportion of such families that were poor went from 53 to 56 percent. An increase in the number of black single-parent households headed by women and a significantly high rate of unemployment among black men (6 out of 10 compared to 1 out of 10 white men) have resulted in higher proportions of blacks than whites living in poverty. A more detailed assessment of demographic shifts and the resulting consequences in poverty rates is shown in Table 4–4.

The progress against poverty is decidedly uneven by demographic groups. By post–transfer estimates, the poverty rate among the aged has dropped most dramatically, while the poverty rate among female-headed families has increased and the poverty rate among the disabled has been very stable. A glimpse of these changes is shown in Table 4–5.

A GENERAL PERSPECTIVE

In Western democracies, the basic social expectation is that the individual will work, saving for the days when work is no longer feasible or desirable. It also is expected that workers within families will care for those within their own families who do not work and that the basic responsibility of the government is to manage the economy in such a way that the opportunity to work is available. It now is recognized that governments have a responsibility to structure, operate, and finance programs that guarantee that a basic standard of living will be met for those truly in need. There is a tension between these social expectations and the two public responsibilities. First, it is expected that public guarantees will not diminish social incentives to work, to save, and to care for one's own. If, for example, a generous guarantee to support single-parent households exists, it is reasonable to expect that some households will break-up because aid is available. Despite claims to the contrary, however, there is no evidence to suggest that family splitting is "caused" by welfare. Second, it is suggested that public funds spent on income assistance transfers divert, at least partially, funds available for investments, which would provide jobs that would obliterate the need for welfare transfers. Again, there is no credible evidence to suggest that economic growth is slowed as a result of social spending (see Table 4–6).

In understanding the problems associated with poverty, it is necessary to understand the public and private systems within our society that attempt to ensure that all households have an opportunity to acquire the basic goods and

Table 4–4   **Poverty Status of Families, by Family Type and Race: 1969 and 1982 (numbers in thousands)**

Characteristic	1982		1969		Percent Change 1969–1982
	Number	Percent of All Families	Number	Percent of All Families	
All Income Levels					
All Races:					
All families	61,393	100.0	51,588	100.0	19.0
With female householder, no husband present	9,469	15.4	5,593	10.8	69.3
All other families	51,924	84.6	45,995	89.2	12.9
White:					
All families	53,407	100.0	46,261	100.0	15.4
with female householder, no husband present	6,507	12.2	4,165	9.0	56.2
All other families	46,900	87.8	42,096	91.0	11.4
Black:					
All families	6,530	100.0	4,889	100.0	33.6
with female householder, no husband present	2,734	41.9	1,384	28.3	97.5
All other families	3,796	58.1	3,505	71.7	8.3
Below Poverty Level					
All Races:					
All families	7,512	100.0	5,008	100.0	50.0
with female householder, no husband present	3,434	45.7	1,827	36.5	88.0
All other families	4,079	54.3	3,181	63.5	28.2
White:					
All families	5,118	100.0	3,575	100.0	43.2
with female householder, no husband present	1,813	35.4	1,069	29.9	69.6
All other families	3,306	64.6	2,506	70.1	31.9
Black:					
All families	2,158	100.0	1,366	100.0	58.0
with female householder, no husband present	1,535	71.1	737	54.0	108.3
All other families	622	28.8	629	46.0	-1.1

Source: U.S. Congress, House Ways and Means Committee Paper 98–55, November, 1983.

services required for a good life. Depending on how specific one cares to be, it is usually sufficient to focus on four basic interacting systems and a fifth system structured specifically to deal with the failure and/or breakdown of those four basic systems. The four basic systems are the family system, the employment system, the social insurance system, and the private insurance system. When, for whatever reason, one of these systems malfunctions and the family is left unable to acquire basic necessities of life, the income welfare system is expected to anticipate, respond to, and correct that deficiency. Since

Table 4 –5

Composition of Households with Incomes Below the Poverty Line, Official Measure, 1967 and 1982

Percentage of Poor Households Where Head Is	1967		1982	
	Pretransfer Poor	Posttransfer Poor	Pretransfer Poor	Posttransfer Poor
Over 65 years of age	50.56	40.43	43.31	22.01
Female, with children under six	5.48	6.97	7.74	12.61
Student	4.05	5.54	4.08	6.56
Disabled	9.36	10.00	10.01	11.09
Persons working full-time, full-year	14.74	19.11	8.51	13.07
Single persons working less than full-time, full-year	6.25	7.59	10.52	14.78
Male family head, working less than full-time, full-year	5.47	6.18	10.31	11.95
Female family head, no children under six, working less than full-time, full-year	4.10	4.18	5.54	7.92
Total	100.00	100.00	100.00	100.00
Number of households (millions)	15.5	10.8	25.3	14.2

Note: Classification is mutually exclusive and hierarchical: Any household head who fits in more than one category has been classified only in the one closest to the top of the table.

Source: Sheldon Danziger, Robert Haveman, Robert Plotnick. Computations by authors from March 1968 and 1983 Current Population Survey data tapes. "Antipoverty Policy: Effects on the Poor and the Nonpoor." Paper read at the Institute for Research on Poverty Conference, "Poverty and Policy: Retrospects & Prospects," December 1984.

from a systems perspective, success or failure in one system generates success or failure in other systems, it is useful to briefly explain each system's functions and its interactions, then focus our primary attention on the welfare system.

THE FAMILY SYSTEM

The family is the primary social unit of Western society. Each family member contributes to and receives from the social productivity of the family. It is a social ideal that marriage is a lifetime commitment, and that parents assume the major responsibilities for home care and work so that the children's needs are met as well as their own. The children, in turn, assume responsibility for care of aged parents. The factual reality is a distant cousin to this idealized perception. Half of all marriages are terminated before death of a spouse. At any moment in time, almost one-quarter of all children live apart from a living parent, and only a small share of aged persons are dependent on their adult children. The welfare system needs to respond to this objective reality.

Table 4 –6   **Social Expenditure and Economic Growth in Six Industrialized Countries, 1960–1981**

	Social Expenditure as Percentage of GDP[a]		GDP per Capita 1981[b]	Annual Growth in GDP per Capita 1960–1981[c]
	1960	1981		
Germany	18.0	26.5	$11,080	3.1
France	13.4	23.8	10,550	3.6
Italy	12.7	22.7	6,120	3.6
United Kingdom	10.3	18.9	8,880	1.8
United States	7.3	14.9	12,650	2.1
Japan	4.0	13.8	9,610	6.4

Source: Gary Burtless, "Public Spending for the Poor: Trends, Prospects, and Economic Limits," Institute for Research on Poverty Conference Paper. Data is from publications of the Organization for Economic Co-operation and Development. *Focus,* 8, no. 2 (Summer 1985): 22.

[a] Government outlays on pensions, health care, and other income maintenance as a percentage of gross domestic product.

[b] Measured in U.S. dollars at 1981 prices and exchange rates.

[c] Measured in constant 1970 prices.

THE EMPLOYMENT SYSTEM

Our basic social expectation is that those who are physically and mentally able to work will work. We exempt from this responsibility those who are in school or training programs, those who have accepted basic family care responsibilities, the disabled, and the aged. The basic public expectation is that governments will manage the economy and education programs so that there is a fit between job seekers and jobs. Generally speaking, the number of jobs available ebbs and flows with progress and decline in the overall economy: when the number of jobs decreases, the poverty rate increases. A vigorous economy is the best way to combat poverty. Poverty rates rise faster than the economy in general falls, when the economy is hurting. When the economy improves, poverty rates fall faster than the economy rises. Those who live at the edge of the poverty line are particularly responsive to even small shifts in the nation's economic well being.

THE SOCIAL AND PRIVATE INSURANCE SYSTEM

Most persons now recognize that the family's income cannot always be met from employment-related income and needs to be supplemented by insurance. The function of employment-related insurance is to replace the flow of income from work when that flow is disrupted due to unemployment, disability, retirement, or death. This replacement system is expected to constitute the second line of defense against poverty. There are two basic categories of employment-related insurance. *Private insurance* for health care and untimely death is purchased on the open market, often by employers who then make these plans available to their employees. *Social insurance* is provided by government. The two major types of social insurance in the United States are unemployment insurance and old age insurance.

The better the employment system works, the better the private and social insurance system works. This is true for two reasons. First, full employment means less strain on social insurance, and second, most of our private and social insurance plans are designed so that the premiums are paid out of wages. The larger the share of the population tied directly to the labor force by regular work or tied indirectly by the labor-force participation of a family member, the larger is the share of the population protected by earning-related insurance. This means that fewer persons have to look to the third line of defense: the direct welfare system. Table 4–7 shows how public and private insurance programs work together to close income gaps generated by the various factors that cause a disruption or cessation of wage income.

Wage premiums and private payments to support insurance in the public and private sectors are dependent on the vibrancy of the employment system. Public and private life insurance provides for the continuance of income to families following the premature death of the breadwinner. When the insurance system fails, the residual demand is placed on the welfare system. When this residual demand is reduced by broader and more effective public and

Table 4 –7 **The Social and Private Insurance System**	**Reason for Earnings Loss**	**Earnings Replacement Program**
	Temporary unemployment	Unemployment Insurance (UI)
	Disability	
	Resulting from work, total and partial	Workmen's Compensation (WC) Veteran's Compensation
	Not resulting from work	Sick leave (provided by public and private employers)
	Short term	Temporary Disability Insurance (TDI) (both public and private)
	Long term, total	Social Security (OASDI) Long-term disability insurance, Early retirement pensions
	Retirement	
	Low- to middle-income retirees	Social Security (OASDI) Some private provision (pensions, annuities)
	Middle- to upper-income retirees	Social Security (OASDI) Considerable private provision
	Death	Life Insurance Social Security

Source: Michael C. Barth, George J. Carcagno, John L. Palm, "Toward an Effective Income Support System: Problems, Prospects, and Choices," Institute for Research on Poverty, U. of Wisconsin—Madison, 1974.

private insurance programs, it allows the welfare system to concentrate its efforts more effectively on that which it does best, the coverage of those at the bottom of the income scale experiencing emergency difficulties.

The principal function of private and social insurance programs is to secure for all households a guarantee against a precipitous fall in income as a result of the death, retirement, or unemployment of the primary breadwinner. All of the components of public-sponsored social insurance programs are in need of strengthening. The most significant part of the insurance system is the old age, survivors, and disability insurance (OASDI) programs, often called Social Security. This program currently is funded out of payroll deductions for salaries up to $40,000 that place a 6.65 percent wage tax equally on the employer and the worker. Monies generated from these wage taxes provide income to a governmentally run trust fund. The trust fund is expected to pay for current benefits to the aged, the disabled, and survivors of deceased employees, with the future flow into the trust fund projected to be sufficiently large enough to pay for later demands on the trust to pay benefits to present and future employees and their survivors as they need them. When this system originally was conceived, the economy was expected to continue to expand and the proportion of the retired population to the total working population was expected to stabilize. In fact, world economic circumstances have changed significantly, and the U.S. economy has faltered in its growth. More significant for social insurance planning is the increase in the ratio of retired persons to working persons. This situation will be compounded in the early part of the next century.

If social insurance collections are to pay for social insurance benefits, then tax rate and benefit schedules need periodic adjustment. Since the total tax on all workers eventually must equal the total benefit to all retirees, a critical relationship emerges. If workers are expected to support retirees through their tax payments, then the size of the tax and the size of the benefit in relation to wages is dependent on the ratio of workers to retirees.

$$\text{Average Wage Taxed} \times \left(\frac{\text{Number of Workers}}{\text{Number of Retirees}} \right) = \frac{\text{Average Benefit}}{\text{Average Wage}}$$

If, as a consequence of demographic shifts such as lower birth rates or longer life expectancies and earlier retirements, the ratio of workers to beneficiaries falls, governments are required either to lower the ratio of benefits to wages, to raise the tax, or to increase the retirement age.

Demographic shifts in the age composition of the population, which result from more births in a given time period followed by longer life spans and earlier retirements, produce a tension in the forward plans of social insurance schemes such as OASDI.

This demographic shift does not mean that the social insurance trust fund is going broke. It does mean that constant adjustments will need to be made. The recent U.S. Pension Commission proposed corrections to the schedule of taxes and benefits that are expected to carry the system safely forward well into the middle of the twenty-first century.

The next section of this chapter focuses on the public assistance system, for which social workers bear the principal responsibility.

PUBLIC ASSISTANCE

Public assistance programs are the welfare programs that provide income, medical care, and social services to those poor persons whose income from wages, property, private transfers, and social and public insurance is inadequate to provide a socially established minimum standard. The standard is not the same for all classes of persons and varies rather considerably from state to state. The distinguishing characteristic of public assistance programs is that they have been designed to aid very particular categories of persons in need of income assistance. Other characteristics of assistance programs distinguish this form of aid from social insurance. First, applicants for public assistance programs have to demonstrate that they are unable to meet their basic needs from current income, sale of assets, or claims on other individuals. This is to say they must pass a "means test." Second, public assistance benefits are funded out of the current general revenues of government and not by a special tax or trust fund. Third, in this country but not elsewhere, public assistance programs are complicated by an uneasy alliance of all three levels of government: federal, state, and local. Finally, as suggested earlier, public assistance programs are different for the different classes of persons in need. Table 4–8 illustrates the breakdown of welfare payments at both the state and federal levels.

Three major types of public income assistance programs—SSI, AFDC, and general assistance—provide cash assistance to recipients. Two major types of public assistance give in-kind benefits: food stamps and Medicaid. All of these programs are in a constant stage of transition, and the demand for welfare reform really means reform of public assistance.

Table 4 –8 **Total Federal and State Welfare Payments (in millions of dollars)**	Recipients (millions)	Federal Payments	State Payments
December 1974	4.0	$341	$110
December 1975	4.3	374	119
December 1976	4.2	386	121
December 1977	4.2	403	125
December 1978	4.2	420	126
December 1979	4.2	457	189
October 1980	4.2	533	168
December 1981	4.1	575	158
December 1982	3.8	607	148
December 1983	3.9	678	147
December 1984	4.1	725	156
December 1985	4.1	763	172

Source: Congressional Research Service, *Welfare Background Paper,* Report 81–124 EPW. Washington, D.C.: Library of Congress, 1981.

Supplemental Security Income

Supplemental Security Income (SSI) was adopted in this country in 1972 and became effective in 1974. It replaced three separate programs: Aid to the Blind (AB), Aid to the Permanently and Totally Disabled (APTD), and Old Age Assistance (OAA). The SSI program is federally funded and administered. In 1986, in a low-paying state where there is no supplementation, a couple living independently in a home or apartment received a benefit of just over $500. In most cases, this couple also would have been eligible for food stamps and medicaid benefits. If, in fact, a couple had no other income or assets and received all of the benefits for which they were theoretically eligible, the couple would be raised above the poverty line on the strength of their welfare benefits. A significant number of aged, blind, and disabled persons are left poor due to glitches in the determination of their eligibility, the failure of some such persons to avail themselves of assistance, and most particularly, the failure of most jurisdictions to search out beneficiaries aggressively. The SSI program works in conjunction with the social security insurance program to aid the poorest of the aged, the disabled, and the blind.

Aid to Families with Dependent Children

The Aid to Families with Dependent Children (AFDC) program is intended to provide cash assistance to families with children, when those children are in need because of the loss of financial support as a consequence of death, disability, or continued absence of a parent from the home. In essence, AFDC is a financial assistance program for the single-parent family. A federal-state program, federal legislation provides matching grants to states. For each dollar spent by a state for AFDC, the federal government reimburses the state a specific amount, which varies by state depending on the state's per capita income. In other words, the poorer the state, the greater the federal match. AFDC programs are administered by the states, subject to federal regulations and audits. Thirty-two states operate the program in cooperation with local governments, channeling their federal funds to be administered directly at the local, usually the county, level.

Originally conceived principally as an aid program for "half orphans," the AFDC program today is a program to aid children living with one parent. Most often this is a consequence of divorce, desertion, or unmarried parenthood. Because AFDC requires that funding only be for single-parent families, it has been suggested that this program encourages fathers to leave to provide government support for their children. In 1962, federal legislation allowed states to provide aid to children in need in intact families, where the family's principal breadwinner was unemployed. This subprogram (AFDC–U) accounts for only 5 percent of program costs and is operative in only twenty-six states. Each state sets its own AFDC benefit standards, and in all states except Wisconsin and California, these benefits have eroded as the inflation rate has increased far more rapidly than the rate at which benefits have been increased (see Table 4–9). For the median state, this decline has been 33 percent, even though in current dollars the benefits were increased from $221 to $399.

Table 4–9   **AFDC Maximum Benefit for a 4–Person Family, by State, Selected Years**

	July 1970	July 1975	July 1980	January 1985[1]	January 1986[1]	Percent Change in 1970–1986 in Constant Dollars
Alabama	$81	$135	$148	$147	$147	−33
Alaska	375	400	514	800	823	−19
Arizona	167	183	244	282	353	−22
Arkansas	100	140	188	191	224	−17
California	221	349	563	660	698	+17
Colorado	235	264	351	420	420	−34
Connecticut	330	403	477	636	664	−26
Delaware	187	258	312	336	349	−31
District of Columbia	238	297	349	399	399	−38
Florida	134	170	230	284	298	−18
Georgia	133	153	193	245	264	−27
Hawaii	263	497	546	546	546	−23
Idaho	242	344	367	344	344	−48
Illinois	282	317	350	368	385	−50
Indiana	150	250	315	316	316	−22
Iowa	243	356	419	419	443	−33
Kansas	244	353	390	422	450	−32
Kentucky	187	235	235	246	246	−51
Louisiana	109	158	213[1]	234	234	−21
Maine	168	219	352	465	489	+8
Maryland	196	242	326	376	395	−26
Massachusetts	314	368[2]	419[1]	463	505	−41
Michigan	NA	453	531[1]	594	618	NA
(Detroit)	(263)	(399)	(501)	(564)	(588)	(−18)
Minnesota	299	385	486	611	616	−24
Mississippi	70	60	120	120	144	−24
Missouri	130	150	290	308	320	−9
Montana	228	227	331	425	426	−31
Nebraska	200	245	370	420	420	−23
Nevada	143	230	314	279	341	−12
New Hampshire	294	346	392	429	442	−45
New Jersey	347	356	414	443	465	−51
New Mexico	182	206	267	313	313	−37
New York	NA	476[1]	563[1]	676	706	NA
(New York City)	(336)	(400)	(476)	(566)	(596)	(−35)
North Carolina	158	200	210	244	269	−37
North Dakota	261	347	408	454	454	−36
Ohio	200	254	327	360	374	−31
Oklahoma	185	264	349	349	384	−23
Oregon	225	413	441[1, 3]	468	482	−21

Pennsylvania	313	349	381	444	466	−45
Rhode Island	263	319	389	547	574[4]	−19[5]
South Carolina	103	117	158	229	239	−14
South Dakota	300	329	361	371	371	−54
Tennessee	129	132	148	168	186	−47
Texas	179	140	140	201	221	−54
Utah	212	306	429	425	439	−24
Vermont	304	367	552	622	651	−21
Virginia	261	311	305[1]	379	410	−42
Washington	303	370	536	561	578	−30
West Virginia	138	249	249	249	312	−17
Wisconsin	217	403	529	636	649	+10
Wyoming	227	250	340	390	390	−37
Guam	NR	NR	307	310	310	NA
Puerto Rico	53	53	66	114	114	−21
Virgin Islands	NR	166	210	215	215	NA
Median State[6]	221	264	350	379	399	−33

[1] CRS survey data.

[2] Includes quarterly grant pro-rated monthly, (CRS survey).

[3] Oregon-based benefits on age of child. The figure assumes all children are under 6.

[4] Winter rate (Nov.–April). Summer rate was $467.

[5] Change calculated on basis of summer 1985 rate.

[6] Among 50 States and D.C.

NR = Not reported.

NA = Not available.

Note: Table compiled by the Congressional Research Service (CRS) on the basis of data from the Department of Health and Human Services and, where noted, from CRS itself. The last column of the table was computed using the CPI–U Consumer Price Index. A projection of 327.9 was assumed for January 1986.

Source: "Background Material and Data on Programs Within the Jurisdiction of the Committee on Ways and Means," 1986 edition. March 3, 1986: 378–9.

Despite declines in real benefits, the AFDC program expanded in terms of recipients until 1975 (see Table 4–10). During the last years of the Carter Administration and first few years of the Reagan Administration, program enrollment declined as a consequence of more strictly enforced eligibility standards.

General Assistance

General assistance is the generic term used to designate public assistance programs that provide financial aid to persons who are in need but do not

Table 4-10 Enrollment in AFDC Program		Program Recipient (000)	Percent Change	Cost in 1980 Dollars (billions)	Percent Change
	1945	943			
	1950	2,223	135.7	.685	175.7
	1955	2,192	−.01	1.889	.00
	1960	3,073	40.2	1.902	46.5
	1965	4,396	43.1	2.786	55.7
	1970	9,659	119.7	4.339	137.5
	1975	11,404	18.1	10.306	36.9
	1980	11,101	−.03	14.113	−11.6
	1981	10,613	−.04	12.475	+.04
	1982	10,504	−.01	12.862	−.01
	1983	10,865	+.03	12.839	−.001

Source: Calculated by J. Heffernan from various volumes of the Social Security Bulletin.

qualify for cash assistance under federally aided and authorized programs. It is financed by state governments with, in some cases, local administrative and/or fiscal responsibility. It goes under various names: home relief, direct relief, often just welfare. Assistance typically is in the form of direct cash aid and vendor payments for medical care, housing, energy payments, and the like. It truly is the aid program at the bottom of the barrel. Thirty-four states provide aid on the basis of need alone, but sixteen have various forms of work or work registration requirements in order to be eligible for the assistance.

There is no federal legislation for general assistance; programs are authorized by laws in the fifty states, resulting in highly varied programs among the states. The following list, assembled from various state and federal sources, attempts to provide an overview of these variations:

Caseloads and Costs (October 1980):
    794,791 cases; 1,002,342 recipients
    Total Payments: $125,364,017
    Average/Case: $157.73
    Average/Recipient: $125.07

Source of Funding:
    State Funding Only: 18 states
    State and Local Funding: 16 states
    Local Funding Only: 17 states

Administering Unit:
    County Administered: 40 states

Township Administered: 8 states

Combination of County and Township: 3 states

State Public Assistance Agency Administered Through Local Offices: 16 states

Local Office Administered, State Agency Supervised: 9 states

Local Office Administered, Not State Supervised: 20 states

Local Office Administered, State Supervised Only If State Funded: 4 states

The basic eligibility requirement for general assistance is need. The definition of need varies, and policies on assistance with respect to need vary by local jurisdiction in twenty-eight states. Needs standards usually are similar to those of federal categorical assistance programs.

Nineteen states grant assistance only to unemployable persons. Thirty-four states will assist employable persons; twenty of these require both registration with the state employment service and acceptance of available work. Nine states grant assistance without regard to employability but continue assistance only to the unemployable. Five states (and certain counties in four other states) permit general assistance to supplement earnings. In two of these states, such aid is limited to families with dependent children.

States with Highest Average Payments per Case (1980):

Hawaii $279.63

New York 204.41

Michigan 189.08

Rhode Island 182.86

Massachusetts 180.27

States with Lowest Average Payments per Case (1980):

Mississippi $15.47

West Virginia 28.25

Indiana 29.44

Oklahoma 35.00

Table 4–11 shows the growth of general assistance programs since 1945.

IN KIND ASSISTANCE PROGRAMS

Food Stamps

The Food Stamp Program is designed to supplement the food purchasing power of an eligible, low-income household in order to allow the family to consume a minimally adequate nutritious diet. A second goal of the program is to expand the market for agricultural goods. Over the years, the welfare objective has come to dominate the agricultural objective. Nevertheless, the program still is administered by the Food and Nutrition Service of the U.S. Department of Agriculture, with street-level administration provided by state

Table 4–11
Growth of General Assistance, 1945–1980

	Case Recipients (thousands)	Average Payment	Estimated (millions)	Annual Benefits
December 1945	257	507	16.55	87.9
December 1950	413	866	22.25	298.3
December 1955	314	743	23.30	214.2
December 1960	431	1244	24.85	322.5
December 1965	310	677	31.65	259.2
December 1970	54	1056	57.85	618.3
December 1975	692	977	102.07	1138.2
December 1980	795	1002	125.07	1504.4
December 1981	861	1046	NA	NA
December 1982	1019	1542	NA	NA
December 1983	1086	1349	NA	NA

Source: *Ibid*. Table 10–4.

and local social service offices. The benefit to the household is provided in the form of purchased bonus coupons or stamps issued to the head of household to be used in retail stores to purchase food items. Eligibility for the program and the full value of the stamps received are determined by the individual household size and monthly net income. Adult recipients, in most cases, are required to be registered for employment. The full value of the coupon allotment is based on the Department of Agriculture's "thrifty food plan," and is estimated at a value equal to the cost of a nutritionally adequate diet for a household of that size. The benefit is indexed each January to reflect changes in food prices (Table 4–12). The specific benefit to a household is determined by a basic benefit reduction rate, which reduces the coupons to be made available by 30 percent of income after standard deduction and expenses. The standard deduction is $85 per month plus 20 percent of earnings. In some cases, larger deductions are allowed to compensate for authorized child care and unusual medical costs. There also is an adjustment for costs of shelter. In addition, food-stamp eligible families without an aged or disabled person may not have gross incomes more than 130 percent above the poverty line. Table 4–13 shows the growth of the Food Stamp Program from 1970 to 1980.

Medicaid

Medicaid is a federal grant-in-aid program to the states to assist them in providing comprehensive medical care to low-income individuals and families. All states participate; however, Arizona recently signed an agreement to implement a statewide alternative plan. Forty-nine states and the District of Columbia are given an open-ended matching payment from the federal government, matching 50–78 percent of the amount the state contributes, depending on the *state's* per capita income. The state proportion is calculated

Table 4–12
Maximum
Monthly Food
Stamp
Allotments
(through September 1986)

Household Size	48 States and D.C.	Alaska[1]	Hawaii	Virgin Islands	Guam
1 person	$80	$111	$124	$103	$118
2 persons	147	204	228	189	217
3 persons	211	293	327	271	311
4 persons	268	372	415	345	395
5 persons	318	442	493	409	470
6 persons	382	530	592	491	564
7 persons	422	586	654	543	623
8 persons	483	670	748	621	712
Each additional person	+60	+84	+94	+78	+89

[1] These allotment levels are for urban Alaska. Benefit levels for rural Alaska are increased by about 40 percent to account for higher food prices in rural areas.

Source: "Background Material and Data on Programs within the Jurisdiction of the Committee on Ways and Means," 1986 edition. March 3, 1986:451.

Table 4–13
Growth of
Food Stamp
Program

	Average Monthly Participants (000)	Percent of Increase	Annual Benefit Expenditure (millions)	Percent of Increase
1970	4,300		551	
1971	9,400	118.6	1,523	176.4
1972	11,100	18.1	1,842	20.1
1973	12,200	9.9	2,136	16.0
1974	12,900	5.7	2,728	27.7
1975	17,100	32.6	4,389	60.1
1976	18,600	8.8	5,306	20.9
1977	17,100	−8.1	5,038	−5.1
1978	16,000	−6.4	5,165	2.5
1979	17,700	10.1	5,165	0.0
1980	17,710	10.1	6,460	25.1
1981	21,000	19.1	9,210	42.6

Source: Congressional Resource Service, *Welfare Background Paper,* Report 81–124 EPW, p. 74. Washington, D.C.: Library of Congress, 1981.

biannually by the federal Office of Research and Statistics, Social Security Administration.

The effect of the formula used is that a state with a mean income of the national average would receive a reimbursement of 55 percent. The formula is structured so that states with per capita incomes below the national average pay a lower proportionate share, and states with a higher-than-average income pay a higher share. The formula is truncated so that no state receives less than a 50 percent reimbursement.

States are required to provide basic medical and hospital services to AFDC recipients and, in most instances, to SSI recipients. A state also may extend aid to the medically needy, those persons whose income and resources are adequate to cover daily living expenses according to the AFDC/SSI standard of the states but not sufficient to pay for medical care. The federal and state governments share the administrative costs to operate medicaid. The history of federal and state costs in the delivery of medicaid benefits is shown in Table 4–14.

An examination of this table reflects a $35 billion increase since the program's rather modest start in 1966, the first full year of operation. The primary reason for this increase is the inflation rate of the costs of medical care. In recent years, federal incentives and state actions have slowed the rate of growth. The total number of program recipients has been static over the last ten years as shown in Table 4–15.

Procedures used to curb the inflation rate of medicaid have been criticized by medical vendors, particularly physicians and nursing homes. A very critical issue for the next decade will be whether it is possible to continue to curb costs and still maintain high-quality medical care.

DYNAMICS OF THE POVERTY POPULATION

A critically important issue regarding the progress against poverty is the question of whether families fall into poverty for relatively short time periods or remain in poverty for extended time periods. Related questions deal with the issues surrounding the circumstances that first plunge a family into poverty and the circumstances that lead to their escape. To a large degree, this is a serious problem of research methods. As long as poverty is measured in terms of movements across a rather arbitrary but none the less precise line, very small shifts in income may appear falsely to be significant shifts in a family's circumstance. A family one dollar over the poverty line, for all realistic purposes, lives identically to a family one dollar below the line. Despite the research problems to be overcome, it now generally is agreed that poverty is more widespread and less persistent than was once thought. One research study found that, over a ten year period, only 0.7 percent of all individuals were income poor throughout the duration of the study (Duncan 1984). Similarly, the study found that roughly 25 percent of all individuals were poor in at least one of the ten years.

Bane and Ellwood (1983) used the same Michigan data to focus specifically on poverty among the nonelderly. Their study shows that for male-headed families, the principal cause for entry into poverty was loss of earnings, while the second most frequent factor was a child becoming independent. Children leaving home in families near the poverty line have high incidences of poverty. Ninety-two percent of all male-headed households escape poverty by an increase in earnings.

Table 4–14

History of Medicaid Program Costs

Fiscal year	Total Dollars (in millions)	Total Percent increase	Federal Dollars (in millions)	Federal Percent increase	State Dollars (in millions)	State Percent increase
1966[1]	$1,658		$ 789		$ 869	
1967[1]	2,368	42.9	1,209	53.2	1,159	33.5
1968[1]	3,659	55.6	1,837	51.9	1,849	59.5
1969[1]	4,166	13.0	2,276	23.9	1,890	2.2
1970[1]	4,852	16.5	2,617	15.0	2,235	18.3
1971	6,176	27.3	3,374	28.9	2,802	25.3
1972[2]	8,434	36.6	4,361	29.2	4,074	45.4
1973	9,111	8.0	4,998	14.6	4,113	1.0
1974	10,229	12.3	5,833	16.7	4,396	6.9
1975	12,637	23.5	7,060	21.0	5,578	26.9
1976	14,644	15.9	8,312	17.7	6,332	13.5
TQ[3]	4,106	NA	2,354	NA	1,752	NA
1977	17,103	16.8[4]	9,713	16.9[4]	7,389	16.7 [4]
1978	18,949	10.8	10,680	10.0	8,269	11.9
1979	21,755	14.8	12,267	14.9	9,489	14.8
1980	25,781	18.5	14,550	18.6	11,231	18.4
1981	30,377	17.8	17,074	17.3	13,303	18.4
1982	32,446	6.8	17,514	2.6	14,931	12.2
1983	34,956	7.7	18,985	8.4	15,971	7.0
1984	37,631	7.7	20,094	5.8	17,537	9.8
1985[5]	41,150	10.9	22,655[6]	12.7	18,495[6]	5.5
1986 (current law estimate)[5]	44,860	9.0	24,686	9.0	20,175	9.1
1987 (current law estimate)[5]	47,786	6.5	25,880	4.8	21,906	8.6

[1] Includes related programs which are not separately identified though for each successive year a larger portion of the total represents Medicaid expenditures. As of Jan. 1, 1970, Federal matching was only available under Medicaid.

[2] Intermediate care facilities (ICFs) transferred from the cash assistance programs to Medicaid effective January 1, 1972; data for prior periods do not include these costs.

[3] Transitional quarter (beginning of Federal fiscal year moved from July 1 to Oct. 1).

[4] Represents increase over fiscal year 1976, i.e., five calendar quarters.

[5] Includes transfer of function of State fraud control units to Medicaid from Office of Inspector General.

[6] Temporary reductions in Federal payments authorized for fiscal years 1982–84 will be discontinued in fiscal year 1985.

Note: Totals may not add due to rounding.

Source: Background Material. Committee on Ways & Means, WMCP 99–14, March, 1986.

Table 4–15   **Unduplicated Number of Medicaid Recipients by Eligibility Category, Fiscal Years 1972–1987 (number in thousands)**

Fiscal Year	Total	Aged 65 or over	Blindness	Permanent and total disability	Dependent children under age 21	Adults in families with dependent children	Other [1]
Ending June:							
1972	17,606	3,318	108	1,625	7,841	3,137	1,576
1973	19,622	3,496	101	1,804	8,659	4,066	1,495
1974	21,462	3,732	135	2,222	9,478	4,392	1,502
1975	22,007	3,615	109	2,355	9,598	4,529	1,800
1976	22,815	3,612	97	2,572	9,924	4,774	1,836
Ending September:							
1977[2]	22,831	3,636	92	2,710	9,651	4,785	1,959
1978	21,965	3,376	82	2,636	9,376	4,643	1,852
1979	21,520	3,364	79	2,674	9,106	4,570	1,727
1980[3]	21,605	3,440	92	2,819	9,333	4,877	1,499
1981[3]	21,980	3,367	86	2,993	9,581	5,187	1,364
1982[3]	21,603	3,240	84	2,806	9,563	5,356	1,434
1983[3]	21,494	3,247	76	2,956	9,418	5,467	1,325
1984[3]	21,915	3,097	74	2,865	9,221	5,347	1,311
1985[3]	22,183	3,124	79	2,838	9,423	5,516	1,203
1986 (current law estimate)[3]	22,894	3,226	81	2,934	9,720	5,632	1,301
1987 (current law estimate)[3]	23,599	3,317	84	3,030	9,996	5,772	1,400

[1] This category is composed predominantly of children not meeting the definition of "dependent" children, i.e., "Ribicoff children."

[2] Fiscal year 1977 began in October 1976 and was the first year of the new Federal fiscal cycle. Before 1977, the fiscal year began in July.

[3] Beginning in fiscal year 1980, recipients' categories do not add to the unduplicated total due to the small number of recipients that are in more than one category during the year.

Source: *Ibid.* Table 4–14.

For female-headed households, the most frequent "cause" of poverty is the simple fact of becoming a female-headed household; that is to say, the husband left, leaving the former spouse and children poor. Most frequently, in the first year after separation, the husband also experienced income poverty. For women, finding a job was the most frequent factor ending poverty, with remarriage a strong second factor.

Labor force attachment also is clearly critical in keeping individuals above the poverty line, almost exclusively so for men. For women, divorce, separation, or child-bearing out of marriage most often forces them into poverty. Fully 75 percent of all AFDC recipients first begin receiving AFDC because of a relationship change that places them in female-headed households. For 48 percent of women going on AFDC, finding a job enables them to go off welfare within two years. It is not what happens to women on AFDC that makes much difference; it is what happens to them within the job market and in their relationships with men. Though the evidence is far from conclusive, public assistance pays the bills while women deal with their condition of poverty. It is not very exciting, but the facts are such that public assistance neither perpetuates nor causes poverty, nor is the amount of assistance given while a person is on welfare sufficient to allow for an avenue for escape. That escape, except for the elderly, lies with what happens in the economy. While individuals are poor, however, public assistance can make their lives a great deal more free of want and insecurity.

SUMMARY

The concept of poverty is complex and attempting to define it often results in considerable debate. Because there are a number of different ways to measure poverty, its incidence varies depending on the definition and measurement used. No matter what the definition, the progress against poverty in the U.S. has been uneven historically. Many people remain poor. Those most at risk to live in poverty are children, women, the elderly, the disabled, and members of ethnic minorities. Because of the economic downturn in the U.S. in recent years, increased numbers of working citizens, including married couples, are also joining the ranks of the poor.

Public assistance programs for the poor are insufficient to meet individual needs and to assist individuals living in poverty to become self-sufficient. Social workers are joining other groups in calling for welfare reform which could provide social services, education, employment training, health care, child care, and other resources to enable larger numbers to move out of poverty. However, the U.S. economic structure and availability of jobs are the factors which influence poverty most strongly. Welfare reform, no matter how well–planned and implemented, is not solely sufficient to significantly reduce poverty in the United States.

KEY TERMS

categorical assistance	SSI
official poverty	AFDC
public assistance	general assistance
relative poverty	food stamps
social insurance	Medicaid

DISCUSSION QUESTIONS

1. Do you believe that a preference for welfare keeps AFDC recipients out of the work force?
2. How does the changing shape of American demographics change the shape of American poverty?
3. To what degree is the number (or percent) of poor a good measure of a society's commitment to social welfare?

REFERENCES

Bane, M.J. and D. Ellwood. 1983. *The Dynamics of Dependency*. Cambridge, Mass.: The John F. Kennedy School.

Danziger, Sheldon, and Daniel Weinberg. 1986. *Fighting Poverty: What Works and What Doesn't*. Cambridge, Mass.: Harvard University Press.

Duncan, G.J. 1984. *Years of Poverty, Years of Plenty*. Ann Arbor, Mich.: Institute for Social Research.

Editorial Research Reports. 1984. *America's Needy: Care and Cutbacks*. Washington, D.C.: Editorial Research Reports.

Gilder, George. 1981. *Wealth and Poverty*. New York: Basic Books.

Harrington, Michael. 1984. *The New American Poverty*. New York: Holt-Reinholt.

Moynihan, Daniel P. 1969. *On Understanding Poverty*. New York: Basic Books.

Murray, Charles. 1984. *Losing Ground: American Social Policy, 1950–1980*. New York: Basic Books.

Romanyshyn, John. 1971. *Social Welfare: Charity to Justice*. New York: Random House.

Stockman, David. *Poverty Rate Increase Hearings, Series 98–55*. Washington, D.C.: U.S. Office of Management and Budget.

SELECTED FURTHER READINGS

Garfinkel, Irv, ed. 1974. *Toward an Effective Income Support Policy*. Madison, Wis.: Institute for Research on Poverty.

Gilbert, Dennis, and Joseph Kahl. 1987. *The New American Class Structure: A New Synthesis*. Homewood, Ill.: Dorsey Press.

Mead, Lawrence. *Beyond Entitlement*. New York, The Free Press, 1986.

Moynihan, Daniel P. *The Politics of a Guaranteed Income*. New York, Random House, 1973.

5 Mental Health and Developmental Disabilities

T wenty-four-year old Jamie Collins currently lives in a halfway house in the inner city of a large southern city. She has lived there for three months, since being released from her tenth stay at the state mental hospital since the age of eighteen. Jamie and her roommates earn money for food and part of the rent by working for an industrial cleaning company. They are supervised by a social worker from the local mental health outreach center, who meets with them as a group twice a week and is available on an on-call basis whenever they need support. Jamie and her social worker are planning for her to enroll in a job-training program next month and to move into her own apartment with one of the other residents of the halfway house within the next three months. Jamie is excited about the opportunity to live on her own.

Jamie enjoyed a relatively stable childhood, growing up in a rural area of the South with her middle-class parents and three sisters. During high school, she began to experience what she terms black outs and had occasional seizures, for which a doctor was unable to find any physical reason. At about age seventeen, Jamie's behavior changed from calm and stable to erratic, ranging from screaming rages to long periods of crying to fun-loving, carefree behavior. Her family had difficulty coping with her behavior. After numerous arguments, Jamie quit school and moved to California, where she held a series of temporary jobs.

In California, Jamie was hospitalized for the first time, after becoming violent on the job. At this time, she was diagnosed as having schizophrenic tendencies, kept in the hospital for ten days, and released

with a prescription for drugs and an appointment to
see a mental health worker at a local mental health
center. Jamie saw the worker and took medication
for about a month. However, after being fired from
a new job, she left the area and began a series of short
stays in cities in the South, working at menial jobs
and barely coping with life. Three years ago, she and
a friend came to the city where she presently resides.
When the friend left her, finding it difficult to cope
with her rapidly changing moods, Jamie began her
succession of short visits to the state mental hospital.
She was released often from the hospital with no job
and no place to go. On one occasion during the
winter, she arrived at the hospital asking to be
admitted because she was tired, hungry, and without
money or shelter.

Fortunately, when Jamie was released from her
last hospital stay, she was referred to a new halfway
house and hired in a job she is able to handle. The
group experience with the other residents and the
support of the social worker have enabled Jamie to
develop a support system of friends whom she feels
care about her. Jamie has been able to see that she has
many strengths and that she is a likeable person. For
the first time in many years, she is excited about life
and looking forward to the future.

The mental health needs of Americans are receiving increased attention.
The 1980 National Commission on Mental Health concluded that 15 percent
of the U.S. population at any given time is in need of mental health services
and that 25 percent of the population suffers from some type of emotional
problem. However, services are available to only one out of every eight individuals who need them. Because of increases in individual stress, financial pressures, divorce and marital problems, and work-related pressures, most
individuals will experience emotional problems at some point in their lives.

How does one determine who needs mental health services and who should
receive them? The stigma placed on individuals with mental health problems
and the stereotypes about the services provided them cause many individuals
with mental health problems to avoid seeking services. People think of mental
health services and those who receive them as portrayed in popular movies and
books, such as *One Flew Over the Cuckoo's Nest* (Kesey 1962). For this reason,
as attempts to move those with mental health problems but not in need of institutionalization into the community take place, many communities and
neighborhoods are developing zoning ordinances and other means to keep
such residents out.

The rights of those with mental health problems also are receiving increased
attention. Should persons be forced to be hospitalized, receive electric shock
treatments, or receive drug therapy against their wishes? Or, like Jamie, when

they so desperately need treatment that is not available due to scarce resources, do they have a right to demand services, especially if it means that they will be less likely to need more intensive services, such as institutionalization, in the future? Does someone in an institution, who could function in a less restrictive environment, have the right to demand such a placement? What about the rights of those in our society who may encounter persons with serious mental health problems? Concern is being expressed about the accountability of those with serious mental health problems and what should happen when such individuals become dangerous to themselves and others. This was exemplified by several recent court cases. The young adult who shot President Reagan was not sentenced for the act due to "reasons of insanity." At the same time, a young adult who killed a number of women over a several year period, diagnosed by a number of psychiatrists as having severe psychological problems, recently was sentenced to death in a Florida court, and a retarded young adult who aided in a murder at the age of seventeen, when his mental age was about six, recently was put to death in that same state.

Current studies also show a strong relationship between individuals with mental health problems and health problems. When persons do not get help in addressing their mental health problems, they are much more likely to become physically ill. A study conducted by IBM found that 50 percent of persons coming to company physicians with health-related problems were experiencing mental health problems (Comprehensive Care Corporation 1981). The high costs of health care could be reduced if more attention were given to the mental health needs of individuals.

Mental health problems, if left untreated, also disrupt families and increase the financial costs to taxpayers, as well as decrease productivity at the workplace. A recent study found that mental health problems cost the United States $64.2 billion in 1980 (U.S. Department of Health, Education, and Welfare 1980). Over half of the individuals providing mental health services are social workers employed in state mental hospitals, private psychiatric treatment facilities, community outreach facilities, schools for the developmentally disabled, child guidance clinics and family service agencies, alcohol and drug treatment facilities, emergency hotlines, and crisis centers. Thus, the areas of mental health and developmental disabilities are rapidly growing and offer many critical roles for social workers.

Topics discussed in this chapter will include defining mental health, mental illness, and developmental disabilities. Critical incidents that have shaped the way individuals with mental health problems are viewed and the types of services provided will also be addressed. Current service needs and issues will be considered, and the roles that social workers play in meeting service needs and addressing these issues will be discussed.

MENTAL HEALTH OR MENTAL ILLNESS?
DEFINITIONAL ISSUES

Societies have always developed their own systems for labeling acceptable and nonacceptable behavior. What is tolerated in one society may not be in another. It might be said that for each society, there is a continuum, with behavior that is definitely unacceptable and inappropriate at one end and behavior that is definitely acceptable and appropriate at the other. Typically, although the behaviors at either end of the continuum are almost uniformly agreed upon by most members of that society, the behaviors in the middle of the continuum tend to cause much debate and disagreement. For example, while murder would be considered a definitely unacceptable behavior by most, where on the continuum would continually talking to oneself fall, or being convinced that you were King Tut? Some societies tolerate little deviance from acceptable behavior. For example, for a brief period in colonial times in Salem, Massachusetts, some persons whose behavior was considered "deviant" were labeled as witches possessed by the devil, and they were tortured and burned at the stake. Later research showed that many of these individuals had severe psychological problems. In other societies, those whose behavior deviates from the norm are given special roles and, in some instances, elevated to status positions within the society. For example, in many American Indian tribes, nonconforming individuals often became shamans, or medicine men, high status positions within the tribes.

Historically, those labeled as mentally ill or retarded often were isolated or punished. In colonial times, individuals were often locked in attics or cellars or warehoused in lunatic asylums. Today, our society is still ambivalent about how such individuals should be regarded. Attempts at deinstitutionalization or mainstreaming emotionally disturbed and handicapped individuals into classrooms and communities have met with much resistance. Goffman (1961) and others suggest that for many individuals who have emotional or developmental problems, the stigma attached to the labels they are given is far more damaging to them than the extent of their problems (Mechanic 1980). David Mechanic, a prominent social policy analyst in the mental health field, argues that definitions of mental illness are made at varying levels in the social structure. Early informal definitions are made in groups within which the person operates, usually family members or coworkers. Such definitions depend on the norms of the particular group and what is tolerated as well as the position the person occupies within the group. A boss' behavior, for example, may be defined as outside of the group norms much less quickly than a file clerk's. Definitions of this type also depend on whether or not the other members of the group can empathize or understand the other's behavior; in other words, whether they can fit that behavior into their own frames of reference. For example, a person who continually talks to his recently-deceased mother while on the job is more likely to be tolerated if the group is aware that the individual had a close relationship with her. However, if there is no apparent context for the behavior or if such behavior persists, such individuals are likely to labeled as *strange* or *odd* (Mechanic 1980).

Definitions of so-called abnormal behaviors typically are based on visible symptoms, such as talking to people who are not present, rather than the severity of the actual problems. Any time one is attempting to define a condition based on nonvisible factors, such as what is going on inside an individual's mind, specific definitions are difficult to achieve. Only those who in some way enter the mental health system are likely to be specifically defined as having some type of emotional problem. The mental health system, in spite of its problems, is likely to accept, at least for short periods of time, almost all individuals who seek its services, including the unwanted, aged, indigent, lonely, and those with nowhere else to go. At times, this results in overestimates of the number of individuals defined as having emotional problems who may not and underestimates of those who do not enter the system but should.

Mental Illness

Formal definitions of mental illness traditionally have followed a medical model, focusing on severe emotional problems caused by brain dysfunction or intrapsychic causes, with little attention to systems or environmental influences. Mental illness has been viewed from a genetic or physiological perspective as a disease of the mind or a disturbance in the functioning of the individual. The American Psychiatric Association has attempted to monitor the classification and definitional aspects of various types of emotional disorders through a classification system termed the *Diagnostic and Statistical Manual of Mental Disorders,* or the **DSM.** This classification system, revised significantly in 1980 and again in 1987, uses a multiaxial system for evaluation, which focuses on the psychological, biological, and social aspects of an individual's functioning. The system incorporates information from five axes in diagnosing an individual. Axes 1 and 2 incorporate all of the mental disorders, such as schizophrenic and psychotic disorders. Axis 3 incorporates physical disorders and conditions. Axes 4 and 5 rate the severity of the psychosocial stressors that have contributed to the development or the maintenance of the disorder and the highest level of adaptive functioning that the individual has maintained during the previous year (Williams 1987, 389).

The DSM classification system is an important one for social work professionals, as it incorporates a systems-ecological perspective in assessing an individual, allowing a focus on either organic factors or environmental factors, or both, that affect an individual's condition. It also allows for the incorporation of the individual's strengths as well as problems when completing an assessment. This classification system has been used increasingly in recent years for third-party insurance reimbursement when mental health services are provided.

Mental Health

Many individuals view mental health and mental illness at opposite ends of a continuum. Others, like Thomas Szasz, suggest that mental health and emotional problems are issues that defy specific boundaries. Szasz objects to labeling the mentally ill and argues that there is no such thing as mental illness. He agrees that there are illnesses due to neurological impairment of the brain but believes that such illnesses are brain diseases rather than mental illnesses. Although he acknowledges the existence of emotional problems, Szasz contends that labeling nonorganic emotional problems implies a deviation from some clearly specified norm. He feels that the label not only stigmatizes the individual, but may cause him or her to actually assume those behaviors.

Szasz argues that instead of talking about definitions of mental illness, we should talk about problems of living. He advocates that it is an individual's struggle with the problem of how to live in our world that requires attention. He and others suggest that positive mental health is promoted by one's competence in dealing with the environment and one's confidence of being able, when necessary, to cause desired effects. Szasz advocates a systems or ecological perspective for viewing mental health. Within his framework, problems in living can be viewed as being due to biological/physiological, economic, political, psychological, or sociological constraints. Promoting positive interactions between individuals and their environments is viewed as congruent with the promotion of optimal mental health and social functioning for individuals. Szasz (1960) proposes a classification system with the following categories of mental health problems:

1.   personal disabilities, such as depression, fears, inadequacy, and excessive anxiety;

2.   antisocial acts, such as violent and criminal behaviors;

3.   deterioration of the brain, such as Altzheimer's disease, alcoholism, and brain damage.

Many mental health experts prefer this system and its emphasis on healthy functioning to a system that emphasizes mental illness. This system accepts that all individuals have difficulties at some point negotiating their complex environments. Mental health services are viewed as available to and needed by all individuals at some time during their lives rather than as something to be avoided.

There is considerable debate on how mental health problems are created. In many instances, it is difficult, if not impossible, to say that any one specific factor *caused* a mental health problem. More than likely, mental health problems are the result of a variety of factors. Research suggests a number of possible explanations.

Heredity, Biological, and Genetic Factors   Research has identified possible genetic traits that suggest that individuals with the same gene pools may be prone to certain mental health disorders. For example, high correlations have been found between the incidence of schizophrenia and identical twins, even when twins were separated at birth and raised in different environments. Some researchers suggest that genetic factors alone do not cause mental health disorders, but that some individuals are predisposed to certain problems through heredity, and that under certain environmental conditions, this predisposition is triggered, resulting in the emotional problem. A variation of this position is that, due to genetic traits or physiological characteristics, some individuals are biologically less capable of coping with environmental stress.

Psychosocial Developmental Factors   This perspective, based on the work of Erik Erikson and others, suggests that mental health problems result from environmental experiences during childhood. Research shows that individuals who experience severe trauma during childhood—such as physical or sexual abuse, separation from a close family member, or alcoholism or drug abuse among family members—are much more likely to experience mental health problems later in life.

Social Learning   The social learning perspective suggests that mental health problems are the result of learned behaviors. Such behaviors may be learned by observing parents or other role models or as survival mechanisms to cope with difficult life experiences.

Social Stress   This perspective, based on the work of Thomas Szasz, focuses on the relationship between environmental stress and mental health, suggesting that individuals who are under greater stress—including the poor, ethnic minorities, and women—are more likely to experience mental health problems.

Societal Reactions and Labeling   This perspective suggests that society creates individuals with mental health problems through a societal reaction process. By establishing social norms and treating as deviant those who do not subscribe to the norms, individuals with mental health problems are identified. Additionally, individuals identified or labeled as somehow different will assume the role prescribed to them; that is, individuals labeled as having mental health problems will behave as they would be expected to if they had the problem.

Systems Perspective   This perspective suggests that mental health problems are the result of a variety of factors that interact in a complex fashion and vary according to the uniqueness of the individual and the environment within which he or she interacts. Family members, peer groups, the neighborhood and community in which the individual functions, and cultural and societal expectations in relation to a person's self-concept, competence, and behaviors—all these can be addressed within the systems perspective. The systems perspective can include a combination of the other perspectives identified earlier as well. For example, a person may be predisposed biologically to experience mental health problems, may have suffered as a child from sexual abuse, may have had a parent who also experienced mental health problems, and currently may be in an extremely stressful living situation (an unhappy marriage, a stressful job, experiencing financial problems). If such an individual experienced mental health problems, it would be impossible to state which of those factors was directly responsible for the problems. A systems perspective allows us to focus on all of the factors within an individual's past and present environment, as well as the individual's physiological characteristics, in addressing mental health problems. If we know which factors are most important, we are much more likely to be able to intervene successfully in alleviating the problems. This focus on both the individual and the individual's environment allows the social worker and the client to "map out" the critical factors most likely to account for the problems, and then to develop an intervention plan that specifically addresses those factors.

Whether one takes a mental illness perspective or a broader perspective, how and when an individual's emotional problems are identified and defined depend on a number of factors:

1. *the visibility, recognizability, or perpetual occurrence of inappropriate/deviant behaviors and symptoms;*

2. *the extent to which the person perceives the symptoms as serious;*

3. *the extent to which the symptoms disrupt family, work, and other activities;*

4. *the frequency of the appearance of the signs and symptoms, or their persistence;*

5. *the tolerance threshold of those who are exposed to and evaluate the signs and symptoms;*

6. *the information available to, the knowledge of, and the cultural assumptions and understandings of the evaluator;*

7. *the degree to which processes that distort reality are present;*

8. *the presence of needs within the family/environment that conflict with the recognition of problems or the assumption of the "sick" role;*

9. *the possibility that competing interpretations can be assigned to the behaviors/signs once they are recognized;*

10. *the availability of treatment/intervention resources, their physical proximity and costs of money, time, and effort as well as costs of stigmatization and humiliation. (Mechanic 1980, 68–69)*

The identification of individuals with mental health problems and the ways those problems are defined are issues of considerable debate among mental health professionals. A number of years ago, psychologist David Rosenhan and his associates conducted a study that exemplifies this concern. Rosenhan and his seven associates went separately to the admissions offices of twelve

Positive nurturing and support during childhood can prevent mental health problems during adolescence and adulthood.

psychiatric hospitals in five different states, all claiming that they were hearing voices. In every instance, they were admitted to the hospitals as patients. Immediately upon admission, they all assumed normal behavior. Even so, professionals at the hospitals were unable to distinguish them from other patients, although in some instances, the other patients determined that they were not mentally ill! Rosenhan and his associates remained at the hospitals as patients from time periods ranging from seven to fifty-two days, with an average stay of nineteen days. The diagnosis at discharge for each of them was "schizophrenia in remission" (Rosenhan 1973).

Developmental Disabilities

Generally, the term **developmental disability** refers to developmental problems such as mental retardation or cerebral palsy, which developed prior to adulthood. Although, in the past, these persons were often referred to as *mentally retarded* or *mentally handicapped,* the term *developmental disability* is preferred, as it is viewed as less negative.

In 1984, the U.S. Congress passed the Developmental Disabilities Assistance and Bill of Rights Act (P.L. 98–527), which defined *developmental disability* as

> *A severe, chronic disability of a person which (a) is attributable to a mental or physical impairment or combination of mental and physical impairments; (b) is manifested before the person attains age twenty-two; (c) is likely to continue indefinitely; (d) results in substantial functional limitations in three or more of the following areas of major life activity: (i) self-care, (ii) receptive and expressive language, (iii) learning, (iv) mobility, (v) self-direction, (vi) capacity for independent living, and (vii) economic self-sufficiency; and (e) reflects the person's need for a combination and sequence of special, interdisciplinary, or generic care, treatment, or other services which are of lifelong or extended duration and are individually planned and coordinated. (P.L. 98–527, Title V, 1984)*

Although over 75 percent of those classified as having developmental disabilities are mentally retarded, other individuals also may be so classified due to cerebral palsy, epilepsy, autism, spina bifida, or speech, hearing, or vision handicaps. Of those individuals classified as mentally retarded, 75 percent are only mildly retarded and can be educated to function fairly independently or with some supervision; 20 percent are moderately retarded; and only 5 percent are profoundly retarded and need constant care and supervision. A number of factors are associated with developmental disabilities:

Preconceptual/hereditary factors: Factors such as metabolic disorders, brain malfunctions, or chromosomal abnormalities can result in disabilities such as Tay Sachs and Down syndrome.

Prenatal factors: Chemical and alcohol addiction, radiation, and infections such as rubella (a form of measles) can result in disabilities, as can fetal malnutrition if mothers do not receive adequate prenatal care.

Perinatal factors: Premature birth, trauma at birth, and infections transmitted during birth such as herpes can result in disabilities.

Postnatal factors: Postnatal infections such as meningitis, trauma as a result of automobile accidents or child abuse, lack of oxygen during illness or an accident, and nutritional deficiencies can result in developmental disabilities. Environmental factors, such as lead poisoning, parents with severe emotional problems, or parental deprivation also are important factors that often result in developmental disabilities. Children who do not receive appropriate nurturance, especially during their early years, are often developmentally delayed, and if intervention does not occur soon enough, mental retardation, learning disabilities, or other types of problems can result and may be permanent.

Specific causes of developmental disabilities often cannot be identified. Many parents who give birth to children with such problems often spend a great deal of time—sometimes their entire lives—blaming themselves because their children have disabilities. Research has enabled the early identification of many types of disabilities, such as phenylketonuria (PKU) which results in retardation. A simple test at birth can allow for immediate treatment, which has virtually eliminated this problem in most Western countries. More attention needs to be given to understanding how and why such disabilities occur.

THE EVOLUTION OF VIEWS TOWARD MENTAL HEALTH AND DEVELOPMENTAL DISABILITIES

The early treatment of individuals with mental health and developmental disabilities depended primarily on the reactions of the individuals' families. In most cases, individuals remained at home and were at the mercy of family members. Although, in some instances, individuals were treated humanely, many were chained in attics and cellars, and sometimes they were killed. When there were no family members to provide for them, they were often transported to the next town and abandoned. Later, almshouses were established. Some mentally ill or developmentally disabled individuals were placed in jails, if they were deemed too dangerous for the almshouse.

The Pennsylvania colony's hospital, established in 1751 for the sick poor and "the reception and care of lunatics," was the first hospital in the United States that provided care for the mentally ill, although treatment of mentally ill patients was little better than it had been in jails and almshouses. Individuals deemed mentally ill were assigned to hospital cellars and placed in bolted cells, where they were watched over by attendants carrying whips, which they used freely. Sightseers paid admission fees on Sundays to watch the cellar activities.

From Inhumane to Moral Treatment

During the late 1700s, people throughout the world began to seek better approaches to address the needs of the mentally ill. What mental health historians describe as the first of four revolutions in caring for the mentally ill actually began in France rather than the United States, with a shift from inhumane to **moral treatment.** Philippe Pinel, director of two hospitals in Paris, ordered "striking off the chains" of the patients in 1793, first at the Bicetre Hospital for the Insane in Paris. Pinel advocated the establishment of a philosophy of moral treatment, which included offering patients hope, guidance, and support, and treatment with respect in small familylike institutions.

The moral treatment movement soon spread to America. Benjamin Rush, a signer of the Declaration of Independence, wrote the first American text on psychiatry, advocating that the mentally ill had a moral right to humane treatment. However, not until the 1840s, through the efforts of a schoolteacher, Dorothea Dix, did the mentally ill in the United States actually began to receive more humane treatment. Dix became aware of the plight of the mentally ill through teaching Sunday School for a group of patients in a Massachusetts hospital. Appalled by what she saw, she gave speeches, wrote newspaper articles, and met with government officials to bring attention to the inhumane and abusive treatment she observed in the many facilities she visited. As a result of her efforts, a bill was introduced in Congress to use the proceeds from the sale of western land to purchase land for use in caring for the mentally ill. This bill was vetoed by President Pierce, which set a precedent for the federal government's refusal to be involved in state social services programs that remained unchanged until the New Deal era.

Refusing to give up, Dix turned her efforts to the individual states. By 1900, thirty-two states had established state mental hospitals. However, Dix and other advocates for the humane treatment of the mentally ill soon had additional cause for concern. What began in many hospitals as humane treatment changed as hospitals became overused and overcrowded, admitting all who couldn't be cared for elsewhere. State insane asylums became warehouses, commonly described as *snake pits*.

Dorothea Dix and her group of reformers demanded that strict guidelines be established for the treatment of mental hospital patients. Again, states responded and expanding facilities soon were heavily bound by detailed procedures. While there were dramatic decreases in abuse and neglect of patients, the guidelines left little room for innovation, and until the 1960s, patients in state mental hospitals received little more than custodial care. In the years immediately following the Dix reform, nearly half of patients who had been admitted were released, often only to make room for new admissions and to alleviate overcrowding. Once the population stabilized somewhat, however, long stays in mental hospitals became the norm, with discharge rates falling to as low as 5 percent. While these state institutions had been intended to house a transitory patient population, the absence of a treatment technology forced the retention of many patients until their deaths. The desire for single state facilities to house large populations of mentally ill patients resulted in their location in rural areas, where land was less expensive and expansion of facilities possible. Thus, the state mental hospital became and, in many instances, still is the "principal industry" in the area where it is located.

In spite of the efforts of Dorothea Dix and others, overcrowded conditions and neglect of patients still existed in many state facilities. Facilities continued to be overcrowded, with large numbers of immigrant patients. While the staff could provide moral treatment, love, and respect to some patients, it was difficult for many to transfer this philosophy to foreigners. Additionally, it was increasingly difficult to seek medical staff willing to work in state mental institutions. Graduates from medical school often were repelled by the foreigners, alcoholics, and severely disturbed individuals who populated the institutions.

A second effort to reform conditions in state mental hospitals was undertaken in the early 1900s by Clifford Beers, a Yale graduate from a wealthy family who had been hospitalized in a Connecticut mental hospital for three years. After his release, Beers almost immediately suffered a relapse and was hospitalized for a second time. During this stay, he began to formulate plans for more effective treatment of the mentally ill. He kept careful notes of the maltreatment he received from physicians and the well-intended but ineffective care he received from caretakers. After his release in 1908, Beers wrote a book, *A Mind that Found Itself,* which was intended to be a parallel to *Uncle Tom's Cabin* but focused on conditions in mental hospitals. This book led to the formation of state mental health advocacy organizations, such as the Connecticut Society for Mental Health. Later, state organizations formed the National Association for Mental Hygiene, which became a lobbying force for the continual reform of state hospitals and the development of alternative systems of care.

The Introduction of Psychoanalysis

What is described as the second revolution in the mental health field occurred in the early 1900s with the introduction of Sigmund Freud's writings and the use of **psychoanalysis** in the United States. Professional mental health workers trained in Freud's techniques attempted to gain cooperation and insight through verbal or nonverbal communication with patients, seeing them at regular intervals over long periods of time.

The first social workers hired to work in state mental hospitals actually were hired before Freud's teachings were introduced into the United States. Their primary role was to provide therapy to clients, but it was based on a limited knowledge about what the therapy should entail. As psychoanalysis gained popularity in the United States, psychiatric social workers, like others working with the mentally ill, were quick to adopt a system of therapy that was reportedly much more effective than the often haphazard treatment they were using. In 1905, Massachusetts General Hospital in Boston and Bellevue Hospital in New York City hired psychiatric social workers to provide therapy to patients. However, because of staff shortages and the large numbers of patients, few patients actually received psychotherapy, which requires highly trained therapists, fairly verbal patients who speak the same language as the therapist, and long hours of treatment to be effective. In most instances, psychotherapy as a treatment approach for dealing with mental health problems was used more in outpatient facilities, either private practices established by psychiatrists or child guidance centers, which were established in the United States in the 1920s and focused primarily on promoting healthy relationships among middle-class children and their parents.

The Shift to Community Mental Health Programs

The third revolution in mental health, a shift in the care of individuals with mental health problems from institutions to local communities, began in the 1940s and still continues. Public interest in mental health issues and treatment of the mentally ill remained at a fairly constant level until the 1940s and the onset of World War II. The military draft brought mental health problems to the attention of Congress. Military statistics showed that 12 percent of all men drafted into the Armed Forces were rejected for psychiatric reasons. Of the total number rejected for any reason, 40 percent were rejected for psychiatric reasons (Felix 1967). Serious questions began to be raised about the magnitude of mental health problems within the entire U.S. population.

After the war ended, state hospitals, which had been neglected during the war, again began to receive attention. Albert Deutsch wrote a series of exposes on state mental hospitals, later published as *Shame of the States* (1949). This stimulated a series of similar books, one which was made into a film, *The Snake Pit*. The attention resulted in a widespread public outcry and created a climate for reform. In 1946, Congress passed the National Mental Health Act, which enabled states to establish community mental health programs aimed at preventing and treating mental health problems. The act also provided for the establishment of research and educational programs and mandated that each state establish a single state entity to receive and allocate federal funds provided for by the act.

In 1949, the U.S. Governors' Conference sponsored a study of mental health programs in the United States. That same year, Congress created the **National Institute of Mental Health**, the first federal entity to address mental health concerns. In 1955, with impetus from a working coalition of leadership from the National Institute of Mental Health and the **National Association of Mental Health**, university medical schools and schools of social work, and organizations of former mental patients and their families, the National Mental Health Study Act was passed. This act signified the belief among both mental health experts and government officials that large custodial institutions could not deal effectively with mental illness. The act authorized an appropriation to the Joint Commission on Mental Illness and Health to study and make recommendations in the area of mental health policy. The commission published a series of documents in the late 1950s and early 1960s calling for reform. Commission reports called for a doubling of expenditures within five years and a tripling within ten years in mental health expenditures to be used for comprehensive community mental health facilities, increased recruitment and training programs for staff, and long-term mental health research. The commission suggested expanding treatment programs for the acutely mentally ill in all facilities while limiting the numbers of patients at each hospital to no more than 1000 inpatients.

The commission also recommended that the majority of emphasis be placed on community programs, including preventive, outpatient treatment, and aftercare services that could reduce the numbers of institutionalized patients and allow for their successful treatment within their local communities. Additionally, it was recommended that less burden be placed on states to provide services and that the federal role be increased in addressing mental health needs. President Kennedy also made mental health issues a high priority and strongly supported the efforts of the commission, becoming the first U.S. President to publicly address mental health concerns. Furthermore, the public was beginning to see the effectiveness of psychotropic drugs in the treatment of the mentally ill and was becoming more receptive to the idea of community care as a result.

Congress passed the Mentally Retarded Facilities and Community Mental Health Center Construction Act in 1963. This act provided major funding to build community mental health centers and community facilities for the developmentally disabled. This and subsequent legislation mandated that centers built with federal funds must be located in areas accessible to the populations they serve and must provide the following basic services components: inpatient services, outpatient services, partial hospitalization (day, night, or weekend care) emergency services, consultation, and educational services. By 1980, there were over 700 community mental health centers in the United States partially funded with federal funds. The intent of the community mental health care legislation was to replace the custodial care within a large-scale institution with therapeutic care within a community through the provision of a comprehensive array of services available locally. Emphasis was to be placed on **deinstitutionalization**, or keeping individuals from placement in hospitals whenever possible, and on least restrictive alternatives, or providing the least restrictive type of care appropriate. Such programs were not only deemed cost effective, as many individuals could work at paid jobs and live in situations requiring less expense than an institution, but also were seen as increasing individual self-esteem and feelings of contributing to society.

The community mental health center legislation, coupled with the use of psychotropic drugs, significantly reduced the numbers of individuals in mental institutions. In 1955, 77.4 percent of all patients received inpatient services; 22.6 percent received outpatient services. By 1980, the numbers virtually had reversed themselves, with only 28 percent receiving inpatient services and 72 percent outpatient services (Mechanic 1980). Emphasis on treatment had shifted from custodial care, shock treatment, or long-term psychotherapy to short-term treatment, group therapy, helping individuals cope with their environments, and drug treatment.

Use of Psychotropic Drugs

What has been described as the fourth revolution in mental health has been the discovery and use of **psychotropic drugs** in the treatment of mental health problems. Use of psychotropic drugs began in the 1950s, when it was discovered that certain drugs could reduce extremely high levels of anxiety, depression, and tension, making it possible for many individuals to function outside of a hospital setting. Drug treatment has been a major factor in reducing the numbers of patients in state mental institutions. Today, patients are likely to be admitted to a state hospital for assessment and diagnosis, with drugs prescribed as the primary method of treatment. Once a patient has been given medication and its effects have been observed, the patient usually is discharged to the care of a local community mental health facility. Largely as a result of this treatment approach, inpatient stays are much shorter. The average stay per patient since 1960 has dropped from just under 1500 days per patient to just under 350 days per patient; and many stay only 7–10 days (Mechanic 1980).

Physicians face a dilemma in balancing the benefits of psychotropic drugs against the dangers of their abuse or misuse. Some drugs have unpleasant side effects, whereas others can be addictive. Taking tranquilizers, for example, may result in heavy sedation. Drugs used for mania conditions often result in increased fatigue, nausea, tremors, thirst, edema, and weight gain. Long-term use of some antipsychotic and antidepressant drugs can result in permanent and devastating neurological disorders. Antidepressant drugs often do not become effective for several weeks, and patients may stop taking the drugs before they benefit from them. In many instances, patients receive heavier doses of the drugs while hospitalized and are released before the best type of drug and most appropriate dosage can be determined. After they leave the hospital, many patients stop taking the medication because they feel too heavily medicated or experience other side effects. Others do not keep appointments with the local mental health center, which would allow for better monitoring of their health.

While use of drugs is not a cure for mental illness, they have been effective in reducing many of the symptoms associated with mental illness. However, more research is needed in ascertaining the long-term effects of such drugs, as well as in developing new drugs that are better able to treat some types of mental illness, such as schizophrenia. Persons with schizophrenia respond less well to drug therapy than those with other illnesses and have high readmission rates to institutions.

More attention also needs to be given to the use of drugs as a treatment approach within the broader context of both the mental hospital and the patient's environment. In many instances, drugs are overadministered to patients in public mental hospitals. This often is due to a lack of knowledge about specific drug therapies, as well as the fact that many hospitals are short on adequately trained personnel who can spend the time needed with patients to appropriately determine the types and dosages of medications they need. In other instances, drugs function as agents of social control both for the hospital and for the broader society once the patient is released from the hospital. While drugs make patients easier to manage, they often simply mask, rather than treat, the problem. This means that patients who could benefit from other therapies, such as counseling, often do not receive them.

CURRENT ISSUES IN MENTAL HEALTH AND DEVELOPMENTAL DISABILITIES

Availability of Resources and Responsibility for Care

Perhaps the most overriding issue in the mental health and developmental disabilities arena relates to how to manage limited resources to best address the needs of those who require services. The mentally ill and developmentally disabled, unable to advocate well for themselves, often fail to receive their just share of funding. Many of the gains in mental health and developmental disabilities programs established in the 1960s have been lost as governments battle over who should have the responsibility for the care of the mentally ill and the disabled and what the level of services should be. While attitudes have changed significantly since colonial times, there is still much change to be made.

Deinstitutionalization

While a number of states and local communities have successfully moved large numbers of mentally ill and developmentally disabled individuals from institutions to community programs and facilities, some are reluctant to do so. Some states are under court order, as a result of suits brought by citizen advocate groups, to move more quickly to deinstitutionalize. Reasons for resistance to deinstitutionalization include inadequate funds and other resources, economic disruption caused by shutting down institutions in areas where they are the major source of employment, and lack of appropriate facilities at the community level to house individuals who could be deinstitutionalized.

In some instances, deinstitutionalization has resulted in individuals, like Jamie, falling through the cracks. Many individuals who could function well within an institutional setting do not do as well in a community setting, particularly with little day-to-day supervision. Deinstitutionalization also means decentralization, and the potential for shoddy standards of maintenance and the failure to provide follow-up services to clients. This decentralization points to the necessity for a case-management system, where social workers or other mental health professionals are responsible for a specific number of clients, ensuring that their living conditions are appropriate, that they are maintaining health care and taking medication, and that their other needs are being met. Some deinstitutionalization programs, however, have been extremely successful. For example, George Fairweather, a noted mental health expert, has established a series of community programs for individuals who previously have been institutionalized. Called Fairweather lodges, these facilities provide supervised living for individuals in small groups, with residents sharing housekeeping chores. Residents also work in the community, with a lodge coordinator who ensures that residents are successful in the workplace. The coordinator also facilitates support group meetings for residents' families as well as for lodge members. The rate of recidivism for this program has been extremely low. While some communities that have established lodge programs were reluctant to do so at first, they now view the lodges and their residents as important parts of the community.

Other successful community programs that have been established include partial hospitalization, where persons attend hospital day programs and receive treatment, returning to their homes at night or to work in the community and return to the hospital for treatment and monitoring in the evenings; and halfway houses and apartment complexes that have been refurbished, with resident supervisors who oversee and lend support to residents. Many persons have been able to return to their own homes. Some go to adult or special children's day care centers during the day while parents work, returning home at night.

Respite care programs established in some communities, using trained volunteers, make it possible for family members to find substitute caretakers so they can have some time away from the person on occasion to regain their energies.

Many residents of both state mental hospitals and state schools for the developmentally disabled were found to be elderly persons who could function in a less restrictive environment if they had someone to care for them. A number of elderly individuals have been placed in nursing homes, often in integrated facilities that take persons without mental health or disability problems, with great success.

The passage of Public Law 94–142, the Education for All Handicapped Children Act (1975), also has made deinstitutionalization more feasible for children. This law mandates that public school systems provide educational and social services for children with a range of disabilities, including speech, vision, and hearing, learning disabilities, emotional disturbances, and mental retardation. Parents and educators are required to jointly develop an individualized educational plan (IEP) for each child. The law also requires each child to be placed in the least restrictive setting possible, with the intent that children with disabilities and emotional problems be placed in the regular classroom to the extent possible and in special education classes as a last alternative.

Many deinstitutionalized individuals have difficulty adjusting to community living, particularly when adequate programs are not available. As one former state hospital resident stated, "At the hospital, I had hot coffee every morning, three meals a day and a warm bed every night, and people to talk to if I wanted to talk. Here, I have the street and that's about it. No food on a regular basis, no bed, and no one to talk to. I didn't have a bad life at the hospital." The biggest problem with deinstitutionalization is the fact that large numbers of individuals have been released from institutions to communities that have been unable to respond quickly enough to develop programs at the community level to adequately meet their needs.

Legal Rights of Patients

Mental health experts have identified patients' rights as the next revolution in the mental health arena. With the increased number of options available to individuals with mental health and developmental disabilities problems, including placement in less restrictive facilities, new counseling techniques, and drug treatment, a number of legal issues also have surfaced. On one hand, do individuals have the right to refuse treatment if they so choose? On the other hand, if treatment technology or knowledge about more appropriate types of treatment exists but such treatment is not available, do individuals have the right to demand treatment? In some states, class action suits have been brought on behalf of patients in institutions demanding that they be placed in less restrictive settings and receive treatment not available to them in the institutions.

The National Association of Mental Health and other advocacy organizations have forced the U.S. court system to establish a series of patients' rights, which include the right to treatment, the right to privacy and dignity, and the right to the least restrictive condition necessary to achieve the purpose of commitment. The courts also have determined that persons cannot be deemed incompetent to manage their affairs; to hold professional, occupational, or vehicular licenses; to marry and obtain divorces; to register to vote; or to make wills solely because of admission or commitment to a hospital.

Patients in mental institutions have the same rights to visitation and telephone communication as patients in other hospitals, as well as the right to send sealed mail. They also have the right to freedom from excessive medication or physical restraint and experiments and to be able to wear their own clothes and worship within the dictates of their own religion. Finally, patients also have the right to receive needed treatment outside of a hospital environment (Mechanic 1980).

Most states make it difficult to commit a person to an institution involuntarily. In many states, however, a law enforcement agency can order that a person be detained in a state institution for a limited time period without a court hearing. At that time, a court hearing must be held and a nonvoluntary commitment can only be ordered if the person is found to be dangerous to himself or herself or to others. Individuals who are not really capable of functioning on their own but who are not found to be dangerous often are released to be on their own.

Because of this system, many individuals receive what some mental health experts have termed the *revolving door approach* to treatment, getting picked up on the streets because they are too incapacitated to function on their own, admitted to the hospital, given medication and food and rest, and then released quickly because they legally cannot be held any longer against the wishes of the patient.

The rights of children to refuse or to demand treatment is an issue that has received even less attention. In many instances, parents commit children to institutions because they do not want to or are unable to care for them. In other instances, the child's problems are the result of family problems that the parents do not want to accept. At the present time, both the rights of individuals to avoid treatment and the rights of individuals to receive treatment are unclear and need to be clarified further by the U.S. Supreme Court.

The mental health field has been subjected to considerable shock within the last decade. Some individuals have argued that deinstitutionalization has resulted in the "ghettoization" of the mentally ill and disabled, meaning that communities in many instances have neither the funding nor the commitment to accept recently released patients, forcing them to subsist in subhuman conditions in poverty areas.

Two social workers from the Mental Health Law Project visited Mr. Dixon, an individual who won his right to freedom in a class action suit several months after he was transferred from the hospital to a boarding care facility. They gave the following description of their observations in testimony before a Senate subcommittee:

> *The conditions in which we found Mr. Dixon were unconscionable. Mr. Dixon's sleeping room was about halfway below ground level. The only windows in the room were closed and a plate in front of them made it impossible for Mr. Dixon to open them. There was no fan or air conditioner in the room. The room had no phone or buzzer.*

There would be no capacity for Mr. Dixon to contact someone in case of fire or emergency and this is significant in the face of the fact that Mr. Dixon is physically incapacitated. Mr. Dixon had not been served breakfast by 10 A. M.. He stated that meals were highly irregular and he would sometimes get so hungry waiting for lunch that he would ask a roomer to buy him sandwiches. He can remember having only one glass of milk during his entire stay at his new home. (U.S. Senate Subcommittee on Long Term Care 1976, 715)

Shortly after this testimony, Dixon returned to St. Elizabeth Hospital and was placed in a more suitable home. However, there are numerous cases similar to or worse than Mr. Dixon's. The quality of life for those who are mentally or developmentally impaired rests on the fate of federal and state legislation and funding, which is facing serious cutbacks during the 1980s. It is clear that we have both the technology and the capacity to maintain those with mental health problems and developmental disabilities in community settings. However, it also is clear that to adequately meet the needs of these individuals, substantial and continuing resources will be required.

Prevention Versus Treatment

The issue of prevention versus treatment, especially within the confines of scarce resources, is a final consideration. Mental health experts address prevention issues at three levels: **primary prevention,** or prevention targeted at an entire population (e.g., prenatal care for all women to avoid developmental disabilities in their infants, parenting classes for all individuals to decrease mental health problems among children); **secondary prevention,** or prevention targeted at "at risk" populations, those groups more likely to develop mental health problems than others (e.g., individual and group counseling for family members of schizophrenics or alcoholics); and **tertiary prevention,** or prevention targeted at those individuals who have already experienced problems to prevent the problems from recurring (e.g., alcohol treatment groups or mental health programs for those individuals who have attempted suicide).

While numerous studies show that prevention programs are cost effective ways to reduce developmental disabilities and mental health problems, it is difficult to create such programs when resources are scarce and so many individuals are in need of treatment. Still, policy makers often focus on short-term solutions to problems, ignoring long-term and more favorable solutions. While in the short term, for example, drug abuse prevention programs cost money, the costs are far less than those to house individuals in institutions or to provide other extensive treatment programs.

Other mental health problems also are currently in the limelight. These include child physical and sexual abuse, spouse abuse, drug abuse, and alcoholism. These problems, while not new, are being recognized as having significant negative impacts on not only the individuals experiencing these problems but the entire family. This emphasis on intergenerational, cyclical problems has focused attention on the need to provide resources not only to children and their families experiencing these problems but to adults who grew up in such families (see Chapters 7 and 8).

THE ROLE OF SOCIAL WORKERS IN THE PROVISION OF MENTAL HEALTH AND DEVELOPMENTAL DISABILITIES SERVICES

The first social workers credited with providing mental health services were the psychiatric social workers hired in New York and Boston mental hospitals in the early 1900s. They were responsible primarily for providing individual therapy to hospitalized mental patients and overseeing the care of discharged patients in foster homes. The mental health field expanded during the 1920s with the establishment of child guidance centers. At these centers, professionally trained social workers provided services to children and their families, most often psychotherapy with children on an individual basis.

Social workers today are involved in the total continuum of mental health and developmental disabilities services. They provide these services in a variety of settings, including traditional social services agencies—such as community mental health centers, child guidance centers, and public social services departments—as well as nontraditional settings—such as the courts, public schools and colleges and universities, hospitals and health clinics, child care centers, workplaces, and the military. While they fulfill a variety of roles, social workers presently form the largest group of psychotherapists in the United States.

Many social workers in mental health settings still provide individual counseling, including psychotherapy, to clients. However, instead of being referred to as *psychiatric social workers,* most are called **clinical social workers.** The majority of agencies who hire clinical social workers require that they meet the qualifications of the National Association of Social Workers Academy of Certified Social Workers (ACSW) certification or appropriate state certification or licensing. In order to receive ACSW certification, an individual must have a Masters Degree in Social Work (MSW) from an accredited graduate school of social work, two years of social work experience under the direct supervision of an ACSW social worker, and a satisfactory score on a competency examination administered by the National Association of Social Workers. State licensing and certification programs have similar requirements but vary by state.

Many social work jobs also are available in the field of mental health and developmental disabilities for social workers with bachelor's degrees in social work (BSWs). BSW social workers provide such services as crisis intervention for women and their children at battered women's centers and operate suicide, runaway youth, child abuse, and other types of crisis hotlines. They also provide counseling to adolescents and their families at youth serving agencies and work as social workers in state hospitals for the mentally ill and state schools for the developmentally disabled. In these settings, they provide counseling to residents and serve as the primary professional involved with the individual's family.

Social workers also work in schools with troubled students and their families, providing individual counseling, family counseling, and family outreach and leading groups for children and their families in areas such as divorce, child maltreatment, dealing with anger, getting along with adults, and alcohol and drug abuse. Many social workers are employed as counselors in alcohol and drug treatment programs. In fact, wherever mental health services are provided, social workers are likely to be employed. In the 1980s, social workers composed the largest professional group in public mental health services. Over half of the labor force employed in mental health–related jobs are social workers, and over one-third of the federally funded community mental health centers have social workers as their executive directors.

Social workers in the field of mental health provide a variety of functions. Many work in direct practice, clinical settings, providing therapy to individuals, groups, and families. Many mental health programs use a multidisciplinary team approach, hiring social workers, psychiatrists, physicians, psychologists, psychiatric nurses, child development specialists, and community aides, who work together to provide a multitude of services. While social workers on multidisciplinary teams are involved in all aspects of treatment, most often they are given the responsibility of working with the client's family and the community in which the client resides. Because of their training from a systems perspective, if resources from another agency are needed, usually the social worker obtains them and ensures that they are provided.

Many social workers in mental health settings provide case-management services even if they are not employed in agencies that use multidisciplinary teams. Case managers are responsible for monitoring cases to ensure that clients receive needed services. A case manager does not necessarily provide all services directly but manages the case, coordinating others who provide the services. Many states are employing case managers at community mental health centers to oversee clients who are living in the local community, including those previously in institutions, who can function fairly independently with supervision and support. The case manager meets with the client and contacts client's family members, employers, and other appropriate individuals on a regular basis to ensure that the client is functioning adequately.

Still other social workers involved in the mental health field function as advocates. Organizations such as the Association for Retarded Citizens advocate for disabled persons on an individual basis, ensuring that they receive needed services. For example, a fourteen-year-old mentally retarded girl in a junior high school in an urban area was not receiving special education services and had been suspended several times for behavior problems. An advocate assigned to her arranged for the school district to provide the needed testing, saw that she was placed in a special education program that reduced her anxiety level and allowed her to function in a setting where she felt better about herself, and arranged for her to receive counseling. Advocates also work to ensure that groups of citizens are provided for; for example, working within a community to ensure that housing is available to individuals with mental health problems and developmental disabilities.

Social workers also function in the mental health arena as administrators and policy makers. Many direct mental health programs, and others work for government bodies at the local, state, and federal levels. They develop and advocate for legislation, develop policies and procedures to ensure that the needs are met of individuals with mental health and disability problems, and oversee governing bodies that monitor programs to ensure that services are provided.

New Trends in Services and Social Work Roles

Although the intent of the Community Mental Health Act was to provide services to individuals within a specific geographic area, studies have shown that in many instances persons receiving services largely have been middle class and white. The Commission on Mental Health established by President Carter in the 1970s found that minorities, children, adolescents, and the elderly were underserved, as were residents of rural and poor urban areas. The commission also found that many services provided were inappropriate, particularly for those persons with differing cultural backgrounds and lifestyles. In many instances when mental health centers were first established, they were directed by psychiatrists trained in psychotherapy or influenced by educational psychologists accustomed to providing testing and working with students. As a result, the staff members often were inexperienced at dealing with nonvoluntary clients, who did not want to be seen, failed to keep appointments, and were unfamiliar with the concept of one-hour therapy sessions. They often were also unequipped to deal with problems such as family violence, child abuse, and sexual abuse.

As programs developed, many centers became skilled at reaching special populations and developing more effective ways of addressing client needs. In the 1970s, centers were required to establish special children's mental health programs. Currently, many centers provide programs that address special populations such as abused children, individuals with alcohol and drug abuse problems, and Vietnam veterans. Mental health professionals also assist in the establishment of self-help groups, such as Alcoholics Anonymous, Adult Children of Alcoholics, Alateen, Parents Without Partners, and Parents Anonymous (a child abuse self-help program).

Today, social workers in mental health settings provide crisis intervention, operate telephone hotlines, conduct suicide prevention programs, and provide alcoholism and drug abuse services. Mental health services increasingly are provided in settings other than mental health centers, including churches, nursing homes, police departments, schools, day care centers, the workplace, and health and medical settings. Problems addressed by mental health professionals have expanded to include loneliness and isolation, finances, spouse and child abuse, male/female relationships, housing, drugs, and alcohol. Mental health staff members have become more multidisciplinary in nature, using teams of professionals, as well as volunteers. Increasingly, the focus of services has been on case management and short-term counseling.

SUMMARY

Services for individuals with mental health needs and developmental disabilities have changed significantly since colonial times. Four major revolutions have occurred in the area of mental health, including the shift from inhumane to moral treatment; the introduction of psychoanalytic therapy; the move from institutions to community programs; and the development of psychotropic drugs that effectively treat many types of mental health problems.

Current issues in the mental health field include scarce resources and conflict over the roles of federal, state, and local governments in providing services; the legal rights of clients and whether they should be able to refuse or demand treatment; the need for more effective services for women, minority groups, and individuals in rural settings; and additional services that address problems such as child maltreatment, alcohol and drug abuse, posttrauma stress for Vietnam veterans, and the special needs of rural and ethnic populations. Social workers currently play a critical role in the provision of mental health services, serving as therapists, advocates, case managers, administrators, and policy makers. These roles are expected to continue and expand in the future. With increased social change and the resulting stress to all individuals in our society, it is anticipated that the mental health needs of all individuals will become an even more important area of focus.

KEY TERMS

clinical social worker
deinstitutionalization
Diagnostic and Statistical Manual
   (DSM)
developmental disability
mental retardation
moral treatment
National Association of Mental
   Health

National Institute of Mental
   Health
primary prevention
psychoanalysis
psychotropic drugs
secondary prevention
tertiary prevention

DISCUSSION QUESTIONS

1. Discuss the problems in defining mental illness.
2. Identify and briefly describe at least four frameworks that can be used in understanding mental health problems.
3. Identify the four major revolutions in the field of mental health.
4. Discuss the meaning of the term *developmental disabilities*. How does this term contrast with previously used terminology to identify persons within this category?
5. Discuss the advantages and disadvantages of current efforts at deinstitutionalization.
6. Identify at least five areas in which social workers employed in mental health settings might work. What are some of the roles in which they might function?
7. Do you agree with Szasz' concept of mental health? Discuss your rationale for either agreeing or disagreeing.

REFERENCES

Comprehensive Care Corporation. 1981. *Employee Assistance Programs: A Dollar and Sense Issue.* Newport Beach, Calif.: Comprehensive Care Corporation.

Deutsch, A. 1949. *Shame of the States.* New York: Columbia University Press.

Diagnostic and Statistical Manual of Mental Disorders 1980. 3rd ed. Washington, D.C.: American Psychiatric Association.

Felix, R. 1967. *Mental Illness: Progress and Prospects.* New York: Columbia University Press.

Goffman, E. 1961. *Asylums: Essays on the Social Situation of Mental Patients and Other Inmates.* Garden City, N.Y.: Doubleday.

Kesey, K. 1962. *One Flew Over the Cuckoo's Nest.* New York: Basic Books.

Mechanic, D. 1980. *Mental Health and Social Policy.* Englewood Cliffs, N.J.: Prentice–Hall.

Public Law 98–257. 1984. *Developmental Disabilities Assistance and Bill of Rights Act.* Washington, D.C.: 98th Congress.

Rosenhan, D. 1973. On Being Sane in Insane Places. *Science* 179: 250–57.

Szasz, T. 1960. The Myth of Mental Illness. *American Psychologist* 15 February: 113–18.

U.S. Department of Health, Education, and Welfare. 1980. *Health: United States, 1980.* Washington, D.C.: USDHEW.

U.S. Senate Subcommittee on Long–Term Care. 1976. Hearings on Long Term Care, p. 715. Washington, D.C.: USDHEW.

Williams, J.B. 1987. Diagnostic and Statistical Manual (DSM). In *Encyclopedia of Social Work,* vol. 1, pp. 389–93. 18th ed. Silver Springs, Md.: National Association of Social Workers.

SELECTED FURTHER READINGS

Green, Hannah. 1964. *I Never Promised You a Rose Garden.* New York: Holt, Rinehart and Winston.

The President's Commission on Mental Health. 1978. Washington, D.C.: Government Printing Office.

Scheff, Thomas. 1966. *Being Mentally Ill.* Chicago: Aldine.

Szasz, T. 1970. *The Manufacture of Madness.* New York: Harper and Row.

6 Health Care

B ill and Carmen Elliott and their one-year-old son, Carl, live in a rural community in the Midwest. Until two years ago, Bill and Carmen managed a family farm; however, because of the downturn in the economy, they were forced to declare bankruptcy. Bill has worked seasonally as a construction worker, and Carmen has worked as a waitress in a local cafe. Two years ago, Carmen became pregnant. Because she and Bill did not have health insurance, Carmen waited until she was five months pregnant to see a doctor. Two months later, she gave birth to a premature son. Shortly after the birth, the baby began experiencing severe respiratory and cardiac problems, and it was decided to fly him to the regional neonatal center 200 miles away. The baby remained at the neonatal center for two months, requiring heart surgery and intensive care.

When the baby finally was allowed to return home, he required extensive care, and Carmen was unable to return to work. Already financially strapped, Bill and Carmen were now faced with a $30,000 medical bill for the delivery and Carl's care. A visit to the local human services department to seek Medicaid was unsuccessful. Although Bill and Carmen's income was considered well below the poverty level, Bill's earnings as a construction worker were too high to qualify for the medical assistance. Bill's boss and other friends held a dance to raise money for the family, which netted $3000.

At this point, Bill and Carmen are overwhelmed with medical bills and are unsure if they will ever be

able to pay them all. Doctors say that Carl will need
extensive physical therapy and possibly more surgery
later on. Over the last six months, Bill has developed
kidney problems, which have already resulted in his
missing five work days. However, he feels that he
can't afford to see a doctor with the already-exten-
sive medical bills and so is hoping that whatever is
wrong will clear up by itself.

At the present time, health care in America is in a crisis state. On one hand,
many of America's citizens like Bill and Carmen Elliott are faced with the
payment of mammoth medical bills as a result of life-threatening situations.
Thirty-five million Americans do not have any health insurance at all; most
have health insurance that provides only limited coverage (*Children's Defense
Fund*, 1986).

On the other hand, national expenses for health care have increased from
$12.7 billion in 1950 to $247.2 billion in 1980 and presently comprise almost
10 percent of the U.S. gross national product (Bureau of the Census, 1981).
The health care industry is the third largest in the United States, preceded only
by agriculture and construction.

Debates over national health care issues focus on two primary concerns:
First, how much of our country's resources should be allocated to health care?
And second, how should those resources be allocated? As our knowledge and
technology in the health care arena continue to expand, decisions in the area of
health care increasingly will become moral and ethical. Given scarce resources,
for example, should an infant who requires tens of thousands of dollars to be
kept alive be given maximum treatment to save its life, particularly when the
child may live a life continually fraught with health problems and possibly
retardation? And what about organ transplants and kidney dialysis—should
these be made available to everyone? And if not, who should get them? With
more U.S. citizens living longer, to what extent should resources be allocated
toward health care for older persons? And to what extent should attention be
given to environmental concerns, such as nuclear power, sanitation, and pollution and their impact on personal health? Finally, given the high costs of
health care, who should pay for health care for the indigent—the federal
government, states, local communities, or individuals and their families themselves? And if individuals cannot afford health care, should it be denied to
them?

Increasingly, social workers will play a central role in helping policy
makers, medical practitioners, and family members make these critical decisions. Social workers also will continue to provide services in a variety of
health-related settings, ranging from traditional hospitals to family planning
clinics, rape crisis centers, and hospice programs for dying individuals and
their families. Studies project that the area of health care, particularly as it
relates to the elderly, is the fastest growing area of employment for social
workers today.

This chapter will provide an overview of our country's present health care
system, the problems it faces, and the types of health care policies and pro-

grams currently available. The roles social workers play in making those policies and programs possible also will be discussed.

A SYSTEMS APPROACH TO HEALTH CARE

Because the systems perspective was first introduced as a mechanism to explain the functioning of the human body, this perspective has a longer history within the health care arena than other arenas in which social workers function. As early as the Greek and Roman eras of civilization, it was observed that many health problems were precipitated by changes in the environment. An ancient Greek medical text, said to be authored by Hippocrates, *Airs, Waters, and Places,* explained health problems in terms of person–environment relationships. This work attributed human functioning to four body fluids: blood, phlegm, and black and yellow bile. As long as these body fluids were in equilibrium, an individual was healthy. However, Hippocrates attributed changes in the balance of these fluids to ecological variations in temperature, ventilation, and an individual's life-style in relation to eating, drinking, and work. Negative influences in the environment caused these fluids to become unbalanced, which in turn resulted in illness to the individual.

Other early works subscribed to germ theory, which is based on the premise that illness is a function of the interactions among an organism's adaptive capacities in an environment full of infectious agents, toxins, and safety hazards. The Greeks and Romans also were cognizant of the relationship between sanitation and illness. Early Roman writings suggested that one could predict and control health through the environment and prevent epidemic diseases by avoiding marshes, standing water, winds, and high temperatures. Public baths, sewers, and free medical care were all ways that early civilizations used to promote health and reduce disease (Catalano 1979).

The focus on the relationship between individual health and the environment continued during later centuries. Frank's medical treatise, *System of a Complete Medical Policy,* written in 1774–1821, advocated education of midwives and new mothers, a healthy school environment, personal hygiene, nutrition, sewers and sanitation, accident prevention, collection of vital statistics such as births and deaths, and efficient administration of hospitals to care for the sick.

Numerous studies throughout the years have attributed incidence of infant mortality, heart disease, and cancer to environmental influences. A number of studies, such as Dohrenwend and Dohrenwend's well-known research (1974), show strong relationships between stressful life events and the subsequent development of physical disorders, supporting Hippocrates' earlier theories of the ways that a negative life-style can affect one's health. Brenner (1973) demonstrated the relationships between health problems such as heart disease, infant and adult mortality rates, and other health indicators and national employment rates between 1915 and 1967. He found that when employment rates were high, health problems were low, and that low employment rates were associated with higher incidences of health problems.

As can be seen in Table 6–1, the greatest contributions to premature death are not individual hereditary factors, but environmental and life-style factors. Studies show that the following factors affect health status significantly.

Table 6–1
Major Factors Contributing to Premature Death: Estimated Percent Contribution to Cause Of Death

Leading Causes of Death	Lifestyle	Environment	Inadequacy of Health Care Services	Biology
Heart Disease	54%	9%	12%	25%
Cancer	37	24	10	29
Motor Vehicle Accidents	69	18	12	1
All Other Accidents	51	31	14	4
Stroke	50	22	7	21
Homicide	63	35	0	2
Suicide	60	35	3	2
Cirrhosis	70	9	3	18
Influenza/Pneumonia	23	20	18	39
Diabetes	34	0	6	60
TOTAL: All 10 Causes Together	51	19	10	20

Source: Centers for Disease Control. *Ten Leading Causes of Death in the U.S., 1975.* U.S. Department of Health, Education and Welfare, 1978.

Income

The higher one's income, the more likely one is to be in good health. The poor are much more likely to have health problems. This can be attributed to the fact that individuals with higher incomes are more likely to have health insurance, seek medical care earlier and more often and also be able to afford more nutritious food and experience less mental stress. The poor also are more likely to live in areas that are environmentally negative, such as areas with poor sanitation or close to hazardous wastes.

Ethnicity

Primarily because of income, whites as a group enjoy better health than non-whites. **Infant mortality rates** are twice as high for nonwhites as for whites, and life expectancies for nonwhites are much shorter: 70.6 years for white men compared to 65.5 for nonwhite men, and 78.3 for white women compared to 74.5 for nonwhite women.

Age

Older individuals experience poorer health than younger ones. This is a result of both the aging process and the fact that one-third of today's elderly are poor and do not seek health care as needed due to the high costs. The aging factor will be of greater significance as the U.S. population continues to age: by the year 2000, 13 percent of the population will be over 65.

Disability

Individuals with both permanent and temporary disability are much more at risk to have serious health problems than nondisabled persons.

Rural/Urban

Individuals living in extremely rural or highly populated urban areas are more at risk to have health problems. This can be attributed to the increasing environmental hazards such as pollution and increased stress from living in a highly populated urban area and the lack of medical facilities for prevention and early medical care found in extremely rural areas.

It is vital that a systems perspective that focuses on the interaction and interdependence between person and environment be used in understanding **health risk factors** and health conditions (see Table 6–2). A 1979 national health report, *Healthy People,* emphasized the important link between physical and mental health, noting the "importance of strong family ties, the assistance and support of friends, and the use of common support systems" in promoting healthy individuals (U.S. Surgeon General 1979).

The current emphasis on holistic health care stems from a systems approach to health care. This perspective views all aspects of an individual's health in relation to how that individual interacts with family members, the workplace, and the community and how the environment, including community quality of life as well as legislation and funding available to support quality of life, has an impact on a person's health. This perspective slowly is replacing the more traditional medical model used by health practitioners, which often only focuses on symptoms and malfunctions of one part of the body without focusing on other body systems or the environment within which the individual interacts.

THE EVOLUTION OF HEALTH CARE IN AMERICA

Early emphasis of health care in the United States focused on keeping people alive. Persons born in the U.S. 200 years ago only had a 50 percent chance of surviving long enough to celebrate their twenty-first birthdays. One third of all deaths were of children less than five years old. Even then, nonwhites had higher death rates. In the late eighteenth century, the death rate was 30/1000 for whites and 70/1000 for slaves (U.S. Public Health Service 1977). Health practitioners at that time were limited in number and in training and faced great difficulties in keeping their patients alive due to environmental constraints, such as poor sanitation and extreme poverty. Many illnesses resulted in catastrophic epidemics, which claimed the lives of entire families. In 1793 during a yellow fever epidemic in Philadelphia, three physicians were available to care for 6000 patients stricken with the disease. Thus, early attempts to improve health care in the United States included national and state legislation relating to control of communicable diseases, sanitation measures such as pasteurization of milk, and education for midwives, physicians, and young mothers.

Although more recent legislation and programs have focused on control of chronic, degenerative diseases such as heart disease and cancer, as well as those illnesses that are self-inflicted, such as cirrhosis of the liver, and other health problems such as accidents and violence, most efforts are still directed to restoring health *after* illness has occurred. The health care system in the United

Table 6–2   Health Risk Factors and Associated Health Conditions

Health Risk Factor	Cancers						Cardiovascular Diseases			Cirrhosis and Chronic Liver Disease	Dental and Oral Diseases		Diabetes	Injuries				Mental Health Problems	Osteoporosis	Pregnancy/Birth Complications			Respiratory Diseases	
	Lung	Breast	Colorectal	Uterine	Oral	Skin	Heart Disease	Stroke	Hypertension		Tooth Decay	Periodontal Disease		Motor Vehicle Accident	Accidental Falls	Violent Injury	Other Injury			Low Birthweight	Congenital Anomalies	Other	Chronic Lung Disease	Influenza and Pneumonia
Misuse of Alcohol					X				X	X			X	X	X	X	X	X	X	X	X	X		
Smoking	X				X		X	X	X									X	X	X		X	X	X
Chewing Tobacco					X																			
Inadequate Nutrition	X	X	X				X	X	X		X	X	X					X	X	X				
Insufficient Exercise							X	X	X						X		X	X	X					
Non-use of Auto Safety Restraints														X										
Poor Oral Hygiene											X	X												
Insufficient Preventive Dental Care											X	X												
Excessive Stress or Inability to Manage Stress							X								X			X						
Teen Pregnancy																		X		X	X	X		
Lack of Protection Against Sexually Transmitted Disease				X																	X	X		
Violence and Abuse																X	X	X						
Failure to Obtain Immunizations																		X						
Insufficient Prenatal Care																		X		X	X	X		
Unsafe Working Conditions														X	X		X							
Exposure to Hazardous Substances	X	X			X													X	X		X	X	X	
Excessive Exposure to Sun						X																		

Source: St. Paul Metropolitan Council. *Prescription for Health.* (St. Paul: Metropolitan Council/Metropolitan Health Planning Board, 1985), p. 18.

States still allows large numbers of U.S. citizens to remain unserved or underserved and mortality rates remain higher than in many developed countries. In spite of the fact that the United States currently spends more on health care than any other country, it ranks fifteenth from lowest to highest when infant death rates are compared among developed countries, and almost one-fourth of all U.S. women who deliver babies at public hospitals have received no prenatal care.

CRITICAL ISSUES IN CURRENT HEALTH CARE DELIVERY

Funding and Costs of Health Care

Emphasis during the 1950s and 1960s was on providing the best possible health care to all Americans and improving health personnel, services, and research. However, as costs for health care skyrocketed in the 1970s and 1980s, attention has shifted to ways to control costs and who should pay for what expenditures. In 1980, the U.S. health care system provided over 1 billion physical examinations, treated over 33 million persons in over 8000 hospitals, provided care to over 1 million persons, mostly elderly, in over 19,000 nursing homes, and treated over 181 million persons in outpatient visits to hospitals. **Private insurance** paid for 26 percent of the costs of this care; consumers paid for 34 percent of the care directly; **public insurance,** including various levels of government, paid for 40 percent of care, mostly through federal Medicaid and Medicare programs. While costs of health care have increased due to inflation, like costs in other areas, other reasons also must be considered. Some attribute increased costs to more extensive use of medical resources by a more educated population interested in preventive health care. They argue that accessibility to group insurance plans through the workplace and the increase in health maintenance organizations and other health programs aimed at reducing health costs actually increase costs because of more extensive use. Statistics show, however, that many Americans, particularly poor persons—minorities, single-parent females, and the elderly—work for employers who do not offer health insurance or are paid such low wages that they cannot afford the health insurance offered. Thus, they are less apt to use health care resources, but when they do, they are more likely to need more costly services because they have not sought preventive care.

However, even with today's emphasis on wellness and public awareness about the damages smoking, alcohol and drug consumption, and lack of exercise can do to one's health, few dollars are spent on prevention by private citizens and by all levels of U.S. government, even though studies show that dollars spent for prevention pay for themselves as much as eight times over in the long run (Comprehensive Care Corporation 1981).

There are other, more reliable explanations for the extreme costs of health care in the United States. First, because of increased access to health care, improved knowledge and technology, and a better quality of life, people are living longer, resulting in increased need for medical care for those 65 and older. Composing approximately 11 percent of the population and more likely to be poor and unable to pay for health care than other groups, persons over 65 have three times more health problems and needs than persons in other age groups.

This infant was born 2½ months prematurely. Prenatal care can prevent early delivery that often results in extremely high costs for health care.

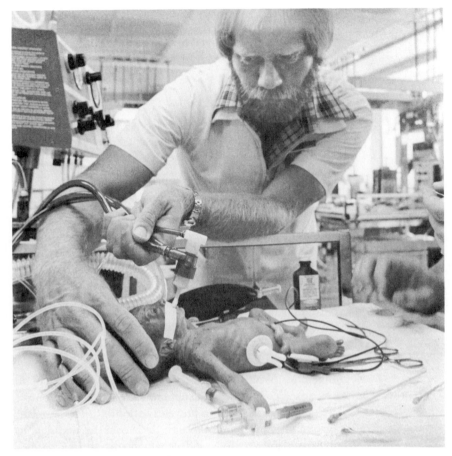

A second factor is the greater availability of knowledge and technology for saving lives: neonatal procedures for infants born prematurely; heart, lung, and other organ transplants; and heart surgery to restore circulation and reduce incidence of heart attacks and other cardiac problems. Currently, the extent and knowledge of technology exceed the dollars necessary to support such sophisticated systems and make them available to everyone in need (see Box 6–1). Additionally, with increased numbers of private hospitals and the difficulties public hospitals face in remaining solvent, health care has become increasingly competitive. This has resulted in duplicative purchases of expensive equipment by hospitals in close proximity in many instances.

A third factor that has been suggested is the use of third-party billing by many medical practitioners (billing an insurance company directly rather than billing the patient). Many physicians and hospitals charge the maximum amount allowable under an insurance system, while they might otherwise be reluctant to charge individual clients the same amount if they knew the clients would be paying for the services directly. However, efforts to reduce Medicaid and Medicare expenditures by setting ceilings for reimbursable costs have led some physicians and nursing homes to refuse to accept clients under these

Box 6–1
Pennsylvania
Girl Sees End
to 'Catch–22'

DANVILLE, Pa. (AP)—The case of 16–month–old Megan Demchak, whose life began 12 weeks prematurely and has been a struggle since, is a classic medical "Catch–22," her doctors say.

The 11–pound–5–ounce, 24½–inch baby has spent her entire life in the hospital, trying to recuperate from the severe lung problems associated with her premature birth. Finally, she is well enough to go home.

However, because doctors were able to wean Megan from the breathing machine that kept her alive for a year, neither federal nor state money would cover the cost of her at-home care, unless an exception was made.

For Megan, that exception came Friday. Denise Niedzielski, the Legal Services attorney who represents Megan's mother, Maryellen, said she had received a letter from the Department of Public Welfare saying it had agreed to abide by a hearing officer's decision to make an exception in Megan's case and pay for the private-duty nursing the little girl needed to go home.

Megan is one of thousands of so-called "high-tech" children. No one is sure of the exact number, though one national organization estimates about 10,000. Their lives are literally dependent on medicine's machines, but because public funds do not generally cover their at-home care, they remain hospitalized at a higher cost.

"It's becoming a very, very recurring theme, not just here but all across America. We have the ability to take care of these kids at home at a more cost-effective way of doing it," said Dr. Stephen Wolf, Megan's physician.

Megan's hospital bill so far is about $550,000 and growing daily. Megan's home care has been estimated to cost between $36,000 and $49,000 a year, depending on the duration and intensity of care.

Source: Associated Press. Used with permission.

health care assistance plans, claiming they lose too much money because the actual costs are much higher than the ceilings allowed.

Even though there are problems with the medicaid system of health care for the poor and with group insurance programs, of greater concern are the large numbers of persons who have no health coverage at all. Over half of the poor in the United States are either not covered by Medicaid or do not use the system. Those persons who have neither Medicaid nor other health insurance coverage often become destitute immediately when they or members of their family suffer health problems. Few families can afford even several thousand dollars in health care costs, and many health problems can easily cost a family over $10,000. Unfortunately, when individuals and other available health care programs cannot pay for health care, local communities and taxpayers must bear the costs. Many local public hospitals that must accept all patients are operating in the red; one local hospital has already spent over $1.5 million on a young child with serious health problems, as the child is not covered by any type of private or public health care plan. Thus, the hospital—and the local taxpayers—are absorbing the costs of her care.

Our society's tendency toward lawsuits is another cost-raising factor. Many medical practitioners fear the increasing number of malpractice suits being filed. One study found that all practitioners face at least one suit during their careers no matter how competent they are. This has resulted in extremely high costs for malpractice insurance, and practitioners who feel compelled to order numerous tests, exploratory surgery, and other medical procedures when they are not sure what is wrong with an individual, to eliminate the risk of a law suit for a wrong decision.

Current Major Health Problems

Heart Disease and Cancer   Although many health problems that faced Americans in the past have all but been eliminated, new ones arise upon which attention must be focused. It is estimated that almost 50 percent of U.S. citizens will die from heart disease, and that cancer will eventually strike one out of every three persons. While new technology and medications have made treatment of these diseases more effective, they remain major causes of death.

AIDS   **Acquired Immunodeficiency Syndrome (AIDS)** is presently of great concern. Those people who are diagnosed with AIDS rarely live more than two years and the disease is spreading. Little is known about how the disease can be treated effectively and current research efforts have yet to find a cure or vaccine to prevent its spread. Because of a long incubation period, most of those who will die of AIDS do not know that they have the disease. Most AIDS victims lose their jobs and most often their health insurance before the disease takes their lives. Currently, little funding has been made available for research, treatment, or public education, and the disease remains a controversial one that has caused panic in many parts of the country.

Other Illnesses and Diseases   Other illnesses receiving increased attention are diabetes, musculoskeletal diseases such as arthritis and osteoporosis, and respiratory diseases.

Catastrophic Illness   Increased national attention is also being given to the problems encountered by families when a **catastrophic illness** occurs. While many families can provide health care for themselves during typical, less serious health problems, a catastrophic illness most often can wipe out the savings of even a fairly wealthy family. Proposals are being made for national legislation to provide national health insurance for individuals and families who experience a catastrophic illness when their available health insurance is exhausted and the costs for the care have reached a certain limit.

Teen-Age Pregnancy   Attention has been directed toward at-risk groups that generate additional health problems. Recently, the group most publicized has been teen-age parents. Studies show that pregnant teens receive little or no prenatal care, poor nutrition during pregnancy, and limited services. As a result, they are at more risk of miscarriages, premature births, and giving birth to infants with low birth weight or congenital problems. While availability of family planning and other preventive services, as well as prenatal health care, are seen by many as a moral issue because such services are seen by some to promote teen pregnancy, such services are cost effective and more likely to result in healthy infants better able to grow up to become healthy adults.

Environmental Factors   Increased attention also is being paid to environmental factors and their impact on the health of individuals. These include hazardous household substances and other poisons, as well as the quality of household building materials, such as lead-based paints and formaldehyde in insulation. Workplaces also present risks to health, and increased attention is being given to environmental protections for employees from dangerous chemicals, pollutants in the air, and hazardous jobs. An estimated one-fifth of all cancer deaths are associated with occupational hazards. Smoking is being seen increasingly as an environmental hazard. In many workplaces and communities, smoking is only allowed in public areas and employers place smokers and nonsmokers in separate work areas. Communities and states are paying increased attention to road and traffic safety; unsafe housing; contaminated food, meat, and dairy products; pest and animal control; biomedical and consumer product safety; and other public health risks, such as inappropriate disposal of chemical and human wastes, storage and treatment of water, and control of nuclear energy plants.

Prevention and Wellness Programs   Increased attention is also being given to preventive aspects of health care, although prevention is still secondary to intervention after a health problem has occurred. The 1979 Surgeon General's report, *Healthy People,* found that the United States spends only about 5 percent of health care dollars on promotion of preventive measures. However, some businesses have established wellness programs, with exercise and fitness programs, nutrition and weight control programs, stop-smoking workshops and other health prevention efforts. A number of employers are working with insurance companies to offer incentives to employees who are low health risks, such as salary bonuses or reduced insurance rates.

Ethical Issues

As health care costs continue to increase, more people need health care and new technology and knowledge make it possible to keep people alive who previously could not have been helped. For these reasons, ethical dilemmas in the area of health care continue to increase. Many of these issues are already before our courts. When infants born three and four months premature can be saved, at what point, if at all, should abortion be prohibited? When infants require extensive neonatal care in order to survive, should such care be made available (see Box 6–2), even if the parents cannot afford the costs? Should the circumstances change to provide such care if the infant can survive but with serious mental and/or physical disabilities? If technology for heart and lung transplants is available, should everyone of all ages and income groups have equal access to these procedures? If a person can survive with medical care or special procedures, should they have a right to decide whether to receive the care or to be allowed to die? Do persons have the right to choose unsafe lifestyles, such as riding motorcycles without helmets, not using seat belts, or using drugs or alcohol heavily, when injuries or other health problems may result in high costs to others—taxpayers, state, and local governments, others in the same' insurance group? Does a pregnant woman have the right to drink, smoke, or use drugs if it can compromise the survival of her child? Who makes such decisions? What are the rights of the individual? Of the parents if the person is a child? Of the state or local governments if they are to pay for the care? Several recent court cases have attempted to address some of these issues. In the early 1980s, the Baby Doe case received national attention. This case involved an infant born with serious health problems who would have been seriously disabled, physically and mentally, with surgery and would have died immediately without surgery. The parents wanted the child to not have surgery, to not suffer, and to die a peaceful death. Some members of the hospital staff wanted the child to have the surgery, and others wanted the child to die. Concern has been raised in similar situations throughout the country. In some instances, it was reported that infants had been starved to death or had

Box 6–2
Wanted: Heart
for Baby Jesse

PASADENA, Calif. (AP)—Doctors sought a donor heart for a dying baby Friday as his parents expressed joy at a hospital's decision to reverse its refusal to list him as a transplant candidate.

"It's a lot easier to wake up in the morning with a little hope," Jesse Sepulveda, 26, told reporters after he and the mother, Deana Binkley, 17, signed over custody of their 12–day–old son, Jesse Dean Sepulveda, to Sepulveda's parents in Los Angeles County Superior Court.

The grandparents, whose names were not disclosed, took formal custody Friday when Judge Robert Olsen signed the guardianship order, which stipulated that the parents would not attempt to regain custody "without the prior written consent of Loma Linda hospital."

Loma Linda University Medical Center agreed Thursday to make Baby Jesse, who at birth was given no more than two weeks to live because of a fatally underdeveloped heart, a candidate for transplant.

The hospital initially rejected Jesse for transplant because doctors felt the young, unwed parents would be unable to provide adequate post-surgical care, according to family representatives who included a Roman Catholic priest.

The infant remained in critical but stable condition Friday at Huntington Memorial Hospital in Pasadena, where he was born May 25 with a fatal underdevelopment of the left side of his heart.

The baby's father said that the legal action "doesn't mean we're going to step aside."

Source: Associated Press. Used with permission.

experienced great pain when life supports were removed from them before they died. Special legislation was introduced that would have required local child welfare agencies to handle all such situations as child protective services cases and conduct investigations before medical decisions were made to ensure that children were being protected. The legislation was changed before it passed so that this did not happen, but it did mandate that hospitals establish special review boards to deal with such cases.

In many instances, such ethical dilemmas can be avoided, and dollars saved, by providing accessible and affordable health care before the problem occurs. For example, pregnant women who don't receive care during the first three months of pregnancy are 30 percent more likely to deliver infants with low birth weights. Costs for providing such infants neonatal intensive care average $20,000. Not only is $772 saved for each day that an infant remains in its mother's uterus between the twenty-ninth and thirty-fourth week of pregnancy, but the ethical dilemmas that often occur with such cases also are avoided (Metropolitan Council 1985).

Health Planning

To eliminate problems in costs of health care, duplication of care in some areas and gaps in others, and interface of public and private sector health care delivery, several important pieces of legislation have been passed. These include the following.

Hill–Burton Act   This act, passed in 1946, funded construction of a number of rural hospitals. Amendments in 1964 authorized the development of areawide hospital planning councils and the concept of areawide hospital planning. The act also specifies that hospitals who receive funding through this legislation cannot refuse to serve clients if they are unable to pay for services.

Medicare and Medicaid   These programs provide the majority of federal financing for health care. Medicare is a special health care program for the elderly to be used as a supplement to their other insurance programs (see Chapter 12), while Medicaid is available only to low-income individuals and families (see Chapter 4). The growth of both programs has been extensive, with the annual cost for both programs now almost $50 billion.

Comprehensive Health Planning Act   This act, passed in 1966, expands on the concept of local health planning districts to coordinate services and also requires review of other factors affecting the health of area residents, such as life-style and environmental conditions. The National Health Planning and Resources Development Act of 1974 further mandates the establishment of health systems agencies and statewide health coordinating councils to monitor hospital bed supply and occupancy rates, obstetric and neonatal special care units, pediatric beds, open heart surgery, and availability of expensive technological equipment such as megavoltage radiation equipment. The focus of this legislation is to increase availability of services in rural or other underserved areas and eliminate duplication in other areas, as well as to provide high-quality care at reduced costs by requiring rate review panels and professional standards of care.

Health Maintenance Organization Act   Passed in 1972, this act allows the development of **health maintenance organizations (HMOs)** to reduce health care costs for individuals. Most HMOs require a monthly fee, which allows free or low-cost visits to a special facility or group of facilities for health care. HMOs are intended to reduce health costs and encourage preventive health care.

Proposed Legislation

Efforts continue to be made through legislation and other policy arenas to balance health care costs with quality of care. Under the Reagan Administration, proposals for legislation to provide national health insurance for catastrophic health problems have been considered. Other proposals advocate providing Medicaid or some other type of health insurance or program for the poor for one year after they leave public assistance, since health care problems often force persons back on public assistance after they have been able to find jobs, sometimes without health insurance.

Many advocates are calling for a national health insurance program for all types of health care, not just catastrophic illness. Those in favor of such a program argue that costs for health insurance are too high for large numbers of individuals to afford, that many local hospitals are going in debt because they are having to pay health care costs for the increasing numbers of indigent persons, and that health costs are higher because persons are not seeking preventive health care, which would be more likely were there a national health insurance program with such an emphasis. Those against such a program argue that it means going to a system of socialized medicine, that the costs would be too high, and that people would clog the health care delivery system with trivial health problems that do not require medical attention. Proponents of such programs have proposed a variety of alternatives, including having the federal government collect funds for the program from various taxes, with the program administered by private insurance companies; having the government collect and administer the program, developing an expanded Medicare program available to everyone; having persons claim a tax credit on their income tax form if they use health care; and providing health coverage only for catastrophic illnesses.

Local states also are passing health care legislation, limiting the amounts that can be collected in malpractice suits in an attempt to keep medical costs down, mandating availability of health care for indigent persons and reducing the burden on local hospitals in poor areas of states, and establishing procedures for decision making about organ transplants and life-threatening situations.

THE ROLE OF SOCIAL WORKERS IN THE DELIVERY OF HEALTH SERVICES

Today, social workers play many roles in a variety of health care settings. Both roles and settings have increased significantly since the first social worker was employed at Massachusetts General Hospital in Boston in 1905. At that time, hospitals and general physicians were the major sources of health care. The social worker worked with the physician, other hospital staff, and the patient's family to ensure that high-quality care and attention continued after the patient returned home. Although responsibility for care after a patient leaves the hospital is still a major one for many social workers in health care settings, today social workers in these settings provide a variety of other tasks as well. Social workers often serve as a liaison between the patient's family and health care staff. They help the staff understand family concerns and how family constraints and other environmental factors may affect a patient's ability to recover. They also help patients and their families understand the implications of illness and issues relating to recovery and care. In many instances, the social worker provides support to the family when a death occurs or a patient's condition worsens.

Social workers in health care settings provide a number of functions, including:

1. social services to patients and their families, such as individual counseling to help a patient deal with a major illness or loss of previous capabilities due to accident or illness, helping family members grieve over a dying individual, or helping a teen-age mother accept her decision to place her child for adoption;

2. liaison with other social and health services agencies regarding patient needs, such as helping arrange for financial assistance to pay hospital bills, nursing home or home health care for patients when they leave the hospital, or emergency childcare for a single parent who is hospitalized;

3. serving as a member of a health care team and helping others understand a patient's emotional needs and home/family situation;

4. representing the hospital and providing consultation to other community agencies, such as child protective services agencies in child abuse cases;

5. providing preventive education and counseling to individuals relating to family planning, nutrition, prenatal care, and human growth and development;

6. providing health planning and policy recommendations to local communities, states, and the federal government in areas such as hospital care, community health care, environmental protection, and control of contagious diseases.

Whereas many social workers function in agencies administered by and hiring primarily social workers, called **primary settings,** health care settings are considered **secondary settings** because they are administered and staffed largely by non-social work professionals. Social workers in health care settings must be comfortable with their roles and be able to articulate their roles and functions clearly to non-social workers. A strong professional identity is important for health care social workers. Additionally, social workers in health care settings must be able to work comfortably within a medical setting. Knowledge and understanding of the medical profession and health care are important for social workers, as is the ability to function as a team member with representatives from a variety of disciplines. Social workers in health care

settings, particularly hospital settings, must be able to handle crisis intervention and most often prefer short-term social work services rather than long-
term client relationships. They must also be able to work well under pressure
and high stress and be comfortable with death and dying.

Hospital Settings

The American Hospital Association requires that a hospital maintain a social
services department as a condition of accreditation. Social workers in hospitals
may provide services to all patients who need them or may provide specialized
services. Larger hospitals employ emergency room social workers, pediatric
social workers, intensive care social workers, and social workers who work
primarily on cardiac, cancer, or other specialized wards. M. D. Anderson Hospital in Houston, Texas, for example, has over twenty social workers. It is a
large hospital that specializes in treating cancer patients. A number of large
hospitals have added social workers who provide social services primarily to
AIDS patients. Other hospitals use social workers in preventive efforts,
providing outreach services, including home visits to mothers identified
during their hospital stay as potentially at risk to abuse or neglect their children. Still others use social workers to coordinate rehabilitative services, serving as a case manager to ensure that occupational, physical, recreational,
speech, and vocational therapy is provided. Social workers work in both public and private hospitals, providing both inpatient and outpatient care. Many
are employed by Veterans Administration (VA) Hospitals, which have a long-
time tradition of using social workers to work with persons who have served
in the Armed Forces. Many VA social workers provide specialized counseling
relating to physical disabilities and alcohol and drug abuse. A number of VA
social workers now specialize in post-Vietnam stress syndrome and provide
services to Vietnam veterans and their families.

Because of accreditation standards, most hospital social workers must have
master's degrees in social work. Many schools of social work offer specializations in medical or health care.

Long–Term Care Facilities and Nursing Homes

Many persons who suffer from illness or disability do not need the intensive
services of a hospital but cannot care for themselves in their own homes
without assistance. For some individuals, particularly the frail elderly, **long-
term care facilities** and nursing homes are most appropriate. There are
various levels of care facilities, with licensing and accreditation requirements
for each. From 1965 to 1972, social work services were mandated for all
nursing homes that cared for residents covered by Medicare. Although such
services are no longer required, they are reimbursable by Medicare and many
nursing homes have found it beneficial to employ social workers. Social
workers in these settings help residents adjust to the nursing home environment, help families deal with their guilt and feelings of loss after such
placements, serve as liaisons to other social services and health care agencies,
and provide individual and group counseling and other social services for
nursing home residents and their families.

It is suggested that provision of social work services to the elderly in health care settings is the fastest growing area in the field of social work, and many schools of social work are offering specializations at the master's degree level in health and gerontology and special courses at the BSW level in these areas to meet the demand.

Community–Based Health Care Programs

Many social workers, both at the BSW and MSW levels, are employed in local community-based health care programs. Most state health departments operate local health clinics, which provide a variety of health services available to low-income residents as well as community education programs for all residents. Such programs include immunizations, family planning services, prenatal care, well-baby and pediatric services, nutrition and other types of education programs, and basic health care. Many health clinics employ social workers to work with patients and their families as other health care services are provided. For example, some clinics operate high-risk infant clinics, which include social services for parents of infants at risk for abuse, neglect, or other serious health problems or those who already have serious health problems and whose parents need monitoring and support. Social workers also work with local community groups and schools, providing outreach programs to publicize such concerns as sexually transmitted diseases and teen pregnancy.

Social workers are also employed in family planning clinics, such as Planned Parenthood, providing counseling and help in decision making regarding pregnancy prevention or intervention, such as planning for adoptive services in an unwanted pregnancy. With new technology that can diagnose problems in embryos in the uterus, many health providers also are employing social workers to provide genetic counseling, helping patients to understand possibilities of giving birth to infants with potential problems, and to make appropriate decisions regarding whether to become pregnant or to terminate a pregnancy.

Increasingly, other health care settings are recognizing the relationship between environmental concerns and mental health and outcomes to the individual that impair physical health. To help address the relationship, previously traditional health care settings increasingly are employing social workers. In many areas, for example, local physicians' clinics, usually operated by a small group of physicians who share a practice, are hiring social workers to provide counseling to patients in an effort to improve mental health and reduce stress. HMOs are also hiring social workers to perform similar functions.

Home Health Care

Many states and communities are recognizing the need for services that enable persons with health problems to remain in their own homes. **Home health care** services most often preserve self-esteem and longevity for the individual and are far less costly than hospital or nursing home care. Trained nurses and home health aides, as well as social workers, make home visits to provide health care in a person's home. Social workers provide counseling to both the client and family and ensure that emotional functioning is appropriate.

State Departments of Health and Health Planning Agencies

Many social workers at both the BSW and MSW levels are employed in health care policy and planning jobs. They help make critical decisions regarding funding, policies, and programs for state legislatures, federal officials, and state and local health departments and planning agencies. The impact of environmental changes on individuals, disease prevention and control, monitoring of solid waste and water facilities, and emergency and disaster planning are other areas in which social workers in these programs become involved. Many social workers have become heavily involved in policies and studies relating to the impact of AIDS in the United States, for example. State health departments provide services relating to dental health, family planning, nutrition, and teen-age pregnancy; nutrition programs for pregnant women and young children; periodic health screening programs for infants and young children; drug and alcohol programs; and teen-age parent services.

The national Public Health Service provides similar services to indigent populations in areas with few medical practitioners, such as Indian reservations and migrant areas. The service also monitors communicable diseases and provides research in a variety of health areas. Other federal programs such as the National Institute of Health (NIH) also provide research and policy alternatives. Both of these programs also employ social workers at the BSW and MSW levels.

Other Health Care Settings

There are numerous other health-related programs in which social workers are involved. Many work for the American Red Cross, for example, providing emergency services to families when disaster strikes. Recently developed health programs that often employ social workers include women's health clinics, which presently number over 1000 and provide gynecological and primary care using a holistic health approach; genetic counseling centers; and rape crisis centers. Many EMS (emergency medical service) programs in large cities are employing social workers to assist in crisis intervention during family violence, child maltreatment, rape, and homicide.

Hospices are multiplying throughout the country and employing social workers in their agencies. Originally begun in England, hospice programs allow terminally ill persons to die at home or in a homelike setting surrounded by family members rather than in an often alien hospital environment. Using the stages of grief described by Elizabeth Kubler–Ross as a framework, many hospices employ social workers to work with families and the dying person or to supervise a cadre of volunteers who provide similar services. As critical issues in health care continue to be identified, the functions of social workers in health care settings will continue to expand.

SUMMARY

Issues relating to health care continue to be controversial and complex. As health care costs continue to rise, new technology and medical discoveries continue to be made, and with more and more persons living longer, concerns about health care will become more evident. Finding a balance of health care that is available, accessible, acceptable, and affordable, yet accountable to funding sources, is the highest priority for the United States in the next decade. Whatever the balance established, social workers will play an ever-increasing role in both the planning and the delivery of health care services.

KEY TERMS

Acquired Immunodeficiency
        Syndrome (AIDS)
catastrophic illness
health maintenance organization
        (HMO)
health risk factors
home health care

hospice
infant mortality rates
long-term care facility
primary setting
private insurance
public insurance
secondary setting

DISCUSSION QUESTIONS

1. Discuss some of the changes in the focus of health care that have taken place in the United States since colonial times.
2. Identify at least three reasons why health care costs have increased.
3. What are some of the ethical issues faced by health care providers and policy makers? Who do you think should receive priority in access to health care if costs prevent it being available to everyone?
4. What are some preventive programs social workers can implement to reduce the need for health care in the United States?
5. Identify at least five roles social workers can play in the delivery of health care services. How do careers for social workers in health care compare to careers in other areas in terms of availability and opportunity? Why?

REFERENCES

Associated Press. 1987. Pennsylvania Girl Sees End to 'Catch-22'. Austin, TX.: *Austin American Statesman*.

Associated Press. 1987. Wanted: Heart for Baby Jesse. Austin, TX.: *Austin American Statesman*.

Brenner, M.H. 1973. "Fetal, Infant and Maternal Mortality During Periods of Economic Stress," *International Journal of Health Sciences* 3, 145–59.

Catalano, R. 1979. *Health Behavior and the Community: An Ecological Perspective*. New York: Pergamon Press.

Children's Defense Fund. 1986. *Children's Defense Fund Budget: An Analysis of the FY 1987 Federal Budget and Children*. Washington, D.C.: Children's Defense Fund.

Comprehensive Care Corporation. 1981. *Employee Assistance Programs: A Dollars and Sense Issue.* Newport Beach, Calif.: Comprehensive Care Corporation.

Dohrenwend, B.S., and B.P. Dohrenwend, eds. 1974. *Stressful Life Events: Their Nature and Effects.* New York: Wiley.

Metropolitan Council/Metropolitan Health Planning Board. 1985. *Prescription for Health.* St. Paul, Minn.: Metropolitan Council.

Nacman, M. 1977. Social Work in Health Settings: A Historical Review. *Social Work in Health Care,* 2 (Summer): 407–17.

Office of Technology Assessment. 1981. *The Implications of Cost-effectiveness Analysis of Medical Technology: Case Study No. 10: The Costs and Effectiveness of Neotatal Intensive Care.* Washington, D.C.: Congress of the United States.

U.S. Bureau of the Census. 1981. *Statistical Abstract of the United States.* Washington, D.C.: U.S. Bureau of the Census.

U.S. Public Health Service. 1977. "200 Years of Child Health," in E. Grotberg, ed., *200 Years of Children.* Washington, D.C.: U.S. Department of Health, Education, and Welfare.

U.S. Surgeon General. 1979. *Healthy People: The Surgeon General's Report on Health Promotion and Disease Prevention.* Washington, D.C.: U.S. Department of Health, Education, and Welfare, Public Health Service.

SELECTED FURTHER READINGS

Bracht, N. 1978. *Social Work in Health Care.* New York: Haworth Press.

Estes, R. 1984. *Social Work in Health Care.* St. Louis: Green.

Marmor, T., and Christianson, J. 1982. *Health Care Policy: A Political Economy Approach.* Beverly Hills, Calif.: Sage Publications.

7 The Needs of Children, Youth, and Families

Divorced for two years, Marjorie White is struggling to survive. Her five children are in a foster home while she tries to stabilize her life. Mrs. White is looking forward to the day when she and her children can live together as a family again.

Mrs. White came from a large family. Her father often drank and beat her mother and Mrs. White. Pregnant at age fifteen and afraid of what her father would do, she eloped with the father of her child, a twenty-one-year-old high school graduate who worked as an auto mechanic. The first year was fairly peaceful, although money was a continual problem. Lacking health insurance, it took them several years to pay the bills for the birth of the baby. However, both the Whites were excited about the baby, and Mrs. White worked hard to provide a good home for her husband and her baby.

The Whites had four more children during the next seven years. Because two of the children had many medical problems, financial pressures continued to mount, and life became increasingly stressful. Mr. White began to drink heavily and beat Mrs. White often. He also beat the oldest child, who was diagnosed as mildly retarded. When Mrs. White was pregnant with her youngest child, her husband left her. Since that time, he has paid child support only for four months.

After her husband left, Mrs. White moved in with a sister, who had four children. She got a job at a fast food restaurant, and a second one cleaning a bank, while her sister took care of the children. This arrangement ended after several months because of continual arguments over money, space, and childrearing.

At that point, Mrs. White applied for food stamps and medical assistance and moved into the subsidized home she still lives in. She hired a teen-age girl to take care of the children while she worked as a waitress. Tired and overwhelmed, Mrs. White had little time to spend taking care of the children or the house. She became increasingly abusive toward her children. The older children did poorly in school and were continually fighting, stealing, and vandalizing. Neighbors saw the younger children outside at all hours, unsupervised, often wearing only diapers. They often heard screaming and the baby crying throughout the night.

One evening when the screams were unusually loud, a neighbor called the police. One of the boys had been badly beaten, with numerous bruises and a broken arm. The local child protective services department determined that Mrs. White's children were being abused and neglected. Mrs. White was overwhelmed, angry, and felt extremely guilty about what had happened. The children were placed in foster care with an older, nurturing couple. With more structure, the children began doing better in school and were able to develop some positive relationships with others. Mrs. White visited the children often, and began to see the foster parents as caring individuals who seemed almost like parents to her.

She enrolled in a job-training program and was hired as a health care aide for a local hospital. She enjoys her job and is talking about getting her high school equivalency certificate and going to nursing school. Mrs. White's social worker encouraged her to join Parents Anonymous, a support group for abusive parents. For the first time, Mrs. White has developed positive trusting relationships with others. She and her social worker are making plans to have the children return home on a permanent basis.

For all individuals, the **family** is probably the most significant social system within which they function. Within the family we first develop trusting relationships, a special identity, and a sense of self-worth. Traditionally, despite difficulties in society, the family has been looked upon as a safe, protective haven where individuals can receive nurturing, love, and support. It is increasingly difficult for children and their families to grow up in today's complex and rapidly changing world. Daily, children are confronted with family financial pressures, the need for one or both parents to work long hours, or the physical or mental illness or loss of a family member. Unable to cope with these pressures, family members often turn to alcoholism or drug abuse, resort to violence, or withdraw from other family members and do not respond to their needs. Sometimes, because they did not receive love and nurturance when they were children, the parents are unable to provide this for their own children. Other parents don't know how to provide for their own children because they have never learned what children need at certain ages or what to expect from them. Other families, although generally functioning well, may be unable to adequately meet the needs of family members during some type of crisis, such as death or a serious illness.

How well a family is able to meet the needs of its members also depends on other systems within the family's environment. The workplace, the neighborhood, the community, and the society with which that family interacts have a tremendous impact on its well-being. Urie Bronfenbrenner (1979) and James Garbarino (1982), two researchers interested in the development of children and families, suggest that more attention should be given to intervention in these broader systems than in the past, rather than just providing services to individual family members. A family that functions within an unsupportive environment is much more susceptible to family problems than a family functioning within a supportive environment. If the family lives in a community that has no programs available to family members, that also may threaten the family's well being.

Consider Mrs. White's situation. Her children were at risk for many reasons. Abused as a child, she learned to distrust others and failed to have her emotional needs met during her childhood. This left Mrs. White feeling worthless and inadequate. Individuals with low self-esteem are more likely to get pregnant during their teenage years. They also are more likely to be beaten by their spouses. Additionally, individuals experiencing financial and marital problems are more likely to abuse their children than other parents. Parents like Mrs. White also have learned from their own parents that anger is dealt with by hitting. Like Mrs. White, they may be used to living with an alcoholic and may have learned many behavior patterns that they carry into their own lives.

This chapter will discuss general issues and trends that must be considered when focusing on the needs of children, youth, and families; the types and extent of problems that can have an impact on children and their families; and factors that place families more at risk to experience those problems. Chapter 8 will focus on services and policies that prevent or alleviate problems experienced by children, youth, and families. The roles that social workers play in providing these services and developing and implementing policies also will be discussed in Chapter 8.

ISSUES TO CONSIDER WHEN ADDRESSING CHILD AND FAMILY NEEDS

What Is a Family?

The typical American family in the post-World War II era included a husband, wife, and 2.6 children. Today, only about 10 percent of American families are of this type. Twenty percent of all families are headed by only one parent, usually a woman, although an increasing number of men are assuming responsibility for raising children following a divorce or separation. Many families have extended family members, such as grandparents, aunts, uncles, or cousins living with them. Others have children adopted through the court system or taken in informally; still others have foster children. It is also becoming more and more common for individuals to live together who are not related by blood or marriage.

During the 1970s, a program was funded by the federal government to develop a national policy that supported families. The program's first task was to define a family. The program staff determined that this task was impossible! Others, however, provide a broad definition of a family, exemplified by the following: Any group of individuals who are bonded together through marriage, kinship, adoption, or mutual agreement (Goode 1964). When referring to needs of children and families, a family is referred to within the context of a parent figure or figures, and at least one child. Perhaps the most important issue in relation to what constitutes a family is that whereas all children and families have similar needs—to be loved, wanted, accepted, fed, clothed, given shelter, and protected—no two families are alike. Each family may be viewed as its own system, and each family system must be viewed as unique unto itself.

How Are Family Problems Defined?

What constitutes a family problem depends a great deal on the perspective of the individual defining the problem. How a problem is defined depends on a variety of factors, including the social and historical context within which the problem takes place; the attitudes and values of the culture or society of the family; the attitudes and values of the community in which the family resides and the norms of the community; the attitudes, values, culture, previous life experiences, and professional background of the person defining the problem; legal definitions of the problem; and the availability of resources to address the problem.

Cultural attitudes, values and practices shape how family problems are defined. In cultures where women become sexually active as soon as they reach menses, teen-age pregnancy is not likely to be considered a problem. Some cultures think it abusive that we make young children sit in a dental chair and force them to open their mouths and have their teeth pulled out. Some family policy experts suggest that the United States as a society is less supportive of children and families than other countries, when legislation and programs supportive of families are considered. In many Scandinavian countries, for example, the government provides free health care to children, subsidies for working parents to stay home when their children are young, and free child care. Other policy experts suggest that our country's fascination with violence as exemplified through the media and sports events has a strong impact on the high incidence of violence within the family, and that the emphasis placed on sex in the media contributes to the high incidence of teen-age pregnancy.

The *norms and values of the community* also shape the way family problems are defined. If everyone within a community is unemployed and lives in housing without plumbing and with dirt floors and all children are poorly fed and clothed, the families within that community living under those circumstances are not likely to be considered as neglecting their children. However, a family living like that in a wealthy community with high employment and stability most likely would be considered neglectful. Whipping a child with a belt is not as likely to be considered child maltreatment in some communities or parts of the country as in others.

The *attitudes, values, personal life experiences, and professional background of the person* defining the problem also influence how a problem is defined. A person raised in a conservative family, where drinking of any alcoholic beverages was considered taboo, might define alcoholism differently than a person raised in a family where drinking alcoholic beverages was commonplace. A physician may be more likely to define child abuse only in terms of bruises or broken bones, whereas a social worker may be more likely to argue that emotional neglect or harassment also constitutes an important form of child abuse.

Legal statutes also provide definitions of some types of family problems. These definitions vary by country and state and often leave a great deal of room for interpretation at the personal, professional, and community level. For example, child maltreatment has been defined at the national level as "the physical or mental injury, or threatened physical or mental injury, of a child by the acts or omissions of the child's parent or other person responsible for the child's welfare" (National Center on Child Abuse and Neglect 1980). Terms such as *mental injury, threatened,* and *acts or omissions* often are difficult to interpret. At the same time, they allow leeway for additional protection of children who may be subject to just as much risk as a child in a more easily defined situation. For example, a child who is constantly threatened with a knife or gun, even though never actually hurt, is at risk of emotional problems.

The *availability of resources* to address the problem may be the most important factor of all in how a problem is defined. The broader the definition, the more children and families will be identified with the problem and in need of assistance; the narrower the definition, the fewer identified with the problem and in need of assistance. The legal definition just given, for example, allows for the inclusion of neglected and emotionally maltreated children. In fact, when a similar state definition was first implemented, three times as many cases of child neglect were reported as cases of child abuse. Almost ten years later, due to scarce resources and significantly more cases reported, physical abuse and neglect cases are investigated and substantiated about equally, and only the most serious cases are defined as such. Resources are so stretched to their limits in many states that more narrow definitions of child maltreatment are being used. During the Kennedy and Johnson Administrations, when resources to address domestic social problems were abundant, the emphasis was on developing programs to "achieve the maximum potential of all children." The emphasis shifted under the Nixon Administration to "meeting minimum levels of care for children and their families," thus significantly narrowing the numbers of families and children who fit within the definition of needed services (Steiner 1976).

What Causes Families to Have Problems?

Families have problems for many reasons—and some families experience similar problems but for different reasons. There is no single cause for a given problem, which is why it is important to use a systems perspective in addressing family problems. It also is more appropriate to say that there are certain factors *associated* with specific family problems, rather than factors that *cause* those problems. This means that a family experiencing a problem may have other problems as well, but it is often difficult to determine which problem ·caused the other.

We know that problems often go together. One is likely to find child abuse, spouse abuse, alcoholism, teen-age pregnancy, and divorce within the same family. Individuals with these problems are more likely to be under stress, worried about financial pressures whether rich or poor, have low self-esteem, and come from families where similar problems existed when they were children than individuals in families without these problems.

Services for children and families often are provided by problem area—for example, specialized services for alcoholism, child abuse and neglect, and spouse abuse—rather than services that focus on the family as a system. This largely is due to the categorical basis on which state and federal funding generally is allocated. This categorical funding system has resulted in fragmented and duplicated services, as well as gaps in services in which client groups "fall through the cracks" or lack a specific funding focus.

How Do Cultural and Gender Differences Affect Family Problems?

While statistics show that more children and families who experience family problems in the United States are white and headed by two parents, that is only because there are more white, two-parent families than other types of families. Thus, it is important to consider not only raw counts but rates; that is, numbers of individuals of a certain group experiencing problems compared to the total population of that group. Such comparisons show that some groups are more vulnerable, or at risk, to experience certain problems than other groups.

Single women with children and members of ethnic minority groups are more at risk to experience family problems in the United States than men and whites. The reader should not infer from this statement that women and members of ethnic minority groups are in any way less competent, genetically impaired, more prone toward violence, or interested only in themselves. There are a number of very critical reasons why women and minority members are more at risk than other groups. A black or Hispanic child growing up in the United States is more likely to grow up in a poor family than a white child. Whereas one out of five children in the United States grows up in poverty, nearly half of all black children and nearly two out of five Hispanic children are poor (Children's Defense Fund 1986). The unemployment rate in this country in 1980 was 16 percent for white youth age 16–24 and not enrolled in school and 39 percent for black youth. More than 50 percent of all households headed by women fall below the poverty level, while only 13 percent of all two-parent households are below this level (Children's Defense Fund 1986). In

1985, 80 percent of all white children, 70 percent of all Hispanic children, and 48 percent of all black children lived in two-parent families. It is estimated that by the year 2000, 70 percent of black families will be headed by single-parent women and 30 percent of black men will be unemployed (Moyers 1986).

Because individuals who experience poverty are far more likely to experience stress, they are far more at risk of experiencing other family problems. Thus, women and minority groups, by the very nature of their positions within the socioeconomic hierarchy, are more likely to experience family problems. Additionally, these groups traditionally have had less power than other groups and are more vulnerable to being ignored or blamed for the problems they cause than being able to advocate for solutions and resources to address them. Women, for example, are often paid less and hired into lower level jobs than men. Those who re-enter the workplace after or while in more traditional marriages where they have not been employed outside the home ("displaced homemakers") are at a disadvantage of getting jobs that allow them to adequately support their families. They also most often must bear the brunt of child care and other child-related needs. Traditional attitudes about women and ethnic minorities are changing, but because of a scarcity of resources available to address their needs, they continue to be at the bottom of the social structure in our country.

Children growing up in families where social support is not available are more likely to experience problems in development, have low self-esteem, drop out of school, become pregnant at an early age, and have difficulty in finding adequate employment. Because they often lack appropriate role models and have been raised in an environment of hopelessness and despair, having children is often the only way they feel competent as people. With few skills and even fewer resources, the cycle of the at-risk family is repeated with their own children.

Although some attention is being given to the special needs of women and minorities and their families, this attention does not always address the problems from a broad context. For example, with the increased divorce rate and increase in numbers of people having children out of marriage, women have been targeted as "America's new poor," and much attention has been given to the **feminization of poverty.** However, in addition to providing more social supports to women and their families, the problem needs to be addressed from a systems perspective—women alone are not responsible for pregnancy or divorce, and men's responsibility in such situations also must be addressed.

Additional factors also must be taken into account when considering the relationship between family problems and minorities and women. While such families also are more likely to experience poverty and stress and, thus, more likely to experience alcoholism or spouse or child abuse or be too overwhelmed by these pressures to parent their children adequately, they are also more likely to be labeled as having such problems. A black parent who abuses a child, for example, is much more likely to take the child to a public hospital or clinic for treatment, where the case is likely to be reported to authorities. A white parent, however, is much more likely to take the child to a private physician, and perhaps to a different private physician if the child is reabused. Minority families and single-women parents also are more likely to seek help for family problems at public services agencies, such as local mental health centers, than at private psychological counseling programs. White parents having problems with children are far more likely to be able to afford to send them to residential treatment facilities for therapy, whereas minority children are much more likely to be sent to juvenile detention centers, where such treatment usually is not available.

Not all minority or women-headed families have problems, and one must be careful not to stereotype such families. However, individuals studying social problems need to be aware that children who grow up in families headed by minorities and women are more vulnerable than children growing up in other families. Family problems must be considered within the context of the broader environment, and these considerations are important as we work to shape the environment to make it more supportive to children and their families.

TYPES OF FAMILY PROBLEMS

Divorce and Separation

The divorce rate in the United States has increased dramatically during the past several decades. In 1980, it was projected that over one-third of married persons of child-rearing age would divorce, with each marriage involving an estimated two children. Current projections suggest that over half of today's children will spend at least some time in a single-parent household (Children's Defense Fund 1982). Divorce and separation result in crises for family members. For adults, the separation or divorce signifies the loss of an intimate relationship that also brought security and support. Separation or divorce also signifies a loss of hopes and dreams as well as feelings of failure. Although there may be relief over the divorce, being alone also brings fear, anxiety, loneliness, and guilt, especially if there are children involved. Initially, parents are so caught up in dealing with their own emotions that they have little energy left to help their children cope. Thus, at a time when their children need them most, many adults find themselves unable to function adequately as parents.

For children, the initial impact of the divorce almost always is traumatic. If a great deal of fighting existed in the family, children may feel a sense of relief. However, they, too, experience anger, guilt, fear, and sadness. Often, children blame themselves for their parents' divorce. Many times, they try to change their behavior, either acting overly good or overly bad in the hope that this will bring their parents back together. Parents often fail to say anything to their children about an impending divorce, because of their own grieving and the belief that their children will cope better if they are not burdened with adult problems.

Studies suggest that the most important factor that helps children get through a divorce is having someone to listen and provide support to them. Parents need to explain that they are divorcing each other and not the child, and that both of them will continue to love and spend time with the child. Some children may not react visibly when they are informed that their parents are separating or divorcing. However, if children do not react immediately after the divorce, they are likely to hold their feelings inside and express them at a later age (Wallerstein & Kelly 1979).

Talking about the divorce and giving them a chance to express their feelings are important aspects in helping children cope with divorce. Children experiencing a divorce in their family usually regress at the time of the divorce; studies show that it takes children an average of two to three years to work through the divorce and be on an equal footing developmentally with their peers. Children may exhibit such behaviors as nightmares and bedwetting, thumb sucking, behavioral problems at school and at home, drop in academic performance in school, listlessness and daydreaming, changes in eating habits, and increases in illness. Particularly if one parent has much less contact than in the past, they may develop extreme fears that they will be abandoned by the other parent or worry about what will happen to them if the parent they are living with dies (Wallerstein & Kelly 1980).

Although children are likely to cope better with divorce if the adults involved cope well, it usually takes them longer to recover, primarily because they have no control over the situation. Children fare better after a divorce if they maintain a positive relationship with both parents and if the parents do not speak negatively about each other to the children or use the children to fight their battles with each other.

Custody and visitation problems often have a negative impact on a child following a divorce. Although the situation is changing, mothers are much more likely to obtain custody in a divorce, with fathers, as the noncustodial parents, having children visit them on holidays and during summer vacations. Courts have placed emphasis on a long-held doctrine that, in a child's "tender years," the mother is more important in the child's life, and unless totally unfit, she should receive custody of children in a divorce. Although in many instances today, fathers want custody and are equally and often more capable of caring for children, less than 10 percent of divorces result in children living with their fathers. Because the average woman's income decreases significantly following a divorce, whereas the average man's income increases, children of divorce often view their fathers as "Santa Clauses" who buy them presents and take them special places, let them stay up later, and let them have fewer rules than their mothers who are buying the necessities and maintaining the daily routine, which usually requires more discipline. Mothers resent that they cannot give their children the same fun aspects of life, whereas fathers often find visitation time with their children artificial and awkward and don't know what else to do with them.

Parents also often expect the child to decide where to live and where to spend holidays, creating undue pressure on the child, who knows he or she will be forced to hurt one parent no matter what the decision. Experts recommend that children be allowed to give input in such decisions, but that final decisions be made by either the parents, or if they cannot agree, by a trained mediator skilled in divorce conflicts, or by the court (Gardner 1970).

Increasingly, parents are opting for joint custody, where both parents equally share custody and often time spent living with the child. Some parents alternate the child's living with them every three or four days, while others have the child with them for six months and then switch the living arrangements. In some instances, to maintain stability for the child, the parents move in with the child, who remains in the same home, one at a time for a specified period of time. Studies conflict as to the benefits of different types of custody. Many experts suggest shared custody if the parents have a positive relationship with each other, as this provides the child with two strong role models who love and pay attention to the child and communicates that the child is wanted and loved by both parents equally. Other experts suggest that shared custody, particularly if it involves a great deal of moving back and forth on the child's part, creates instability and a lack of permanence, and that the child has no place to truly call his or her own.

The need for support to families experiencing divorce, particularly for children, is receiving increased attention. Many cities have established family **mediation** centers, where a team of social workers and attorneys work together with families in the divorce process. This helps parents maintain positive relationships with each other in an adult way, resolving conflicts together rather than forcing them to take adversarial roles, as is often the case when individuals have separate attorneys and a court action. Public schools and family service agencies also have established special programs and support groups for children experiencing divorce and their parents.

Single Parenting

Presently, 20 percent of families in the United States are headed by a **single parent,** either because of divorce or separation or, increasingly, because of unmarried women giving birth to children. Currently, the majority of all black children are being raised in single-parent homes. As indicated earlier, projections suggest that, by 1990, the number of children of all ethnic groups being raised in single-parent homes will increase significantly. There is no evidence that suggests that growing up in a single-parent family is inherently positive or negative. However, single-parent families are more likely to be associated with factors that place the children in these families more at risk of other types of family problems, such as alcoholism, child maltreatment, teen-age pregnancy, and juvenile delinquency.

These families, with a single income most often earned by a woman, are more likely to be poor and, if not within the poverty definition of poor, experiencing financial stress. In addition to financial pressure, single parents must maintain sole responsibility for overseeing the household and childrearing. As a result, children growing up in single-parent families often are used to different life-styles than others. It is a paradox of children growing up in single-parent families that, on one hand, they are likely to have more freedom than other children, and on the other hand, they must take on much more responsibility. Children of single parents often have increased freedom because they must spend more time by themselves while their parents are working. Because childcare is so expensive, many children of single parents, especially school-age children, become "latch key" children, responsible for themselves until their parent gets home from work. Others must be responsible for caring for younger siblings. It is not unusual for a child of a single parent to come from school alone, do homework and household chores, and prepare the evening meal. Single-parent children also must assume more responsibility for themselves because of the unavailability of supervision.

Single-parent children who are the same gender as the parent who has left the home also may assume many of the roles of the absent parent, for example, mowing the lawn and doing household repairs. They also may serve as companions to their parents, who may be lonely or too busy or hurt to establish adult relationships. Parents may confide in children about money, relationships with their ex-spouse, and other adult matters, and expect children to accompany them on activities such as shopping trips, meetings, or parties. They also may place children in a situation of role reversal, expecting children to comfort them and meet their needs. Other parents become overly protective, worrying that since they have lost a significant relationship with an ex-spouse, they also may lose the relationship with the child.

Children in single-parent families may experience inconsistent discipline. A parent may be too tired to discipline at some times or likely to be stressed and to overdiscipline at others. Parents' dating and development of opposite-sex relationships also can be stressful to children in single-parent families. Many children, particularly if they feel abandoned by the absent parent or do not have a positive relationship with that parent, may be anxious for the parent with whom they reside to remarry. Other children, particularly older children who have been in a single-parent family for a longer period of time, may see any dating by their parent as a threat to their own relationship and may do everything possible to destroy such relationships. Such issues as how much to tell children about dating, how involved they should be in decision making about serious relationships or remarriage, handling "overnight" guests and live-in boy friends, and how to help children handle a relationship that has ended are of concern to single-parent children and their families.

Children growing up in single-parent families also may have fewer options regarding long-range plans for their future. Income and time limitations of such families may preclude college or other post-high school education.

Other issues children growing up in single-parent families may face include kidnapping or fear of being kidnapped by the noncustodial parent, sexual abuse or other types of child maltreatment by the parent or parent's friends, alcoholism or drug abuse by one or both parents, and concerns about the child's own sexuality and ability to establish long-term, opposite-sex relationships.

Increasingly, schools, child guidance centers, and community mental health centers are offering special programs for children growing up in single-parent families. Programs include individual and group counseling, family counseling, and the development of self-help groups for children. Big Brother and Big Sister programs, which match adult role models in one-to-one relationships with children, also help children in single-parent families develop healthy relationships with adults of the opposite sex of the custodial parent figure to ensure that children experience positive relationships with both male and female adults. A number of books and other materials are also available to help both children with single parents and their families. Longitudinal studies of children growing up in single-parent families are also helping to identify strengths of such families, as well as problem areas, to be better able to help children growing up in this type of family constellation.

Stepparenting and Blended Families

With increased numbers of single-parent families, second marriages also are on the increase. Eighty percent of divorced adults remarry, and 60 percent of remarriages involve at least one child. In 1980, 13 percent of children in the United States were living in a stepparent family (U.S. Department of Health and Human Services 1980). A number of these families involve marriages between partners who each have children from previous marriages. Such families are often referred to as **blended families.**

Remarriage typically generates a number of strong feelings among both children and adults involved. While adults may feel a sense of joyousness and security, children are likely to feel a sense of loss in relation to the parent, who must now be shared with the spouse, as well as anxiety over what the addition of another adult will mean to their own well being. They also may experience concern about balancing the stepparent relationship with that of the absent birth parent. If the new marriage brings other children, relationships between stepsiblings may bring forth feelings of competition and jealousy.

The development of stepfamily relationships can be a difficult process, and time and effort are required on the part of all family members to make the new family constellation work. Children frequently feel distant from their new stepparent and may see that parent as a replacement for their absent parent. Even if they like the stepparent, conflicts over loyalty to their birth parent may prevent them from establishing a positive relationship. If the child functioned as more of a "partner" in the family than a child, feelings of displacement and jealousy toward the stepparent can occur. Additionally, many children, no matter how old, still have fantasies of their birth parents reuniting, and the remarriage represents a threat to these fantasies. Stepsiblings also mean less attention for birth children, as well as possible competition outside of the family boundaries regarding friends, sports, and school.

In addition to the development of emotional bonds among family members, adjustments to changing family roles, responsibilities, and family identity must be made in a blended family. Rules often are readjusted, and many times are more strict, than they were in the single-parent household. If children are still in major contact with their other birth parent, they are now essentially members of two households, each with its own distinct culture and rules. Problems regarding multiple role models and parental figures can create confusion to children. Some experts in stepparent family relationships suggest that the stepparent should not in any way undermine the absent birth parent relationship but should establish himself or herself as a parental figure in the family and take an active role in immediate family issues such as rules and discipline. Other experts argue that the parenting should be left completely to the child's parents, with the stepparent working to establish a positive bond with the child, but as an adult friend rather than a parental figure, staying out of decisions regarding rules and discipline.

While remarriage can increase the stability, security, and financial aspects for children, working through the implications of such changes takes a great deal of time before there is acceptance. Special parent education classes for stepparents, support groups for stepparents, spouses, and children in stepparent families, and family counseling programs are available in many communities to help focus on strengths of such families and provide support in working through problem areas.

Alcoholism and Drug Abuse

Current evidence indicates that over 10 percent of individuals in the United States are being raised or were raised in alcoholic homes. An increasing number of childen are being raised in homes where abuse of drugs is common. There are 30 to 50 million children of alcohol and drug abusers in the United States (Ackerman 1983). Until recently, alcohol and drug abuse has been viewed as an individual disease rather than a family problem. However, recent studies have found that individuals raised in such families are five times as likely to become substance abusers themselves. Twenty percent of juvenile delinquents and children seen in child guidance and mental health clinics come from homes where alcohol abuse is a problem. Other studies show high correlations between alcohol and drug abuse and family violence (Gelles 1979). Children who manage to "survive" in substance abusive families without such problems seldom escape unscathed. Experts in substance abuse suggest that adult children of alcoholics manifest coping characteristics they developed as children within their own families, including a compulsion to control, a need to overachieve, and a need to please others continually (Black 1979).

In looking at a substance abusive family from a systems perspective, the family develops a way of functioning with the abuser as the central family member that, although dysfunctional to outsiders, is functional to the family in that it facilitates survival. Family members or others who facilitate continuation of substance abuse are called **enablers**. For example, a spouse may assume the major responsibility for maintaining the family, protecting the children from the substance abuser, and making excuses for his or her behavior. An older child may take on a "hero" role, believing that by being a perfect child and pleasing the parents, the substance abuse will stop or be less likely to disrupt the family. This child is likely to get excellent grades in school, take care of younger children, nurture both parents, and work toward keeping family members happy no matter what the costs to the child. Another child in the family may take on a "scapegoat" role, subconsciously believing that negative attention directed at him or her will take the attention away from the parent who is the substance abuser. Conflict between the parents over the substance abuse may instead be directed at the child, who is always getting in trouble at home, at school, and in the neighborhood. Yet another child may assume the role of the "lost child," believing that by being scarce the family is better able to cope. These children are always in their rooms, under the table or in the corner, or at friends' homes. They seek little attention and, in fact, go out of their way not to call any attention to themselves at all. A final role a child in such families may assume is the "mascot" role. These children, often the youngest, become the pets or clowns of the family, always available to be cuddled when cuddling is demanded or to entertain when entertainment can alleviate some of the family's pain (Ackerman 1983).

Ackerman and others who have identified such roles in substance abusive families, however, point out the enormous costs of these roles on the individual family members throughout their whole lives, as well as the total family. Such roles actually promote the substance abuse, and family members are seen as unknowingly encouraging the substance abuse. This is why current substance abuse intervention strategies view the abuse as a family systems problem; if communication patterns and roles within families are not changed concurrently with treatment for the substance abuser, the substance abusive behavior is likely to return quickly, reinforced by the behaviors of other family members.

The ways that families typically cope with substance abuse can be divided into four phases. The first phase is the reactive phase, in which family members deny that the substance abuse exists and develop their own coping strategies around the substance abusive parent usually, sometimes intentionally, enabling the abuse to continue. These strategies range from nagging, to making excuses or covering up abuse (without direct confrontation that there is a substance abuse problem), to staying at home to try to prevent the substance abuse, to denying emotional feelings. Children in such families may be victims of birth defects as a result of the substance abuse, may be torn between parents wondering why one is angry or feeling sorry for or angry at the abuser, may avoid activities with peers because of fear and shame, may not trust others, and may learn destructive and negative ways to get attention (Ackerman 1983).

The second is the active phase, where family members become aware that there is a substance abuse problem, that this is not a normally functioning family, and that help is available. Family members begin to realize that the abuser does not control the family and that they have the power to make changes in their own behaviors and cannot assume responsibility for the substance abuser. At this point, members may join self-help groups such as Alanon or Alateen, where others going through similar experiences within their own families can lend support. The third phase in a substance abusive family is the disequilibrium phase. This phase is difficult for all family members but must be experienced if the problem is to be alleviated. This phase occurs after family members are aware that a problem exists, but all efforts to change the abuser or the family dynamics have been unsuccessful. During this phase, family members consider openly whether disruption is the only alternative. This often leads to polarization among family members. This phase often ends in divorce with subsequent separation of family members. It is doubly traumatic for children, who then have to experience both the problems of alcoholism and divorce. It is estimated that divorce occurs in approximately 40 percent of family situations that reach this phase. For those families who do not choose separation, the traditional family communication patterns may be shaken enough that the family begins to actively change. Whether disruption occurs or the family member who is the substance abuser agrees to make a concerted effort to change, the family is forced to reorganize. This requires new and different roles for family members (Ackerman 1983).

The final phase that families involved in substance abuse experience is the family unity phase. Many families with substance abuse problems either disrupt or maintain the substance abuse problem and never reach this phase. Being free of substance abuse is central to this phase; however, it is not enough. Acceptance of the family member as a non-substance abuser and lasting changes in family communication patterns must take place if the family is to remain free of recurring substance abuse problems.

Many children grow up in disrupted or dysfunctional families who experience the repercussions of substance abuse, violence or neglect.

Treatment programs for substance abusers must involve the entire family if they are to be successful and must focus on not only an understanding of the aspects of substance abuse, but also of how family communication patterns facilitate the abuse. Individual, group, and family counseling sessions, self-help groups for all family members, and residential treatment programs in some combination have been found to be most effective in alleviating substance abuse.

Spouse Abuse

While definitions of **family violence** differ across state lines, a general definition often used is "an act carried out by one family member against another family member that causes or is intended to cause physical pain or injury to that person." Family violence typically has been separated into two major categories: spouse abuse and child abuse. Recent attention also has focused on elder abuse and children battering their parents. Child abuse first received attention as a major national issue in the 1960s, with impetus from the medical profession and other professionals and concerned child advocates; however, spouse abuse did not gain attention until a number of years later. Attempts to combine forces by women's advocates were met with resistance from child abuse advocates. Early attempts to develop programs and secure legislation for spouse abuse were spin-offs from rape crisis centers, which often were run by feminists at the grassroots level.

Professionals, particularly those from the medical profession, were concerned that joining forces with feminists might place child abuse programming in jeopardy. Thus, as of 1986, there are only limited legislation and centralized programs to deal with spouse abuse, although significant efforts in both legislation and federal programs exist for child abuse. More important, very limited federal dollars have been appropriated for spouse abuse programs. Some states have allocated funding for spouse abuse programs; however, these programs usually are either small adjuncts to child welfare/child abuse departments or under the auspices of special women's commissions, implying that spouse abuse is a woman- or child-related problem rather than a family problem of concern to everyone. Some child abuse programs have funded spouse abuse programs only by suggesting that children raised in a home where spouse abuse is present are emotionally abused.

An additional reason why attention to spouse abuse was late in developing relates to ways men and women are viewed in our society: Men are regarded in power positions both within and outside of the home. Although men are seen as having power over children as well, it is much easier for the general public to become concerned about abused children than abused women. Many individuals still subscribe to the myth that women who are beaten somehow deserve it, or that they must enjoy it or they would not put up with it.

Violence between couples extends beyond the marital relationship. A recent study found that between 22 and 67 percent of dating relationships involve violence of some sort. Milder forms of violence, such as slapping, pushing, and shoving, are more common, but more severe types of violence, including kicking (commonly done in the stomach to pregnant women), biting, punching, and threatening with a knife or gun also are surprisingly common. A sad commentary on the implications of family violence is that more than 25 percent of the victims of the violence and more than 30 percent of the abusers interpreted the violence as a sign of love.

Incidence of family violence among couples is thought to be about one in every four marital relationships. A number of factors commonly are associated with spouse abuse. Men who assault their wives generally have low self-esteem and feel inferior. Feeling powerless outside of the family, they exert their power within the domain of their homes. It is more difficult to interpret factors associated with women who are abused. Lenore Walker has identified "learned helplessness" as a common trait among abused women (1983). She suggests that women have learned to act passive and helpless as a way of coping with their violent spouses and have been conditioned to believe that they are powerless to get out of the violent situation. Many times, abused women have no employable skills and are concerned about being able to survive, particularly if they have children. Other studies show that battered women are not always passive, often seeking help in dealing with the abuse but love their husbands in spite of the violence and believe they will reform. In many violent situations among spouses, the period following the violence is almost like a honeymoon period, with the abusive spouse often crying, being extremely sorry for the violence, threatening suicide if he is deserted, promising never to be violent again, and being extremely loving and supportive. It is difficult for a woman who loves her husband not to be taken in by this Jekyl and Hyde personality, at least initially.

Other studies show that women with low self-esteem, particularly those who were physically or sexually abused as children, feel so worthless that they believe they deserve the violent treatment. Such women are more at risk to be abused than other women. While in some situations, the woman is passive and the man abusive, in other situations both spouses are violent; however, because of size differences, it is most often the woman who is hurt. Other factors that place couples more at risk for spouse abuse include alcohol and drug abuse, financial stress and poverty, and the male's unemployment or underemployment.

Although programs that address spouse abuse are extremely limited, many communities are establishing safe houses and battered women's shelters, where battered spouses and their children can seek refuge. These programs also provide counseling for both women and children, and assist them in legal issues, locating housing and employment if they decide not to return to the batterer, and in developing support networks. Sadly, in 1985, three out of every four women seeking shelter at such a program were turned away because of lack of space. Additionally, while some programs have been developed that focus on helping the batterer to learn to control anger and on communication patterns in couple relationships, most programs usually begin to treat the violence after it has reached an intolerable point and change is difficult.

Child Maltreatment

Child maltreatment has received far more attention, and far more resources, than spouse abuse. However, reported cases of child abuse continue to increase at epidemic rates and current resources are unable to serve the many abused and neglected children and their families who come to the attention of available programs. In 1984, there were 1.7 million reported cases of child abuse and neglect in the United States, a 16 percent increase from the previous year and a 40 percent increase since 1981 (American Humane Association 1986). A recently conducted national study (U.S. Department of Health and Human Services 1981) suggests that reported cases of child maltreatment represent less than one-third of children who actually are maltreated. Exact figures on numbers of abused and neglected children do not exist because most maltreatment happens within the confines of family privacy, and when cases are known to others, they are often not reported.

There are four categories of child maltreatment: physical abuse, neglect, sexual abuse, and emotional maltreatment, which includes emotional abuse and neglect. Neglect is the most frequently reported type of maltreatment, with 42 percent of all reports of this type. Reports of sexual abuse, however, have increased most in recent years. This is likely because of increased awareness about sexual abuse, which has eliminated some of the secrecy that previously surrounded the problem. Children of all ages are maltreated. While infants are most at risk to be abused or neglected severely, most abused children are school age. Large numbers of adolescents are also maltreated; however, because of scarce resources, these cases are least likely to gain the attention of authorities.

Physical Abuse   Most children who are physically abused receive bruises or abrasions; however, children also receive broken bones and burns, as well as internal injuries, as a result of **physical child abuse.** Physical abuse is a result of beating, kicking, spanking too severely, slapping, biting, punching, throwing, burning, or shaking a child. Many times, parents lose their tempers and do not intend to harm the child severely. Many factors are associated with

**Figure 7–2
Conceptual
Presentation of
the Recogni-
tion of Mal-
treated
Children: An
Iceberg**

This figure depicts the estimated incidence of actual cases of child maltreatment and who in the community knows about these cases. As the figure shows, the child protective service agencies that are mandated to provide services in such cases actually know about only 33% of cases that other professionals know about. This percentage does not even include those cases which only neighbors or immediate family members know about, suggesting that known cases of maltreatment are only the "tip of the iceberg" when it comes to how much child maltreatment actually exists.

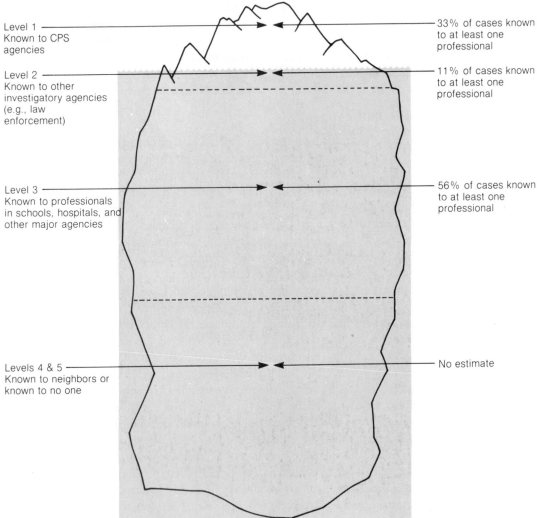

Level 1
Known to CPS
agencies

33% of cases known
to at least one
professional

Level 2
Known to other
investigatory agencies
(e.g., law
enforcement)

11% of cases known
to at least one
professional

Level 3
Known to professionals
in schools, hospitals, and
other major agencies

56% of cases known
to at least one
professional

Levels 4 & 5
Known to neighbors or
known to no one

No estimate

Figure adapted from *National Study of the Incidence and Severity of Child Abuse and Neglect* (1981), Washington, D.C.: U.S. Department of Health and Human Services.

families who physically abuse children, including economic problems (with unemployment and poverty), isolation, unrealistic expectations about child developmental milestones and about children's abilities to meet parental needs for love and attention, alcoholism and drug abuse, abuse or maltreatment of the parent during childhood, lack of education about nonphysical alternatives to discipline, low impulse control and inability to cope well with stress, and marital problems. Children who were born prematurely or with congenital problems, children who somehow do not meet parental expectations or are perceived as different by their parents, and children who are the result of unwanted pregnancies are more at risk to be abused physically than other children.

Using a systems perspective, one can also see that children who grow up in communities with few economic resources and few support systems available to families also are more at risk to be abused. Cultural conditions also have an impact on physical abuse. Studies show that cultures where children are valued and where parenting is shared by extended family members or others beyond the nuclear family have less child abuse than other cultures (Korbin 1982).

Sexual Abuse   **Sexual abuse,** more than any other type of child maltreatment, has received increased attention in recent years. Reported cases of sexual abuse have increased by as much as 65 percent in some states. This has two reasons: with increased public awareness, many more individuals, including the children themselves, are reporting cases; with children today exposed to more adults than in the past, including child care providers, stepparents, and other adults, the likelihood of being abused is increased.

Child sexual abuse can be defined as "contacts or interactions between a child and an adult when the child is being used as an object of gratification for adult needs or desires" (National Center on Child Abuse and Neglect 1980). Thus, child sexual abuse can include acts such as fondling in addition to sexual intercourse. Recent legislation also mandates that state child abuse laws include child pornography and sexual exploitation in definitions of sexual abuse. This expands the definition to include acts such as taking pictures of children in sexual poses or for purposes of sexual gratification. Although the true incidence of sexual abuse is not known, recent studies suggest that one of every four women and one of every seven men have experienced some type of sexual abuse before they reached the age of eighteen (Finkelhor 1984).

While most individuals think of sexual abusers as strangers who accost children in the park, the majority are known and trusted by the children they abuse. The first category of abusers consists of parents. Sexual abuse by birth parents, commonly referred to as **incest,** is considered by many to have the most serious personal and social consequences. Abusers also may be other parent figures, such as stepparents. The second category of abusers consists of family members other than parent figures. This includes siblings, grandparents, and uncles or aunts. Sexual relationships between siblings are reported to be the most common. The broadest definition of *incest* includes sexual relationships between any family members. The third category of sexual abusers includes trusted adults. These may be teachers, babysitters, neighbors, coaches, leaders of children's groups, or other adults. The last, and least frequent, types of sexual abusers are strangers or remote acquaintances.

The reasons why adults sexually abuse children are complex and vary according to the individual abuser. Some experts involved in the treatment of sexual abusers classify them as falling somewhere on a continuum with two opposite types of abusers. At one end of the continuum is an abuser who is primarily interested in having intimate adult relationships but is emotionally unable to feel good enough about himself or herself (although the majority of reported sexual abusers are men) to have a positive emotional relationship with another adult. This type of adult is insecure and usually experiencing some type of personal crisis. They are likely to be married but in relationships that have deteriorated significantly. Feeling too inadequate to seek emotional fulfillment from their spouses, they often turn to their children to meet their needs. While time spent together at first may be nonsexual and regarded by both parent and child as special, over time such fulfillment becomes sexual for the adult as well. In this situation, the adults involved see themselves in an adult relationship and are more than likely also to view the child as a pseudoadult. Individuals involving children in such relationships are far more likely to go from fondling to full intercourse in an attempt to have an adult–adult relationship but feel more comfortable with a child replacing the adult partner because of their own feelings of inadequacy.

At the opposite end of the continuum are adults that view the experience with the child as feeling like a child themselves and seeing the child in a child role. These abusers are more likely to be labeled **pedophiles** (lovers of children). Individuals at this end of the continuum have a sexual fascination with children, but from a child perspective rather than from an adult perspective. Some experts view pedophiles as having arrested stages of sexual development; others suggest that pedophilia may be due to a hormonal imbalance or genetic inclination.

Most abusers engage in a seductive, power role with children with whom they become involved. Children, wanting affection and too young to know how to draw boundaries themselves between positive affection and sexual abuse, initially may become involved and then be too afraid to tell anyone what is going on. Although the sexual abuse acts themselves may not involve physical force on the part of the adult, the child is trapped in the situation because adults are in power positions with children. Some abusers tell children that the relationship is the only thing keeping the family together, or the abuser is the only one who really loves and understands the child. Other abusers threaten physical harm to the child or to other family members if the child refuses to cooperate or tells anyone what is going on. For example, they say that their mother will "go crazy," the child will be taken out of the home, or the adult will sexually abuse a younger sibling.

Studies on the effects of sexual abuse show that it is extremely harmful to children emotionally and that many individuals who have been sexually abused suffer long-term effects. The impact of sexual abuse on children depends on factors such as the age of the child when the abuse occurred, the type of sexual abuse that took place, the relationship of the abuser to the child, the length of time the abuse occurred, how long it was between the time the abuse occurred and someone found out that it was going on, other characteristics of the child's family and available positive support to the child, and the reactions from family members and professionals when the sexual abuse finally is discovered (Sgroi 1982). Many persons who have been sexually abused see themselves as victims due to the trauma of the abuse and have extremely low self-esteem, difficulty in establishing intimate, trusting relationships with others, and problems with their own families and marriages when they become adults. Without intervention for the sexually abused child and the family, persons who have been sexually abused are more at risk than others to turn to alcohol or drugs or suicide to ease their pain. Many communities have established programs that promote public awareness of sexual abuse and early intervention with families once cases are reported to attempt to address such long-term effects.

Child Neglect   **Child neglect** can be defined as "a condition in which a caretaker responsible for the child either deliberately or by extraordinary inattentiveness permits the child to experience available present suffering and/or fails to provide one or more of the ingredients generally deemed essential for developing a person's physical, intellectual and emotional capacities" (National Center on Child Abuse and Neglect 1980). As opposed to child physical abuse, in which damage to a child is inflicted, neglect is characterized by acts of *omission;* this usually means that something that should have been done to or for a child was not done.

Many states include specific categories in their definitions of child neglect, including failure to provide adequate food, clothing, or shelter for a child, often termed *physical neglect;* failure to provide adequate supervision for a child, for example, leaving young children alone for inappropriate periods of time, often termed *lack of supervision;* leaving a child alone or not returning when expected to care for a child, often termed *abandonment;* failure to provide medical care for a child, often termed *medical neglect;* failure to provide an education for a child, often termed *educational neglect;* and failure to provide for a child's emotional needs, often termed emotional neglect.

Although some individuals view neglect as less dangerous to a child than abuse, this is not the case. Studies have shown that just as many children die each year from neglect as from abuse. Many are burned in fires while left alone or with inadequate supervision, some drown in bathtubs while left unsupervised, others die because their parents did not obtain medical care for them soon enough when they became ill. Other studies show that neglected children, in fact, may suffer from more long-term consequences of their maltreatment than abused children. Adults who did not have their physical or emotional needs met as children are much more likely to have problems in finding and maintaining jobs, developing positive relationships with other individuals and remaining in marriages, and parenting their own children adequately.

One type of neglect that is receiving increased attention is **non-organic failure to thrive,** a form of parental deprivation. Failure to thrive has been medically defined as a child who is three percentiles or more below the normal weight for his or her particular age, the child seems to be being fed on a regular basis by its caretakers, and nothing organically wrong can be found with the child, yet it does not gain weight and literally "fails to thrive." Yet when placed in a hospital and given nothing more than regular feedings of its normal diet, coupled with love and attention (e.g., holding and cuddling), the child begins to gain weight immediately. Bowlby's studies of maternal deprivation and children raised in orphanages in Europe without love and attention found a high death rate and significant differences in intelligence quotient (IQ) and physical and emotional development when compared to children raised in environments where they received love and attention (1951). Similar findings are evident among children diagnosed with failure to thrive syndrome.

Parents who neglect their children differ from other parents at the same socioeconomic level. While there is a strong relationship between poverty and neglect, not all parents who are poor neglect their children. Research studies have shown that the typical neglectful parent, as compared with nonneglectful parents also living in poverty, is more isolated, has fewer relationships with others, is less able to plan and less able to control impulses, is less confident about the future, and is more plagued with physical and psychological problems. They also are more likely to say that they have never received love and were unwanted by their parents. Many have been raised by relatives or in foster care. Neglectful parents often began life lonely, and continue to live in isolation. Polansky, Ammons, and Gaudin (1985) found that neglecting parents had difficulty identifying neighbors or friends with whom they could leave their children if they needed emergency childcare or from whom they could borrow five dollars in an emergency. They are extremely isolated from both formal and informal support networks; many neglecting parents describe their social workers as being their best or only friends.

Polansky, et al. (1975), classify two types of neglecting parents. The first type suffers from what they term **apathy-futility syndrome.** These neglecting parents have all but given up on life. They see little hope for the future and view all efforts to try to relate to either their children or others as futile. They convey an attitude of hopelessness and despair. Usually neglected themselves as children and in many instances in the past, beaten down whenever they tried to make a go of life, they lack the physical or emotional energy to relate to their children. A neglectful parent with apathy-futility syndrome is likely to be found lying on the couch in a chaotic household that hasn't been cleaned or cared for, with children unkempt and uncared for, left largely to fend for themselves. Children raised by this type of neglectful parent may suffer from physical, medical, educational, and/or emotional neglect, as well as lack of supervision.

The second type of neglecting parent characterized by Polansky, et al. (1975) is one with **impulse-ridden behavior.** This type of parent may be loving and caring and may provide adequate food, clothing, and medical care most of the time. However, this parent has trouble making appropriate decisions and often behaves impulsively. Such parents suddenly may decide to go to a party and leave their children alone or may answer the telephone and become so engrossed in the telephone conversation that they forget that their child is unattended. They often get in trouble with employers over impulsive behavior at work, with creditors because of impulsive spending habits, and with friends because they make commitments and then impulsively change their minds and go off with others instead. Neglectful parents with impulse-ridden behavior are restless, intolerant of stress, and lacking in consistency. Their children never know exactly what to expect and, in fact, may be abandoned for long periods by an impulsive parent who suddenly decides to go off somewhere on a trip. Such parents can be seen by their social workers as making great progress in being more consistent in their childcare, and then ask their social worker to babysit for their children so they can go off to the beach, or go to the beach and seem to forget completely that their children are left unsupervised. Children of neglecting parents of this type are likely to suffer from abandonment, lack of supervision, and emotional neglect. Additionally, because of the inconsistency they experience, they are likely to have difficulty trusting others, developing positive relationships, and being consistent themselves.

Neglecting parents often are more difficult to help than abusive parents, particularly those who are apathetic and feel hopeless. Unlike abusive parents, who still have enough spirit to be angry, many neglecting parents experience feelings of despair and futility. These feelings are much more difficult to change. By helping neglecting parents develop trust in other individuals and increase their self-esteem, particularly through links with supportive individuals, social workers can help them begin to care adequately for their own children. Most of the attention and resources in the area of child maltreatment has gone to child physical and sexual abuse rather than to neglect. Because studies show that neglect is just as detrimental to children as abuse—and in some instances, more so—increased concern needs to be given to this type of child maltreatment.

Emotional Maltreatment   Emotional maltreatment is the most elusive form of child maltreatment. It is the most difficult to define, the most difficult to substantiate, and the most difficult to obtain resources for. It probably, however, also is the most common type of child maltreatment, and like other types of child maltreatment, it can result in serious long-term consequences for the child. Experts suggest that there are two types of emotional maltreatment: emotional abuse and emotional neglect (Whiting 1978). Definitions parallel those of abuse and neglect. **Emotional abuse** is viewed as acts of commission, or emotional acts against a child. Emotional abuse is often verbal; it includes being told continually how bad the child is, perhaps that parents wish the child had never been born, and being blamed for all the parents' and family's problems. Almost all parents emotionally abuse their children at some times; one child development expert notes that children receive six negative messages about what they do for every one positive message (Ginott 1965). However, continual emotional abuse can lower self-esteem and undermine a child's feelings of competence. Parents also emotionally abuse children in other ways; some parents, for example, give away children's prize possessions to "another child who will appreciate it," telling children that they don't deserve special things because "they are bad." Less often, parents emotionally abuse children by shaving their heads or cutting their hair or doing other humiliating things as forms of punishment. Children who are forced to watch parents or others in the family being beaten or otherwise abused also exemplify emotional abuse. Children forced to experience sexual abuse are emotionally abused; in fact, some experts suggest that the emotional abuse has just as severe, if not more severe, consequences for the sexually abused child than the sexual abuse (National Center on Child Abuse and Neglect 1980).

Emotional neglect, like neglect itself, relates to acts of omission involving a child and includes the failure to meet the child's emotional needs. Parents who emotionally neglect children may provide for their physical needs, but they usually interact very little with their children in an emotional sense. Common parent–child activities such as cuddling, holding, reading or singing to, going places with, or just talking with a child are nonexistent for children who are emotionally neglected. Not having their emotional needs met when they are children is likely to result in adults who cannot give emotionally to their own children. Such adults may not only emotionally neglect their own children but also subject them to other types of maltreatment.

Problems Associated with Adolescents

Little attention has been given to the special needs of adolescents in literature about children and family problems. Many family development experts are quick to point out that prevention and early intervention efforts aimed at young children and families would eliminate many adolescent problems. They note that adolescents who come through the juvenile justice system as delinquents, runaways, or due to pregnancy come from families who have experienced many of the problems discussed in this chapter but have not received appropriate services and support. Presently in the United States, because of the scarcity of resources available to address family problems, most resources are targeted toward younger children, who are more vulnerable than adolescents. In one state with few resources, school personnel find themselves agreeing with teenagers when they determine that their only recourse to escape a serious family situation is to run away from home. Because youth shelters and services are limited, a youth advocate in another state suggested that her only alternative to ensure that teens had safe shelter was to suggest that they get arrested so they could be booked into the juvenile detention center! Adolescents labeled as *delinquent* often should more appropriately be considered "throwaways" or "push-outs," as more and more families fail to provide for the needs of their children and find themselves with emotionally damaged adolescents (Children's Defense Fund 1986). Estimates suggest that 1.2–1.5 million children and adolescents run away each year; most of these are teenagers who are gone only a night or two, but many never return to their homes (Children's Defense Fund 1986). Most runaways are running in an attempt to cope with serious problems, including physical and sexual abuse, family alcoholism or drug abuse, divorce or spouse abuse, other family problems, or failure in school. A study of New York runaway youth shelters found that between one- and two-thirds of teens who came to them for help did not feel that they had a home to return to (Children's Defense Fund 1986).

Many adolescents experiencing problems also suffer academically. Family problems often result in learning disabilities and other learning problems, and young persons who do not feel good about themselves and are faced with daily problems at home are not likely to do well in school. Increased concern is being expressed about dropout rates of youth and the high illiteracy rate of both young and older adults. The national dropout rate in 1985 was 25 percent, with significantly higher rates for black and Hispanic youth. In New

York City and Los Angeles, the dropout rate for Hispanics that year was 80 percent.

Youths who do not complete high school suffer in their ability to locate suitable employment. There is a serious lack of employment available for young adults, particularly those who are black and Hispanic, even when they do graduate from high school. In 1983, more than half of all black high school graduates not enrolled in college were unemployed, whereas only approximately 25 percent of white high school dropouts were unemployed (Children's Defense Fund 1986). The limited availability of job skills training and adequate employment suggests that poverty rates, particularly for blacks and Hispanics, will continue to increase.

Another major problem facing our country today is teen pregnancy. In 1983, 1.1 million teenagers became pregnant, resulting in 500,000 births. Over 20 percent of these births were to mothers fifteen years old and younger. Becoming a parent when a teenager is not developmentally prepared interrupts, sometimes permanently, the teen's successful transition into adulthood.

Emotional abuse is probably the most common type of child abuse, but help is available.

Words hit as hard as a fist.

"You're pathetic. You can't do anything right!"

"You disgust me. Just shut up!"

"Hey stupid! Don't you know how to listen."

"Get outta here! I'm sick of looking at your face."

"You're more trouble than you're worth."

"Why don't you go and find some other place to live!"

"I wish you were never born!"

Children believe what their parents tell them. Next time, stop and listen to what you're saying. You might not believe your ears.

Take time out. Don't take it out on your kid.

 Write: National Committee for Prevention of Child Abuse, Box 2866E, Chicago, IL 60690

Teens today are faced with a great deal of pressure from many sources—peers, the media, advertising—to see their primary self-worth in terms of their sexuality. With limited opportunities to be successful in other arenas, such as the family, school, and the workplace, many male and female teens feel that their sexuality, and producing a baby, are the only ways they can feel good about themselves and have someone to love them. The United States has one of the highest pregnancy rates in the Western world, and the number of younger teens, age twelve to fourteen, becoming pregnant is increasing each year. Many factors are associated with teen pregnancy, including poverty, low self-esteem, lack of information about reproduction, school failure, lack of appropriate health care and other services, and poor family relationships. Additionally, emphasis on pregnancy prevention and intervention has focused on teenage girls, and little has been done in regard to prevention and intervention with teenage boys. Even more important, attention to pregnancy prevention often only begins when teens (girls) reach age thirteen. Developing positive self-esteem, effective decision-making skills, a strong value system, and a sense of responsibility for one's self and others—all major deterrents to teen pregnancy—are characteristics shaped from birth on.

Whereas, in the past, most teens who became pregnant relinquished their babies for adoption, either formally through agencies or informally through relatives, today the majority of teens are choosing to keep their babies. This places tremendous pressure on both the teen mothers and their children. Infants born to teenagers are much more likely to have low birth weight, be premature babies, or have congenital and other health problems. Their mothers also are more likely to drop out of school, remain un- or underemployed, and raise their children in poverty than non-teenage parents. The cycle often repeats itself: Teen pregnancy is both a cause and a result of poverty. In 1986, minority teens, more likely to grow up poor, constituted 27 percent of the teenage population, about 50 percent of poor adolescents, and about 40 percent of teen-age mothers (Children's Defense Fund 1986). Nearly 90 percent of babies born to black teens fifteen- to nineteen-years-old are born to single mothers. Teen pregnancy is viewed by many concerned about family problems as the hub of the cycle of poverty in the United States. (*Time Magazine,* 1985).

SUMMARY

There are many reasons why children, youth, and families in the United States experience problems. Many families experience a number of problems, and families who are at risk to experience one type of problem are likely to be at risk to experience others as well. From a systems perspective, factors associated with family problems are complex and interactive. Societal and cultural factors, as well as the level of support available to families from the communities in which they reside, have an impact on the nature and extent of problems experienced by families. Finally, all families have strengths that can be used to draw from when they do experience problems. Effective intervention and prevention programs can capitalize on these strengths when working with children, youth and families. However, effective intervention and prevention efforts must be undertaken within the broader context of understanding the complexities of the family problems discussed above. Chapter 8 will address programs and policies that help families in need and the roles that social workers play in providing these policies and programs.

KEY TERMS

apathy-futility syndrome
blended family
child neglect
custody
emotional abuse
emotional neglect
enabler
family
family violence

feminization of poverty
impulse-ridden behavior
incest
mediation
non-organic failure to thrive
pedophile
physical child abuse
sexual abuse
single parent

DISCUSSION QUESTIONS

1. Identify and discuss at least three of the issues that must be considered when defining a family problem.
2. Discuss briefly at least three issues that often surface in families who experience divorce.
3. Describe at least four roles family members might play where substance abuse is a problem.
4. Identify and briefly describe the four types of child maltreatment.
5. Identify at least five factors likely to be associated with families who abuse or neglect their children.
6. Briefly discuss at least four reasons why teenagers today are likely to become parents.
7. Why are minority children, youth, and families more likely to be at risk of serious problems than white children, youth, and families?

REFERENCES

Ackerman, R. 1983. *Children of Alcoholics.* Holmes Beach, Calif.: Learning Publications.

American Humane Association. 1986. *National Analysis of Child Neglect and Abuse Reporting.* Denver: American Humane Association.

Black, C. 1979. Children of Alcoholics. *Alcohol Health and Research World,* no. 4(1): 23–27.

Bowlby J. 1951. Maternal Care and Mental Health. *Bulletin of the World Health Organization* 3: 355–534.

Bronfenbrenner, U. 1979. *The Ecology of Human Development.* Cambridge, Mass.: Harvard University Press.

Children's Defense Fund. 1986. *Children's Defense Budget: An Analysis of the FY 1987 Federal Budget and Children.* Washington, D.C.: Children's Defense Fund.

Finkelhor, D. 1984. *Sexual Abuse: New Theory and Research.* New York: Free Press.

Garbarino, J. 1982. *Children and Families in the Social Environment.* New York: Aldine Press.

Gardner, R. 1970. *The Boys and Girls Book about Divorce.* New York: Bantam Books.

Gelles, R. 1979. Violence toward Children in the United States. In R. Bourne and E. Newberger, eds., *Critical Perspectives on Child Abuse.* Lexington, Mass.: Lexington.

Ginott, H. 1965. *Between Parent and Child.* New York: Avon Books.

Goode, W. J. 1964. *The Family.* Englewood Cliffs, N.J.: Prentice–Hall.

Korbin, J. 1982. *Crosscultural Perspectives on Child Abuse.* Berkeley: University of California Press.

Moyers, W. 1986. "The Vanishing Black Family." New York: ABC Television.

National Center on Child Abuse and Neglect. 1980. *Neglect: Mobilizing Community Resources.* Washington, D.C.: Department of Health and Human Services.

National Center on Child Abuse and Neglect. 1980. *Selected Readings in Sexual Abuse.* Washington, D.C.: Department of Health and Human Services.

National Center on Child Abuse and Neglect. 1980. *The Role of the Child Protective Services Worker.* Washington, D.C.: Department of Health and Human Services.

Polansky, N.A., G. Hally, and N.F. Polansky. 1975. *Profile of Neglect: A Survey of the State of Knowledge of Child Neglect.* Washington, D.C.: Department of Health, Education, and Welfare.

Polansky, N., P. Ammons, and J. Gaudin. 1985. Loneliness and Isolation in Child Neglect. *Social Casework* (January): 38–47.

Sgroi, S. 1982. *Handbook of Clinical Intervention in Child Sexual Abuse.* Lexington, Mass.: Lexington.

Steiner, G. 1976. *The Children's Cause.* Washington, D.C.: Brookings Institute.

Steinmetz, S., and M. Straus. 1974. *Violence in the Family.* New York: Harper and Row.

Time Magazine. 1985. Children Having Children. December 9: 78–90.

U.S. Department of Health and Human Services. 1980. *Helping Youth and Families of Separation, Divorce, and Remarriage.* Washington, D.C.: Department of Health and Human Services.

U.S. Department of Health and Human Services. 1981. *National Study of the Incidence and Severity of Child Abuse and Neglect.* Washington, D.C.: Department of Health and Human Services.

Walker, L. 1983. The Battered Women's Syndrome Study. In D. Finkelhor, R. Gélles, G. Hotaling, and M. Straus, eds., *The Dark Side of Families.* Beverly Hills, Calif.: Sage Publications, 31–48.

Wallerstein, J. and J. Kelly. 1980. *Surviving the Breakup: How Children and Parents Cope with Divorce.* New York: Basic Books.

Wallerstein, J. and J. Kelly. 1979. Children and Divorce: A Review. *Social Work* (November): 468–75.

Whiting, L. 1978. Emotional Neglect of Children. In *Proceedings of the 2nd Annual National Conference on Child Abuse and Neglect.* Vol. I. Washington, D.C.: Department of Health, Education and Welfare, 209–13.

SELECTED FURTHER READINGS

Billingsley, A., and J. Giovannoni. 1972. *Children of the Storm: Black Children and American Child Welfare.* New York: Harcourt, Brace, Jovannovich.

Garbarino, J., and H. Stocking. 1980. *Child Abuse and Neglect.* New York: Aldine Press.

McGowan, B., and W. Meezan. 1983. *Child Welfare: Current Dilemmas; Future Directions.* Itasca, Ill.: Peacock.

8 Services to Children, Youth, and Families

essie Jones is a social worker with the local family services agency. She is involved in a number of activities that prevent families from becoming dysfunctional, as well as activities that help families when problems occur. Her agency provides several programs in this area. Parenting programs teach childcare to teen-age parents. An outreach program and parent groups seek out and help parents who are under stress or having problems with their children. The agency provides individual, family, and group counseling for children and family members of all ages. Recently, the agency has developed a shelter for adolescents who cannot remain in their own homes. The agency also provides homemaker services, childcare, and employment services to help families remain economically self-sufficient and able to stay together.

Jessie enjoys her job a great deal. Although she finds it difficult to deal with the many problems faced by the families with whom she is assigned to work, especially when children are suffering, she has learned to share small successes with family members. "If I can make things better in some small way each day for one child or one parent, my job is more than worthwhile," she stated in a recent newspaper interview.

Programs and policies that address the needs of children, youth, and families are as diverse as the types of needs experienced. Traditionally, the system that has provided programs and policies that address child and family concerns has been called the **child welfare delivery system.** This system includes the "network of agencies, public and private, denominational and non-denominational, offering direct social services to children and families" (Kadushin 1980, 3).

This chapter will focus on services provided that address the family-related problems discussed in the previous chapter. The roles that social workers play in providing services to children, youth, and families also will be discussed.

CURRENT PHILOSOPHICAL ISSUES

All policies and programs that address the needs of children, youth, and their families not only must consider the social and cultural framework of the child's family, the community, and the broader environment but also a number of current philosophical issues.

The Right to a Permanent, Nurturing Family

The first assumption is that every child has a right to grow up in a permanent, nurturing home and that every attempt must be made to provide such a home whenever possible. This assumes that the child's own home should be seen as the best option for that child whenever possible. Such a philosophical position dictates that services should be provided first to the child's family and that every attempt should be made to keep the child and the family together. This position has led to the development of **own-home services** programs, or services provided to a child and family while they remain together, as opposed to placing a child in a foster home or other type of substitute care. Increasingly, special attention is being given to those services that will keep families together rather than quickly removing the child from his or her family setting.

In the past, many children receiving services in an overloaded service delivery system became lost in the system, with no chance to either return home, be adopted or become emancipated. Concern among many individuals and advocacy organizations has led to legislation at both the state and federal levels that mandates the concept of **permanency planning.** This concept ensures that when a child and family first receive services, a specific plan is developed that states what is planned to help that family remain together if possible and, if not, what will be done to provide a permanent, nurturing home for the child. Specific plans are developed to take place within time limits and, in many instances, are monitored by the court. This way, if a family receives services without making enough progress to provide for a child's most basic needs, the parents' rights can be terminated and the child placed in an adoptive home, rather than the child remaining in limbo in the foster care system. Such planning assists agencies to make more realistic decisions about helping children and their families and ensures that families know specifically what they need to do in order to be allowed to continue to parent their children.

The Best Interests of the Child

Decisions about needs of children and families should be based on what is in the best interests of the child. There are times when, even with the most appropriate intervention, it is questionable whether it is best for children to remain with their own families. In such circumstances, should decisions regarding where a child is placed (e.g., remain with his or her own family or be placed elsewhere) focus on the child's best interests, the parent's best interests, or the family's best interests? While experts agree that the rights of both the parents and their children need to be considered carefully, current trends give attention first to the **best interests of the child.** This means that careful attention must be given before any decision is made to what the most beneficial outcome will be for that particular child.

In *Before the Best Interests of the Child* and *Beyond the Best Interests of the Child,* Goldstein, Freud, and Solnit give careful consideration to this issue. They argue that in considering what is best for a child, the **least detrimental alternative** for that child must be considered. In other words, if it is detrimental for a child to remain with his or her family, what is the least harmful alternative that can be considered?

Another concept discussed by Goldstein, Freud, and Solnit focuses on considering who is most significant and should be involved in planning changes in a child's life. Until recently, decisions regarding where a child should be raised usually involved the child's biological mother, and then father. However, the early rearing of many children is by a relative or a foster parent rather than their biological parents. Goldstein, Freud, Solnit, and others stress the importance of considering the child's **psychological parent** rather than biological parent, who might not always be the same individual.

Considerations before State Intervention

An additional philosophical issue of importance is under what circumstances the community or state should intervene in family matters. As indicated previously, in the past, families were considered sacred, and intervention in family matters seldom took place. Now, with increased attention to such family problems as child abuse, child neglect, spouse abuse, and alcoholism, many children are growing up in unsafe and unnurturing environments. Many family advocates are beginning to suggest that intervention in families should take place only when requested by a parent, such as child custody disputes; when a parent chooses to relinquish the rights of a child and place that child for adoption; or when a parent is seriously abusing a child and the effect of the abuse on the child can be visibly observed. Others argue that early intervention is more likely to result in keeping a family together, as well as protect the child from growing up with severe emotional damage.

Prevention of Family Disruption and Dysfunction

Another major issue is whether scarce resources should be targeted toward prevention or treatment of family problems. And, if toward prevention, should it be primary, secondary, or tertiary? All three are important in strengthening families.

Most intervention with families today is treatment-oriented rather than prevention-oriented, and even those programs are not available to many parents and families in need of such services. Due to scarce resources, little attention is given to any type of prevention at all. Of the few prevention programs available, the focus is tertiary in nature. In many instances, children must be severely abused or families in serious crisis before services are available.

How Accountable Are Parents?

A final issue receiving increased attention is to what extent parents should be held accountable in regard to caring for their children, and what should be done to parents who do not care for them adequately. A number of specialists in family problems suggest that punishment is more likely to make parents angry and less likely to teach them how to be better parents. These specialists hold that effective treatment programs and the availability of resources are much more optimal for children than punishment of their parents and likely separation from them. Other experts suggest that a compromise is most effective: that parents whose family problems pose severe consequences for their children be brought before the court and ordered to receive treatment, with punishment ordered if the treatment is refused.

DEFINING SERVICES TO CHILDREN, YOUTH, AND FAMILIES

Traditionally, services to children, youth, and families have been defined as **child welfare services.** Kadushin (1980, 5) suggests that "child welfare involves providing social services to children and young people whose parents are unable to fulfill their child parenting responsibilities, or whose communities fail to provide the resources and protection that children and families require," and that the goals of child welfare services are "to reinforce, supplement or substitute the functions that parents have difficulty in performing; and to improve conditions for children and their families by modifying existing social institutions or organizing new ones."

The **Social Security Act,** the most significant piece of national legislation ever passed in relation to providing support to children and families, has a specific section (Title IV–B) that mandates states to provide a full range of child welfare services defined as:

> *public social services which supplement, or substitute for parental care and supervision for the purpose of:*
>
> 1. *preventing or remedying, or assisting in the solution of problems which may result in the neglect, abuse, exploitation or delinquency of children,*
>
> 2. *protecting and caring for homeless, dependent, or neglected children,*
>
> 3. *protecting and promoting the welfare of children of working mothers and*
>
> 4. *otherwise protecting and promoting the welfare of children, including the strengthening of their own homes where possible or, where needed, the provision of adequate care of children away from their homes in foster family homes or day care or other child care facilities. (Section 425)*

Because of negative connotations associated with the term *welfare* and the current emphasis on the importance of strengthening the family in order to support the child, *child welfare services* today more often are referred to as *services to children, youth, and families* or *child and family services*. Both Kadushin's definition and the definition in the Social Security Act are broad enough, however, to be congruent with either of the more currently preferred terms.

THE HISTORY OF SERVICES TO CHILDREN, YOUTH, AND FAMILIES

In colonial times, children were considered to be the responsibility of their families, and little attention was given to children whose families were available to provide for them, no matter whether the family actually met the child's needs. Children usually came to the attention of authorities only if they were orphaned and relatives were not available to provide for them. Churches and a few private orphanages cared for some dependent children; however, prior to 1800, most orphans were placed in almshouses, or indentured, given to families to function as servants. Focus during this time period was on survival, as death often occurred at early ages; fewer than half of all children born in the United States prior to the 1800s lived to reach the age of 18.

During the 1800s, increased attention began to be given to the negative effects of placing young children in almshouses along with the insane, retarded, delinquents, and disabled. In 1853, Charles Loring Brace founded the Children's Aide Society of New York, which established orphanages and other programs for children. Brace and others felt that the most appropriate way to "save" the children who came to the attention of their agencies was to give them the opportunity to develop strong, moral characters. To them, this meant removing them from the negative influences of their parents and urban life.

Brace viewed rural Protestant families as ideal parents for such children, and recruited large numbers of foster families from the rural Midwest to serve as foster parents. During the mid–1800s, "orphan trains" carrying hundreds of children stopped at depots throughout the Midwest, leaving behind those children selected by families at each stop.

By 1880, the Children's Aide Society of New York had sent 40,000 children to live with rural farm families (Bremner 1974). This move was strongly criticized by a number of individuals and organizations. While some called attention to the negative effects of separating children from their parents, the greatest criticism raised was because of religious conflicts. The majority of children placed in foster homes were from Irish immigrant families who were predominantly Catholic, whereas their foster families were primarily German and Scandinavian Protestants. The outcry led to more emphasis placed on the development of Catholic orphanages and foster homes.

Still, there was little attention paid to children living with their own families or with other families as a result of informal placement by their families, and there were no standards nor any system of intervention to address the needs of abused and neglected children and their families. This changed in the 1870s as the result of a now-famous case involving a young girl in New York named Mary Ellen. A visitor to Mary Ellen's neighborhood was appalled at the abusive treatment she was receiving from her caretakers (she was living with relatives) and reported the situation to a number of agencies in New York City. When none would intervene, the visitor, reasoning that Mary Ellen fell under the broad rubric of "animal," finally got the New York Society for the Prevention of Cruelty to Animals to take the case to court and request that the child be moved from the family immediately.

As a result of the Mary Ellen case, New York and other cities established Societies for the Prevention of Cruelty to Children. These organizations, however, focused primarily on prosecution of parents rather than on services to either children or their families. The establishment of Charity Organization Societies (COS) and settlement houses in the late 1800s gave increased attention to children and families, as well as to the environments in which they functioned.

The majority of other efforts in the 1800s and early 1900s focused on the health needs of children. This was because illness was frequent and the death of children was commonplace during this time period and also because middle- and upper-middle-class families saw prevention of disease as a way to keep the diseases of immigrants from spreading to their own children (Bremner 1974). Immunization laws, pasteurized milk legislation, and other sanitation laws passed easily during this time period. Other relevant legislation focused on child labor laws and compulsory school attendance legislation. Increased attention began to be given at both state and national levels to the responsibilities of government to provide for children and families, and many states passed legislation establishing monitoring systems for foster care and separating facilities for dependent, neglected, and delinquent children from those for adults.

The most significant effort toward the establishment of a true service delivery system for children, youth, and families during the early 1900s was the creation of the **U.S. Children's Bureau** in 1912. This was a result of the first White House Conference on Children, held in 1910, and a coalition of child advocates from the settlement houses, COS groups, and state boards of charities and corrections. The legislation establishing the U.S. Children's Bureau was significant, because it was the first national legislation that recognized that the federal government had a responsibility for the welfare of its children. Julia Lathrop was appointed the first chief of the bureau. Its first efforts were aimed at birth registration and maternal and child health programs, in an attempt to reduce the high infant mortality rate and improve the health of children. One of the bureau's first publications, *Infant Care,* a booklet for parents, has undergone over twenty revisions and remains the most popular document available from the Government Printing Office. Today, the Children's Bureau is responsible for a number of federal programs for children, youth, and families and is a part of the U.S. Department of Health and Human Services.

During the first thirty years of the 1900s, states continued to become more involved in services to children, youth, and families, particularly in the South and West, where private agencies did not have the strong hold they held in the East. Many states established public departments of welfare that also were responsible for child and family services, including protecting children from abuse and neglect, providing foster homes, and overseeing orphanages and other institutions for children. The establishment of the American Association for Organizing Family Social Work (which later became the Family Service Association of America) in 1919 and the **Child Welfare League of America** in 1920 gave further impetus to the provision of child and family services. Both of these organizations stressed the role of the social work profession and established recommended standards for the provision of services. During the 1920s, attention turned to parenting and facilitating the development of healthy parent–child relationships. Child guidance centers were established and the emphasis on psychoanalysis led to increased attention to child therapy. Adoption as a formal child welfare service and subsequent adoption legislation also occurred during this period.

Services to children, youth, and families became more formalized with the passage of the Social Security Act in 1935. This act established mother's pensions, which later became the AFDC program, and also mandated states to establish, expand, and strengthen statewide child welfare services, especially in rural areas. The definition of child welfare stated earlier in this chapter incorporated the following trends presently seen in state and federal child welfare services:

1. recognition that poverty is a major factor associated with other child and family problems;
2. a shift from rescuing children from poor families and placing them in substitute care to keeping children in their own homes and providing supportive services to prevent family break up;
3. state intervention in family life to protect children;
4. increased professionalization and bureaucratization of child welfare services;
5. an emphasis at the federal level that it is the responsibility of the federal government to oversee the delivery of child welfare services within states to ensure that all children and families in the United States have access to needed services.

In spite of the Social Security Act, there continued to be problems with the delivery of services to children, youth, and families. Access to services remained unequal and many children continued to grow up in poverty. Some child welfare services, such as adoption, were provided primarily to white middle-class families, and few child welfare services adequately addressed the needs of black and Hispanic children and their families. Many children, particularly minority children, spent their entire childhoods in foster care. What initially was meant to be temporary care until families stabilized enough for their children to return became a permanent way of life for many children.

In the 1960s, the Kennedy and Johnson administrations took a strong interest in children, youth, and families. Services during these administrations were broader, and targeted at prevention and the elimination of poverty. Many of these programs were based on then new studies that suggested that children could be shaped by their environment and that heredity played only a minimal role in individual outcomes. The focus became to "maximize the potential of all individuals" and to help them become productive adults. As a result, programs were implemented such as infant care centers, Head Start (a preschool program focusing on social, emotional, and cognitive development), and increased emphasis was placed on education, as well as job training and employment programs for youth and their parents. With this broad-based focus, traditional child welfare services received less attention in favor of strengthening families and preventive services.

When President Nixon took office, resources were perceived as being more scarce. There was a shift in focus from providing maximum resources to meeting minimum standards in regard to child and family services. With only a few exceptions actively advocated by Congress, services to children, youth, and families narrowed and funding, programs, and policies shifted back to more traditional child welfare services, including protective services to abused and neglected children and their families, foster care, and adoption.

In 1974, attention to the **battered child syndrome**—a medical diagnosis given to a child who comes to a medical setting with a broken bone, and X-rays reveal previously broken bones throughout the body in various stages of healing—resulted in strong advocacy from the medical profession and key Congressional leaders, such as Walter Mondale. As a result, Congress passed the Child Abuse and Neglect Prevention and Treatment Act. This act mandated the establishment of the National Center on Child Abuse and Neglect as part of the Department of Health, Education, and Welfare (now the Department of Health and Human Services). It required states receiving federal dollars to strengthen child maltreatment programs to meet a number of mandates, including state definitions and reporting laws regarding child maltreatment; established research and technical assistance programs to assist states in developing child maltreatment prevention and treatment programs; and established special demonstration programs that could later be adapted by other states. When the act was renewed three years later, a new section was added to strengthen adoption services for children with special needs, or those children

With appropriate intervention, children and adolescents growing up in troubled families can become well-functioning, healthy adults.

who were waiting to be adopted and were considered difficult to find homes for because of ethnicity, age, or developmental disabilities.

During the Nixon administration, because of increased concern about the high costs of child care and the numbers of children left alone because their parents could not afford child care, Congress attempted to pass legislation that would give states funding for child care subsidies for low-income working parents. It was reasoned that this not only would keep more children safe, but also would reduce the numbers of women on AFDC and the numbers of families living in poverty. That legislation, and most other child and family services legislation since that time, failed to pass. Significant legislation that has passed in recent years includes the 1974 Juvenile Justice and Delinquency Prevention Act, which establishes limited funding for runaway youth programs; the Indian Child Welfare Act (1976), which attempts to prevent disruption of American Indian families; and the Education for All Handicapped Children Act (1975), which mandates the provision of educational and social services to handicapped children through public school systems.

In 1980, Congress passed the Adoption Assistance and Child Welfare Reform Act. Advocates had been urging that legislation of this type be passed for many years as they became increasingly concerned about the large numbers of children "drifting" in the foster care system and those who were legally free for adoption but for whom homes were not being found. A number of studies (Maas & Engler 1959; Vasaly 1976) indicated that the child welfare services delivery system perhaps was doing more harm to children than they would experience if they had remained in their own homes. One study found that, while foster care philosophically is intended to be short term (six months or less) while parents prepare for family reunification through counseling and other types of assistance, this was not the experience of many children. The average age of children studied in foster care was approximately thirteen; the average number of years a child had been in foster care was approximately five; the average number of social workers managing the child's case while in foster care was approximately five; and the average number of different foster homes in which the child had lived was approximately five.

The Adoption Assistance and Child Welfare Reform Act has the potential to significantly change the thrust of services to children, youth, and families. Through ceilings on funding allowances, it encourages the establishment of own-home services and reductions in the number of children in foster care; it requires case plans and six-month reviews for all children receiving child welfare services, so that they do not languish in foster care; and it provides federal funding to subsidize the adoption of special needs children. Much of the legislation passed, however, has not received the funding appropriations needed to successfully implement the legislation. Additionally, recent sessions of Congress have placed ceilings on amounts available for child and family services. If current funding allocations remain the same, by 1990, Americans will be spending 21 percent less on poor children and families and 58 percent more on military defense than they did in 1980 (Children's Defense Fund 1986). During the 1980s, increased focus due to publicity has been given to drug abuse, sexual abuse, and teen-age pregnancy. However, due to budgetary constraints and attention to other priorities, funding in these areas has not followed the increased attention.

PREVENTIVE SERVICES TO CHILDREN IN THEIR OWN HOMES

Although preventive services receive less attention than other types of services, there are many programs that strengthen families and reduce chances for family dysfunction.

Natural Support Systems

Given the scarcity of resources, increased attention is being given to the strengthening of **natural support systems** to assist families. Many families develop social networks of friends, relatives, neighbors, or coworkers who provide emotional support; share childcare, transportation, clothing, toys, and other resources; offer the opportunity to observe other children, parents, and family constellations and how they interact; and provide education about child rearing and other family life situations. However, studies show that many families who experience problems are isolated and lack such support systems. Many social services agencies, churches, and other community organizations are assisting communities in the establishment of support systems for new families and other families who lack natural support systems to help them meet their needs. Some communities have established telephone support programs for various groups, such as a Parents' Warmline or Teen Help Line, where individuals can receive support and information about appropriate resources.

Parent Education

While most people are required to learn math and English in school, little attention is given to one of the most important roles they are likely to play as adults—that of being a parent. Many communities offer parenting classes aimed at a wide range of parents: prenatal classes for parents prior to the birth or adoption of their first-born infants, classes for parents of toddlers and pre-schoolers, classes for parents of school-age children, and classes for parents of adolescents. Such programs not only offer education about basic developmental stages of children and adolescents and alternative methods of child-rearing and discipline, but they also encourage the development of mutual support systems among participants who often relax about their roles as parents when they realize that other parents have similar concerns and struggles.

Child Development and Child Care Programs

Accessible and high-quality childcare programs that are affordable for working parents, particularly single parents, also can be seen as preventing family breakdown. Such programs help parents ensure that their children are happy and safe in a comfortable, nurturing environment while parents work, thus reducing parental stress. Many child care programs offer additional opportunities for parents, including parenting education classes, babysitting cooperatives, social programs, and the opportunity to develop support systems with other parents and children. However, affordable, high-quality child care programs often are unavailable to working parents, particularly in rural areas. Child care for infants, for school-age children during vacations and holidays, and when children are sick also is relatively unavailable in most areas of the United States. An additional gap in services is the availability of evening and night child care for parents who must work late shifts.

Special programs are available for low-income parents. However, these are often limited in the hours and in the numbers of children they can serve. **Head Start**, perhaps the most successful program established under the Office of Economic Opportunity in the 1960s, provides not only a developmental learning program for preschool children, but also health care, social services, and parent education. Infant parent centers, which allow parents the opportunity to learn how to interact and play with their children in order to stimulate their development, also are available to some parents on a limited basis.

Recreational, Religious, and Social Programs

Often when discussing services for children, youth, and families, no attention is given to the major roles that community resources other than social services agencies play in meeting family needs. From a systems perspective, the broader social, recreational, and religious programs must be seen as primary services available to all persons and families; and social services agencies are to be viewed as residual services to address the needs of those families not served by these primary services. The church meets the spiritual, emotional, social, and recreational needs of many children, youth, and families and often plays a major role in establishing special preventive services, such as childcare programs, outreach centers, and parent education programs. Increasingly, the business community is providing preventive services through the workplace, including bag lunch programs for working parents, recreational facilities and programs for employees and their families, and the facilitation of coworker support systems. Many communities offer substantial recreational programs for families that are free and provide family entertainment. Serious gaps exist in most communities, however, in providing appropriate recreational programs for adolescents. Some experts attribute increases in adolescent problems, including teen-age pregnancy and delinquency, to the lack of available programs for this age group.

Appropriate Educational Opportunities

Most studies identify strong relationships between difficulties in school and individual and family problems. Programs that provide an opportunity for children to learn in ways that help them feel good about themselves and develop a sense of competence prevent family and child-related problems in the long run. Such children are less likely to become pregnant, drop out of school, and live their lives in poverty. School-based social services allow for close cooperation between children and adolescents, teachers and school administrators, parents, and the community.

Health and Family Planning Programs

Early screening of health problems also reduces child and family problems. Health problems place increased stress on families, and access to affordable health care from prenatal care to adulthood is an important aspect of preventing family breakdown. Additionally, access to programs that provide help in responsible decision making about the decision to become a parent, through family planning clinics, churches, and other community resources, reduces the risk of unwanted children and provides assistance in exploring options when pregnancy occurs.

Education about Family Problems

Finally, education about the various types of family problems, and resources available should they occur, is a significant form of prevention. Many communities provide programs for children that focus on prevention of sexual abuse by teaching them about types of touch and what to do when they find themselves in an uncomfortable situation with an adult or older child. Other communities provide alcohol and drug awareness programs.

SERVICES TO CHILDREN AND FAMILIES AT RISK

Health and Hospital Outreach Programs

Many health clinics and hospitals have established special programs to address the needs of children and families who are "at risk" of family disruption or dysfunction. (These and other services to families at risk are shown in Figure 8–2.) Some clinics have high-risk infant programs, for example, that provide intensive services to teen-age parents; parents of low-birth weight, premature, or handicapped infants; parents with alcohol or drug abuse problems; and parents who never seem to have established appropriate relationships with their children. Clinics offer a variety of services, such as weekly outreach programs conducted by a public health nurse, individual counseling, play groups for children and support groups for parents, role modeling of appropriate child-care, and assistance in obtaining other resources as needed. Hospitals offer similar programs. In some hospitals, specially trained nurses identify at-risk mothers in the delivery room and provide intensive care and support to those mothers during their hospitalization in addition to outreach services to both parents after the hospital stay. In a number of instances, such programs help parents realize they do not wish to be parents and help them relinquish children for adoption or place them in foster care while they receive additional help. More often, such programs prevent child abuse or neglect and help parents establish positive relationships with their children.

In some areas, special clinics are being established to provide services for adolescents. Clinics provide basic health care, information on adolescent development and puberty and sexually transmitted diseases, and in some instances, pregnancy tests, contraceptive information, and prenatal care. Some clinics are located in public high schools. While this has caused some controversy, studies show that physical and emotional problems, sexually

Figure 8–2   **Support Service Options for Families at Risk**

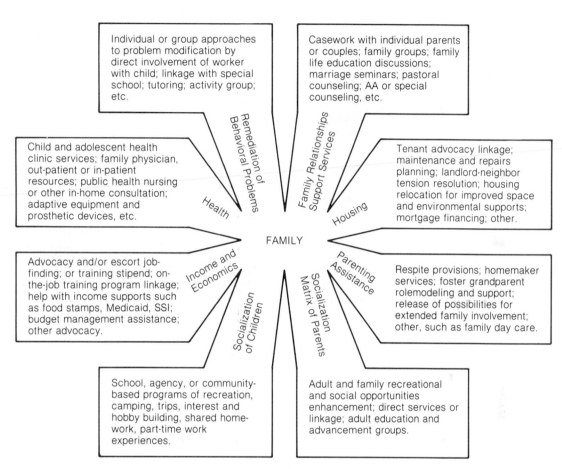

Source: Sr. Mary Paul Janchill, *Guidelines for Decision–Making in Child Welfare.* New York: Human Services Workshops, 1981, p. 13.

transmitted diseases, and pregnancies have decreased significantly in these schools.

Childcare

While most often attention is given to childcare for working parents, childcare also is used as a service for at-risk parents that enables children to remain in their own homes. Many parents need respite from their children and cannot provide for their needs twenty-four hours a day. Childcare provides parents time to meet their own needs and provides children the emotional support they may not be getting at home. It allows families to stay together and is less costly than foster care and less traumatic for the child. In many states, some childcare providers receive special training to enable them to work more effectively with at-risk parents and children. In some instances, childcare providers develop surrogate parent or positive role relationships with parents, giving them much needed emotional support as well as their children.

Many times parents under stress reach a point where they need a break from their child or they will abuse or neglect the child. Other times, emergencies occur and parents lack natural support systems to help them in times of crisis. In other situations, families with severely developmentally disabled children need time for themselves but must cope twenty-four hours a day with them and their needs. Many communities have established various forms of crisis or respite care programs for such families. Some agencies have respite care programs for developmentally disabled children, where specially trained adults care for children evenings or weekends so parents can have time to themselves. Other communities have established crisis nurseries or shelters, where parents under severe stress or in a serious emergency can leave their children for a limited amount of time (usually no more than three days). Some programs even provide emergency transportation for the children; most require counseling for parents under extreme stress while their children are in crisis care.

Some communities provide respite care for adolescents who need time away from their parents. Emergency shelter facilities for teens also most often provide crisis and family counseling to help stabilize the situation so the teen can return home. However, special services for teens are lacking in many areas. In some communities, the only resource available for children as young as twelve or thirteen is the Salvation Army's general shelter.

Homemaker Services

Many agencies provide homemaker services to families who are at risk or who have abused or neglected their children. Homemakers are specially trained individuals, often indigent persons from the community who have been parents themselves and can serve as a nurturing, supportive role model for the parents and children in the home. Homemakers offer practical suggestions and education about housekeeping, childcare, nutrition and cooking, health and safety, shopping, budgeting, and access to community resources. Additionally, they may serve as surrogate parents to both parent and children in the family and often develop positive, trusting relationships with family members who may have been previously isolated. Homemaker services are far more cost effective than foster care and often prevent the necessity to separate children from their parents.

Crisis Intervention Programs

Various community agencies provide **crisis intervention** services to families in crisis, which de-escalate the crisis and often result in a subsequent referral for additional help, such as counseling. Law enforcement agencies in many communities have crisis intervention teams that handle domestic disputes, including situations of spouse and child abuse. Some runaway youth shelters provide crisis intervention for adolescents and their parents. Hospitals also provide crisis intervention services in emergency rooms, dealing with child maltreatment, family violence, and other serious family problems. From a systems perspective, intervention often can be more effective in a crisis situation than in a noncrisis situation, because the family system is thrown into disequilibrium. Studies show that families are more receptive to change and to agreement to services such as counseling during disequilibrium, because regular defenses and the family balance are no longer in tact.

Counseling

Individual, marital, and family counseling services are available in many communities for families experiencing problems. Mental health centers, social services agencies, child and family services agencies, child guidance clinics, employee assistance programs, churches, schools, youth services programs, and hospital outreach programs often provide various types of counseling services. Unfortunately, services often are available on a limited basis, due to scarce resources and the large numbers of persons needing services, and may not always be available at no cost or on a sliding scale. Additionally, counseling to address specialized family problems, such as family violence or sexual abuse, often is unavailable in many communities. For example, only $5 per child was available for counseling services for the large number of sexually abused children in one large city, when one hour of counseling cost $40–80 and children needed long-term counseling in most instances.

Studies show that for many family problems, group counseling is more effective than individual counseling, or a combination of both is more effective than individual counseling alone. For example, when dealing with sexual abuse, children who have been sexually abused need to hear from other children that they are not the only ones who have had such an experience. Sexual and physical abusers as well as others with family problems, often deny that there is a problem, and group therapy sessions with others in similar situations break down their defenses more quickly than in individual counseling in most instances.

Support and Self–Help Groups

Support groups and **self-help groups** also are effective ways of helping children, youth, and families cope with family problems. Such groups help individuals to realize that they are not the only ones coping with a given problem. Additionally, support and self-help groups help members develop new ways to cope as they learn from each other. Perhaps most important, persons who may see themselves as being inadequate have a chance to reach out and give something to someone else. Types of self-help groups include Alcoholics Anonymous for alcoholics, Alanon for family members of alcoholics, Alateen for teen family members of alcoholics, Narcotics Anonymous, Adult Children of Alcoholics, Parents Anonymous for abusive or potentially abusive parents, Parents United for sexually abusive parents, Tough Love for parents of out-of-control adolescents, and Parents Without Partners for single parents. Many communities have established support groups for adults, children, or teens dealing with divorce, stepparenting, death of a loved one or other type of loss, or those living with a developmentally disabled or emotionally disturbed family member.

Volunteer and Outreach Programs

Many traditional social services agencies are overloaded with cases and can provide only limited services—and those only to families with the most severe problems. A number of agencies have established volunteer components, while other agencies have been established that use only volunteers. In many instances, because they can spend more extensive time with families, volunteers can be highly successful in intervention and prevent family disruption. Most volunteer programs have established effective screening mechanisms that recruit volunteers with good nurturing skills who can relate well to clients. Many have been parents themselves, some are grandparents, and others are students or already involved in human services. Volunteers usually receive extensive training and are supervised by a social work case manager. Many communities and states have successful volunteer programs. SCAN (Suspected Child Abuse and Neglect) of Arkansas and Family Outreach Centers established by the National Council of Jewish Women both use highly trained volunteers to work on a one-to-one basis with abusive and neglecting families. The SCAN model is based on a reparenting framework, which focuses on developing trust and then helps the parent work through all the stages of psychosocial development that they missed during their own childhoods. Volunteers in such programs visit often and converse with parents and children, assist in problem solving and accessing community resources, and serve as a surrogate parent/role model/friend to the parent and family members. Similar programs have been developed that pair volunteers with teen-age parents and abused and neglected children. The national Big Brothers/Big Sisters program uses volunteers as friends and role models to children from single-parent families. Studies show that volunteer programs can keep families together. Given the continuing increase in the numbers of families needing services and the lack of availability of resources, volunteer programs are likely to increase.

CHILD PROTECTIVE SERVICES

Families reported as being abusive or neglecting to **child protective services** (CPS) divisions within state human services agencies must be investigated by the agency to ascertain if the maltreatment report can be substantiated. If the social worker (commonly referred to as a *child protective services worker*) finds that abuse or neglect is a problem, the family receives protective services. This is a nonvoluntary program—meaning that the parents did not request or volunteer to receive the services. Child protective services workers most often determine that, although services are required, it is safe to leave the child in the home while the services are being provided. If they feel that the family is resistant to the services, or the state in which they work mandates court involvement, they may take the case to court and request that the court order services, such as counseling. This way, if the family does not comply, the worker can bring the case back into court and request more serious options, such as placing the child in foster care.

Child protective services workers provide a variety of services to the families with whom they work. Their primary goal is to keep the child safe, and they make every effort to ensure that the child can be safe in his or her own home. They often serve as case managers, arranging for community resources such as housing, employment, transportation, counseling, health services, childcare, homemaker services, or financial assistance. They provide counseling, parent education, and support. They may assist a client in getting involved in a church or other support group, or they may suggest (or require) that the client attend Parents Anonymous or be assigned a volunteer. Often, they develop a specific contract with a parent delineating specific goals the family must accomplish in order to be removed from the child protective services caseload.

SUBSTITUTE CARE

Although every attempt is made to keep children in their own homes, sometimes this is not possible. Parents may have too many unmet needs of their own, serious health or emotional problems, or be too little interested in parenting to be able to care for their children adequately. In such situations, **substitute care** is located for the children involved. Unless the situation is an emergency—which many state laws define as a life-threatening situation—a child protective services worker cannot remove a child from a family without a court order. Even with emergency removals, court orders must be obtained, usually within twenty-four hours, and hearings held with parents present. Once a child is placed in substitute care, the child must have a plan developed that focuses on either returning the child home or, less often, terminating the parental rights and placing the child in an adoptive family. Each case must be reviewed, either by a community or a court review panel, every six months to ensure that the child is not in limbo in the foster care system.

Although it is not always the case, every effort should be made if a child does need to be placed in substitute care to ensure that the placement is the least restrictive option. This suggests that relatives, neighbors, and others with whom the child is familiar be considered first if they meet criteria to be positive substitute parents for the child. Consideration also should be given to finding care for the child consistent with his or her cultural background, preferably in the same neighborhood or school area. Since it is important that, if in the best interests of the child, the birth parents visit the child, attention also needs to be given to accessibility of the parents as well. If appropriate relative placements or other suitable arrangements cannot be made, the child most often is placed in a foster family. Foster parents are recruited and trained to relate to children and their birth parents. They often have children of their own and may take in more than one foster child. All states have strict standards regarding numbers of children foster parents can parent, appropriate discipline and treatment of children, and supervision of foster parents. Many foster parents keep in touch with their foster children after they leave, and some adopt the children if they become available for adoption. A number of states train foster parents to parent certain types of children, for example, adolescents or children who have been sexually abused. Foster parents also develop support systems and many belong to local and national foster parent organizations. While foster parents are paid a limited amount each month to care for each child, they often spend more than they receive and in almost all instances give large amounts of love and attention to the children they parent, who are often needy and may take out their frustrations on the foster family.

Some children have difficulty handling the intimacy of a foster family, particularly if they have been seriously abused or neglected. In other instances, a foster family may not be found for a particular child—it is difficult to find foster homes for adolescents, for example. Group homes, which usually have a set of house parents to care for five to ten children or adolescents, are an alternative to foster care. Such homes attempt to maintain a homelike atmosphere and provide rules and structure to children and adolescents. They also may include regular group counseling sessions for residents.

Children and adolescents who need more structure than foster care or group homes can provide may be placed in residential treatment programs. Such programs, more expensive to maintain than foster care and group homes, provide consistent structure for children and adolescents, as well as intensive individual and usually group counseling. Most residential treatment programs help the child establish the boundaries that may be missing from home, focus on building self-esteem and competence, and help the child resolve anger and other issues from his or her family experience. The goal of residential treatment is to develop enough coping skills that the child can return home better able to deal with the family situation. Ideally, the family also has undergone counseling, so they do not enter into old roles that may force the child back into previous behaviors in order to survive. Family counseling does not always occur, however, and it is often up to the child to cope on returning to the family and community.

Children and adolescents with more serious problems may be hospitalized. In hospital settings, more intensive therapy is provided and medication also may be used. In other instances, children or adolescents, primarily delinquent adolescents, are placed in juvenile detention facilities. Studies suggest that white, middle-class children and teens are more likely to be placed in residential treatment or hospital programs, while poor and minority children are more likely to be placed in juvenile detention facilities.

Although recent attempts have been made to strengthen the substitute care system, problems remain. Perhaps the greatest problem is the lack of resources available to birth parents that enable them to reunite with their children. Overloaded service delivery systems often cause social workers to be unable to provide services needed to parents. As a result, social workers are reluctant to terminate parental rights and free children for adoption. On the other hand, because they cannot provide needed services, they are also reluctant to return children to unsafe homes. Thus, children languish in the foster care system. Emlen (1977) shows, however, that when intensive services are provided to parents, even those who have multiple problems and have been separated from their children for long periods of time, children can be reunited successfully with their own parents.

ADOPTION

When parents choose not to or cannot provide for their children, parental rights are terminated by the court and the child becomes legally free for **adoption.** However, many children in the United States, particularly black children, are adopted informally by relatives without a formal court hearing ever taking place. The focus of adoption has changed significantly in recent years. In the past, the emphasis was on finding a perfect child for a couple who biologically could not have children, with an attempt to match the child to the parents according to physical features such as hair and eye color. Today, the emphasis is on finding an appropriate parent for a child, one who can best meet that child's needs.

Most adoptions that take place today are the result of remarriages, with fewer infant adoptions. This is because many young women of all ethnic groups are choosing to keep their babies rather than place them for adoption. However, there are still traditional maternity homes/adoption agencies that provide residential and health care and counseling services before birth and, in some instances, postadoption counseling after birth. Many adoption agencies, however, have changed their focus to the more than 120,000 **special needs children** available for adoption in the United States. Such children, while traditionally considered by many to be unadoptable, have been placed successfully in a variety of family settings. Special needs children are those who are minority, older, physically or emotionally disabled, or members of sibling groups. Agencies also have focused on parents they had not previously considered. While in the 1960s and 1970s emphasis was on transracial adoption, currently most agencies focus on finding parents who are of the same ethnic or cultural background as the child, if possible. Thus, a number of agencies have established special outreach programs to black and Hispanic communities to recruit adoptive parents. Agencies also are recruiting single parents, working parents, foster parents, and parents with large families already. Experience is showing that all of these families can successfully parent. An additional emphasis is on placing siblings together in the same adoptive family. Previously, many siblings were separated, often forever.

The Adoption Assistance Act, previously discussed, allows monthly living allowances and medical expenses for families who could not otherwise afford to adopt special needs children. More assertive outreach efforts, such as Father Clements' "one church, one child" program that recruits adoptive families through black and Hispanic churches, television's "Wednesday's Child" programs that portray children available for adoption, and national computerized services listing waiting children and waiting parents, have resulted in children being adopted who were previously considered unadoptable, including many who in the past would have been relegated to a life in a state institution.

Other current adoption trends include foreign-born adoptions and open adoptions, which allow the birth parent(s) to be involved in the selection of the adoptive parents, and, in some instances, to be able to maintain contact with the child as the child grows up. While adoption services have been strengthened, there are still barriers to successful placements, particularly of special needs children. Agencies and individuals still consider some children unadoptable, and some agencies are reluctant to work on placing children across state lines, even when parents in other states can be located or vice versa. There also is a need for more extensive postadoption services, particularly for special needs children who are adopted. Adoptive parent groups have been instrumental in advocating for legislation, in establishing adoption programs, and in providing support to other adoptive parents. Presently, they provide the primary support after placement in many communities.

Additional issues relating to adoption will continue to be raised in the next decade, including the ethics of paying young pregnant girls large amounts of money for their unborn children without going through an agency, as well as issues relating to surrogate parents.

THE ROLE OF SOCIAL WORKERS IN THE PROVISION OF SERVICES TO CHILDREN, YOUTH, AND FAMILIES

Social workers play many roles in the provision of services to children, youth, and families. In fact, this is the most traditional area of social work practice. The "child welfare worker," first a volunteer during the 1800s and then a trained social worker in the 1900s, is most often the stereotype of the typical social worker. However, the roles of social workers in this area have expanded significantly, and social workers at the BSW, MSW, and Ph.D. level all are actively involved in the provision of services to children, youth, and families. At the BSW level, social workers are involved as childcare workers in group homes and residential treatment centers, as women and children's counselors at battered women's shelters, as counselors at runaway youth shelters, as crisis counselors in law enforcement agencies, and as child protective services and foster care workers in public social services agencies. An entry-level position in the area of child and family services usually provides a broad-based experience that allows a great deal of flexibility to move to other jobs, either into supervisory positions or other areas of social work. Some states require a minimum of a BSW for certain child and family positions, such as child protective services and foster care staff.

A number of social work jobs in this area require a MSW degree. This is partly due to the standards established by the Child Welfare League of America, which many agencies follow, as well as the fact that some child and family services are highly specialized. In almost all instances, an MSW is required of an adoption worker. Most child guidance centers and child and family service agencies also require MSW degrees. Many social work or therapist positions in residential treatment centers require a MSW, as do clinical social work positions in adolescent and child psychiatric treatment programs. Most schools of social work have child and family or child welfare specializations at the graduate level, which provide special course work in this area, as well as field placements in child and family services settings.

With the implementation of the Ph.D. degree in social work, some child guidance or child and family services agencies are attempting to hire agency directors at this level. Additionally, persons who want more highly specialized clinical experience are earning Ph.D. degrees, enabling them to do more intensive therapy with children, youth, and families.

School Social Work

Another specialized field that focuses on services to children, youth, and families is school social work. This refers to social work services provided in a school-based setting. Such services are advantageous for many reasons. First, they allow the social worker to see the child or adolescent in a natural setting, interacting with peers, teachers, and school administrators, which provides a different perspective than seeing a client in an office or an agency. Second, they allow the social worker access to large numbers of children and families in need of services; most children aged five to eighteen attend school. Third, it allows the social worker to help parents and school personnel use a systems approach to leverage the needs of child, focusing on the relationships between the child, home, and school—and the broader community. Often, in school, the focus of staff is on academic performance and school behavior. A social worker with a systems perspective can help school personnel understand the importance of family and community variables in relation to the child's capacity to function in the school setting. In some states, a teaching certificate and teaching experience are required of a school social worker in addition to a BSW or an MSW degree. In other states, only a BSW or MSW is required. Most states have educational certification programs that establish requirements for all school personnel, including social workers. The National Association of Social Workers has a school social work division, and two school social work journals are published nationally.

If students are interested in a social work career in the area of child and family services, there are a number of child welfare and child and family journals, as well as numerous books on all areas discussed in this chapter, readily available. In addition, since many child and family services programs have volunteer programs, volunteer experience also will help students determine if they are interested in this area as well as provide sound social work experience.

SUMMARY

Policies and programs that focus on the needs of children, youth, and families are developed and implemented within the context of society and community attitudes and values, awareness about needs, and the availability of resources. The presently-preferred focus is directed toward prevention and early intervention, keeping families together, and making decisions based on the best interests of the children. However, lack of resources places large numbers of children, youth and families in jeopardy of disruption and serious dysfunction. Because individual and family needs are diverse, as are available programs to address them, there are many opportunities for social workers interested in children, youth, and family services.

KEY TERMS

adoption

battered child syndrome

best interests of child

child protective services

child welfare delivery system

Child Welfare League of
      America

child welfare services

crisis intervention

Head Start

least detrimental alternative

natural support system

own-home services

permanency planning

psychological parent

self-help group

Social Security Act

special needs child

substitute care

U.S. Children's Bureau

DISCUSSION QUESTIONS

1. What is meant by the concepts *in the best interests of the child, least detrimental alternative,* and *psychological parent?*

2. Describe briefly at least three prevention programs used with children and their families.

3. Compare own-home services with substitute care and adoption. What are the advantages and disadvantages of each?

4. Identify at least two areas in which social workers at the BSW and MSW levels might be employed in a child and family services positions.

5. What is meant by *special needs adoption?*

6. Select one of the "family problem areas" discussed in the previous chapter. Identify at least one prevention and one intervention program you would suggest to address that problem area.

7. Identify at least three problems with the current children, youth, and families service delivery system.

REFERENCES

Bremner, R. 1974. *Children and Youth in America.* Cambridge, Mass.: Harvard University Press.

Children's Defense Fund. 1986. *Children's Defense Budget: Analysis of the FY 1987 Federal Budget and Children.* Washington, D.C.: Children's Defense Fund.

Emlen, A. 1977. *Overcoming Barriers to Planning for Children in Foster Care.* Portland, Ore.: Portland State University.

Goldstein, J., A. Freud, and A. Solnit, 1979. *Before the Best Interests of the Child.* New York: Free Press.

Goldstein, J., A. Freud, and A. Solnit. 1973. *Beyond the Best Interests of the Child.* New York: Free Press.

Kadushin, A. 1980. *Child Welfare Services.* New York: Macmillan.

Maas, H., and R. Engler. 1959. *Children in Need of Parents.* New York: Columbia University Press.

McGowan, B., and W. Meezen. 1983. *Child Welfare: Current Trends and Future Directions.* Ithaca, Ill.: Peacock Press.

Social Security Act. 1935. Title IV–B, Section 425. Washington, D.C.: U.S. Congressional Record.

Vasaly, S. 1976. *Foster Care in Five States.* Washington, D.C.: U.S. Department of Health, Education, and Welfare.

SELECTED FURTHER READINGS

Child Welfare. A bimonthly journal published by the Child Welfare League of America, New York.

Janchill, M. 1981. *Guidelines for Decision–Making in Child Welfare.* New York: Human Services Workshops.

U.S. Department of Health, Education, and Welfare. 1978. *Child Welfare Strategy in the Coming Years.* Washington, D.C.: U.S. Department of Health, Education, and Welfare.

9 Criminal Justice

J oe is a thirty-two-year-old man whose current address is Huntsville State Prison. He is serving a twenty-year sentence for armed robbery. This is not Joe's first term in prison, but he hopes that it will be his last.

Joe first came to the attention of the criminal justice system when he was fourteen years old. He was arrested for stealing a car. The third child in a family of six children, Joe grew up with his mother and siblings in a poverty-stricken area in a large eastern city. He was abused physically during his childhood and received little positive attention from his mother. From first grade on, Joe had difficulty in school. He had a short attention span, disrupted the classroom, and rarely completed his schoolwork.

At the time of his first arrest, Joe was in the seventh grade for the second time. He was placed on probation and his family was referred for counseling. However, because his mother worked long hours, she was never able to arrange the sessions. Joe became more of a problem in school and the neighborhood. He began skipping school, experimenting with drugs, and committing a series of burglaries. His mother could not handle his frequent bursts of anger nor get Joe to respond to her limits.

When Joe was sixteen, he spent three months in a juvenile detention facility, where he did well with the structure provided by the program. When he left the program, he was assigned a probation officer and returned to his family. His conditions of probation stipulated that he attend school on a regular basis, maintain a specified curfew, and report to his probation officer monthly. Joe followed these conditions for several months; however, he continued to have difficulty in school and dropped out four months after he returned home. He held a series of jobs at fast food restaurants, but had difficulty coming to work regularly and became frustrated because he was not earning very much money. Increasingly, he gravitated toward older young adults who hung out on the street and seemed to have the freedom and the money he yearned for. They liked Joe, and he felt accepted by them and enjoyed being with them. Joe soon became involved with them in selling drugs and committing burglaries.

Joe then began a series of arrests for drug dealing, burglary, and assault, which resulted in several stays in various detention facilities. Just before his last arrest, Joe married a nineteen-year-old who recently had their baby. He is anxious to get out of prison and begin to get to know his son and support his family. He is frustrated by the limited work programs and the lack of counseling available at the prison. He has enrolled in a prison education program to try to earn his high school equivalency certificate and hopes to be released to a community halfway house and enroll in a job training program. He knows that he will need job skills and help in dealing with his anger and frustration if he is to maintain a successful marriage and job and to stay out of prison.

Public social problems are specific conditions in the society that are perceived as sufficiently bothersome to merit intervention by government. Crime is clearly such a condition. Citizens have a right to expect government protection from crime. Society has a need to apprehend suspected offenders, to convict the guilty and free the innocent, and to appropriately punish and rehabilitate the convicted. These steps constitute the ordered processes of the criminal justice system.

The criminal justice system is expected to act as both a specific and general deterrent to crime. A **specific deterrent** is structured to prevent crimes very directly. In capital cases, for example, the execution itself is obviously a specific deterrent; the fear of capital punishment serves as a further **general deterrent**. This does not mean a society can impose capital punishment without cost.

In our society the criminal justice system is evaluated not only by its capacity to contain crime but also by the justice meted out by the system. That is why we refer to the *criminal justice system* rather than the *criminal containment system*. The system's dual responsibility to protect the citizenship rights of criminals as well as their victims constitutes the core of the criminal justice system. The constitutional safeguards of our society are expected to follow criminals from their first apprehensions by police, through their arraignments, trials, imprisonments, and reentries into society. That these constitutional safe-guards increase the costs and, perhaps, lower the effectiveness of police, courts, and prisons in containing crime is seen as one of the costs of democracy.

All systems of public policy face policy dilemmas, but the dilemma of the criminal justice system is particularly acute. This is reflected by the rise of vigilantism, a public expression of discontent with the balance that has been struck within the criminal justice system. This system is charged with the deterrence of crime and the maintenance of justice. Its desired goals include (1) efficient, but not intrusive police work; (2) fair and impartial trials for the accused, and an awareness of the rights of the victims; (3) safe, yet secure and humane prisons; and (4) parole programs that provide reentry into the free society of ex-offenders but protect the community at large.

Law-abiding citizens want to be protected from criminal behavior but also want protection from unwarranted intrusion of the criminal justice system into their private lives. The duality of these demands imposes costs and constraints on police, court officers, and prison and parole officials. Since in the final analysis "law and order" exponents and "civil libertarians" want the same things, where does the policy problem lie? It lies in the question of emphasis and balance. The pendulum of criminal justice is almost never perceived as lying at a perpendicular position.

VIEWS OF CRIMINAL BEHAVIOR

A number of views of criminal behavior compete to explain why people commit crimes. Crime can be viewed as psychologically aberrant behavior, as socially induced behavior, as a consequence of rational thought where criminals simply see crime as just another way to make a living, or as a complex interactive process of an individual's personal characteristics and the many factors that constitute his or her environment. The explanation accepted by various citizens constitutes the structure upon which they wish the criminal justice system to be built.

Psychological Views of the Criminal Personality

One school of thought suggests that criminals differ from noncriminals in some fundamental way, other than the obvious one of having been convicted. The distinguishing trait has been found over the years to be reflected in body or head shape, skull size, chromosome structure, specific patterns of response to projective tests, or in the complex labeling process of psychiatric diagnosis. Of course, there is a circular reasoning process in all of the psychological-physiological attempts to establish a criminal type. There also is a kind of satisfaction in the notion of a criminal type, because crime policy then becomes, simply, segregation of the criminals from the rest of society.

A second psychological interpretation of the **etiology of crime** is only slightly more sophisticated. Crime is seen simply as a manifestation of a compulsion derived from unresolved conflicts between the super ego and the id. Someone with a criminal personality, by definition a defective ego, is unable to overcome the desire to defy social taboos, yet the conflict reflects itself in an unconscious desire to be caught.

Anecdotal evidence suggests that criminals do operate this way—they may deliberately, albeit unconsciously, leave the clues that lead to their arrests. Were it not for the seriousness of the incidents, this behavior often would be truly comic. One young criminal brought a pair of slacks to the cleaners and, after being presented with the claim check, he pulled a gun and robbed the attendant. He returned three days later with the stub of the claim check to pick up his slacks and was patient enough to wait when the same attendant said the slacks were on the way. The young man waited calmly for the police to come and arrest him. Another pair of criminals left the motor running in the getaway car, but because they had failed to check the fuel gauge before the robbery, their car ran out of gas while they were holding up the bank. Anecdotal, but not systematic, evidence suggests such a pattern in all crime (Silberman 1980). If there is any basis for such a theory of crime, it leads to the conclusion that punishment is not a deterrent to crime but, in fact, is a stimulant.

A more sophisticated psychological theory of the etiology also contains in its assumptions the prescription for a proper anticrime policy. The following is a summation of what can be classed as a psychosocial theory of crime:

1. criminal behavior is learned;
2. learning criminal behavior occurs in a socially correlated way. Certain classes of persons will learn different ways of crime;
3. the processes involved in learning criminal behavior are the same as those in learning other behavior that involves learning a technique as well as values.

This view of criminality is less encompassing than the more simple etiological-psychological views of crime. It does not attempt to explain which people will commit crimes, an impossible task, but rather, why and how those who have committed crimes are systematically different from those who do not.

Social Views of Criminal Behavior

Another perspective suggests that crime is not caused by individual physical or mental deficiencies but rather by societal breakdown. Proponents of this perspective focus on industrialization, racism, poverty, and family breakdown as major factors that create social disorganization and, in turn, increases in crime. Discussions of crime and society too often are a battle of straw men. Each side sets up a straw man opponent that is denounced soundly. Charles Silberman and James Q. Wilson are often cited as prototypes of opposing views. In fact, both see the relationship between crime and social conditions as inordinately complex. Whereas Wilson believes that criminal sanctions would deter crime, Silberman places more faith in indirect social reforms. Both would argue that we need more carrots (job opportunities, antipoverty programs, etc.) and more sticks (swift and certain prison terms as a deterrent), but they would disagree on mix and emphasis.

Sociological inquiries into crime frequently are based on statistical correlates, such as the increasing breakdown of the traditional family or variations in unemployment and crime rates. The more sophisticated inquiries fall short of establishing a direct path of causation. Crime is seen as a result of many factors within the context of the offender's society. Street crime and white collar crime are seen as very different expressions of social maladjustment. Regardless of specifics, the essence of the sociological perspective is that general deterrence, rehabilitation, and reeducation of offenders constitute the best safeguards against repeated crimes.

The "social view of crime" advocates a criminal justice system that offers a variety of social intervention strategies (Cullen 1982). One such strategy of importance to social work practitioners is collaboration between social worker and police officer at the earliest intervention point. When the suspected offender is first in police custody, social workers and police officers are expected to concur on the case disposition. The argument is made that, despite their disparate professional orientations, both social workers and police officers are experienced in dealing with troubled people at crisis points in their lives. Individualization of response is seen as the critical mode (Treger 1975).

No one sociological perspective is seen as dominant. Rather, a number of theories are offered, depending on the type of crime committed. Marshall Clinard (1967) suggests the following classification of crimes:

1. violent personal crimes: i.e., murder;
2. sexual offenses;
3. occupational/white collar crimes;
4. political crimes;
5. organized crimes;
6. professional crimes;
7. crimes without victims.

Each of these types of crime has its own sociological pattern, and each crime type places a unique set of demands on the criminal justice system.

Economic Rationale of Crime

A final perspective is that crime is simply another form of entrepreneurship, which happens to be illegal. This view sees the criminal as an amoral person who calculates the costs and benefits of a particular crime, much as a business person calculates the costs and benefits of opening a new store. In the economic formulation, potential criminals assess the costs of getting caught and sentenced against the probable benefits of successful completion of the crime. They decide to be criminal or not, depending upon the outcomes of their calculations. People who are not poor commit fewer crimes because the costs of going to prison (in lost wages, deprivation of status, amenities of life, etc.) are higher for them than for others. If we subscribe to this theoretical perspective, to contain crime, all we need to do is increase the probable chances of being caught, sentenced, and sent to jail. There is little or no empirical evidence to suggest a valid basis for this theory (Hillman 1980).

Each of these views of crime, and we have listed only three, provides a policy paradigm for the criminal justice system, from the role of the arresting officer to the responsibilities of the parole and probation workers. One's beliefs as to the reasons criminals commit crimes are the obvious sources of ideas of how to contain crime.

PROGRAM ALTERNATIVES WITHIN THE CRIMINAL JUSTICE SYSTEM

For every thirty-six crimes committed, one person is sentenced to prison. Only one crime in every four reported results in an arrest of a suspected offender. There is roughly one arraignment for every three arrests, and although nearly 95 percent of all criminal arraignments result in criminal conviction or guilty pleas, only one in three results in a prison term. These numbers mislead as much as they reveal; for in fact tracking a particular crime (acknowledging that crimes are greatly underreported) to a particular sentence is a Herculean statistical task. One thing that is unambiguous in these numbers is the enormous amount of discretion that operates within the criminal justice system.

The American criminal justice system largely is an English invention, but it includes some important innovations that are the peculiar products of the United States. These American innovations are the elements of the system in which social work is most explicitly and importantly involved; these are the programs of probation, parole, and juvenile procedures. The American system is perhaps more fragmented than the criminal justice system in most countries. The criminal justice system can be seen first as composed of three parts: police, courts, and correctional arrangements. With federal, state, and local involvement at each level and a separation into adult and juvenile divisions, a multipartite system emerges. More dramatic is the fact that no subsystem views the criminal problem from a total perspective. Each entity is busily resolving its own problems. The result is a highly fractured system that is difficult to describe, evaluate, or control.

Despite the lack of cohesion and internal tensions, it is clear that actions within one subsystem have reverberations throughout the entire system. "Success" or "failure" in one part may generate significant problems for another part. Should state and local police, by virtue of more personnel or better investigation apprehend 25 percent more offenders, both the courts and the correctional system would have to absorb more defendants and prisoners. If the prison system released a higher proportion of recidivists, police and the courts would have to deal with a larger population of criminals. On the other hand, overcrowded prisons generate backups in local jails. All of the elements of the criminal justice system must respond to the factors in the larger society that accelerate criminal behavior. Because the criminal justice system is not examined or funded as an entity, each component accepts and adopts its own strategies. Not infrequently, the functional adaptation for one part produces particular problems for another entity within the system.

The Police

A suspect formally becomes involved in the criminal justice system at the point when he or she is questioned in connection with a crime. Arrest does not always occur. If arrest is followed by a formal charge, the path may lead to *indictment* and trial. Frequently, if not most frequently, the questioning does not even lead to arrest; the questioning of a suspect could lead to the conclusion that "successful" prosecution is unlikely.

The Courts

After the indictment, the suspect moves into the court stage of the process. An *arraignment* is held, where the suspect, now a defendant, is able to enter a plea of guilty or not guilty. If the defendant enters a guilty plea, a date is set for sentencing. The defendant who enters a not guilty plea may request a jury trial or to be tried by the court without a jury. At the time of that plea, the court has the opportunity to dismiss the charges for lack of sufficient evidence and remove the defendant from the criminal justice system.

The *prosecutor* is the public official in the criminal justice system charged with presenting the evidence that the state has against a defendant. Prosecutors are officers of the court (attorneys) but in fact have responsibilities that go beyond this. A conceptualization of the role of the prosecutor has some limitations and caveats. Prosecutors are in a critical position in the criminal justice system. Because they work in close cooperation with the police, the courts, and the correctional arrangement, they are the persons most likely to provide leadership in any efforts to coordinate the activities of the various agencies within the system. The criteria utilized by the prosecutor in deciding whether to proceed within the criminal justice system or to divert the case in a particular direction is of central importance. The prosecutor has the opportunity to drop the charge or to engage in various forms of plea bargaining to facilitate the operations with regard to a particular defendant.

In a criminal trial a human being's freedom is at stake. The *defense attorney* is the person whose performance in large measure will determine whether the individual receives a fair shake from the state. Prosecutors and judicial officials have divided loyalties. By the ethics of our judicial system, the defense attorney's loyalty primarily is to his or her client. Indigent defendants are represented through the public defender system. The rights of defendants was established in the famous case of *Gideon vs. Wainwright* (Lewis 1964).

The judge is the principal officer of the court, who presides over the court and has the final responsibility for organizing the process at the trial stage to ensure that justice is administered. The nature of the judge's office is unique in the system of criminal justice. Because of the nature of their duties and their power, the staffs of judges are critical to the conduct of their offices and thus of the entire criminal justice system. No other individual within the criminal justice system has as much largely unsupervised discretion as the judge. The President's Commission on Law Enforcement and Administration of Justice has recommended that state criminal justice systems be strengthened by improving the quality of judicial officials. An important ancillary to improving the quality of the judicial system is to provide judges with adequate staffs.

A major problem with the criminal justice system is that it is so overloaded, particularly the court system. Public defenders' offices, public prosecuting attorneys' offices, and judges often are unable to devote the appropriate time to their cases needed to ensure that judicial decisions are fair to both society and the individuals who come before the courts.

Corrections

The corrections component of the criminal justice system includes those programs that deal with a criminal after sentencing by the court. Corrections programs include various types of incarceration or detention facilities (such as prisons and jails), parole, and probation.

The state penitentiary is one of America's most unchanged social institutions. The striped suit and the ball and chain have disappeared but the social climate of the *prison* remains. The type of prison constructed in 1819 remains as a prototype, though simple prison crowding has eliminated the separate cells. The notion of enforced degradation and hopelessness has proven to be a costly failure in the war against crime.

The confusion about the purposes of imprisonment remains a hallmark of the American system. What is the mission of the prison? Is it *reform*—to alter the perception of inmates so that crime is no longer seen as acceptable behavior? Is it *isolation*—the mere sequestering of the criminal from society so that the only opportunity for crime is against one another? Is it *retribution*—a mechanism for society to "get even," to extract its revenge on those who lawlessly punish others? Is it general deterrence—for the prisons to serve as a reminder to those contemplating crime how costly to the perpetrator the crime could be? Each mission requires a differently structured prison operation. There is considerable evidence to suggest that in trying to perform all four missions, the American prison performs no mission whatsoever (Silberman 1980).

The quality of United States prisons varies greatly and in many dimensions: security, therapeutic mode, rehabilitation potential, even basic human amenities. As a general rule, federal prisons are more tolerable than state prisons, which, in turn, are better than jails. The one common denominator is that all prisons are horrible places. With rising costs and lower societal expectations of prisons, several states have turned to contracting with private enterprise, not only to build but to actually operate the prisons.

Some states are turning to other types of detention facilities than large-scale prisons. A number of states and communities have established minimum security centers for nonviolent offenders and those guilty of less serious crimes. These centers allow them to work in the community but otherwise be incarcerated. Other states and communities have set up halfway houses for persons who have served time in prison but are not yet ready to be released into the community without some sort of structure and supervision. A new type of incarceration made possible by modern technology allows persons to be incarcerated in their own homes. A person wears an unremovable band with a radio transmitter that trips a signal in a correction-monitoring center when the person goes beyond the front yard. This system is cost effective and may reduce significantly the numbers of persons in prison facilities. Studies show that prison may actually teach more about crime than reform, creating persons likely to return to prison for more serious offenses than their first ones. Thus, this system also may serve to reduce repeat offenses, as well as allow already scarce rehabilitation programs within prisons to focus more intensively on fewer individuals.

Probation is an official correctional option in which the offender is given an opportunity to remain free from detention or have a fine held in abeyance in return for accepting supervised living. The supervisional constraints could not legally be placed on a free citizen but are accepted by the convicted person as a contract in lieu of detention or fine. Rather than going to prison, the offender is supervised by a probation officer who monitors his or her activities and ensures that the conditions of probation are met. These conditions can include abstinence from drugs and/or alcohol, a curfew, not leaving the county of residence, holding a job, and counseling. If the conditions are violated, the offender can be ordered back before the court, the probation revoked, and a prison sentence given instead.

Parole is the opportunity given to a person who has been imprisoned to serve the remainder of the sentence outside of prison in a supervised situation. Again, the constraints could not be placed on the free citizen, but a prisoner may choose to accept parole as a means for an earlier reentry into society. Originally conceived of as a policy available to individualize the rehabilitation of the offender, both probation and parole now principally are mechanisms for managing of the size of the prison population.

Judges grant probation, often as part of a prearranged plea bargain, where a defendant agrees to plead guilty to or to accept a guilty finding for a lesser

Social workers participate in the criminal justice system and are often called to testify in court cases.

crime rather than risk a guilty finding for a more serious offense and a possible prison term. It should be noted that suspension of sentence is unconditional, whereas probation is conditional. If the individual fails to live up to the conditions of probation, there are civil and criminal procedures to revoke probation and impose the sentence. In unconditional suspension, the individual is found guilty but the judge feels that conviction alone is sufficient, and thus suspension has the effect of satisfying the offender's criminal liability.

If suspension or probation is not appropriate, a sentence is imposed. After serving some portion of the sentence in detention, the prisoner is considered for parole, either automatically or by petition. Probation and parole decisions essentially are similar. The judge in probation, or a citizen board in the case of a parolee, considers a report that includes information about the crime, the social history of the individual, social support available to the person, present conditions, etc. These reports are now highly uniform in accordance with a court decision on procedural rights. The philosophy of individualized decision making remains, but the reality of practice is a largely semiautomatic procedure for parole and/or bargained probation. Myth and reality stand far apart in probation and parole practice.

Diversion

Clearly, there is a need to divert persons from the criminal justice system, because the size and complexity of running all those guilty of criminal behavior through the system would overload and break down the system. **Diversion** is the formalization of the old process by which police officers did not make arrests in certain crimes and/or crime areas, or prosecutors dismissed charges, diverting individuals to other programs, such as counseling or DWI classes. Much criminal behavior is better dealt with outside the criminal justice system and inside the social services network. Police and prosecutors often view crimes likely to be diverted as either not serious or beyond their purview but too important as social problems to be either condoned or ignored (Nimmer 1974).

Traditional or old style diversion procedures have been criticized for the ad hoc nature of their operation. One police officer may think that a crime was committed in a family dispute and enter one or more members into the criminal justice system, while a second officer may respond to the identical circumstance with counseling on the scene. A third may extract a promise from the family to contact a social services agency as the price of nonarrest. These ad hoc judgments violate equity. A number of communities have elected to formalize the diversion procedure. Two such procedures will be discussed.

Court Employment Programs (CEPs) originally were funded in part by the federal government. Local communities, using their own unique but jurisdictionwide criteria, established alternative paths to prosecution or disposition. Social work counselors contacted the clients prior to disposition and referred them to employment and/or vocational training programs from a list of participating private employers. The counselors would seek 120–day adjournments and, if the case appeared to be headed toward resolution, the traditional path of prosecution, trial, prison and parole was cut short. A second and far more common practice was to establish local "dispute settlement services," such as New York's Family Crisis Intervention Unit. The process is the same as just described: the social services unit contacted the client and established a treatment strategy that might include individual or family counseling, or substance abuse treatment, and prosecution was postponed. If this intervention was successful, the case would not proceed through the criminal justice system.

The Juvenile Court

The juvenile courts in this country were first established in Cook County, Illinois, in 1899. The philosophy of the juvenile courts then as now is that the courts should be structured to act in the best interest of the child. In essence, juvenile courts thus have a treatment and rehabilitation orientation that sometimes dominates its adjudicative function. In adult criminal proceedings, the focus is on a specific crime. In contrast, the focus of juvenile courts is often on the psychological, physical, emotional, and educational needs of the defendant, as opposed to the child's specific guilt in a unique case. Of course, not all juvenile court judges live up to these principles and there is the ever-present danger that the juvenile court process can be subverted.

Gerald Gault, a 15-year-old youth, was tried in the Arizona juvenile court for allegedly making an obscene phone call to a neighbor. Neither the accused nor his parents was given advance notice of the charges against him. He was not informed of his legal rights and, if found guilty, could have been held within the criminal justice system until he reached the age of majority. The procedures used by the Arizona officials in the Gault proceeding were not unreasonable. They were in accord with the thinking of the times, that advance notice and formal trial are likely to stigmatize a child and violate many confidentialities. The focus of concern was of the state as a parent rather than the state as the embodiment of a social conscience. Thus, Gault was brought before the juvenile court and tried without proper safeguards.

In 1967, the case went to the Supreme Court. The majority opinion, written by Justice Abe Fortas, vehemently criticized the juvenile correctional establishment and made it clear that regardless of intent, juveniles should not be deprived of their liberty without the full set of due process rights available to an adult. This case restored to juvenile procedures safeguards that often had been ignored, including notification of charges, protection from self-incrimination, confrontation, cross-examination, and the like (Niger 1967).

The wisdom of the Gault decision is still disputed. There is no doubt that it gives minors the same basic constitutional rights enjoyed by adults. They should never have lost them. However, the return to a focus on whether or not a young person has committed a crime often masks the need for help exhibited by young persons caught up in the court processes. This case has brought about a critical reassessment of juvenile procedures and has suggested that the treatment, rehabilitative role of the juvenile correctional system must take a second stage to the process of protecting the rights of the juvenile before the criminal justice system. Youth crime is a particularly troublesome problem to society. The way in which we have addressed this in the past has been either to treat juveniles as though they were adults or to treat juveniles in such a fashion that their basic rights were not protected. The necessity to reassess this responsibility is one of the most challenging problems that social work will face in the 1980s.

THE ROLE OF SOCIAL WORK IN THE CRIMINAL JUSTICE SYSTEM

The role played by the social work community in the criminal justice system has been relegated almost exclusively to the correctional components of the system. Police agencies only recently have begun to use social workers; these social work functions have low priority in the police budgets and fall quickly to budget cuts. Adult courts have made relatively little use of professional social workers. Social workers most frequently work in the criminal justice system in the juvenile courts, rehabilitation centers, prisons, and parole programs. Such uses of social workers, however, need to be assessed within a systemwide context.

Some law enforcement experts suggest that the majority of police calls are family- or crisis-oriented rather than crime-related. When crimes occur, they often are the result of family problems—many homicides, for example, occur among family members rather than outside of the family. Increasingly, crime is associated with other social problems, such as alcohol or drug abuse.

Social workers play a number of roles in police departments. Many departments have crisis intervention teams, consisting of both police officers and social workers, that respond to domestic violence calls or calls to assist victims of rape or other violent crimes. Some police departments have established special victim assistance programs. Often staffed by social workers, these programs provide follow-up services to victims of crime, helping them work through their feelings. They also help victims locate emergency funding, shelter, employment, counseling, and other needed services.

Many police departments also have special child abuse or sex crimes units, which include social workers on their staffs. The social workers assist in investigating suspected cases, interviewing children and other individuals involved, contacting other agencies such as child welfare departments and hospitals, and arranging for emergency services when needed. A number of police departments also hire social workers to work in youth programs. In Pittsburgh, for example, social workers operate inner-city recreation programs. The Austin, Texas, police department has a social worker managing a dropout prevention program in the public schools. Such social workers provide counseling and drug and alcohol education, and serve as positive law enforcement role models to youth at risk of becoming involved in crime.

The role of the social worker in prison and prison life is very much peripheral. The social worker most likely is involved only when convicts enter or leave prison. The classification and assignment process at entry point is heavily influenced by social work practice. The pardon and parole recommendation also is influenced by social workers. The provision of service within the walls themselves, while influenced by social work knowledge, typically is done by others.

SUMMARY

In the sad history of crime and punishment, reform is always just beyond the horizon. As the chapter shows, a dreary picture is drawn from practice and current procedures. The practice of police does not deter crime, the courts do not dispense justice, the corrections system does not correct, and the parole system does not facilitate reentry into society as law-abiding citizens. Clearly, part of the problem is that insufficient funds are spent on the criminal justice system. Too much is expected for too little expended (Felkenes 1978).

Funds alone are not the problem. Despite a considerable and growing body of knowledge of what works and what does not work in police, court, and correctional settings, there is insufficient attention to integration within the system. Each unit of the system seeks to improve its operation and to clarify its mission, but at the expense of other components within the system. A more effective integration of police, court, and prison practices is required.

The failure of the criminal justice system also is due to an uncertainty of what it is expected to deliver: Is it safe streets? Is it a just system? Is it effective rehabilitation? Or, is it simple containment? Effective policies require clarity, choice, commitment, and closure. The segmented structure of the criminal justice system eschews all of these. As a consequence, during some periods society throws money at certain aspects of the overall problem; during other periods, other aspects are funded. What is absent is a careful diagnosis and prescription.

KEY TERMS

diversion	parole
etiology of crime	probation
general deterrent	specific deterrent

DISCUSSION QUESTIONS

1. To what extent is the policy dilemma of the criminal justice system reflected in the juvenile justice system? To what extent does the juvenile system have its own unique policy dilemma?
2. Which of the three views of crime, if any, is most consistent with social work practice theory?
3. If systems integration is the central problem of the criminal justice system, how can the contemporary social worker enhance the probability of that integration?

REFERENCES

Clinard, Marshall. 1967. *Criminal Behavior Systems.* New York: Holt, Reinhart and Winston.

Cullen, F. T. 1982. *Rethinking Crime and Deviance.* Totowa, N.J.: Rowman and Allanheld.

Felkenes, G. T. 1978. *The Criminal Justice System: Its Functions.* Englewood Cliffs: Prentice–Hall.

Hillman, Darrell. 1980. *The Economics of Crime.* New York: Routine Press.

Lewis, Anthony. 1964. *Gideon's Trumphet.* New York: Random House.

Niger, Allen. 1967. "The Gault Decision, Due Process and the Juvenile Court." *Federal Register* 31, no. 4: 8–18.

Nimmer, Raymond. 1974. *Diversion: The Search for Alternatives.* Chicago: American Bar Foundation.

Silberman, Charles. 1980. *Criminal Violence and Criminal Justice.* New York: Random House.

Treger, H. T. 1975. *Police and Social Work Teams.* Springfield, Ill.: Charles C. Thomas.

Wilson, James Q. 1983. *Thinking About Crime.* New York: Basic Books.

SELECTED FURTHER READINGS

Byrne, J. M., and R. J. Sampson. 1986. *The Social Ecology of Crime.* New York: Springer–Verlag.

Curtis, Lynn A. 1985. *American Violence and Public Policy.* New Haven, Conn.: Yale University Press.

Feinman, Clarice. 1986. *Women in the Criminal Justice System.* New York: Prager.

Scheingold, Stuart A. 1984. *The Politics of Law and Order: Street Crime and Public Policy.* New York: Longman.

Wilson, Colin. 1984. *A Criminal History of Mankind.* New York: Putnams.

10 Services at the Workplace

erry and Barbara Watson, both twenty-six years old, live in a small house in a rapidly deteriorating part of the city with their three children, ages two, four, and seven. Jerry works at a large automobile parts manufacturing plant, supervising a largely automated assembly line. Barbara works as a computer programmer for a large company. The Watsons' two youngest children attend a day care center, and their oldest child attends school.

Until recently, Jerry's job has been the most important aspect of his life. He is well liked as a supervisor, and in the neighborhood, his job is viewed as desirable and well paying. However, Jerry is finding that his job is a lot less meaningful to him than it has been in the past. His raises are less frequent and don't go very far in paying for necessities, let alone anything else. Most automobile companies are buying their parts from abroad, and Jerry's company increasingly is automating its operations, reducing the need for employees. There is even talk of shutting down the company. Jerry is frustrated about the lack of pay and concerned about how long his job will last. Although he knows that his wife has to work in order to make ends meet, Jerry resents the fact that she has less time for him and feels bad because he can't provide for his family on his own.

Within the last two years, Jerry has begun drinking heavily. He has beaten Barbara several times, and finds himself yelling at the children and spanking them more often. Jerry's supervisor has noticed a change in his job performance and is ready to give him formal notification that he needs to improve or risk being fired. Jerry feels tired, financially pressured, and emotionally defeated.

Barbara also finds herself strained emotionally. In addition to her job, Barbara maintains most of the responsibility for taking care of the house and the children. She gets up at 5:30 A.M. and it is always after midnight before she has everything done and can collapse into bed. Because the day care for the Watsons' two children costs over half of Barbara's take-home pay, they can't afford child care for their oldest daughter before and after school. Barbara worries about her being at home alone and makes several telephone calls to her each afternoon. Additionally, neither of the companies the Watsons work for allows employees to take sick leave when their children are sick, and all three children have been sick a lot lately. Barbara has missed six days of work in the last two months to care for her sick children. On three other occasions, Barbara has kept her oldest daughter home from school to take care of the younger children.

Recently, Barbara has been having difficulty sleeping and has had stomach problems. Her doctor prescribed tranquilizers, which she takes more often than the prescription calls for. Barbara's coworkers are worried about her but resent having to do extra work when she is absent or not able to work as quickly as she usually does. Her boss has commented on her slip in job performance. Barbara likes her job very much but also is very worried about her husband and her children. She feels guilty because her working places extra pressures on her family. Her oldest daughter is not doing well in school and Barbara is too tired to help her. All of the children vie constantly for her attention. Barbara feels caught between the pressures of work and her family, and she is becoming increasingly overwhelmed by the demands of both.

Most individuals over the age of eighteen have two major domains in which they interact: the family and the workplace. While attention to social problems and individual needs usually includes an emphasis on the family, rarely is there any focus on the relationship between the individual and the workplace. This omission has caused us to help individuals and their families less often and not as effectively as we could.

Consider again the systems perspective to understanding problems discussed in Chapter 3—the way systems overlap and interact with each other and the individuals who function within those systems. Think about this perpective in relation to the Watson family. Though until recently the Watsons have been a close-knit family, work is a primary focus in their lives. It produces the economic resources needed to provide food, clothing, shelter, and the recreational activities affordable to them. When someone meets Mr. or Mrs. Watson, a frequent first question asked is not "to what family do you belong?" but rather "where do you work?" In our society, a person's status in life is defined largely by occupation. Much of our self-respect, self-fulfillment, identity, and status is defined by the type of work that we do. Until recently, both Mr. and Mrs. Watson received positive fulfillment from their workplaces. They got along well with coworkers and received raises, recognition for jobs well done.

At first, their two jobs allowed the Watsons to support their family adequately. The positive aspects of work spilled over into the family, and they also maintained positive support within the family. However, the overlaps between the two domains began to create additional pressures for both Mr. and Mrs. Watson. Conflicts began about which came first—home or work— when there didn't seem to be enough energy for both; what to do when children were sick; how much money to spend on child care, eating out when tired or cooking meals at home, and other items; and what types of jobs and career paths to pursue when the type of work available seemed to be changing. All these had an impact on Jerry and Barbara's relationships and ability to function, both at home and at work.

For both Barbara and Jerry Watson, work presently has many negative implications. Ideally, they will seek help from some type of social service program before either their family or their jobs become jeopardized further. A social worker or other helping professional who becomes involved with the Watsons' problems cannot help them effectively if work issues are not taken into consideration.

This chapter will explore current and projected demographics regarding the work force; the changing nature and meaning of work; problems within the family and at the workplace created by work and family tensions; and the roles the workplace and social workers can play in attempting to prevent such problems from occurring or recurring.

A HISTORICAL PERSPECTIVE ON WORK AND FAMILY RELATIONSHIPS

In most Western countries, particularly in the United States, much of the basis of society can be traced to the Protestant work ethic, which stems from the Protestant Reformation of the seventeenth century. The work ethic suggests that work is the will of God and that laziness is sinful. Attitudes toward paupers during the early colonization of the United States and toward welfare recipients today stem from the impact of the work ethic on our society.

For women, however, the emphasis was different; the primary role of women was to maintain the family and to support the ability of men in the family to work outside the home. Until the 1970s, this pattern changed only during wartime, when women were needed in the factories because men were away at war. However, as soon as peace returned, women returned home and men to the workplace. Those women who did work outside of the home, because of either necessity or interest or both, often were considered to be outside of their appropriate role. It is interesting to note, for example, that until the 1970s, most studies regarding work focused on the negative impact of the *unemployed man* on his family, or on the negative impact of the *employed woman* on her family (Bronfenbrenner & Crouter 1982).

Within recent years, much has changed in regard to the relationship between the individual and the workplace. Probably the biggest change has been due to the large numbers of women who are working, including those with children. Other changes have taken place as well. Individuals today expect more from the workplace then just a paycheck: recognition, a say in decision making, benefits, flexible working hours. Numerous studies have focused on the alienation of some workers and the fact that many workers today put other priorities ahead of their jobs. Additional problems receiving increased attention from the workplace include alcoholism and drug abuse; increased costs of health care and other benefits; how to provide maternity, paternity, and sick leave; and the overall increase in stress of employees (Kanter 1977). Figure 10–1 shows some trends, past and future, with regard to employee characteristics of households.

A growing number of experts view the relationiship between work and family life as one of the most critical policy issues to be addressed during the next decade. In many instances, special social services and other programs have been established within the workplace to assist employees and their families in order to maintain or increase productivity.

Industrial social work (also called occupational social work) has emerged as a growing field for social workers. By applying a systems perspective, social workers have the potential to play a major role in strengthening relationships between the individual, the family, and the workplace.

THE CHANGING NATURE OF THE WORK FORCE

The majority of today's work-related programs and policies are based on work and family demographics as they existed during the 1950s: an almost totally male work force and a male breadwinner supporting his stay-at-home wife and 2.6 children. However, in 1985 only about 10 percent of American families could be classified this way. Over 50 percent of two-parent families have *both* parents employed full-time within the work force. Over 50 percent of all working women have children, and over half of those working women have children under six years of age. In 1982, 42 percent of women with children under one year of age were employed outside the home. Over half of all women are now working, with women accounting for over 40 percent of the total work force (U.S. Bureau of Labor Statistics 1984).

It is estimated that by 1990, 75 percent of all women of child-bearing age will be employed beyond the family setting, and that slightly over half the labor force will be female (Children's Defense Fund 1982). As Figure 10–2 indicates, the increase in the number of women employed outside of the family has been fairly sudden, leaving both employers and families unprepared to deal adequately with the resulting implications.

Many individuals argue that the reason for this phenomenon has been primarily economic; that the majority of women work as an economic necessity rather than by choice. Others argue that the women's movement, and the

Figure 10–1
**Employment
Characteristics
of Households,
1960, 1975, and
1990**

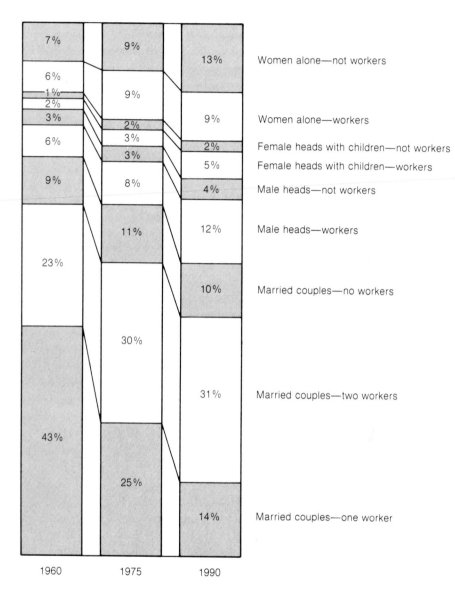

Source: Masnick, G. and M.J. Bane. *The Nation's Families: 1960–1990.* Cambridge, Mass. Joint Center for Urban Studies at MIT and Harvard University, 1980.

realization that women have choices open to them other than remaining at home, has created this shift. Still others counter that the women's movement was a result of women being forced to enter the work force, and, once getting there and dealing with unfair conditions, began lobbying for changes and more options from which to choose. Still others argue that more women are working because of the increased emphasis on self-fulfillment (the "me" generation) and consumption among both genders.

Figure 10–2
Labor Force Participation Rates for Married Women in the United States, 1950–1984

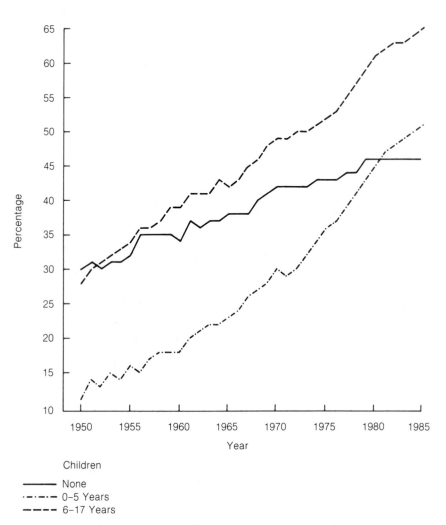

Source: U.S. Department of Commerce, Bureau of the Census. *Current Population Survey.* March 1950–1984.

Whatever the reason or reasons for the increased number of women in the labor force, this factor more than any other has focused attention on the relationship between work and family. As Kanter (1977) explains, when only one family member left the home each day and operated within the work system, there was less necessity for overlap or interaction between the work and family systems, and it was fairly easy to keep them separate. However, when two family members become involved in the work system, it is impossible to keep the two systems separate.

Other demographic shifts require special attention as well. In 1980, 20 percent of all families in the United States were one-parent families, most headed by women (Children's Defense Fund 1982). Nationally, women in general earn less than their male counterparts in the work force. For every dollar that a man earns, a woman earns sixty-four cents. In 1981, the 42 million working husbands in the U.S. averaged $20,870 in income, while the average earnings for the 27.7 million working wives was $8,600. The average income for married couples was $25,550. Economically, single-parent families headed by women fare much worse than other families. Persons living in over half of the single-parent female-headed households in the United States live in poverty and earn an average income that is 50 percent of the median of male-headed households (U.S. Bureau of the Census 1984).

For these families, issues such as affordable child care, flexible working hours, transportation to and from work, and job training, in addition to salary and benefits, are crucial. For their employers, absenteeism and tardiness, sick leave, and employee stress become factors no matter how competent and hard working their employees are.

The increase in divorce, the fact that Americans are more mobile than in the past, and the fact that women are living longer than their spouses have also resulted in an increased number of individuals who live alone. Recent figures indicate that 25 percent of all Americans live alone. By 1990, this percentage is expected to increase significantly (Masnick & Bane 1980). There also is a shift in the age of today's workers. Nearly half of today's work force is less than 35 years of age, and almost one-fourth, between 16 and 24. This trend toward a younger work force has been coupled with many older workers taking early retirement, or not seeking other employment after retirement due to social security regulations that place restrictions on earning above a certain amount. However, problems in financing social security may reverse these trends. As older individuals remain healthier for longer periods of time, mandatory retirement laws also may change and elective retirement may decline. Similarly, as increased numbers of women in the work force grow older, especially since women enjoy better health than men as they age, they, too, are more likely to remain in the work force.

Given these trends, the potential will increase for large numbers of young, relatively inexperienced workers entering the workplace with values and expectations different than those of the older members of the work force. Because younger workers are more likely to be better educated, and command lower wages initially, workplaces may be encouraged to hire the young at the expense of the old. Given the large numbers of older workers in top-level positions and the fact that many companies have streamlined their operations and eliminated many upper and middle management positions, futurists are projecting that newer workers will have fewer opportunities for promotion than their older counterparts have enjoyed in the past.

The types of jobs in which workers are employed also have changed. In the past, the majority of workers have been employed in blue-collar jobs. However, as the United States has shifted from a manufacturing-based society to a services-based society (Katzell 1979), more and more workers are employed in white collar jobs. In 1984, over 50 percent of the work force was in white-collar jobs (U.S. Bureau of Labor Statistics 1984). Additionally, today's workers also are much better educated than in the past. Most have high school degrees; one-third have attended at least one year of college; and one-sixth have college degrees. As a result, the younger members of today's work force earn a significantly higher salary than older workers earned at the same age, thereby increasing salary expectations for this age group (Stapleton & Young 1984).

The ethnic composition of the workforce also has changed, with many more nonwhites being hired, particularly in clerical, blue-collar, and service positions. In some areas, undocumented aliens from Mexico and South and Central American countries also have contributed to the expansion of the work force; one sociologist estimates that undocumented workers account for over 30 percent of the growth in the work force attributed to ethnic minorities (Freeman 1979).

The shift in jobs away from major industrial centers in the North and East to the Sunbelt and West Coast states, as well as the move away from small agricultural production, also has had a significant impact on the work force and their families. Many individuals and families who have remained in industrial centers or farm areas have been forced to take lower paying jobs or to receive financial assistance for the first time in their lives. They often have lost their homes, farms, and businesses, and depleted their savings, and face an unpredictable future.

THE CHANGING NATURE OF WORK

Futurists disagree when discussing projections regarding the workplace of the future. Some speculate that the heavy decline in manufacturing jobs will be counterbalanced by increases in service jobs, including the provision of childcare and care of the aging, since working individuals will be unable to provide these supports to either their children or their parents. Others project fewer jobs due to automation and the general decline of labor-intensive industries (Etzioni 1984; Friedman 1983; Galambos 1984; Katzell 1979). Such issues have important implications when addressing employee concerns and the roles social workers and others can play in dealing with them. These contradictory projections make it difficult to predict accurately the future needs of employees and their families, how those needs will surface at the workplace, and which strategies are most likely to meet them.

Although employed individuals often bring numerous problems to their families and vice versa, the ramifications of unemployment are far more serious. Layoffs and unemployment are expected to increase as the nature of work continues to change. Because work not only provides economic support to families but is a basic definition of an individual's self-worth, increased unemployment is an issue of national concern. Studies show that unemployment and low economic status are associated with poor family cohesion and family deterioration (Bronfenbrenner & Crouter 1982).

Many individuals and their families faced with unemployment or underemployment relocate to a supposedly more opportune area. Such areas, however, usually are largely unprepared to address the many needs created by a rapidly expanding population. Housing and other necessities are unavailable or more expensive than anticipated; the availability of work for certain types of workers is inflated or exaggerated; and transportation, utilities, and education are often lacking or underdeveloped. The absence of support from family and friends also plagues those relocating; and social services agencies, overwhelmed by the population influx, are unable to provide resources to meet many employee and family needs.

For employees and their families who remain in unproductive areas, as well as for those who relocate to new areas, stress increases significantly. Social services agencies in these areas report significant increases in suicides, family violence, alcoholism and drug abuse, marital problems, juvenile delinquency, and other mental health problems. They also report significant increases in family financial problems and pressures.

THE CHANGING WORK FORCE: ATTITUDES AND VALUES

Demographic changes in the work force have had a considerable impact on changing attitudes and values toward work. While most employees continue to be fairly satisfied with their jobs, there is a growing discontent among certain segments of the labor force over the nature and meaning of work. Employees today are experiencing a new type of worker, described by one policy analyst, Daniel Yankelovich (1979), as the *new breed worker*. Yankelovich contrasts today's worker with the "organization man" described by Theodore Whyte in the 1950s (1956). (This term would be considered sexist today, but was appropriate at that time since the work force was primarily male.) Whyte's organization man was one who put the needs of the organization for which he worked above all else. He came to the company intending to remain there for his entire career, worked long hours, willingly traveled and relocated for the company, and viewed his paycheck as his primary reward for his loyalty and hard work.

As Yankelovich and others note, today's worker is much different from Whyte's organization man. Concerns about quality of life and a willingness to express such concerns to employers have forced an emphasis on additional incentives beyond the paycheck. An insistence on individual accomplishment and self-fulfillment, priorities given to interests outside of the workplace, and personal recognition on the job suggests that employees expect work to have additional meaning beyond the extrinsic rewards of a paycheck. Not only is the meaning of work changing, but it must be viewed differently for different individuals. A recent study conducted by Yankelovich for *Working Woman* magazine found that men viewed the meaning of work and satisfaction with their jobs along two dimensions, salary and a say in decisions. Women, however, viewed job satisfaction among six different dimensions, primarily related to relationships with and recognition from coworkers and supervisors (Kagan 1983).

Bureaucratization of the workplace has resulted in a lack of clarity regarding the self-identity of individuals and what should be valued most in a person's life: job as was true for individuals in the past, or family, or one's self and one's own needs. Less support from family members and lack of time to develop supportive relationships with others have resulted in a growing number of individuals who maintain a strong identity with the workplace and expect the majority of their needs to be met by their work. One recent study found that employees were more likely to seek help when dealing with problems, including marital and other family problems, from coworkers than from neighbors or family members (Anderson 1985).

In addition to the increased expectations that the workplace should meet personal needs, a growing number of younger, more educated workers expect high salaries, rapid promotions, and challenging jobs (Katzell 1979). Because of increased acceptance of alternate life-styles and the fact that the cost of refusing a job is reduced due to an extensive social welfare system and the large number of families where more than one individual is employed, Yankelovich and others suggest that for many workers, the traditional work ethic has diminished significantly.

The changes in the types of workers in today's work force and their attitudes toward work have occurred so rapidly that the workplace, for the most part, has been unable to adjust at a comparable pace. Many workplaces still expect the loyalty of the organization man to which they were accustomed, and also expect the employee's wife and 2.6 children to remain at home and out of the realm of the workplace.

IMPLICATIONS FOR EMPLOYEES AND THEIR FAMILIES

Most of the attention relating to changes in the types of individuals now in the workplace has been directed toward the impact on the family rather than on the workplace. The majority of this attention has been focused on two-parent families. As we have suggested earlier it is when multiple members of the family work that the work and family domains begin to overlap and, in many instances, create conflict. Such conflicts result in lack of time for individuals for themselves and family members; stress caused by balancing work and family schedules and priorities; problems in obtaining adequate childcare and other parenting issues; feelings of isolation due to lack of time and energy to develop friends and support systems; and financial difficulties (Kamerman & Hayes 1982; Kanter 1977; Piotrkowski 1978).

Several studies focusing on the impact of work on family life have stemmed from Wilensky's (1960) suggestion that people experience a **spillover effect,** where feelings, attitudes, and behaviors from the workplace spill over into leisure life and vice versa. Evans and Bartolome (1980), suggest five possible work–family relationships:

1. *Spillover Effect,* where one domain affects the other in either a positive or negative way—for example, if you really like your job, this will add satisfaction to your family life;

2. *Independent,* where work and family life exist side by side but are independent from each other—making it possible to be satisfied and successful with your job but not your family, for example;

3. *Conflict,* where work and family are in conflict with each other and cannot be reconciled. In a conflict relationship, sacrifices are required in one area in order to be satisfied and successful in the other—for example, spending less time at home with family members in order to be successful at your job;

4. *Instrumental,* where one domain is primarily a means to obtain something for the other—for example, a job is seen only as a way to earn money to maintain a satisfying family life;

5. *Compensation,* where one domain is a way of making up for what is missing in another—for example, a recently divorced man puts all of his energies into his job, works long hours, and socializes only with coworkers.

In helping both employees and their family members understand how they can better balance work and family life, it is useful for social workers and other helping professionals to help them look at how they view their work-family relationships.

When examining the impact of work on the individual and family, one additional perspective that deserves attention is the importance of life events. Rapoport and Rapoport (1980) advocate the use of a life-span model, in which the meaning of work and family changes as individuals move through childhood, adolescence, youth, adulthood, mid-life, and old age. Individuals often are pressured to give full attention to both work and family life at the same period of life—for example, learning and beginning a successful career at the same time that they have just married and are beginning to have children. Some policy analysts suggest that companies should consider not focusing on promotions and moves up the career ladder for their employees until they are middle-aged and have already dealt with the childrearing years. The importance of looking at life span can also be seen when focusing on the large number of individuals who make mid-life career changes, not because they are necessarily just unhappy with their jobs, but because they are dealing with personal developmental issues that are age-related.

The majority of attention given to the impact of work on the family has been devoted to working wives and mothers. For all families where mothers work, the impact on the family, particularly the children, is an issue that has been well-researched. Current findings indicate that, taken by itself, a mother's employment outside the home has no negative effects on the child. Factors that may affect children of working mothers include the quality of childcare which the child receives while the mother is working; the overall stability of the family itself; the type of employment; the socioeconomic status of the family; and the quality and quantity of time from either parent spent with the child (Bronfenbrenner & Crouter 1982).

Not surprisingly, the majority of studies focusing on work and family issues find that increased stress on the employed family member and the family itself is the factor most often identified by those individuals studied. Some mental health experts suggest that the tremendous increase in the number of individuals seeking mental health services can be attributed to increased pressures faced by more and more individuals trying to balance the demands of job and family.

Recent studies have also focused on **dual-career families,** particularly in relation to the changes in family roles and responsibilities when both parents work. Although most studies find that both parents in dual-career families experience stress and less time for themselves and family members, it is the wives and mothers who feel these pressures the most. While in many dual-career families, husbands share more in childrearing responsibilities, the majority of childrearing responsibility still falls on the wife. Studies also show that although husbands take on more of the parenting tasks, housekeeping responsibilities fall almost totally on the wives, even among families where both husbands and wives view themselves as being less traditional in the division of household tasks than other couples (Klein 1983). Both men and women from dual-career families list strengths as being additional income, greater opportunities for meaningful communication and growth because both individuals are stimulated by jobs, and more sharing in parenting roles. However, women in such families face numerous role conflicts, citing lack of time to accomplish tasks both at home and at work, lack of time for self, lack of time for spouse, and lack of time for children as major concerns. Furthermore, some studies find that career families are not having as many children as in the past. When families do have children, childbearing occurs within a shorter span of years so that parents can continue working (Portner 1978).

In addition to increased stress, individual and family finances is another area of work-family problems. Even many families where both parents are employed outside of the home are below or barely above the poverty level. Financial pressures are especially great for women, minorities, and other workers less likely to be well educated or trained and, as a result, more likely to be employed in low-paying jobs. Those individuals who are single parents (also most likely to be women and minorities) are especially vulnerable to financial pressures. Additionally, 25 percent of the U.S. work force is not covered by employee health insurance. These employees, more likely to be women and minorities, have eight times as many dependents as individuals who are covered by insurance. When these families do have health crises, they are likely to face severe financial problems. For women employees who become pregnant, maternity leave (without pay) is only available 29 percent of the time. Paid vacations, taken for granted by most individuals, are unavailable to 20 percent of the work force (Kamerman & Kingston 1982).

Accidents and other on-the-job health hazards create additional stresses for employees and their families. Coal miners whose daily contact with coal dust results in black lung disease; workers in chemical plants who contract cancer and miscarry or produce children born with congenital deformities; and construction workers who may be hurt by heavy equipment place themselves and their families in jeopardy. A number of individuals have successfully sued employers for mental anguish experienced by themselves and their families as a result of such situations.

Nationally, an estimated 5.2 million children under the age of 14 are without adequate child care while parents work. Often, infants and toddlers are left sleeping alone at night by working parents. It is not unusual for children ages four and five to be left at home alone for long periods of time, and children as young as eight are often left in charge of much younger children. Increased numbers of children are being injured, often fatally, as a result of fire or other accidents while left unsupervised by working parents. In New York recently, five children five years old and younger died in a fire. They had been left alone in a locked apartment while their mother worked as a waitress. The same day in Texas, a twelve-year-old girl, left in charge of her ten-year-old brother while her parents worked, heard a noise in the front yard and, becoming scared, got out her father's gun. The gun went off accidentally, killing her younger brother. The noise was being made by the family dog. Increases in vandalism and other youth-related delinquent acts, as well as increases in teen-age pregnancy, are being attributed partly to the lack of supervision provided to adolescents while their parents work.

Escalating divorce rates and numbers of individuals living alone have left the affiliational needs of many individuals largely unmet. Increasingly, employees and their families, lacking a support system and unable to cope with life's pressures, succumb to divorce, family violence, alcoholism or drug abuse, suicide, or to other health or emotional problems. A study conducted for the IBM Corporation found that 50 percent of individuals seen by the company's medical department had problems that were emotional or psychological in nature (Compucare Corporation 1981). For workers and their families facing such pressures, however, options often are limited. Many individuals work because they have to in order to support their families, often as the sole source of support for those families. For those who earn low wages and cannot rely on other family members for emotional support or to meet family needs such as childcare, the toll on them and their families can be extensive. Even for those who have more options, such as being able to afford childcare or rely on relatives, or who work different hours than other family members, balancing work and family pressures is still difficult.

IMPLICATIONS FOR THE WORKPLACE

The problems that have an impact on the individual employee and his or her family also have a significant effect on the workplace. The United States is currently ranked eighth in productivity among Western countries. Productivity in the private sector decreased from 3.2 percent in 1965 to 1.8 percent in 1979, but has increased slightly since 1980 (U.S. Bureau of Labor Statistics 1984). Job turnover, absenteeism, and other costs created by employee and family problems are expensive to both the workplace and the consumer, who ultimately is forced to absorb these costs.

A 1975 study determined that a typical manufacturing company invested an average cost of over $1000 per worker during the first year of employment for training. The turnover rate was as high as 31 percent, resulting in a substantial loss of dollars for those companies each time an employee left. Of those individuals who left the companies, 76 percent listed childcare problems as the major reason for leaving, while 95 percent listed it as either the first or second reason (Texas Industrial Commission 1977). Absenteeism and lost work time to deal with parenting issues are also costly to employers; a number of Houston, Texas, companies indicate that their telephone lines are completely tied up between three and four o'clock in the afternoon when children arrive home from school (University of Texas Center for Social Work Research 1983).

Although childcare problems have received much attention in relation to the workplace in recent years with the increased numbers of mothers in the work force, other employee problems are even more costly. In 1980, lost productivity due to alcoholism in the United States totaled $30.1 billion. Drug abuse cost $8.3 billion in productivity, and other mental health problems cost $25.8 billion (U.S. Department of Health, Education, and Welfare 1980). Forty percent of industrial fatalities and 47 percent of industrial accidents are related to alcohol use, and the average cost of one employee grievance relating to poor job performance due to alcoholism is over $1500. At General Motors Corporation, absenteeism costs $1 billion each year, and costs related to alcohol, drug abuse, and other mental health problems add hundreds of dollars to the costs of each automobile. One recent study found that consumers pay an additional $237 per automobile just due to alcohol alone (Compucare Corporation 1981). Such costs are not only attributed to the individual with the problem; one study found that individuals from families where one person was an alcoholic were absent from work ten times more often than persons from families where alcohol was not known to be a problem (Hopson 1977).

Many studies suggest that increased individual and family problems that are emotionally based exact a heavy toll on both the individual and the workplace in relation to health care costs. In 1983, fringe benefits accounted for almost 37 percent of salaries and wages paid by employers in the United States. The average hourly worker received benefits worth $7,582 in that year (U.S. Chamber of Commerce 1984). Wages increased 20 percent between 1969 and 1984, and benefits increased 171 percent (U.S. Bureau of Labor Statistics, 1984). The high cost of health care is a major issue for employers. Many are not only increasing employee-paid costs of health care but are also reducing the extent of benefits available.

The fact that more and more workers are looking to the workplace to meet affiliational needs has created additional problems on the job. Coworkers and supervisors find themselves spending increased amounts of worktime listening

Employee problems in the workplace are costly in monetary and human terms.

to employee problems, ranging from marital disputes to more serious problems such as alcoholism, drug abuse, and spouse abuse. A supervisor for a large company who oversees fifteen employees recently noted that in one day she had helped find temporary shelter for a woman employee who had been beaten the previous night by her husband, listened to another employee whose son was in jail for cocaine abuse and theft and referred him to a counseling center, confronted an employee regarding a job error and learned that he was in the midst of a divorce from a twenty-five-year marriage, and covered for another worker who had to leave early because she had a sick child.

ADDRESSING WORK AND FAMILY PROBLEMS: WHOSE RESPONSIBILITY?

Given the serious costs of employee and family-related problems to workers, their families, and the workplace, many groups have become involved in developing strategies to address these problems. Social services counselors are much more likely to address factors related to the job when working with individuals and family members than they have in the past. Many communities have developed task forces and programs to provide affordable childcare and transportation for employees. A number of public schools have established before- and after-school childcare programs, and some schools schedule parent-teacher conferences and other events during evening hours so that most working parents can attend. Social services agencies in some communities have come into the workplace to provide noon-time seminars and other programs relating to topics such as coping with divorce, alcoholism and drug abuse, and parenting.

A growing number of employers have also realized that they have a social responsibility to address such problems. Some companies have established **Employee Assistance Programs (EAPs),** which provide counseling and other social services to employees, and often their families, through the company. Others have expanded health coverage to cover alcoholism, drug abuse and mental health counseling, and dental care. A number of both public and private employers have established flexible working hours for their employees, sharing of jobs, and the creation of permanent part-time jobs. Still other employers have stress reduction and health promotion programs, including on-site fitness centers where employees and their families can exercise. Some employers also provide on-site childcare for employees, or have established other programs that provide childcare; several companies have even established special programs that provide care for school-age children during the summer or when the children are sick.

EMPLOYEE ASSISTANCE PROGRAMS

Nationally, over 5000 organizations have established formal employee assistance programs (EAPs) to provide counseling to their employees. Originally, these programs were established to provide counseling and treatment for employees with alcohol problems and usually employed a recovered alcoholic, often one of the company's own employees, as the program coordinator. Today, a wide variety of EAPs are available. While many are still primarily alcohol-related, others are "broad-brush" programs, addressing a wide range of employee problems, including divorce, child-rearing, spouse abuse, and financial problems (Shain & Groeneveld 1979).

A number of EAPs have a full-time coordinator employed by the company who trains supervisors in how to recognize troubled employees and make referrals and publicizes the program within the company. This coordinator provides the initial screening of employees to ensure that the EAP services are appropriate; however, a referral is then made to a contracting social services agency outside of the company that provides the services. In other instances, the coordinator oversees an "in-house" EAP, where the majority of services, including counseling, are provided directly by company employees, often social workers. Studies have found such programs to reduce employee absenteeism as well as health care costs and increase employee productivity. General Motors Corporation found that it saved $3700 per year for each employee successfully enrolled in its EAP, or a total of $37 million in a single year alone (Compucare Corporation 1981).

CHILDCARE PROGRAMS

Companies are responding to the needs of employees in other ways. Many organizations have helped to establish a variety of childcare programs. In some instances, companies have established on-site childcare programs, allowing parents to bring children to the program on their way to work, to see them during their lunch periods, and to be close by if a child should become sick. Other companies have worked with communities in establishing childcare referral systems, helping employees to locate appropriate childcare that best meets individual needs. Some companies provide vouchers for childcare, allowing parents to contribute a portion of their employee benefits for child care of their choice. Others provide a variety of after-school and summer childcare programs and programs for sick children. One company, realizing the amount of money lost every time a child is sick, provides nurses to go to parents' homes and care for children, paying a portion of the cost for this service.

While less well-documented, childcare programs appear cost-effective to employers. The turnover rate for one company was 1.8 percent for those employees with children in its childcare program compared to 6.4 percent for employees with no children enrolled. One company in Houston, Texas, reported saving 3700 hours in absenteeism in one year after its childcare program was established. The company had a waiting list of potential job applicants, whereas a similar company without child care was having difficulty recruiting workers (Center for Social Work Research 1983). Still, nationally, only about 1800 organizations provide or assist in the provision of child care for their employees. About half of these are hospitals (Friedman 1985). Although a limited number of worksites have special provisions for sick children, most organizations do not even allow employees to take personal leave time when children are sick. A study conducted in 1980 by the Conference Board, a national organization that focuses on workplace issues and programs, found that only 13 percent of U.S. companies provide personal leave time when children are sick.

Some firms have implemented other programs to increase productivity, including flexible work schedules, health and wellness programs, transportation systems, recreation teams, and employee work groups that work together to improve the workplace and its environment. Co-workers also play an important role in lending support to other employees and their families. Many coworkers are turning to their fellow employees for support during times of crisis. Help with childcare, transportation, advice about coping with teen-agers or divorce—all these are types of assistance provided increasingly by coworkers rather than neighbors, friends, or relatives.

SOCIAL WORK IN THE WORKPLACE

One of the areas in which the profession of social work is expanding is in the provision of social services in the workplace. Termed *industrial social work* or *occupational social work,* many view this specialization in social work as relatively new; however, this is not the case. In fact, it is interesting to note that the profession of social work owes its name to industry. The term *social work,* introduced in the United States in the early 1890s apparently as a direct translation of the German phrase *arbeiten sozial,* was used to refer to housing, canteens, health care, and other resources provided to employees by Krupp munitions plants to support the industrial work force (Carter 1977). Although in many other countries, industry is the largest field in which social workers practice, in the United States industrial social work developed and was in effect between 1890 and 1920, then was largely dormant until the 1970s.

The development of welfare and social work programs in industry began with mutual aid societies and volunteer programs established as a result of many of the progressive reform movements during the late 1800s and early 1900s. Positions of "social secretary," "welfare manager," or "welfare secretary" existed in many American industries, including textile mills in the South, Kimberly Clark, and International Harvester.

Welfare secretaries had backgrounds primarily in religious or humanitarian work, with little previous experience in either social work or industry. In general, they were responsible for overseeing the physical welfare (safety, health, sanitation, and housing), cultural welfare (recreation, libraries, and education programs), economic welfare (loans, pensions, rehabilitation, hiring, and firing), and personal welfare, which included social work (then called *case work*) with employees and their families (Carter 1977).

A Bureau of Labor Statistics survey reported that by 1926, 80 percent of the 1500 largest companies in the United States had at least one type of welfare program and about half had comprehensive programs. Sociologist Teresa Haveren recently reviewed old records and conducted a historical study of work and family relationships at the Amoskeag Textile Mill in New Hampshire in the late 1800s and early 1900s. The company, like many other industries during that time period, provided corporate housing close to the mill for working parents; boarding houses for young single employees; English, sewing, cooking, and gardening classes; nurses who provided instruction in housekeeping, health care, and medical aid and visited the sick and elderly regularly to provide food and assistance; a charity department to provide needy families with clothing, food, and coal and assistance to widows with large families if their husbands died or were injured on the job or were former employees; a hospital ward for employees injured on the job; a dentist for employees' families; a childcare program and kindergarten; a children's playground with attendants to supervise the children; a swimming pool and ice skating rink; an Americanization program; an athletic field and showers; lectures, concerts, and fairs; and a Boy Scouts program (Haveren 1982). While many companies were generous with assistance, services were denied if an individual refused to work. Thus, the system was designed to encourage loyalty to the organization. As many industries employed entire families, often in the same work unit, it can also be argued that this system made it less difficult for workers to make the transition from family to factory, with many family members seeing little difference between work life and family life.

During the late 1920s, opposition to these programs came from a number of fronts, including employees themselves. Many employees were immigrants, including women. As they became more acculturated within the United States, they saw such welfare programs as paternalistic. The rise of the labor movement also increased negativism toward corporate welfare programs.

Labor leaders considered such programs antiunion, believing that the welfare secretary diffused employee unrest without bringing about changes that would improve working conditions for employees. The emergence of scientific management of the workplace turned the focus to improving efficiency of workers. Later, scientific management and welfare work merged into a new field, personnel management. At the same time, public and private social services agencies became more prevalent, decreasing the need for business to provide the many services they had previously provided. Thus, corporate welfare programs declined.

During World War II, The National Maritime Union and United Seaman's Service provided an extensive industrial social work program, providing assistance to the families of the more than 5000 union members who had been killed during the war. Because unions feared social workers hired by companies would not be sympathetic to unions, other unions initiated industrial social work programs. Until recently, unions were responsible for the majority of industrial social work programs in the United States (Carter 1977).

Historically, industrial social work has served a variety of functions in industry. Profit often has been a major motivation of employers who provided social work services, hoping that these services would increase productivity and morale in the same way that fringe benefits have been used. However, social workers have affected the workplace in addition to providing social services to employees and their families. Social work also has played a role in integrating new groups of inexperienced workers such as women, minorities, and immigrants into the work world; providing affirmative action consultation; strengthening relationships between the corporate world and the community; and in organizational development through redesign of work to make the workplace more humane for employees. In addition to expertise in working with troubled individuals and families, social workers also are trained in the art of effective communication and negotiation, skills that lend themselves well to advocating for employee needs or working to improve conditions within a workplace or understanding between employees and employers.

It seems logical that social workers should become more actively involved in the workplace. Industrial social work lends itself to the provision of services within a natural setting—the majority of adults, after all, are employed. The opportunity for a universal service delivery system that goes beyond services to the poor, the elderly, and the sick also is ideal for the provision of preventive services, an area that is almost negligible from the broader perspective of total services provided.

While individuals with specializations in fields other than social work, such as personnel management and industrial psychology, also are employed in human relations capacities in business, such as in personnel or employee counseling positions, social work as a profession is strengthening its interests and capabilities in the area of industrial social work (see Box 10–1). The two major professional bodies that guide the profession, the National Association of Social Workers and the Council on Social Work Education, have established task forces, developed publications, and held conferences that focus on industrial social work. In some instances, these programs are interdisciplinary in nature and operate jointly with other departments such as business administration. All programs provide future industrial social workers with knowledge and skill in dealing with alcoholism and drug abuse, marriage and family problems, and other individual and family problems. They also offer courses relevant to working in organizations and the corporate world. To be successful in the workplace, social workers need additional knowledge and skill in business principles, planning and management, marketing, financial management, personnel administration, family counseling, and organizational behavior. Students in industrial social work programs also are placed in field internships in corporations, where they work directly with troubled employees and their families or are involved in administration and planning activities within the corporation.

Much of the focus of industrial social work to date has been on the client as a worker. Although it is important that social work as a profession recognize the importance of work within the individual's life, the emphasis of industrial social work has been primarily at the individual casework level through employee assistance programs and other forms of one-to-one counseling or information and referral services. The central focus appears to be on the relationships of work to emotional problems. Social workers have also played a role in addressing work-related social policy issues such as the appropriate division between corporate and social welfare sectors in the provision of social services; the relationships between work and family roles for men and women; the impact of affirmative action programs on women, minorities and disabled individuals; and unemployment. However, little attention has been given to the role social work might play from an organizational change perspective.

Because social workers operate from a systems perspective, focusing on the interaction between the individual and his or her environment, they are well

Box 10–1
The Industrial
Social Worker

A job description for an industrial social worker might include the following:

> Counseling and carrying out activities with troubled employees and their families to assist them with their personal problems and to achieve maintenance of their productive performance;
>
> Advising on the use of community services to meet client needs and establishing linkages with such programs;
>
> Training front line personnel to enable them to (1) identify when changes in job performance warrant referral to a social service unit and (2) carry out an appropriate approach to the employee that will result in such referral;
>
> Developing and overseeing the operation of a management information system, which will record service information and provide data for analysis of the unit's program;
>
> Developing a plan for future programmatic direction and staffing of the industrial social work program;
>
> Offering consultation to management decision makers concerning human resource policy;
>
> Helping to initiate health, welfare, recreational, or educational programs for employees;
>
> Advising on corporate giving and on organizational positions in relation to pending social welfare legislation.

From S. Akabas, and P. Kurzman, "The Industrial Social Welfare Specialist: What's So Special?" In S. Akabas and P. Kurzman, eds. *Work, Workers, and Work Organizations: A View From Social Work,* pp. 201–202. Englewood Cliffs, N.J.: Prentice–Hall, 1982.

equipped to develop strategies of intervention at a variety of levels of systems within which the individual functions (see Box 10–2). Consider again, for example, the Watson family discussed at the beginning of this chapter. Social work intervention could include individual counseling for Jerry and Barbara Watson relating to their respective jobs. However, because the problems which the Watsons face are associated with their relationship to each other, a social worker might propose marital counseling for the couple, seeing both of them together. Remember, though, that the Watson children also were having difficulties within the family. It also might be appropriate for a social worker to provide counseling for the entire Watson family.

Other individuals within the systems in which the Watsons operate may need to be involved, too. Coworkers and supervisors with whom the Watsons interact may be exacerbating their problems. The oldest daughter's teacher also

Box 10–2
Assessment of
Problem(s)

A comprehensive social worker's assessment of a worker's problem(s)
should include the following:

I.   Worker
   A.   Work History
   B.   Current Position—Occupation, Hours, Salary, Fringe Benefits
   C.   Job Duties and Responsibilities
   D.   Adequacy of Job Performance
   E.   Degree and Type of Autonomy and Control in Work Role
   F.   Relationships with Colleagues, Supervisors, Subordinates
   G.   Specific Work Strains and Satisfactions
   H.   Career Goals
   I.   Self–Concept as a Worker

II.   Work Organization
   A.   Size, Location, Function, Physical Setting
   B.   General Ambiance
   C.   Organizational Structure
   D.   Opportunities Provided Worker for Advancement
   E.   Expectations re Loyalty, Performance, etc.

III.   Interface Between Work and Family
   A.   Mesh between Worker's Time and Family Time
   B.   Adequacy of Income to Meet Personal and Family Needs
   C.   Degree to which Work Role and Responsibilities Intrude on
       Family Life
   D.   Degree to which Family Roles and Responsibilities Intrude on
       Work Life
   E.   Degree to which Work Role Meets Expectations of Significant
       Others, e.g., Spouse, Children, Family of Origin, Friends
   F.   Overlap between Work and Leisure Activities

From J. Cohen and B. McGowan, "What Do You Do?" An Inquiry into the Potential of
Work–Related Research. In S. Akabas and P. Kurzman, eds., *Work, Workers and Work Organizations: A View from Social Work*, pp. 126–27. Englewood Cliffs, N.J.: Prentice–Hall, 1982.

might be helpful in providing insight into the girl's problems. A social worker
might wish to work with these individuals in addition to the Watsons, to help
others with whom they interact be more supportive of their needs. There may
also be other resources within the community that the social worker might
refer the Watsons to a low cost after-school childcare or recreational program
for the daughter; parenting classes; Alcoholics Anonymous; a battered wom-
en's program.

The role of a social worker can go beyond the individual and family intervention level. Perhaps, the social worker might realize that there are numerous individuals at the workplace experiencing the same kinds of problems as the Watsons. The social worker might establish support groups for employees with similar concerns and needs. An additional role of the social worker could be to advocate with management for company policies that better support the needs of employees like the Watsons. The social worker might work with others within the workplace to implement childcare programs, flexible work hours, and adequate sick leave policies and, perhaps, also work with others beyond the workplace to develop state and federal legislation to mandate policies that are more supportive of employees and their families, such as maternity leave, and sick leave policies that incorporate illness among family members.

The University of Pittsburgh has developed three models of service for industrial social workers that incorporate a variety of roles inherent to the profession of social work. The first model, the *employee service model,* focuses primarily on the micro level of the systems within which employees and their families function. In this model, social work functions include counseling employees and their families; providing educational programs to employees; referring employees to other agencies; implementing recreational programs; consulting with management regarding individual employee problems; and training supervisors in recognizing and dealing appropriately with employee problems.

The second model, the *consumer service model,* focuses on intervention at a broader level within the same systems. This model views employees as consumers and assists them in identifying needs and advocating to get those needs met. Social workers work with consumers-employees in assessing their needs; in developing strategies to best meet the needs identified; identifying and providing community resources to meet the needs; serving as a liaison between consumer-employee groups and social services agencies; and developing outreach programs to meet employee needs.

The third model, the *corporate social responsibility model,* focuses on intervention at a macro level within the various systems in which employees and their families function. Social workers operating within the realm of this model work with the workplace, community, and society in general in developing and strengthening programs that support individual employees and their families. They provide consultation about human resources, policy, and donations to tax exempt activities within the workplace, analyze relevant legislation and make recommendations for additional legislation, administer health and welfare benefits, conduct research to document needs and evaluate programs and policies, and serve as community developers, providing a link between social service, social policy, and corporate interests (Akabas & Kurzman 1982).

These models often overlap in actuality, with social workers in industrial settings providing tasks that fall within more than one model. The majority of social work activity in the workplace to date has been with the employee service model. It is anticipated that as more and more social workers practice within an industrial setting, more of their activity will fall within the other two models.

SUMMARY

A systems approach to social problems focuses on the interactions between the individual and his or her environment. Until recently, little attention has been given to the interactions between the individual, the individual's place of employment, and the individual's family. However, as more women, both with and without children, enter the workplace, and as rapid social change continues to have a negative impact on many individuals, the relationship between the workplace and the family can be ignored no longer. Individuals experiencing stresses at the workplace invariably bring their stresses home. Conversely, individuals experiencing stresses at home bring their stresses to the workplace. The costs of employee and family alcoholism, drug abuse, marital problems, parenting problems, and other mental health problems are extensive to both the family and the workplace.

A number of communities and workplaces have developed programs that assist individual employees and their families to better balance work and family pressures. These include employee assistance programs, childcare, transportation, and health and wellness programs. Studies show that these programs are effective in preventing family and workplace dysfunction. The field of industrial social work is emerging as an area where some impact can be made through intervention in the workplace to improve family functioning, as well as increasing profitability and productivity for the work organization. It is anticipated that social work as a profession will begin to play a more major role in developing programs within the workplace, as well as appropriate policies and legislation, that provide increased support to employees and their families.

KEY TERMS

dual-career family	job sharing
Employee Assistance Programs	life-span model
(EAPs)	outsourcing
industrial social work	spillover effect

DISCUSSION QUESTIONS

1. List four ways that the composition of the workplace has changed over the past thirty years. How have these changes had an impact on the workplace?

2. Using a systems perspective, discuss the relationships between an individual, his or her workplace, and his or her family.

3. Name three types of employee and family-related problems and describe how these problems affect the workplace.

4. Name three types of work-related problems that an employee might experience. In what ways might these problems affect the employee's family?

5. Describe five types of programs employers have established to address employee and family needs.

6. Describe the three models on which an industrial social work program might be based. List at least three of the roles an industrial social worker employed in a workplace setting might play.

REFERENCES

Akabas, S., and P. Kurzman. 1982. The Industrial Welfare Specialist: What's So Special? In S. Akabas and P. Kurzman, eds. *Work, Workers, and Work Organizations: A View from Social Work.* Englewood Cliffs, N.J.: Prentice–Hall.

Anderson, R. 1985. *Employer-Based Support to Employees and Their Families.* Austin: University of Texas at Austin.

Bronfenbrenner, U., and A. Crouter. 1982. Work and Family through Time and Space. In S. Kamerman and C. Hayes, eds., *Families that Work: Children in a Changing World.* Washington, D.C.: National Academy Press.

Bureau of Business Research. 1984. *Private Sector Employee Benefits in Texas: The Relevance to Working Families.* Austin: University of Texas at Austin.

Carter, L. 1977. Social Work in Industry: A History and a Viewpoint. *Social Thought* 3:7–17.

Center for Social Work Research. 1983. *Achieving Organizational Excellence: Issues of Personal and Family Life—A Report of the Texas Corporate Leadership Forums.* Austin: University of Texas at Austin, School of Social Work.

Center for Social Work Research. 1983. *Work and Family Life Issues: A Report of a Series of Corporate Forums Held with Selected Work-related Organizations in Texas.* Austin, Texas: Center for Social Work Research, The University of Texas.

Children's Defense Fund. 1982. *America's Children and Their Families: Key Facts.* Washington, D.C.: Children's Defense Fund.

Cohen, J., and B. McGowan. 1982. "What Do You Do?" An Inquiry into the Potential of Work-Related Research. In S. Akabas and P. Kurzman, eds., *Work, Workers and Work Organizations: A View from Social Work.* Englewood Cliffs, N.J.: Prentice–Hall.

Compucare Corporation. 1981. *Employee Assistance Programs: A Dollar and Sense Issue.* Newport Beach, Calif.: Compucare Corporation.

Etzioni, A. 1984. The Two–Track Society. *National Forum: The Phi Kappa Phi Journal* 64(3):3–5.

Evans, P., and F. Bartolome. 1980. The Relationship Between Professional Life and Personal Life. In C. Derr, ed., *Work, Family, and the Career: New Frontiers in Theory and Research.* New York: Praeger.

Freeman, R. 1979. The Workforce of the Future: An Overview. In C. Kerr and J. Rosow, eds., *Work in America: The Decade Ahead.* New York: Van Nostrand Reinhold.

Friedman, D. 1983. *Encouraging Employer Support to Working Parents: Community Strategies for Change.* New York: Carnegie Corporation.

Friedman, D. 1985. *Report of Corporate Child Care Assistance.* New York: Conference Board.

Galambos, E. 1984. A "High–Tech" or a Service Economy Future? *National Forum: The Phi Kappa Phi Journal* 64(3):38–39.

Haveren, T. 1982. *Family Time and Industrial Time.* Cambridge, England: Cambridge University Press.

Hopson, A. 1977. Where Are the Other Victims of Alcoholism? *Labor–Management Alcoholism Journal* 7(2):22–23.

Kagan, J. 1983. Survey: Work in the 1980's and 1990's. *Working Woman* (April 1983):26–28.

Kamerman, S., and C. Hayes. 1982. *Families that Work: Children in a Changing World.* Washington, D.C.: National Academy Press.

Kamerman, S., and P. Kingston. 1982. Employer Responses to the Family Responsibilities of Employees. In S. Kamerman and C. Hayes, eds., *Families that Work: Children in a Changing World.* Washington, D.C.: National Academy Press.

Kanter, R. M. 1977. *Work and Family in the United States: A Critical Review and Agenda for Research and Policy.* New York: Russell Sage Foundation.

Katzell, R. 1979. Changing Attitudes Toward Work. In C. Kerr and J. Rosow, eds., *Work in America: The Decade Ahead.* New York: Van Nostrand Reinhold, 1979.

Kerr, C., and J. Rosow. 1979. *Work in America: The Decade Ahead.* New York: Van Nostrand Reinhold.

Klein, D. 1983. Trends in Employment and Unemployment in Families. *Monthly Labor Review,* 106(12):21–25.

Masnick, G., and M. J. Bane. 1980. *The Nation's Families: 1960–1990.* Cambridge, Mass.: Joint Center for Urban Studies at MIT and Harvard University.

Piotrkowski, C. 1978. *Work and the Family System: A Naturalistic Study of Working Class and Lower Middle Class Families.* New York: Free Press.

Portner, J. 1978. *A Literature Search: Topics Relevant to a Consideration of Impacts of Work on the Family.* Minneapolis: Minnesota Council on Family Relations.

Rapoport, R., and R. Rapoport. 1980. Balancing Work, Family and Leisure: A Triple Helix Model. In C. Derr, eds., *Work, Family and Career: New Frontiers in Theory and Research.* New York: Praeger.

Shain, M., and J. Groeneveld. 1979. *Employee–Assistance Programs: Philosophy, Theory, and Practice.* Lexington, Mass.: Lexington Books.

Stapleton, D., and D. Young. 1984. The Effects of Demographic Change on the Distribution of Wages, 1967–1990. *Journal of Human Resources* 19(2):175–201.

Texas Industrial Commission. 1977. *Industry–Sponsored Child Care: A Question of Productivity.* Austin: Texas Industrial Commission.

U.S. Bureau of the Census. 1984. *Current Population Survey.* Washington, D.C.: U.S. Department of Commerce.

U.S. Bureau of Labor Statistics. 1984. *Employment and Earnings* 31(12). Washington, D.C.: Department of Labor.

U.S. Bureau of Labor Statistics. 1984. *Report of U.S. Growth in Productivity, June 1984.* Washington, D.C.: Department of Labor.

U.S. Chamber of Commerce. 1980. *Employee Benefits, 1979.* Washington, D.C.: U.S. Chamber of Commerce.

U.S. Department of Health, Education, and Welfare. 1980. *Health: United States, 1980.* Washington, D.C.: Department of Health, Education, and Welfare.

Whyte, W. 1956. *The Organization Man.* New York: Doubleday.

Wilensky, H. 1960. Work, Careers and Social Integration. *International Social Science Journal.* 7(4):543–60.

Yankelovich, D. 1979. Work, Values, and the New Breed. In C. Kerr and J. Rosow, eds., *Work in America: The Decade Ahead.* New York: Van Nostrand Reinhold.

SELECTED FURTHER READINGS

Akabas, S., and P. Kurzman. 1982. *Work, Workers, and Work Organizations: A View from Social Work.* Englewood Cliffs, N.J.: Prentice–Hall.

11 Social Work in Rural Settings

al Smith is the County Agent for Joshua County. Hal is a graduate of the state agricultural college, where he majored in the agricultural sciences. He is a native of Joshua County, having grown up on a farm in this area. In college, Hal prepared for a career that would enable him to return to a rural setting. After a number of years serving as an assistant, he was promoted to County Agent. The primary role of the County Agent is to assist the local residents with information and assistance with matters relating to agricultural production, ranching, horticulture, homemaking concerns (such as cooking, canning) and like problems.

Over the course of a year, Hal also becomes involved in matters that are not directly related to his official responsibilities. In making his rounds in Joshua County this past year, he has contacted the local minister to arrange for food and clothing for three rural migrant families, has referred two children to the Lions Club for eyeglasses, has arranged transportation to take an elderly widower to a city hospital for diagnostic work and care, and secured labor to harvest crops for a local farmer who became temporarily disabled in a farm accident. These activities, while incidental to his role as County Agent, are viewed by Hal as opportunities to assist those in need.

Today, millions of Americans live in rural communities like Joshua County that are characterized by limited resources and isolation. Although the majority of our citizens reside and work in urban areas, the population of small towns and outlying areas has experienced an increase in numbers over the past several decades. As more individuals and families become disenchanted with the fast pace and over-crowded conditions of cities, it is likely that the rural population will continue to expand.

Rural areas, with their small towns, farms, and ranches of varying sizes, constitute an appreciably different environment and life-style than that in cities. Although automobile and air travel has provided many rural inhabitants access to the resources of major cities, isolation and long distances continue to typify the conditions under which others must live. On the average, people living in rural areas experience an overall quality of life that is manifested by more limited resources than those experienced by urban residents. Farley et al. (1982) have illuminated many of the urban–rural differences, pointing out that over half of America's substandard houses, half of our poor, the majority of our untreated ill, and substantial numbers of unemployed individuals live in rural areas. In this chapter, we will review some of the more salient characteristics of rural America and identify social welfare and social work resources available in rural areas.

RURAL: AN OPERATIONAL DEFINITION

Arriving at a universally agreed upon definition of *rural* is more difficult than the reader might think. Generally, such definitions are based upon population counts (the census) of a specified area rather than upon the behavioral traits and customs of people. For example, the "hillbillies" from Tennessee, Arkansas, and West Virginia who migrated into many of our northern cities brought along with them their customs, values, and traits. Disadvantaged and unsophisticated in the ways of urban life, they had a great deal of difficulty adapting to the demands of urban life. Uneducated and unskilled, they were relegated to poverty and a continual struggle for survival. Although their customs and habits positioned them clearly as rural transplants, once in the urban environment, they were no longer considered to be rural. Urban dwellers moving into rural areas have experienced similar "culture shock." The point is that definitions of urban or rural are not subject to the behavioral attributes of population groups but rather to population size. Seemingly, such definitions should constitute a rather simple task, yet it is complex.

The United States Census Bureau classifies as rural communities that are composed of 2500 people or fewer. This classification has limited utility in that it only enables us to separate out those communities statistically identified as rural from those that are not. For example, is a small isolated rural community of 2500 in Utah the equivalent of a similarly sized, incorporated, "bedroom" community twenty-five miles from Houston in terms of access to resources? Probably not.

In addition, millions of Americans live on farms or ranches that are some distance from villages, towns, or cities. In many of these areas, small farms are in close proximity to neighbors, while in others, miles may separate families from each other. Rural inhabitants often are identified as *rural-farm* or *rural-nonfarm* to further clarify and differentiate the nature of rural residency. Clearly, there are differences and distinctions in the daily living requirements and patterns of the small town resident and that of the farm dweller.

Farley et al. (1982) have suggested that rural life might be conceptualized as ecological, occupational, and sociocultural. Each conceptual aspect provides a basis for differentiating among rural towns and outlying areas. Many of these characteristics will be reflected in the discussions that follow. The reader should be aware that the life of a small farmer in Georgia may be appreciably different than that of a goat rancher in West Texas.

CHARACTERISTICS OF RURAL POPULATIONS

Data are available that enable us to gain an overview of rural life. Approximately 80 million Americans are living in rural areas, and that number is increasing. Many of the areas in which they live are predominantly agricultural, where crops, poultry, cattle, sheep, or goat commerce serve as the main source of livelihood. Inhabitants may live on small acreages and be self-sufficient or work for large commercial farms. Many attempt to do both. With growing frequency, major industrial developments are seeking out rural areas to establish plants or factories, thus providing opportunities for employment.

SOCIAL ORGANIZATIONS OF RURAL COMMUNITIES

Unlike major metropolitan areas, social networks in rural communities are more personalized and informal. Many of the prominent and powerful community leaders are descendants of early settlers, are often large landowners, and are leaders in community affairs. Residents, both affluent and poor, tend to be known by large numbers of people in the community. Privacy and anonymity are seldom achieved. Good as well as bad news travels through the informal community grapevine network with amazing speed. Reputations are routinely established for residents and are changed only with great effort. Newcomers often find themselves in an "out-group" category and, regardless of their interest or endeavor, find it difficult to be accepted fully into the inner circles of community life. Judgments concerning the character, ability, and competency of individuals tend to be based on subjective assessments. The success or failure of community residents usually is considered to be the result of personal effort and motivation. Hence, the poor, unemployed, or downtrodden are viewed as individuals who lack the determination to achieve. Divorce and poverty typically are classified as personal failures, and strong negative sanctions serve as constant reminders that deviation from the norm is accompanied by increasing social distance and exclusion from free and full participation in community life.

On the other hand, responses to people in need are often quick and personal. A death in the family or farm failure stimulates neighbors to respond with goods and services designed to assist the needy through the crisis situation. Droughts, floods, tornadoes, and other natural disasters create a bond among farmers and ranchers and a unity of purpose with shared concern. Reciprocity typically is manifested in the sharing of labor for harvesting crops, assisting others in times of need, and organizing to counteract threats to community life. Politically conservative, rural communities are characterized by resistance to innovation and skepticism concerning modern technological innovations. City slickers are viewed with disdain and are not to be trusted until proven worthy of trust. They are considered to be uninformed as to the needs of rural residents. Honesty and strong character are valued as desirable traits.

The action hub of rural communities centers around the church, the local bank, the county extension office, small businesses, the feed store, and the local school system. As a consequence, the local banker, ministers, county agent, store owners, and school administrators usually hold powerful influence over community life. County government is typically relegated to the county judge and county commissioners. Law enforcement is invested in the sheriff's office, although many small towns also have a police force. Violations of the law are considered to be a personal offense against the community, and mitigating circumstances are usually downplayed or viewed as irrelevant. Ginsberg (1976, 7) suggests that rural communities have a style of living that is scaled down from urban areas and states that

> *a smaller scale of life does not imply simplicity. Rural communities are often as socially complicated as cities. Many of the things that happen may be based upon little-remembered but enduringly important family conflicts, church schisms, and crimes. It may require months of investigation before a newcomer in a rural area fully understands the power relationships of the community's institutions. Things are often not as they are supposed to be . . . . a single civic club may have a disproportionate influence over governmental matters, while the government may be weak.*

The social organization of rural communities is as varied as the locations in which they occur. Although there are common threads of roles and relationships that knit the community together in any setting, variances are common and idiosyncratic to each locale.

SUPPORT SERVICES IN THE RURAL COMMUNITY

Many of the support services that urban residents take for granted are often scarce or nonexistent in rural communities. It is not uncommon to find an absence of doctors, nurses, social workers, dentists, or attorneys in small rural towns. Adequately staffed hospitals with modern up-to-date equipment are expensive to develop and maintain, and small communities lack the resources to finance them. As a consequence, many health-related problems go unattended or rely upon traditional cures or folk medicine. Resources for the treatment of mental illness are particularly lacking. However, individuals exhibiting "peculiar" behavior often find acceptance in rural areas, and their families may experience considerable understanding and social support from neighbors. Social work and social services are distributed sparsely in rural areas, often the result of the community's mores or limited financial support capabilities.

As discussed earlier, the church is a significant institution in rural life. Congregations are quick to respond to those in need and set the pace for community action in time of crisis. The church also is the center for community activities, sponsoring various social get-togethers and recreational opportunities. Religion typically plays a vital role in setting the moral tone and in meeting the spiritual needs of rural residents. Ministers are viewed not only as spiritual advisors but also as community leaders.

In agricultural areas, the county extension office, funded by the **U.S. Department of Agriculture**, provides many services valued by the farm community to assist rural areas, and the county liaison office provides a variety of community and family services. Technical assistance is made available for planting crops, harvesting, ranch management, disease control, care of livestock, food preparation, home canning, and other activities related to farm, ranch, and home management. Informally, the county agent often becomes aware of personal problems and serves as counselor, case manager, and resource finder. It is not uncommon for the county agent to function as an advocate or broker for farmers experiencing financial disaster (with the local banker or other lending agencies).

Recreational activities are often limited in rural areas. The absence of a local movie house, skating rink, parks, libraries, and other outlets for children and teen-agers severely restricts opportunities for leisure time activities. Many small communities literally "roll up the sidewalks" at dark. As a consequence, the local school often is a prominent source for recreational get-togethers and sponsors dances and holiday programs. Athletic events are usually well attended and serve as the central focus for young people and adults to meet and socialize. The school, along with the church, is among the primary institutions for social organization in the rural community.

SOCIAL PROBLEMS IN RURAL AREAS

Many health and social problems in rural America often are overlooked or undisclosed, due to the lack of emphasis and attention given them in rural environments. Health indicators reflect that infant mortality and chronic disease rates are higher in rural areas than in urban ones. Some estimates suggest that over "50 percent of the rural aged suffer from continuing poor health, with 87 percent of these suffering from some form of chronic illness" (Hyde 1978, 21). Case finding and treatment are limited by inadequate or nonexistent health care networks and the lack of qualified medical personnel.

Lower incomes and erratic employment opportunities contribute to higher rates of poverty and disease in rural areas. A Wisconsin study reported that 81 percent of the rural elderly had incomes under $4000 in 1977 and that 60 percent of the minority population living in totally rural environments had incomes below the poverty level (Hyde 1978). Many minority group members are engaged in crop harvesting, which is often unpredictable, pays poor wages, and may require families to move from place to place to secure employment. Although many of these families are no longer migrants, they are generally referred to as migrant workers.

The children of migrant workers, like their parents, receive less education than their counterparts living in urban areas. Disease rates and higher infant mortality rates reflect the substandard conditions under which the majority live. Small town school systems already strained for financial resources are not diligent in enforcing mandatory school attendance laws. As a result, many migrant farm children are not encouraged to pursue education. Many of them must work alongside their parents in order to assist the family in making enough income for a minimal level of survival. As a result, a vicious cycle is set in motion resulting in the perpetuation of intergenerational farm laborers who are poor and lack resources or opportunities to break the poverty cycle.

Rural communities are also more segregated than urban areas. Morrison (1976) reports that racial segregation, limited political participation, and impoverishment continue to characterize the plight of minorities in rural communities. Attempts to organize farm labor and implement civil rights legislation have met with only limited success due, primarily, to the resistance of large landowners and commercial farmers who seek to maintain the status quo and exert sufficient power to assure that reform does not occur. In states that border Mexico, such as Texas, New Mexico, Arizona, and California, large numbers of undocumented aliens are viewed negatively by many, because they are seen as compounding the problems crowding the farm labor market since they work for lower wages. However, experience has shown that they do jobs that otherwise go unfilled or are outsourced. Since most undocumented aliens are concerned with being detected by Federal Immigration Officials (and returned to Mexico), they are vulnerable to exploitation by landowners who seek cheap labor. The recent decline in the value of the peso has further exacerbated the problem and prompted large numbers of undocumented aliens to cross the border to seek work and better living conditions.

Poor white farm workers experience many of the same problems. Typically less educated than urban whites, they are viewed stereotypically as people with less incentive and motivation to succeed. Limited resources and skill levels keep them on the farm. Illiteracy rates are higher and poverty more pervasive among rural whites than urban whites. When rural whites do migrate to cities, they are relegated to low-paying jobs and often experience considerable difficulty in becoming assimilated into the urban environment.

The Farm Crisis

Inflation, low farm prices, high production costs, imports, and economic recession have converged to create a crisis for the small landowner farmer. Within the past decade, farm and ranch foreclosures have increased dramatically, resulting in the displacement of large numbers of farmers and ranchers who depended upon agricultural production for their livelihood. It is not uncommon for intergenerational farms to be lost through foreclosure. Displaced farmers often lack the skills to become absorbed readily into other aspects of the labor market, particularly older farmers or ranchers. Major commercial farm operations have contributed to the demise of small farm operations through volume production that lowers unit prices for products. The small operator, even under optimum conditions, has great difficulty competing.

Currently, in the United States, few resources are available to assist the small farmer in maintaining property and purchasing the equipment essential for a successful operation. The federal government's preoccupation with reducing deficit spending has taken its toll on farm supports. Along with these problems, the stress and tension associated with the loss (or imminent loss) of one's farm create havoc for the families of small farmers and serve as a disincentive for prospective new farmers to engage in agricultural occupations. Many jobs are lost and a way of life destroyed. Many of the victims, once productive and self-sustaining, must turn to welfare as a means of survival. Urbanites must be reminded continually that their survival also depends upon a healthy agricultural industry.

SOCIAL WELFARE IN RURAL COMMUNITIES

There are many times more small communities and towns in the United States than cities or major metropolitan complexes. Those located east of the Mississippi River are in more densely populated states. These communities vary in size and proximity from major metropolitan areas. For example, Tilden, Texas, a county seat town of approximately 350 residents is situated in a county that covers approximately 1400 square miles. It is the largest town in the county. What type of organized social welfare programs would one find in this community? What is needed? To what extent could the community support social welfare services?

The reader should be wary about generalizations concerning the nature and extent of organized social welfare programs in small towns and rural areas due to their size, diverse nature, and ability to finance needed services. Many rural areas have very few services. Services that are provided tend to be basic in nature. Typically, public welfare services, mental health and mental retardation

Because resources are sparse in rural areas, social workers most often provide general services.

outreach centers and public health services are found in rural areas, although they usually are minimally staffed, offer only limited assistance, and often may be reached only by a drive of several hundred miles. It is not unusual for counties to offer a limited welfare assistance program and for county administrative officials (usually the county judge) to administer benefits along with their other duties. A few rural communities have Community Action Agencies (a residual of the War on Poverty programs), although attempts to organize rural areas, in general, have been unsuccessful (Morrison 1976). Senior citizens' luncheon programs may be provided by a branch of an areawide agency on aging. Employment agencies, family planning services, and family counseling agencies and related services are not typically found in rural areas. Ginsberg (1976) suggests some innovative changes that would increase the service capacity to meet the needs of rural populations:

1. *The public, basic services must often expand their activities to include functions that they might not carry in cities. For example, a public welfare office might be charged with much more responsibility for family counseling, community development, and social welfare planning simply because it exists, is staffed with knowledgeable people, and needs to help meet problems that occur, despite the absence of agencies. Similarly, a community mental health program may be required to carry some youth services activities that its urban counterparts would leave to other agencies.*

2. *Many activities are voluntary and depend, therefore, on the good will and interest of their supporters rather than upon full-time professional staff. This is particularly true of social welfare planning efforts, which are often the result of social welfare professionals working together without additional compensation to create and sustain a structure for coordination and planning. Some direct service and community development activities are conducted in a similar manner.*

3. *Although formal structures may not exist, many informal services are offered in rural communities. In fact, it is the nature of communities, both rural and metropolitan, to develop services for overcoming human problems. For example, the functions carried by Travelers' Aid agencies in large cities may be performed in rural communities by the police or the sheriff's office. A single individual may carry out a program serving children. Churches may assume responsibility for everything from food baskets to family counseling. It is important for social workers in all communities to understand the nature of the service delivery system. In rural America that structure may be hard to identify because of its informal nature.*

4. *Some formal agencies in rural areas may carry expanded functions. Youth-serving programs such as 4–H, the Boy Scouts, Girl Scouts, and Campfire Girls may be the only resource for activities that in a larger area would be handled by the YMCA, YWCA, and other programs.*

5.   *The importance of individuals and families in serving social welfare needs should not be overlooked. As has already been suggested, one public spirited woman may function almost as effectively as an agency or office. Knowing about such people and gaining their assistance is crucial for the rural worker.*

6.   *Perhaps most important is the fact that some formal organizations exist in rural areas that are important but different from those one finds in urban settings. The best example is probably the cooperative extension services, which are sponsored by each state (along with Department of Agriculture standards and funds), usually under the supervision of state land-grant universities. The traditional function of such programs is to provide consultation on agricultural activities to farmers and ranchers as well as homemaking information to rural women. However, they have expanded their functions dramatically, with many cooperative extension programs now heavily committed to community improvement and development programs in areas as diverse as housing, drug abuse treatment, and social welfare planning. Working with such organizations, which are most prominent in rural areas, is essential for the rural worker.*

In general, it might be concluded that organized social welfare services in rural areas are underdeveloped and not sufficient to meet the existing needs. Additional resources must be channelled into rural areas if services equivalent to those in urban areas are to exist.

SOCIAL WORK IN RURAL SETTINGS

The practice of social work in rural communities is both similar and different from that practiced in urban areas. The core of knowledge, methods, and skills of social work practice undergird practice in both environments. As the preceding pages suggest, the nature of rural settings, the problems experienced, and the lack of resources converge to confront the social worker with a unique set of challenges. Creativity and the ability to innovate and influence community members to mobilize in meeting needs are paramount among the skills essential for successful practice in rural settings. Bruxton states that

> *No other environment compares with rural practice in carrying out the dictum of the "total individual" in the "total environment." The rural social worker by her- or himself must often provide the rural dweller with services, support, and hope while simultaneously helping to change the environment in order to provide better transportation, increased medical care, and a more responsive community. (1976, 32).*

Unlike urban social workers, the worker in a rural area may find frustrating the absence of fellow professionals and a social service network. Opportunities for consultation and feedback are limited, with the result that decision making is often difficult and problematic.

Social workers who both live and practice in rural areas find that they are neighbors as well as professional practitioners. Almost everyone in the community knows who they are, and they may be called upon at home as well as the office to provide a wide range of services. Their service constituency may consist of children, adults, the mentally ill, the incarcerated, the bedridden, the distressed, and the abandoned (Bruxton 1976). At any one time, the worker may be assisting a family in securing a nursing home placement for an older parent, securing resources for a disabled child, counseling with a pregnant teen-ager and her family, collaborating with local ministers in developing leisure time activities for youth, assisting school personnel in management techniques for a hyperactive child, or working with the court in securing rehabilitation resources for a delinquent child. These varied demands require that the worker be flexible, have good communication skills, engage both private and public resources, and have a basic understanding of community values and practices.

As Fenby (1978) suggests, practicing social work in a rural setting subjects the worker to a life in a "gold-fish bowl." Everyone tends to know the worker both professionally and personally. The private life of the worker is closely scrutinized. Since workers, like other community people, have problems, the way they are managed becomes a matter of community concern. Like ministers, the worker is expected to meet high personal and moral standards, and any deviation may lower community esteem. In rural communities, the ability to separate personal life from professional competence is difficult. Often, the credibility of the worker is at stake should personal problems go unresolved.

Maintaining client confidentiality is difficult to achieve. Neighbors may become clients. Community residents typically know when problems are being experienced and when professional assistance has been sought. A casual encounter at the grocery store may prompt a resident to inquire as to how a client is progressing. As Fenby has indicated:

> At times a client will be open about his or her knowledge. "I hear you had oil burner problems this morning and Art sent his truck out." At times there is a subtle change in the therapy hour, and the therapist cannot discount the fact that information from the "outside" is affecting the interaction "inside." For example, a client who had been working well in therapy became evasive and distant, although nothing discernible had caused the change. Probing uncovered that the woman had discovered that my husband was on a yearly contract at the college, and had surmised that therefore I would not be staying in the area. She thought that therapy would end in failure, uncompleted. In a small world it is essential to be aware of contamination from outside information in the process of the therapy. (1978, 162)

Social workers who have periodic assignments in the rural area but do not reside there encounter other problems. Typically, they are viewed as outsiders. In some instances, they have not had the opportunity to become aware of community priorities and values. Often, they are viewed as having little vested interest in the community and, as a result, respond to special client problems out of context. Community resistance may become an additional barrier to problem solving. Sensitivity to the importance of interpersonal relationships with community leaders is essential in gaining support for change efforts.

An old social work axiom suggests that "change comes slow." While this premise is open to debate, it is valid in rural social work practice. Time tables and the pace of life tend to be slower. Urgency is offset by practicality and patience. Waiting matters out may be given more credence than intervention. Workers must learn to stifle their frustration and impatience, yet retain their persistent efforts in the helping process. As the credibility and competence of the worker become more established, community resistance will turn into support, and the contribution made to the community as a problem solver will become enhanced.

RURAL SOCIAL WORK AS GENERALIST PRACTICE

By now it should be apparent to the reader that the variety and diversity of the tasks inherent in rural social work practice can best be accomplished by the generalist practitioner. Workers in rural communities are called upon to work with individuals, families, groups, and in community organization. Administrative and management skills are essential in rendering needed services (see Box 11–1). The ability to define problems operationally, collect and analyze data, and translate findings into practical solutions are requisites for enriched practice. The rural practitioner is a multimethod worker who appropriately facilitates in the problem-solving process. Knowledge of resources, resource development, methods of linking clients with resources, and case management are basic skills required of the rural social worker. Other essential requirements for generalist social work practice are discussed earlier in this book.

Box 11–1
Some
Characteristics
of Effective
Rural Social
Workers

1. They are especially skillful in working with a variety of helping persons who are not social workers or who may not be related to the profession of social work, as well as with peers and colleagues.

2. They are able to carry out careful study, analysis, and other methods of inquiry in order to understand the community in which they find themselves.

3. They utilize their knowledge of the customs, traditions, heritage and contemporary culture of the rural people with whom they are working to provide services to the people with special awareness and sensitivity.

4. They are able to identify and mobilize a broad range of resources which are applicable to problem resolution in rural areas. These include existing and potential resources on the local, state, regional and federal levels.

5. They are able to assist communities in developing new resources or ways in which already existing resources may be better or more fully utilized to benefit the rural community.

6. They are able to identify with and practice in accordance with the values of the profession and grow in their ability and effectiveness as professional social workers in situations and settings where they may be the only professional social worker.

7. They are able to identify and analyze the strengths and/or gaps and shortcomings in governmental and nongovernmental social policies as they affect the needs of people in rural areas.

8. They accept their professional responsibility to develop appropriate measures to promote more responsiveness to the needs of people in rural areas from governmental and nongovernmental organizations.

9. They are able to help identify and create new and different helping roles in order to respond to the needs and problems of rural communities.

10. They initiate and provide technical assistance to rural governing bodies and other organized groups in rural communities.

11. They are able to practice as generalists, carrying out a wide range of roles, to solve a wide range of problems of individuals and groups as well as of the larger community.

12. They are able to communicate and interact appropriately with people in the rural community, and adapt their personal life-style to the professional tasks to be done.

13. They are able to evaluate their own professional performance.

14. They are able to work within an agency or organization and plan for and initiate change in agency policy and practice when such change is indicated.

15. On the basis of continuous careful observation, they contribute knowledge about effective practice in rural areas.

Statement on "Educational Assumptions for Rural Social Work" by Southern Regional Education Board, Manpower Education and Training Project Rural Task Force.

THE BACCALAUREATE SOCIAL WORKER AND RURAL SOCIAL WORK PRACTICE

Social work in rural communities is both challenging and rewarding. Self-reliance and the ability to work apart from social work support systems are attributes that rural social workers must have in order to function effectively. Many undergraduate social work programs are located in small cities or large towns adjacent to rural areas and specialize in rural social work practice. Field placements typically utilize rural agencies to familiarize students with skills essential for practice in those settings.

The baccalaureate social worker's generalist practice perspective will prove invaluable in working with rural populations. The opportunity to engage existing formal and informal organizations in extending or developing resources to meet community needs is a continuing challenge the BSW worker can address competently. The worker also will find that individuals and families in rural areas often have problems and need assistance in problem solving. The knowledge and expertise of the worker in problem identification, outreach, linking target systems with resources, resource development, education, and problem solving help to enrich the lives of rural inhabitants as well as to strengthen community support systems. The ability to understand community value systems and to experiment with innovative techniques in working with community residents are essential assets for productive practice.

Until recently, social workers have not been inclined to engage in rural social work practice. Fortunately, this attitude is changing. Job opportunities in rural communities are increasing, and the potential for a satisfying and rewarding career in rural social work practice is greater now than ever before.

SUMMARY

In this chapter, we reviewed some of the characteristics that typify rural community life in America, identified the more salient problems experienced by people living in rural areas, examined the social organization of rural communities, and presented an overview of the more typical social support networks in rural areas. The methods and functions of social work practice in rural areas have been presented, and the role of the generalist practitioner outlined. Rural social work is a setting ideally suited for the baccalaureate social worker. Job opportunities are increasing, and the challenges for a successful career in providing needed services for rural communities are attracting social workers in greater numbers into rural areas.

KEY TERMS

rural
U.S. Department of Agriculture

DISCUSSION QUESTIONS

1. What problems are involved in defining rural populations?
2. Identify the major "activity" centers in rural communities. Who appears to be among the more significant power brokers in rural areas?
3. Describe the types of problems that are more likely to be found in rural areas. What type of informal network exists to assist with these problems?
4. What types of formal welfare services generally are found in rural areas? How do these services interact with other community resources?

5. What types of services will the social worker more likely be offering in rural areas? What problems will be encountered? Indicate the skills essential in rural social work practice.

6. What roles would the BSW social worker play in rural areas?

REFERENCES

Bruxton, Edward B. 1976. "Delivering Social Services in Rural Areas." In Leon H. Ginsberg, ed., *Social Work in Rural Communities: A Book of Readings,* pp. 29–38. New York: Council on Social Work Education.

Farley, O. William, Kenneth A. Griffiths, Rex Skidmore, and Milton G. Thackery. 1982. *Rural Social Work Practice.* New York: The Free Press.

Fenby, Barbara L. 1978. "Social Work in a Rural Setting," *Social Work* 23, 2 (March): 162–63.

Ginsberg, Leon H. 1976. "An Overview of Social Work Education for Rural Areas." In Leon H. Ginsberg, ed., *Social Work in Rural Communities: A Book of Readings,* pp. 6–8. New York: Council on Social Work Education.

Hyde, Henry. 1978. "Rural Development, What's Coming—What's Needed," *Human Services in the Rural Environment.* Madison: Center for Social Service, University of Wisconsin.

Morrison, Jim. 1976. "Community Organization in Rural Areas." In Leon H. Ginsberg, ed., *Social Work in Rural Communities: A Book of Readings,* pp. 57–61. New York: Council on Social Work Education.

SELECTED FURTHER READINGS

Clark, Frank, Jon Bertsche, and Edward V. Bates. 1980. "Informal Helping in a Rural Boom Town," *Human Service in the Rural Environment* 5 (May–June): 19–24.

Martinez–Brawley, Emilia E. 1981. *Seven Decades of Rural Social Work.* New York: Praeger Publishing.

Martinez–Brawley, Emilia E. 1982. *Rural Social and Community Work in the U.S. and Britain.* New York: Praeger Publishers.

Munson, Carlton E. 1980. "Urban–Rural Differences: Implications for Education and Training," *Journal of Education for Social Work* 16 (Winter): 95–103.

Summers, Anne, Joe M. Schriver, Paul Sundet, and Roland Meinert, eds. 1987. *Social Work in Rural Areas.* Batesville: Arkansas College.

Weber, Gwen K. 1976. "Preparing Social Workers for Practice in Rural Social Systems," *Journal of Education for Social Work* 12 (Fall): 110–111.

Whitaker, William H., ed. 1985. *Social Work in Rural Areas.* Proceedings of the Ninth National/Second International Institute on Social Work in Rural Areas. Orono: University of Maine.

12 Old Age: Issues, Problems, and Services

loise Earnest is an 81–year–old widow who lives alone. She has been unable to care for herself, and her home lacks an adequate heating system. Living on limited income derived from her husband's social security benefits and Supplemental Security Income, she has been the object of concern to many in the community for some time; however, she has frustrated all those who have attempted to assist her. Both her personal appearance and home are in a deplorable state. Besides being filthy, Mrs. Earnest has many large sores on her hands, face, and legs. Communication is difficult because she is unable to hear. She also cannot see without her glasses. Her conversation consists of delusional and paranoid comments about her neighbor, who she claims is responsible for the condition of her home.

Mrs. Earnest has two sons and one daughter, who live in an adjacent city some seventy-five miles from her. They feel that she should be in some type of protective environment, such as a nursing home, but have been unwilling to become involved in forcing her to enter such a living situation. Efforts by community agencies have been rebuffed, and the dilemma over whether to forcibly intervene and provide Mrs. Earnest with adequate health treatment and a protective environment continues.

While not all older Americans experience problems similar to those of Mrs. Earnest, a growing number struggle to survive on meager resources. Many older adults experience a sense of satisfaction, accomplishment and contentment. However, many others must struggle to survive, which limits their ability to enjoy life. There is perhaps as much variation among the old as there is between the young and the old.

Today the number of people reaching old age is much greater. Life expectancy has increased dramatically since the early 1900s, when only 3 out of every 100 Americans were 65 years of age or over. By 1980, 10 out of every 100 were 65 or over. By the year 2030, 16 out of every 100 will have reached the age of 65 years. On the average, each day of every year results in another 1700 persons who reach their 65th birthdays! At no time in recorded history have as many older adults populated a society as is the case in America today. Not only are more individuals reaching age 65; they are also living longer (see Table 12–1). In 1977, the average life expectancy was 72 years, with more and more individuals living into their eighties and nineties. Some experts suggest that we should talk about two groups of elderly, the "old," and the "old-old." Increasingly, older individuals in their sixties are caring for their own parents in their eighties and nineties.

While living a long life is a goal to which most of us aspire, the consequences to society have the potential of being catastrophic. Assuring that essential resources are available to meet the needs of the older population places a heavy burden on government and private resources, including families. More and more, middle-aged Americans are becoming the "sandwich generation," having to provide for their children at the same time they also are providing for their elderly parents. However, many families cannot provide such support, especially when major health problems occur, and many elderly do not have families available to provide even emotional support. Thus, there is an increasing reliance on federal and state government to provide for such needs. For example, it is estimated that one-fourth of the federal government's expenditures is allocated to meeting the needs of the older population. With continually increasing numbers of older adults in our society, even larger government allocations will be necessary in the future (see Figure 12–1).

In this chapter, we will examine the more salient issues and problems an older population creates for society, review their problems of adaptation, and identify resources that have been developed to provide physical and social support systems designed to meet their needs.

Table 12–1   **Growth of Each State's Elderly Population 1970–1980 and 1980–1984 (numbers in thousands)**

State	1980 all ages		1980 65 plus				Percent Increase, 1970–1980	1984 65 plus		Percent Increase, 1980–1984
	Number	Rank	Number	Rank	Percent	Rank		Number	Percent	
Alabama	3,894	22	440	19	11.3	24	35.0	476	11.9	8.3
Alaska	402	51	12	51	2.9	51	67.7	15	3.1	32.6
Arizona	2,718	29	307	28	11.3	25	90.4	375	12.3	21.9
Arkansas	2,286	33	312	27	13.7	2	31.4	336	14.3	7.4
California	23,668	1	2,414	1	10.2	34	34.1	2,693	10.5	11.5
Colorado	2,890	28	247	33	8.6	46	31.6	280	8.8	13.4
Connecticut	3,108	25	365	26	11.7	18	26.3	407	12.9	11.6

Delaware	594	48	59	48	10.0	36	35.0	67	11.0	13.8
D.C.	638	47	74	46	11.6	20	4.9	75	12.1	1.5
Florida	9,746	7	1,688	3	17.3	1	70.6	1,931	17.6	14.4
Georgia	5,463	13	517	16	9.5	41	40.6	577	9.9	11.7
Hawaii	965	39	76	45	7.9	49	72.4	94	9.0	22.9
Idaho	944	41	94	41	9.9	37	38.2	108	10.8	14.9
Illinois	11,427	5	1,262	6	11.0	29	15.4	1,356	11.8	7.5
Indiana	5,490	12	585	13	10.7	31	18.5	638	11.6	8.9
Iowa	2,913	27	388	24	13.3	4	10.7	410	14.1	5.9
Kansas	2,364	32	306	29	13.0	8	15.1	323	13.3	5.6
Kentucky	3,661	23	410	21	11.2	27	21.5	438	11.8	6.8
Louisiana	4,206	19	404	22	9.6	39	31.8	435	9.7	7.5
Maine	1,125	38	141	36	12.5	11	23.0	152	13.1	7.6
Maryland	4,217	18	396	23	9.4	42	32.0	447	10.3	13.0
Massachusetts	5,737	11	727	10	12.7	10	14.2	777	13.4	6.9
Michigan	9,262	8	912	8	9.9	38	21.2	1,007	11.1	10.3
Minnesota	4,076	21	480	18	11.8	17	17.3	517	12.4	7.7
Mississippi	2,521	31	289	31	11.5	21	30.1	306	11.8	5.9
Missouri	4,917	15	648	11	13.2	5	15.6	682	13.6	5.3
Montana	787	44	85	43	10.8	32	23.0	,096	11.6	13.2
Nebraska	1,570	35	206	35	13.1	7	12.1	216	13.4	4.8
Nevada	800	43	66	47	8.2	47	112.3	87	9.5	32.2
New Hampshire	921	42	103	40	11.2	28	31.3	114	11.7	10.6
New Jersey	7,365	9	860	9	11.7	19	23.4	942	12.5	9.6
New Mexico	1,303	37	116	38	8.9	45	64.2	135	9.5	16.6
New York	17,558	2	2,161	2	12.3	13	10.2	2,247	12.7	4.0
North Carolina	5,882	10	603	12	10.2	35	45.7	688	11.2	14.1
North Dakota	653	46	80	44	12.3	14	21.2	87	12.6	7.6
Ohio	10,798	6	1,169	7	10.8	30	17.2	1,280	11.9	9.5
Oklahoma	3,025	26	376	25	12.4	12	25.5	401	12.1	6.5
Oregon	2,633	30	303	30	11.5	22	33.8	344	12.9	13.4
Pennsylvania	11,864	4	1,531	4	12.9	9	20.3	1,676	14.1	9.5
Rhode Island	947	40	127	37	13.4	3	22.1	138	14.3	8.7
South Carolina	3,122	24	287	32	9.2	44	50.5	331	10.0	15.1
South Dakota	691	45	91	42	13.2	6	13.1	96	13.6	5.8
Tennessee	4,591	17	518	15	11.3	26	34.8	566	12.0	9.4
Texas	14,229	3	1,371	5	9.6	40	38.2	1,514	9.5	10.4
Utah	1,461	36	109	39	7.5	50	40.8	128	7.7	16.9
Vermont	511	49	58	49	11.4	23	22.5	63	11.8	7.8
Virginia	5,346	14	505	17	9.5	43	38.1	572	10.2	13.2
Washington	4,132	20	432	20	10.4	33	34.0	492	11.3	14.0
West Virginia	1,950	34	238	34	12.2	15	22.3	255	13.0	7.1
Wisconsin	4,705	16	564	14	12.0	16	19.3	611	12.8	8.4
Wyoming	470	50	37	50	7.9	48	23.1	42	8.2	12.3

Source: U.S. Bureau of the Census, Decennial Census of the Population "Estimates of Population of States, by Age: July 1, 1981–83," *Current Population Reports,* Series P–25, No. 95, and "State Population Estimates, by Age and Components of Change: 1980–1984," *Current Population Reports,* Series P–25, No. 970.

Figure 12–1   **Population 55 Years and Over by Age: 1900–2050**

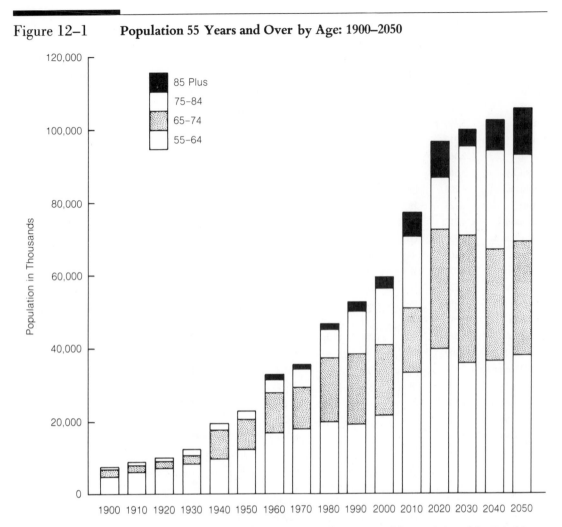

Source: U.S. Census of Population, 1890–1980 and projections of the population of the United States: 1983–2080. *Current Population Reports,* Series P–25, No. 952 middle series.

BEHAVIOR AND ADAPTATION TO OLD AGE

Although we do not discuss in detail the developmental processes of later life in this chapter, a few observations are offered to dispel some of the myths that many individuals believe to be true about the aging process. The reader should be aware that **aging** is a normative process and not a fixed dimension of the life-cycle. Young children age, as do older adults. All societies attach significance to various stages of the life-cycle. Aging is not only a chronological process; it has symbolic meaning as well (Karp & Yoels 1982). Cultures determine, for example, the age at which their members should enter school, marry, begin careers, enter the military, have children, become grandparents, and retire. Norms for behavior are prescribed at various developmental stages of the life-cycle. Old age has been viewed too often as a period of dramatic decline. Thus, older adults are expected to be less active, need fewer resources, contribute less to society, and become more content and serene.

Scientific data buttress many of the symbolic definitions assigned to old age. Physiological changes, including the loss of muscular strength, sensory losses, and reduced lung elasticity are but few of the measurable differences between older adults and the young. On the other hand, many of the presumed losses associated with cognitive functioning have been demonstrated to have little substance in fact. Intelligence and intellectual functioning, once thought to decline appreciably in old age, are not measurably affected by the process. Behavior in old age is an individual matter and not attributable to the aging process alone. Any accurate assessment of adaptation in late life must take into consideration the effects of the environment on behavior, as well as the physiological and cognitive characteristics present within the behavioral context.

In recent years, several theories of aging have emerged that seek to explain or describe adaptation in late life. Among the more prominent ones are disengagement theory (Cumming & Henry 1961), activity theory (Havinghurst 1968), exchange theory (Dowd 1975), and developmental theory (Kimmel 1974). *Disengagement theory* assumes that biological degeneration and social withdrawal are coterminous and functional for the individual and society. This theory contends that as older adults decline physically, they have less need and desire for social interaction and progressively become "disengaged" from social roles. However, more penetrating analysis reveals that it is societal discrimination against older adults that limits the social contexts (and thus opportunities) for social interaction. Social barriers, such as mandatory retirement, constrain the opportunities for participation in society. For some this means the limited income resources and fewer social friendship networks of the aged.

Exchange theory attributes social withdrawal of the aged to a loss of power. Having once exchanged their expertise for wages, the aged must comply with mandatory retirement in exchange for pensions, social security payments, and Medicare. Thus, the power advantage has shifted from them as individuals to society (Dowd 1975). The effect of this power loss results in withdrawal from meaningful social interaction and greater dependence upon those holding power over them.

Developmental theory emphasizes positive adaptation and life satisfactions based upon mastering new tasks as the individual moves through the life-cycle, including old age. Life-span development is viewed as a normal process that encompasses new challenges, new tasks, and flexibility in incorporating changes into the repertoire of behaviors. Older adults must accept the physiological changes they experience, reconstruct their physical and psychological life accordingly, and integrate values that validate their worth as older adults (Clark & Anderson 1967).

Activity theory "implies that social activity is the essence of life for all people of all ages" who must maintain adequate levels of activity if they are to age successfully (Barrow 1986, 72). Presumably, more active older adults will achieve greater satisfactions and thus age more adaptively.

Society's role in creating the behavioral and value context for older adults must be examined in order to gain insights into the problems and issues implicit in understanding adaptation in later life. As Simone de Beauvoir has indicated in *The Coming of Age:*

> *Society cares for the individual insofar as he is productive. The young know this. Their anxiety as they enter in upon social life matches the anguish of the old as they are excluded from it. Between the two ages, the problems lie hidden by routine. . . . Once we have understood what the state of the aged really is, we cannot satisfy ourselves with calling for a more generous "old-age policy," higher pensions, decent housing and organized leisure. It is the whole system and our claim cannot be otherwise than radical—change life itself. (1971, 807)*

Our society stresses productivity and distributes varying degrees of rewards and power in relation to it. Retirement serves to disengage older adults from socially recognized productive efforts. Instead of being consumers of their own current productive efforts, older adults are forced to be consumers of the efforts of others. As we now turn our attention to the problems and issues confronting older adults, the reader should keep in mind that there are no simple solutions to problems. Case work with older adults who have problems may bring some relief to those individuals helped, but it does not address the causes of those problems. Changing the social systems that produce the problems is a more tenable solution, albeit more difficult.

ATTITUDES TOWARD GROWING OLD

Negative attitudes toward the aged are among many of the harsh realities one faces in old age. Although there has been a pronounced positive shift in attitudes toward aging in recent years, negative attitudes persist (Butler & Lewis 1977). Our society often has been characterized by its emphasis on youth and productivity. Independence is stressed and is enabled by financial supports gained through employment. Retirement often drastically reduces available income and may contribute to dependency. As a result, older adults are often viewed as being of less value to society.

Negative attitudes also are expressed through the process of exclusion. Media, for example, have avoided the use of older adults in television commercials, while advertisements in newspapers and magazines use younger persons to convey messages. Until recently, older adults, when used in film or advertising, were portrayed as dependent, irascible, or in poor health. Fortunately, there is evidence the media is beginning to present a more accurate portrayal of older adults.

Collectively, many societal practices have reinforced negativism toward old age. Many of these practices, such as mandatory retirement, have supported the idea that older adults are less capable of making contributions through work and to society. Various rules and regulations governing employment limit the opportunity for them to make such contributions. The discrimination or differential treatment based upon age alone is called **ageism.** Like other forms of discrimination, ageism is institutionalized and, as a result, is often subtle. Individuals are often unaware that they reinforce it through their attitudes and practices. Unfortunately, negative attitudes toward older adults may be expressed by professional practitioners as well as the public in general. Riley (1968) identifies nurses, medical doctors, attorneys, clergymen, and social workers, among others, as giving preference to younger individuals as clientele.

As we review other problem areas experienced by older adults, the reader should keep in mind that attitudes, although not always directly linked with behavior, tend to shape our priorities and practices. Viewing the older population as "excess baggage" is not the bedrock upon which positive responses to the needs of older adults will be achieved.

RETIREMENT

The impact of retirement upon human behavior continues to be a topic of major interest. Although retirement often has been viewed as synonymous with old age, that scarcely is the case in our society today. Data indicate that more and more Americans are electing to retire at earlier ages while, on the other hand, many older citizens continue to work either full or part time in the labor force. This mixture of age and work (either full or part time) clouds our ability to arrive at a precise definition, or line of demarcation, that clearly separates those among us who are retired from those who are not. When, for example, is an individual considered to be retired? Is the military "retiree" receiving a full retirement pension from the military, yet working full time in a civil service position, considered to be retired? Or the 72–year–old person receiving full social security benefits from the federal government who works full time as a court bailiff? And what about the 69–year–old housewife receiving Supplemental Security Income (public assistance for the aged)? Certainly, many other examples would further muddy the already murky waters of the definitional dilemma.

As a result, researchers use operational definitions that seldom are accepted universally. Some view individuals as retired if they receive a pension from their employer for past work performed, regardless of their present work status. Others identify retirees as those individuals who receive retirement pension benefits that exceed any monies earned through a present work, and many identify a person in retired status who receives a pension and works half-time or less. Obviously, the retiree living on a pension and not working presents us with far fewer definitional problems. There is agreement that the retired status is achieved only in relation to benefits earned through employment of one type or another (Atchley 1985).

Although it is difficult, primarily due to the definitional problems just described, to ascertain how many individuals are added to the retirement pool each year, it must be large, although 37 percent of those age 65 and over continue to be participants in the labor force (U.S. Department of Labor 1983). For many retirees, income resources often are reduced drastically upon retirement. Few would argue that the quality of life is related to available spendable income, and for many retired individuals meeting basic survival needs is often difficult. Luxurious life-styles and world cruises often portrayed in magazines targeted for the retired "over 50" population and sponsored by associations such as the American Association of Retired Persons are options available only to a relatively small percentage of the retired group. Understandably, many retirees remain concerned over the relative stability of the social security system, which, incidentally, has been the catalyst for retirement on a grand scale. As Riley and Foner (1968) indicate, finances are important in the relationship between age and attitudes toward retirement.

Income, of course, is not the only factor affecting positive adjustment to retirement. Health is a matter of great importance and concern. As the retired population grows older, good health becomes more problematic. Few survive beyond their seventies without some debilitating health problem, such as arthritis, high blood pressure, poor digestion or related problems. For most, such problems impose few restrictions upon mobility or achieving daily living goals. For others with more severe conditions, the role of patient tends to eclipse preferred retirement activities. Concerns over meeting medical expenses, or anticipated expenses, may lead to conservative spending patterns that, in turn, reduce options and activities. Most older adults rely primarily on Medicare, a federal health insurance program available to individuals 65 and older. For the retiree in poor health, health-related problems may diminish the satisfactions desirable in the world away from work.

Future-oriented retirees who have developed interests and activities also seem to achieve greater gratification. It is accepted, generally, that preretirement programs have been successful in promoting greater satisfaction and adjustment in retirement. Unfortunately, such programs are still a rather novel occurrence, although they seem to be growing in popularity.

Many communities have established home health care programs where social workers and other professionals provide conpanionship, medical care and positive support.

The need for research on retirement continues to be crucial. While the past several decades have produced a significant amount of inquiry by social investigators, the relatively untapped potential of retirement-related research becomes more manifest with the growing number of retirees in this country. From past efforts, we have developed an emerging body of knowledge and understanding of the effects of retirement upon individuals. Obviously, there is much more to learn. Appropriate and valid social policies must be undergirded with a sound base of knowledge.

Retirement is emerging as a desirable goal for more Americans as it becomes more commonplace and publicly accepted. Our attention will now be directed in more detail toward the social and adaptive issues related to growing old in our society.

AGING AND MENTAL HEALTH

The state of mental health among older adults is not appreciably different than that of the population in general. Unfortunately, adaptive problems such as disorientation, memory loss, excessive dependency, and senility are assumed to be inherent to the aging process. The pervasiveness of these myths results in the view that older adults, in general, experience mental health problems. Just as individuals in other stages of the life-cycle, older adults may experience problems of a mental nature that result in dysfunction. And, as with younger people, these problems generally are responsive to treatment. In some instances, these adaptive problems have been present throughout the life-cycle and carried on into old age. Other individuals have managed to function adequately and do not develop mental health problems until late in life, often as a result of interpersonal loss, organic deterioration, or some traumatic event. On the other hand, activity and future orientation appear to be associated with good mental health. Maintaining enthusiasm and working toward goals are antithetical to the development of dysfunctional behavior.

Problems experienced in old age also may be analyzed using a systems perspective. The way that an individual interacts within the environment strongly influences that individual's mental health. Many of the symptoms of dysfunctional behavior that appear in old age may be attributable to environmental factors. Social isolation and loneliness often appear to produce maladaptive behaviors. Overmedication often results in memory loss, disorientation, loss of vigor, or loss of appetite. Depression, one of the more common mental health problems in late life, may be caused by bereavement, anxiety related to income security, a limited social friendship network, health concerns, relocation, and related factors. Ageism and lack of attention to problems of the elderly have led to increased concern about this group's high suicide rate (Figure 12–2). In 1985, 25 percent of all suicides within the United States were among the over 65 population.

Organic deterioration is more common in late life and results from a condition known as Alzheimer's disease. This disease tends to be progressive, with increasing maladaption. Disorientation, memory loss, wandering, and inappropriate behavior are among the symptoms. Fortunately, relatively few older adults are affected by this disease.

Figure 12–2   **Suicide Rates in the United States by Age, Sex, and Race, 1974**

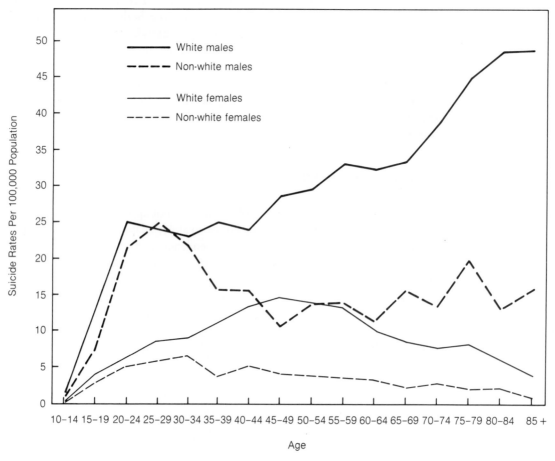

Original Source: The National Center for Health Statistics. As it appears in Marv Miller, *Suicide After Sixty: The Final Alternative,* p. 4. Copyright 1979 by Marv Miller.

Dramatic changes in the mental health of individuals are seldom caused by the aging process alone. Individuals possessing well-integrated personalities who prepare themselves for changes related to retirement, develop leisure-time interests, and plan for the future are less vulnerable to age-related stress factors.

INCOME SECURITY

Justifiably, one of the more persistent anxieties experienced by older adults relates to income security. Inflation, with its consequent effect upon the prices of commodities, has increasingly limited buying power. With few exceptions, income available to individuals after retirement is well below that they received when employed. For many, retirement income is only half of what they received while on the job (Schulz 1980). Few of our present-day older people have earned sufficient incomes to be able to put away money for retirement. Retirement incentive plans such as IRAs, tax-deferred annuities, and Keogh plans were nonexistent during the time of their employment. As a result, the majority of retirees are forced to live on social security payments.

Social Security was never intended to be a complete retirement income plan. It was designed to supplement pension plans provided by the individual's employer. Yet today, 75 percent of retired elderly have only Social Security to meet their financial needs (Barrow & Smith 1983). A smaller number receive Supplemental Security Income (public financial assistance for the elderly) benefits that average only $300 per month. Over 80 percent of the aged have incomes of less than $10,000 per year. Many live at or below the governmentally established poverty level (see Tables 12–2 and 12–3). Older single women, for example, had an average yearly income of $3595 in 1980—well below the poverty level. Their counterparts, older single men, had slightly higher annual incomes of $4367, which borders the poverty line (*Population Bulletin* 1980). Older families with heads over 65 had an annual income of approximately $10,140 per year. As these data suggest, older single women are by far the most jeopardized by limited incomes. With the passing of time, inflation will further reduce the buying power of the nation's aged.

While money does not always produce happiness, it is related to satisfaction in later life. The common myth that older adults need less income to meet their living needs is hardly buttressed by fact. The need for food, clothing, shelter, recreation, transportation, and the ability to buy gifts for grandchildren and family members does not decline with age. Lowered standards of living, unmet needs, and the inability to adequately meet these needs may result in feelings of inadequacy and loss of self-esteem.

Income is an enabling resource and affects the options available in life. As income declines so do those options, including the loss of independence.

Table 12–2   Percentage of Aged Units Below the Poverty Line and 125 Percent of the Poverty Line for One or Two Persons Aged 65 and Older by Gender, Marital Status, and Race, 1982

	White					Black				
Income Status	All Units	Married Couples	Nonmarried Persons Total	Men	Women	All Units	Married Couples	Nonmarried Persons Total	Men	Women
Below poverty line	20	8	29	21	31	52	25	64	49	69
Below 125% of poverty line	32	13	46	34	49	65	39	76	64	80

Note: The money income of aged married couples and nonmarried persons is compared with the official poverty line for aged couples or nonmarried persons living alone. In 1982, the poverty line was $5,836 for two persons 65 and older and $4,626 for one person 65 and older.

Source: Adapted from S. Grad, "Income of the Population 55 and Over, 1982," SSA Publication No. 13–11871, Table 49 (Washington, DC: U.S. Department of Health and Human Services, 1984).

Table 12–3   **Income From Social Security Benefits for Aged Units 65 and Older by Gender, Race, and Marital Status, 1982**

Income (Recipients Only) [a]	White					Black				
	All Units	Married Couples	Nonmarried Persons			All Units	Married Couples	Nonmarried Persons		
			Total	Men	Women			Total	Men	Women
Number of recipients (in thousands)	15,986	6,734	9,252	1,801	7,451	1,527	477	1,049	267	783
Median income [b]	$5,310	$7,670	$4,600	$5,080	$4,490	$3,820	$5,920	$3,210	$3,710	$3,050

[a] Recipients of Social Security may be receiving retired-worker benefits, dependents' or survivors' benefits, transitionally insured, or special age–72 benefits. Units with a person reporting receipt of both Social Security benefits and railroad retirement are excluded (1% of those aged 65 and over).

[b] Rounded to the nearest $10.

Source: Adapted from S. Grad, "Income of the Population 55 and Over, 1982," SSA Publication No. 13–11871, Table 24 (Washington, D.C.: U.S. Department of Health and Human Services, 1984).

Various health and social service resources that have emerged to assist older adults with their needs may not be necessary if retirement income benefits were sufficient to enable the nonworking aged to meet their needs at the marketplace. The United States lags behind other industrialized nations in replacement (retirement) income for its aged, ranking fourth in payments to couples and eighth in income benefits for the single older adult (Wilson 1984).

HEALTH AND HEALTH CARE SERVICES

People of all ages must contend with sickness and health-related problems. In later life, however, the probability of developing health problems becomes more pronounced. Unfortunately, this condition has led many observers to conclude that aging and poor health are synonymous. Such is not the case, if one considers that health problems in old age are treatable and correctable, just as they are at earlier stages in the life-cycle. Older adults are more prone to develop illnesses such as pneumonia, influenza, and gastrointestinal complaints than in the population in general (see Table 12–4). Also, chronic disease, including heart disease, hypertension, cancer, arthritis, diabetes, emphysema, osteoporosis, and visual impairments are more common in old age (Whitney 1976).

Only 5 percent of the older adult population is affected by health problems so severe that their mobility is limited. The majority are able to move about the community even though they may have one or more disease symptoms.

Health care resources are provided primarily through Medicare and Medicaid. **Medicare** is a government health insurance program designed to pay for

Table 12–4   **Death Rates for the Ten Leading Causes of Death for Ages 65 and Over, by Age: 1976 (deaths per 100,000 population)**

Cause of Death by Rank	65 Years and Over	65–74 Years	75–84 Years	85 Years and Over
All causes	5,428.9	3,127.6	7,331.6	15,486.9
1. Diseases of the heart	2,393.5	1,286.9	3,263.7	7,384.3
2. Malignant neoplasms	979.0	786.3	1,248.6	1,441.5
3. Cerebrovascular diseases	694.6	280.1	1,014.0	2,586.8
4. Influenza and pneumonia	211.1	70.1	289.3	959.2
5. Arteriosclerosis	122.2	25.8	152.5	714.3
6. Diabetes mellitus	108.1	70.0	155.8	219.2
7. Accidents	104.5	62.2	134.5	306.7
Motor vehicle	25.2	21.7	32.3	26.0
All other	79.3	40.4	102.2	280.7
8. Bronchitis, emphysema, and asthma	76.8	60.7	101.4	108.5
9. Cirrhosis of liver	36.5	42.6	29.3	18.0
10. Nephritis and nephrosis	25.0	15.2	34.1	64.6
All other causes	677.5	427.8	908.6	1,683.8

Source: National Center for Health Statistics (U.S. Public Health Service), "Advance Report—Final Mortality Statistics, 1976," *Monthly Vital Statistics Report,* vol. 26, No. 12, supplement (2), March 1978; and unpublished data provided by the National Center for Health Statistics.

hospital care and related medical expenses for persons over 65. Due to the escalation of the costs of medical care, the amount of benefits paid by Medicare has decreased to approximately 50 percent of the total cost of the care. The inability of older adults to pay the portion of medical fees not covered by Medicare has resulted in large numbers not seeking necessary medical attention.

Medicaid, a health assistance program for low-income individuals including the aged, is administered at the state level with both state and federal funds used to pay for essential medical treatment. Aged recipients must qualify for the Supplemental Security Income Program in order to establish eligibility for Medicaid benefits. This program pays health care providers for both hospital and related health services. Both Medicare and Medicaid pay for nursing home care where eligibility has been established.

Both Medicare and Medicaid have made it possible for many older adults to obtain needed medical treatment who would not otherwise seek such care. Due to personal cost-related factors, however, many older adults often are forced to delay receiving treatment until health conditions become severe or life threatening. Neither of these health insurance programs is designed to provide funding for preventive health care. Doubtless, many serious health problems could be averted or become less problematic if attention were given to preventive health measures.

As with other government-funded benefit programs, Medicare and Medicaid funds rapidly are approaching deficit spending levels. Various solutions to the financing of health care have been proposed. These include a reduction of benefits and more stringent eligibility requirements and an expansion of government coverage for catastrophic cases. Solutions to financing must be found if the health needs of our older population are to be met.

ABUSE AND NEGLECT

Maltreatment of older adults completes the sequential occurrence of family violence throughout the life-cycle. As is the case with battered children or spouses, the knowledge that old persons are the victims of abuse and neglect is antithetical to our social morality.

Little is known about the form and pervasiveness of abuse and neglect of the elderly due to limited research inquiry. Neglect is the failure to perform the needed activity or task essential for meeting one's daily needs. Abuse is a physical or psychological act intended to inflict harm.

Self-neglect is perhaps the most common. Many older adults lack the necessary resources or skills to provide adequate nutrition or to maintain daily household living tasks, such as washing dishes, cleaning the house, and securing proper health services. Self-neglect is more frequent when older persons are socially isolated and have little involvement with family or friends. Caretakers, usually family members, also may be involved in the neglect of the elderly's physical and emotional needs. Neglect often occurs when an older adult lives with a son or daughter and is dependent. Ignoring daily and special needs, denying transportation, failing to include aged persons as members of family households, ignoring their desires to contribute, and providing improper clothing and diet are among the more common forms of neglect experienced by the aged.

Like neglect, abuse usually occurs when the older adult is living with a relative. Abusers often are overtaxed mentally and emotionally and lash out when demands are made on them by older family members. Physical abuse takes the form of slapping, shoving, punching, or placing the older adults in restraints. Psychological or emotional abuse results from threats (of sending the older adults to nursing homes, etc.), ignoring, ridiculing, taking their social security or other income and giving them no spending money, cursing, and reminding them that they are a burden.

It is estimated that 10 percent of the older population experiences abuse or neglect. The rates are potentially higher, since many victims are reluctant to report experiences for fear of retaliation or placement in a nursing home. Many states have enacted legislation to protect older adults from abuse and neglect. Family violence is an unfortunate and dehumanizing product of our society, which generally focuses upon those dependent upon others for some aspect of their care. Protective services are designed to secure victims from further harm. Unfortunately, such services do little to alleviate the causes of the problem.

NURSING HOME CARE

Most older Americans enjoy reasonably good health, with only 5 percent experiencing health problems so debilitating that they require nursing home care. The contemporary nursing home industry has emerged primarily as a result of Medicare and Medicaid legislation, which allows third-party payments to the providers of health care services. Nursing homes typically are licensed by state health departments, which have the responsibility of periodically reviewing the homes to ensure that minimal standards of care are maintained. In addition, all states require that administrators of homes be licensed, although there is considerable variation in administrator licensing requirements among the states.

Nursing homes often are portrayed as dehumanizing warehouses, where little concern and attention are directed toward the needs of residents. In recent years, more stringent state standards and skillful investigation and evaluation techniques by regulatory agencies have resulted in the provision of high-quality services. Many nursing homes provide excellent patient care and extend special efforts to meet the psychosocial needs of their residents. Other homes are skilled in the delivery of medically related services but lack the foresight, knowledge, and skill to address the psychological and emotional needs of their patients.

The majority of nursing homes in this country are proprietary, that is, they are private profit-making businesses. Some homes are nonprofit and are usually operated through the auspices of religious organizations or units of state or local governments. There appears to be little difference in the quality of care between the private profit-making homes and those of a nonprofit nature. Privately owned facilities are more vulnerable to "shaving" services in order to maximize profit. Strict enforcement of standards, however, minimizes any significant differences in the services provided for residents.

Nursing homes will continue to be the most viable resource for the debilitated elderly. Alternatives such as home health care, visiting nurses, and personal care homes enable the older adult to reside in the community for a longer period of time but tend to defer, not replace, the need for nursing home care (see Figure 12–3). As the need for additional nursing home beds increases (400,000 more by the year 2000), financing the needed care will become more critical. Government financing plans are strained already and should forecasted budget reductions become a reality, alternative financing or other more cost-effective plans must be developed to assure that the debilitated elderly receive essential health care services. In a number of communities, churches, unions, and private profit organizations are developing residential facilities for the elderly.

HOUSING AND TRANSPORTATION

Although the majority of older adults are homeowners, housing often is a major concern for them. The rate of substandard homes among the elderly

Figure 12–3
**Per Capita
Health Care
Expenditures
for the Elderly
by Type of
Care and
Source of Pay-
ment: United
States, 1978**

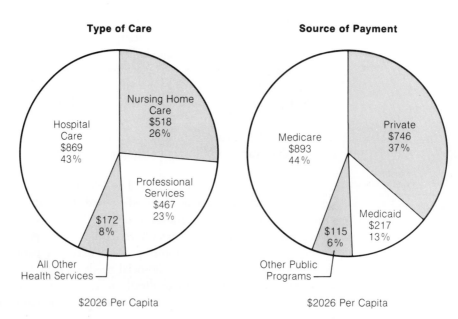

Note: Other health services include drugs and drug sundries, eyeglasses, appliances and other health services.

Source: U.S. Department of Health and Human Services, Federal Council on Aging, *The Need for Long Term Care* (Washington, D.C.: Government Printing Office, 1981), p. 51.

exceeds those of other age groups in the population. Many of their houses become dilapidated over the years, and in later life the ability of older adults to maintain or repair them is limited due to low incomes. In addition, older adults find it very difficult to secure home repair loans. They must be content with progressively deteriorating housing, which often results in inadequate protection from the heat, cold, and other threatening climatic conditions.

Government housing for the aged typically is difficult to secure due to the high demand for low-cost housing units. Even when available, many older adults find low-cost housing unattractive, impersonal, lacking privacy, and too noisy. The advantages include low rent, security, and adequate protection from weather extremes. More units are needed for older adults but are not likely to be forthcoming due to government budgetary limits.

Housing alternatives for the more economically secure aged have recently become more pronounced. High-rise, self-contained apartment complexes have been developed through the auspices of both religious organizations and private sponsorship. These facilities are typically attractive, provide all of the amenities for comfortable living, and assure peer interaction and essential social supports. Many of these facilities also provide differing levels of medical care, nursing services, and meals should individuals become unable to care for themselves in their own apartments. Such facilities, however, are much more costly, and many require substantial down payments before an individual is accepted as a resident. While housing communes are not abundant, they are growing in popularity and provide a family-type living experience for older participants. This type of housing arrangement develops when several older adults pool their resources to rent or purchase a dwelling and share in its up-keep. Basic living costs such as food and utilities are shared, thus enabling each participant to spend less on basic living needs.

Transportation is essential for grocery shopping, attending church services, keeping appointments with doctors and dentists, visiting friends, and maintaining contact with the family. Most older adults must travel some distance in order to procure the necessities for daily living. It often is very difficult for them to do so. Many who once owned an automobile find the hazards of driving and the cost of vehicle maintenance and insurance beyond their capacity to manage. As a result, they depend upon alternate sources of travel. Public transit systems usually are not satisfactory. Bus routes typically are developed for employed workers who regularly use this type of conveyance. Scheduling often results in long walks to bus stops, transfers, and prolonged riding time. In addition, it is extremely difficult for older adults to carry grocery bags onto the bus and walk several blocks from the stop to their residences. A few transit systems have developed specialized services for the handicapped and aged and operate on a door-to-door basis by appointment. Few are available to serve the elderly on an on-call basis. Users must anticipate needs (often as long as two weeks in advance), make the appointment, and hope that they are not forgotten.

Volunteers have been engaged in providing transportation services for the elderly in some communities. Although only a small minority who need this service are able to get it, this option has enabled many older adults to gain mobility for securing needed goods and services. Nutrition programs also have provided transportation to luncheon programs. Some have been able to extend their transportation services to include shopping and social visits. This type of transportation alternative is available only to a comparatively few older adults in need.

The absence of transportation has resulted in many older adults becoming home-bound. Social isolation often is a result. Social isolation leads to the loss of incentive, activity, self-deprecation, and eventually psychological and physical deterioration, thus confirming the public stereotype that older adults elect not to participate in the mainstream of life.

Unfortunately, little has been accomplished in addressing transportation needs of the aged. Indeed, government budget cuts have significantly reduced transportation programs designed for the elderly in many communities. The reader might ask this question: How do we expect older adults to be independent, shop for themselves, attend meetings, and remain engaged with societal institutions if they lack the transportation resources to do so? Such is the case for many of our aged today.

MINORITY GROUP MEMBERS AS OLDER ADULTS

The problems of adaptation discussed earlier in this chapter are also experienced by older minority group members, but to a much greater extent. Life expectancy for both blacks and Hispanics is appreciably less than for whites (see Table 12–5). Approximately 7 percent of the blacks and 4 percent of the Hispanics are 65 or over, compared with 11 percent of the total U.S. population (Watson 1982). Since neither genetics nor heredity has been a factor contributing to a shorter life expectancy for these groups, social and cultural factors are more likely to account for this differential in longevity. As a result of social discrimination, larger proportions of minority populations experience lower incomes, more physically menial and demanding work, and fewer opportunities to achieve essential life-support services. This has resulted in more severe and unattended health problems, inadequate nutrition, fewer opportunities for social advancement, near-poverty wages, and an oppressive cultural environment. Growing old under these adverse conditions has to be difficult. Fortunately, there is some evidence that the social climate is changing and that the opportunity structure in which minorities may compete is becoming more equitable. If such is the case, we can expect to see similar proportions of older blacks and Hispanics achieving late life to those experienced by whites.

Table 12–5   Population 55 Years and Over by Race, 1984 (numbers in thousands)

	Total		White		Black and Other	
	Number	Percent	Number	Percent	Number	Percent
Percent Distribution of Racial Groups by Age:						
All ages	236,416	100	201,555	100	34,861	100
0 to 54	186,220	79	156,420	78	29,809	85
55 to 64	22,210	9	19,805	10	2,400	7
65 to 74	16,596	7	14,959	7	1,637	5
75 to 84	8,793	4	7,981	4	812	2
55 plus	50,195	21	45,136	22	5,509	16
65 plus	27,985	12	25,331	13	2,654	8
85 plus	2,596	1	2,391	2	205	0.1
Percent Distribution of Age Groups by Race:						
All ages	236,416	100	201,555	85	34,861	15
0 to 54	186,220	100	156,420	84	29,809	16
55 to 64	22,210	100	19,805	89	2,400	11
65 to 74	16,596	100	14,959	90	1,637	10
75 to 84	8,793	100	7,981	91	812	9
55 plus	50,195	100	45,136	90	5,059	10
65 plus	27,985	100	25,331	91	2,654	9
85 plus	2,596	100	2,391	92	205	8

Note: Percents may not add to 100 due to rounding.

Source: U.S. Bureau of the Census, *Projections of the Population of the United States, by Age, Sex and Race, 1983 to 2080*, Series P–25, No. 925.

While retirement income benefits for all older adults are relatively low, they are even less for the minority aged (see Table 12–6). For example, in 1983 the percentage of aged white families living below the poverty level was 6.6 percent, compared to 24.3 percent for aged blacks and 15.5 percent for aged Hispanics. The percentage of white women family heads living below the poverty level was 7.0 percent, compared with 26.4 percent for black women family heads. The data are even more revealing when comparing white and black men living alone (18.5 percent and 45.0 percent respectively). For aged white women living alone, the percentage was 24.5 percent compared with 63.4 percent for their black counterparts (Current Population Reports 1977). Accurate income data for aged Hispanics are more difficult to ascertain, but all estimates are that the percentage living below the poverty line is somewhat less than that for blacks.

Many of the necessary support services often are not available to aged minority members due to discrimination, language differences, lack of information concerning eligibility requirements, limited entitlement, pride, and less than vigorous outreach services.

Table 12–6   Number and Percent of Elderly Living in Poverty by Race, Sex, and Living Arrangement, 1983

| | Living arrangement | | | | | |
| | Number (thousands) | | | Percent | | |
Race and sex	In Families	Unrelated Individuals	Total Number	In Families	Unrelated Individuals	Total Percent
White:						
Male	496	298	794	6.1	18.5	8.2
Female	552	1,507	2,059	7.0	24.5	14.7
Total	1,048	1,805	2,853	6.6	23.3	12.0
Black:						
Male	142	105	247	21.9	45.0	28.3
Female	204	340	544	26.4	63.4	41.7
Total	346	445	791	24.3	58.4	36.3
Hispanic Origin:						
Male	38	22	60	17.7	(1)	22.4
Female	35	53	88	13.7	45.7	23.7
Total	73	75	148	15.5	43.7	23.1
All Races:						
Male	656	412	1,072	7.4	22.1	10.0
Female	771	1,861	2,640	8.8	27.7	17.0
Total	1,427	2,273	3,711	8.1	26.5	14.1

Source: Bureau of the Census. Characteristics of the Population Below the Poverty Level: 1983 *Current Population Reports,* Series P–60, No. 147, Table 3.

Unfortunately, growing old as a minority group member only replicates living conditions experienced throughout the life-cycle—but to a greater extent. Poverty, limited options, and discrimination hardly assure that they will attain the security, contentment, and life satisfactions that most older Americans do.

SERVICES FOR OLDER ADULTS

A wide array of social, health, and related support services has either been extended or developed to provide for the needs of the aged. On the federal level, the majority of these programs has their legislative base in either the Social Security Act or the Older Americans Act. Social Security Act programs cover both income maintenance through social insurance and Supplemental Security Income and health services through either Medicare or Medicaid. The Older Americans Act of 1965 provides supplementary services through funding of nutrition programs, transportation, social services, and the coordination of services for the aged.

Through both governmentally and privately sponsored sources, such older citizen participation programs as Foster Grandparents, Green Thumb, and the Retired Seniors Volunteer Program, as well as a variety of self-help programs, have been developed within the past decade. Older adults in the Foster Grandparent Program, for example, are employed part-time to work with children in state schools, hospitals, and day care centers, with pregnant teenagers and with abusive and neglectful parents. Senior Centers provide a site in many communities where older adults can interact, partake of nutritious meals, participate in recreational activities, and pursue hobbies or crafts. Through the auspices of the Older Americans Act, Area Wide Agencies on Aging (AAAs) have been established throughout the country that coordinate services to the aged. Among their many functions are such activities as assessing the needs of the older population, providing or contracting for congregate meals programs, developing transportation services, serving as information and referral resources, and acting as advocates for the aged in assuring that communities will be attentive to their needs.

Meals-on-wheels programs provide hot meals for the home-bound aged and attempt to provide essential social contact with older adults who find it difficult to leave their homes because of limited mobility related to a variety of physical debilities. Adult day care centers enable older adults to remain in the community. Often participants live with a working son or daughter who cannot provide the required daily monitoring for the older person. Day care centers assume caretaking responsibilities during the periods when their children are away at work. These centers usually have a variety of activities and provide health check-ups and supervision for participants. Mental health services are provided through mental health–mental retardation outreach centers, and counseling services usually are available through many local social services agencies to the aged and their families. Older adults living in rural areas often are disadvantaged in that many of these services are not readily available to them, although nutritional and transportation resources usually are offered.

Although the utilization of community services is helpful in meeting the needs of many older adults, they are not widely available in proportion to the numbers in the community that could potentially benefit from them. Outreach efforts have been reasonably successful in securing participation; however, resources are limited and funding levels impose limits on the number that can be served. Often, agencies are not located strategically, and therefore the participation of many older adults is limited. Outreach efforts would be more effective if indigenous workers (older adults) could be employed for that purpose (Stewart et al. 1972).

The need for support services for the aged will continue to expand with the expansion of our older population. New funding sources must be developed to accommodate this growing need. Social, health, and related services are essential in promoting the well being of the older population.

SOCIAL WORK WITH OLDER ADULTS

In recent years, social work practice with the aged has intensified. In 1982, the Bureau of Labor Statistics estimated that 700,000 new jobs would be available in services to the elderly by the year 2000 ("Growth Industries of the Future" 1982). Gerontologists expect most of these jobs to require skills at the BSW social work level or below (McCaslin 1985). Many schools of social work have developed specializations in **gerontology,** and social work research has focused on problems of adaptation and life satisfactions in old age. As a result, research and literature on this topic have developed rapidly, and a beginning knowledge base for intervention is being established. It is now recognized that older adults experience many of the same problems evident at other stages of the life cycle: personal adjustment problems, marital problems, relocation, family conflict, adjusting to separation and loneliness, anxiety over limited income, mental illness, and interpersonal loss, among others. Growing along with this recognition is the acknowledgement that the aged are responsive to social work change efforts.

Direct practice is the most common form of social work intervention with the aged. This type of practice includes working with older adults and their families on specific problems, such as personal adjustment, securing resources to meet their needs, providing emotional support in decision making, dealing with death and dying, mental health counseling, and learning to manage family conflict. Direct practice employs a counseling and guidance approach, stresses problem clarification and the development of options and priorities, and provides an opportunity for the client to express dysfunctional anxiety and emotion.

Community-based practice focuses upon exo-level systems as targets for creating a more responsive opportunity structure for the aged. Using an advocacy approach, the social work function is to "identify issues such as poor housing, lack of transportation, health needs, economic needs, and . . . to mobilize community resources to help bring about change through the development of resources to meet these needs" (Johnson 1983, 234).

Social workers with an older adult clientele must be aware of the special problems they encounter. Many of the aged have been self-sustaining members of society and have developed problems of adaptation only after they reached old age. Accumulated interpersonal losses (i.e., loss of spouse, friends, familiar environment, job, income, physical health, etc.) often produce social and behavioral dysfunctioning that inhibits the achievement of life satisfactions and meeting daily living needs.

Social workers are employed currently in a variety of agencies that serve the elderly, including mental health centers, family service agencies, nursing homes, nutrition programs, recreational centers, hospitals, health and nutrition centers, volunteer programs, transportation and housing programs, protective services programs, and community planning agencies. Social work activity with older adults will continue to be intensified and interventive techniques refined as the theoretical knowledge base expands, resulting in more effective services to the ever-increasing older population in need of them.

SUMMARY

This chapter has examined the problems and issues related to growing old in America. As the older population continues to expand, more creative approaches to meeting their needs must be developed. Problems that must be addressed include inadequate income, ever-increasing costs of health care, housing, and income inadequacies, abuse and neglect, minority status, transportation, and the growing need for services.

The majority of our older adults experience few problems of sufficient magnitude to deprive them of their satisfactions in later life. Far too many, however, suffer from deprivation related to limited resources and unattended health concerns. Social workers can attempt to meet this challenge through the development of more understanding, knowledge, and skill in working with the aged.

KEY TERMS

aging	Medicaid
ageism	Medicare
gerontology	

DISCUSSION QUESTIONS

1. Identify at least three consequences to society because the U.S. population is growing older.
2. Contrast disengagement theory, exchange theory, developmental theory, and activity theory in describing aging.
3. What are the implications of retirement for an elderly person?
4. Why is the suicide rate for the over–65 population increasing?
5. Describe at least four programs available to the elderly to help address their needs.

6.   What are some jobs in the field of gerontology available for a social
worker?

REFERENCES

Atchley, Robert C. 1985. *Social Forces and Aging.* 4th ed. Belmont, Calif.:
Wadsworth Publishing Company.

Barrow, Georgia M. 1986. *Aging, The Individual and Society.* 3d ed. St. Paul,
Minn.: West Publishing Company.

Barrow, Georgia M., and Patricia A. Smith. 1983. *Aging, The Individual, and
Society,* 2d ed. New York: West Publishing Company.

Butler, Robert N., and Myrna I. Lewis. 1977. *Aging and Mental Health,* 2d ed.
St. Louis: The C.V. Cosby Company.

Clark, Margaret, and Barbara Anderson. 1967. *Culture and Aging.* Springfield,
Ill.: Charles C. Thomas.

Cumming, Elaine, and W.E. Henry. 1961. Growing Old: The Process of Disengagement. New York: Basic Books.

Current Population Reports. 1977. *Characteristics of the Population Below the
Poverty Level: 1975.* Series P–60, Number 106. Washington, D.C.: Government Printing Office.

de Beauvoir, Simoe. 1971. *The Coming of Age.* New York: Putnam Publishers.

Dowd, James J. 1975. "Engaging as Exchange: A Preface to Theory," *Journal
of Gerontology* 30 (September): 589–94.

Garvin, R.M., and Robert C. Burger. 1964. *Where They Go to Die: The
Tragedy of America's Aged.* New York: Delacorte Press.

"Growth Industries of the Future." 1982. *Newsweek* (October 18): 83.

Havinghurst, R.J. 1968. "A Social–Psychological Perspective on Aging," *The
Gerontologist* 8, no. 2: 67–71.

Johnson, H. Wayne. 1983. *The Social Services: An Introduction.* Itasca, Ill.: F. E.
Peacock Publishers.

Karp, David A., and William C. Yoels. 1982. *Experiencing The Life Cycle.*
Springfield, Ill.: Charles C. Thomas Publisher.

Kimmel, Douglas. 1974. *Adulthood and Aging: An Interdisciplinary Developmental View.* New York: John Wiley & Sons.

Lauderdale, M., J. Stewart, and G. Shuttlesworth. 1972. "The Poor and the
Motivation Fallacy," *Social Work* (November): 38–42.

McCaslin, Rosemary. 1985. Substantive Specializations in Master's Level
Social Work Curricula.

Riley, Mathilda White. 1968. *Aging and Society.* New York: Russell Sage.

Riley, Mathilda White, and Anne Foener, eds. 1968. *Aging and Society. Volume 1: An Inventory of Research Findings.* New York: Russell Sage.

Schulz, J. 1980. *The Economics of Aging,* 2d ed. Belmont, Calif.: Wadsworth
Publishing Company.

Stewart, James C., Mitchell Lauderdale, and Guy E. Shuttlesworth. 1972. "The Poor and the Motivation Fallacy," *Social Work* 17, no. 6 (November): 34–37.

U.S. Department of Labor. 1983. *Manpower Report to the President, 1983.* Washington, D.C.: Government Printing Office.

Watson, Wilbur H. 1982. *Aging and Social Behavior.* Monterey, Calif.: Wadsworth Health Science Division.

Whitney, Kevin N. 1976. "Health Aspects of Aging." In David B. Oliver, Candace A. Forster, and Kevin H. Whitney, ed., *Human Responses to Aging: Theory and Practice,* pp. 83–104. San Antonio: Trinity University.

Wilson, Albert J. E. III. 1984. *Social Services for Older Persons.* Boston: Little, Brown and Company.

SELECTED FURTHER READINGS

Beaver, Marion L., and Don Miller. 1985. *Clinical Social Work Practice with the Elderly.* Homewood, Ill.: The Dorsey Press.

Burnside, Irene. 1984. *Working with the Elderly: Group Process and Technique.* Monterey, Calif.: Wadsworth, Inc.

Foner, Anne. 1986. *Aging and Old Age.* Englewood Cliffs, N.J.: Prentice–Hall.

Harbert, Anita, and Leon H. Ginsberg. 1979. *Human Services for Older Adults.* Belmont, Calif.: Wadsworth Publishing Co.

Huttman, Elizabeth. 1985. *Social Services for the Elderly.* New York: The Free Press.

Lowy, Louis. 1979. *Social Work with the Aging.* New York: Harper & Row,

III

Social Work:
Its Practice
and Methodology

S ocial work practice and methodology are presented in this section of the book. Chapter 13, "Direct Practice: Social Work with Individuals and Families," examines the most prevalent methodology in professional social work practice, intervention by the social worker with client constituencies who experience problems with social dysfunctioning. Both theory and techniques are discussed as they relate to problem solving strategies with the roles of both social workers and clients identified.

Chapter 14, "Direct Practice: Social Work with Groups," reviews the professional activities of social workers who use the group method in assisting client populations with a variety of problems. Group theory is reviewed briefly and a variety of groups identified. Issues in group formulation, group process, and methods of working with groups are presented.

Chapter 15, "Social Agency Administration," treats the myriad of tasks essential in bringing together the resources, opportunities, roles, and objectives of the social agency in its problem-solving mission. Various strategies of leadership, administration, and management are reviewed as requisites for increasing the efficiency and economy of the agency's activities. The agency's product in relation to the administrative process is analyzed.

The final chapter in this section, Chapter 17, "Research and Practice," treats the utility of social research as an integral part of the problem-solving process. The role of research in policy and practice is explicated to inform the reader of the need to continually buttress practice with data gained from research findings.

The cluster of chapters found in this section provides the reader with an in-depth awareness of basic social work methodology, and its rationale and potential effectiveness in assisting individuals, groups, and communities with problems.

13 Direct Practice: Social Work with Individuals and Families

pproximately seven years ago, Mary Jones, a thirty-six-year-old woman moved to Iowa from West Virginia with her five children. She later was joined by her mother. Mary left two children, both retarded, in West Virginia—a nine-year-old in a state institution and an eight-year-old with friends.

With her in Iowa are Carl, Kate, Bobby, Carol, and Jane. Carl, age nineteen, is a school drop-out who works periodically at mechanic jobs and seems to enjoy them. Kate, age eighteen, completed high school and has clerical skills. Bobby, the eleven-year-old, is physically handicapped and attends school now and then. Carol, age eight, goes to school as often as possible but sometimes stays at home to help around the house with family chores. The youngest child, Jane, age four, is severely retarded and currently residing in an Iowa institution. Four years ago, Mrs. Jones' mother, Shirley, moved to Iowa to live with Mary. She is illiterate and manages the household.

Mary has worked with some degree of regularity as a waitress. She received AFDC in West Virginia and also in Iowa, while living in Clarksville. She moved to Clear Creek, Iowa, a year and one-half ago, where she worked intermittently for Bumps Family Restaurant. Mary was laid off from her job one month ago due to illness, but was promised her job back when her health was better. During her illness, she received health care services at the county out-patient clinic. Records indicate that Mary has never been married.

Mary has come to the local social services agency seeking help with her "down" feelings. She states that she is "about ready to give up" since she never seems to be able to "get on top of her problems." While she now feels reasonably strong, she has not heard from the Bumps Family Restaurant, although they said they would call her as soon as they had an opening. She has considered reapplying for the AFDC program, but she prefers to work. Mary also is concerned because school officials have indicated that Carol must attend school regularly, or they will have the child welfare officials investigate. She is fearful that they might remove Carol from her home. She needs money for rent and food. She says that she has come to the agency as a last resort.

Mary is afraid of her depressed feelings because, in West Virginia, she had been hospitalized for simple schizophrenia. Her family is best characterized as multiproblem. Mary and her social worker identified some immediate objectives that they will work on. First, the social worker will help Mary contact the food bank to arrange food for the family. Mary agrees to go with the social worker to the school to talk with school officials about a plan for Carol. The social worker agrees to assist Mary in contacting the landlord and arranging for emergency rent supports until Mary can find a job or reestablish her eligibility for AFDC. Mary and the social worker also will have weekly conferences to discuss Mary's problems and to develop options for dealing with them.

Unfortunately, the problems Mary is experiencing are neither unusual nor rare. Thousands of individuals like Mary must cope with a variety of problems, and often turn to social agencies for assistance. Social workers who specialize in working with individuals, families, and groups are often the only hope that many people have to find relief for their problems. In this chapter, we will examine how social workers in direct practice with individuals and families assist their clients in finding solutions to their problems.

The society and world in which we live are characterized by rapid transition, change and uncertainty. The technological revolution has contributed to sweeping modifications of life-styles, increased mobility and shifting values. As the capacity to create new products has increased, the shifting job market requires new skills and more adaptable employees. Relationships among individuals have become tenuous and short-lived. As a result, a sense of roots in the community is becoming increasingly more difficult to achieve. Family life has been affected by social and job-related pressures and upward mobility. The pursuit of success has replaced long cherished values regarding the sanctity of family-first goals. The new "liberation movement" has given rise to an emphasis on individuation and happiness as contrasted with strong family commitments. Broken families have become commonplace as marriages are being terminated with ever-increasing frequency.

Emotionally disturbed children, the illicit use of drugs by both adults and children, an increasing burden of caring for older adults, and two-career marriages have created demands on individuals and families that often leave them disrupted, confused, tense, and frustrated.

These and many other social pressures generated by our rapidly changing society are experienced by virtually all of us at one time or another. It is neither unusual nor is it a sign of weakness for individuals and families in stressful situations to seek professional help with the hope of alleviating stress and its **dysfunctional** consequences. All of us have needed the steady guidance of a respected friend or professional at some time. When problems become increasingly stressful and self-help efforts fail to produce solutions, professional assistance may be needed. Direct practice social work is a method of providing that assistance.

Direct practice with individuals, families, and groups is the oldest social work practice method (traditionally referred to as **casework**). As we indicated in Chapter 2, it had its formal developmental roots in the Charity Organization Society Movement, when "scientific charity" was emphasized and the need for trained professional workers became a fundamental prerequisite to a more studied approach in working with client populations. The distinguishing characteristic of **direct practice** (as contrasted with other social work methods) is its face-to-face involvement with individuals, families, and small groups in assisting them to seek solutions to perplexing problems. In this chapter, we will examine the components and characteristics of the direct practice methods used with individuals and families. Direct practice with groups will be explored in the next chapter.

DIRECT PRACTICE: A DEFINITION

A social work direct practitioner assists clients in a change process that focuses on producing a more optimal level of social functioning. Direct practice is both a process and a method. As a process, it involves a more or less orderly sequence of progressive stages in engaging the client in activities and actions that promote the achievement of agreed upon therapeutic goals. As a method, it entails the creative use of techniques and knowledge which guide intervention activities designed by the direct practitioner. Direct practice also is an art that utilizes scientific knowledge about human behavior and the skillful use of relationships to enable the client to activate or develop interpersonal and, if necessary, community resources to achieve a more positive balance with his or her environment (Bowers 1949). Direct practice seeks to improve, restore, maintain, or enhance the client's social functioning (Boehm 1959). The key converging elements in direct practice are

1. it is an art (which involves a skill that results from experience or training);
2. it involves the application of knowledge of human behavior;
3. it is based on client involvement in developing options designed to resolve problems;
4. it emphasizes the use of the client's resources (psychological and physical) as well as those extant in the community in the problem solving process;
5. it is based on an orderly helping process;
6. it is based on planned change efforts; and
7. it focuses on problem solutions.

Although the basis for direct practice was grounded in the philosophy and wisdom of early social work pioneers such as Mary Richmond, Gordon Hamilton, Helen Harris Perlman, Florence Hollis, and others, many changes in practice have occurred over the years. As greater knowledge of human development, ecology, economics, organizational behavior, stress management, social change, and more effective intervention techniques have emerged, direct practice has been enriched and offers a more scientifically buttressed model for intervention. The face-to-face relationship between the social worker and the client has maintained its integrity as a fundamental prerequisite for intervention, as has the emphasis on process (study, assessment, intervention objectives, intervention, evaluation, and follow-up). Democratic decision making and the belief in the dignity, worth, and value of the client system continue to undergird direct practice philosophy. The client's right to self-determinism and confidentiality (privacy) are fundamental practice values in the helping process. These values and practice principles form the fundamental concepts and interventive practice techniques that are identified with direct practice currently.

PREPARATION FOR DIRECT PRACTICE

Earlier in this chapter, we indicated that a requisite for direct practice was an understanding of factors that effect human behavior. The practitioner must not only be armed with an understanding of personality theory and knowledge of the life cycle but must also be able to assess the effects of the environmental context within which behavior occurs. Factors such as race, gender, ethnicity, religion, social class, physical condition, occupation, family structure, health, age, income, and educational achievement are among many of the contributing variables that converge to account for behavior within different social contexts. While it is not possible for practitioners to master all knowledge related to behavior, theories allow us to make guided assumptions about behavior from which we are able to make logical estimates of factors associated with the client's problems. The direct practitioner is able to arrive at probable causes of dysfunction and to establish theoretically plausible interventive activities that will assist client systems in solving problems.

THE DIRECT PRACTICE PROCESS

The orderly process of direct practice consists of social study, assessment, intervention and evaluation. Each step in this process is guided by the application of theory and knowledge of human behavior.

Social Study

The social study consists of obtaining relevant information about the client system and the problem (or problems) being experienced. The client's perception of the problem, its antecedents, how the problem is affecting life satisfaction and performance, attempts at problem management, and outcome goals are important parts of the social study. The practitioner also obtains information regarding the client's ability to function in a variety of roles and collects data that enhance the practitioner's ability to initiate the process of making initial judgements about probable causes and potential actions that might lead to problem resolution. The social study responds to such questions as: Who is the client? What is the nature of the problems as the client sees and experiences them? What has the client done to alleviate the problems? How effective was it? What other individuals or groups are affected by the problems, and how is the client related or associated with them? What are the client's strengths and weaknesses? How motivated is the client to work toward solutions to problems?

Assessment

Assessment consists of making tentative judgements about the meaning of the information derived in the social study. It provides the basis for initiating and establishing intervention objectives and formally engaging the client in the intervention process. At this stage of the direct practice process, the perceived reality of the client's behaviors is filtered through the matrix of theory and understanding of human behavior to arrive at probable causes of the problems. Assessment seeks to answer such questions as: What factors are contributing to the client's problems? What is the potential for initiating a successful change?

Goal Setting

Goal setting is the process where the client and practitioner ascertain intervention options that have the potential to relieve or solve the problem based on the client's abilities and capacities. Short-term and long-term goals are developed after reviewing all options and determining which are most appropriate for the particular client, problem, and situation.

Contracting

In contracting, the practitioner and the client agree to work toward the identified intervention goals. To facilitate and clarify the commitment implied by the contract, the role of the practitioner is identified explicitly and the client agrees to perform tasks related to the solution of the problem. The contract makes visible the agreement both parties have reached and serves as a framework from which they may periodically assess intervention progress.

Contracts may be renegotiated or altered during the course of intervention, as more viable goals become apparent. Contracts also help to maintain the focus of intervention.

Intervention

The focus of direct practice intervention is derived from the social study and assessment and sanctioned by the contract between the practitioner and client. The implementation phase of intervention focuses on the problem and may involve such activities as counseling, role playing, engaging other community resources, establishing support groups, developing resources, finding alternative-care resources, family involvement, play therapy, or related strategies. The goal of **intervention** is to assist the client toward an acceptable resolution of problems. The practitioner must skillfully involve the client throughout the intervention process by providing regular feedback, support, and an honest appraisal of the problem-solving efforts.

Evaluation

Clients are not likely to remain in the intervention process unless they feel some positive movement has been made toward resolving their problems. Evaluation is an ongoing process in which the practitioner and client review intervention activities and assess the impact upon the client's problem situation. Both must intensively examine their behavior, with the goal of understanding the impact upon intervention goals. What has changed? What has not changed? Why? How does the client view the problem at this time? Has social functioning improved? Become more dysfunctional? What is the overall level of progress? Are different interventions needed? Evaluation within this context becomes a self as well as joint assessment process. Based upon the evalua-

Many social workers function in direct practice settings. Here, family members participate in a counseling session with a social worker.

tion, intervention may continue along the same lines or be modified as implied by the evaluative process.

THE DIRECT PRACTICE RELATIONSHIP

Although it has been many years since Biestek (1957) outlined the components of the casework relationship, they continue to be intrinsic to the direct practice relationship. Briefly outlined, these components are as follows:

Self-determinism: Social work practitioners respect their clients' rights to make choices that affect their lives. On occasion, those choices may not appear to be in the best interests of the client; however, the role of the practitioner in such an instance would be to point out the potentially dysfunctional aspects of the choices. Of course, this does not preclude or limit the practitioner's effort to assist the client in making more appropriate choices. However, it does indicate that undue influence or belittling the client is unacceptable behavior in "bringing the client around" to more appropriate choices. Social work is based upon a democratic process, in which self-determinism is a fundamental part.

Confidentiality: The client's right to privacy is guarded by the principle of confidentiality. It is based upon the notion that information shared between the client and practitioner is privileged. The client must not be compromised by making public the content of information disclosed in the intervention process. Confidentiality assures the client that feelings, attitudes, and statements made during intervention sessions will not be misused. This principle also commits the practitioner to using client information only for professional purposes in working with the client.

Individualization and Acceptance: Regardless of the nature of the client's problems, each client has the right to be treated as an individual with needs, desires, strengths, and weaknesses different from those of anyone else. Acceptance is the ability to recognize the dignity and value inherent in all clients, in spite of the complex array of problems that characterizes their behavior.

Nonjudgmental Attitude: Recognizing that all human beings have strengths and weaknesses, experience difficult problems, make improper choices, become angry and frustrated, and often act inappropriately, the practitioner maintains a neutral attitude toward the client's behavior. To judge clients and their behaviors is to implicitly erect a barrier that may block communication with them. From the clients' perspective, judgmentalism places the caseworker in the same category as others who may be making negative judgements about them. Nonjudgmentalism does not limit the right of the caseworker to confront the client with inappropriate behaviors. It does suggest that the client should not be condemned because of them.

Freedom of Expression: The client's need to express feelings and emotions is encouraged. Often, pent up emotions become disabling to the client and result in more problematic behaviors. The client should be encouraged to engage in free and unfettered self-expression within the safety of the direct practice relationship.

The direct practice relationship is the conduit through which assistance is extended by the worker and is received and acted upon by the client. The principles of the relationship just outlined must represent more than a catechism to be learned by the worker, if an effective helping process is to be achieved. These principles must be "experienced" by the client in interaction with the worker. As the client "tests the water" by investing energy in the problem-solving process, trust will be established only if the relationship principles are a distinctive aspect of client–worker interaction.

THE DEVELOPMENT OF PRACTICE SKILLS

The development of competency in using the direct practice method is acquired through study, role playing, and supervised practice. Since direct practice involves the application of knowledge, it is an effective method of problem solving only if employed skillfully. As in other applied professions, skill is an "art" that is enriched and refined continually through the controlled and thoughtful interaction with clients. Just as one would assume that the skill of a surgeon increases with time and experience, those same principles apply to the development of direct practice skills. We will now examine some of the more significant skill areas that are essential for effective direct practice.

Conceptual Skills

The ability to understand the interrelationships of various dimensions of the client's life experiences and problem behaviors and to place them within an appropriate perspective provides a framework from which intervention goals may be established. Conceptual skills enable the worker to view the many incidents and interactions of the client not as discrete entities within themselves but as interacting parts of the client's behavioral repertoire. Without conceptual skills, social study data have little meaning, and assessment may become less accurate. Conceptual skills also involve an ability to place the client's problem within a theoretical framework and to arrive at appropriate intervention strategies directed toward problem solving.

Interviewing Skills

The interview is more than just a conversation with the client. It is a focused, goal-directed activity used to assist clients with their problems. Communication skills are essential in assuring that the interview will be productive. The practitioner must assume the responsibility for maintaining the professional purposes of the interview. Sensitivity to both the client's statements and feelings are necessary. Putting the client at ease, asking questions that enable the client to share observations and experiences, and being a sensitive listener enhance the productivity of the interview. The worker's sensitivity to the client's feelings and ability to communicate an awareness of those feelings strengthen the helping relationship and provide encouragement and support to the client. Empathy (the ability to "put oneself in the client's shoes") is a benchmark quality of the helping relationship. Clients who feel that the worker really "understands" their problems are able to feel more relaxed and hopeful that solutions will be found for them. Not all interviews are conducted for the same purpose. Zastrow (1981) identifies three types of interviews that are used to facilitate the helping process in social work. *Informational interviews* are used primarily to obtain a client history that relates to the problems currently experienced. The history collecting process should not be concerned with all of the life experiences of the client but only selected information that may have an impact on current social functioning. The *diagnostic (assessment) interview* has a more clinical focus, in that it elicits responses that clarify the client's reactions to problems and establishes some sequential ordering of events that enables the practitioner to make initial judgements about events that affect client behaviors. *Therapeutic interviews* are designed to help clients make changes in their life situations that will help alleviate their problem. Not only are the client's feelings and emotions shared in these interviews, but problem-solving options are developed and efforts at change reviewed.

Recording

Maintaining case records that provide insightful information into the client's background (social study data), judgements about the nature of the problem (assessment), and worker–client activity are essential in maintaining the focus of ongoing activities with the client. Practitioners typically carry a large caseload, with many clients over a long period of time. Properly maintained records enable the worker to review the nature of the problem, objectives, and progress in each individual case prior to appointments. In many instances, cases are transferred both within and outside of the agency, and the case record provides an up-to-date accounting of the client's problems and activities directed toward their resolution. Case records also are useful for research purposes. Properly maintained records strengthen the direct practice process. If viewed within this context, record keeping becomes less of an irrelevant chore and more of a vital tool for effective service delivery.

PRACTICE THEORY

Over the years, a number of theoretical approaches to direct practice have emerged. Practitioners have adopted various models and many use an eclectic approach; that is, they integrate different aspects of several theories as a framework for practice. Some often find that one particular theoretical model is viable for one type of problem situation, whereas another may have greater utility in other situations. For example, a caseworker may use behavior therapy with children and ego psychology with adults. The point is that there are many different approaches to practice, each offering the practitioner a theoretical framework for intervention. A few of the more widely accepted social work treatment theories will be reviewed here.

Systems/Ecological Framework

This framework for practice, discussed extensively in Chapter 3, is based upon the observation that individuals and their environment are in a continual state of interaction and that problematic behavior is the result of disequilibrium between these entities (i.e., the individual and the environment). Since people live in a constantly changing environment, adaptive skills are required in order to maintain coping abilities consonant with environmental demands. Adequate coping skills are predicated upon the abilities of individuals, families, and groups to both integrate the consequences of environmental forces into their adaptive response repertoires and to influence (and change) those environmental factors involved in creating dysfunctional stress. As Brieland, Costin, and Atherton (1985, 145) state:

> *The human being and the environment shape each other. Styles of coping with stress emerge from their perceptions of environmental demands and their capabilities for response. The "ecological" model seeks a match between personal and adaptive needs and the qualities of the environment.*

The systems/ecological framework directs the attention of the social worker to the necessity of not only reviewing the adaptive responses of the client system but also to examine the environment within which that system interacts: family, groups, neighborhood, economy, etc. This framework is most useful in the assessment phase of the helping process.

Ego Psychology

Often referred to as psychosocial treatment theory, **ego psychology** stresses the interplay between the individual's internal state and the external environment (see Box 13–1). The individual's developmental experiences, fears, hostilities, failures, successes, and feelings of love and acceptance all converge to form an estimate of self through which life experiences are filtered and responded to. A main feature of this theory deals with the individual's ability to cope with external pressures and to respond in such a way as to produce satisfaction and feelings of security and self-worth. Often, internal stress results from the inability to solve problems of a mental or physical nature. Inappropriate or underdeveloped coping skills aggravate and intensify the problems, thus causing the person to become apprehensive, insecure, unwilling to risk, anxious, or in extreme cases, mentally ill.

Ego psychology also is concerned with environmental factors that affect the individual's adaptive abilities. Job loss, immobility, death, divorce, poverty, discrimination, and child management are among many potentially stressful conditions that may overextend coping capacities. Because stress is experienced individually, practitioners must give individualized consideration to the client in the problem situation. Knowledge of stress management, personality organization, and the effectiveness of coping mechanisms is essential in the assessment process. Ego psychology is an "insight" therapy. Help comes to clients through developing an awareness of their problem and reaction to it and learning to develop more adaptive coping skills, which results from this understanding. Perhaps the "key" principle associated with using ego psychology as a treatment therapy is that of enabling the individual to develop more adaptive coping skills. The result should be the reduction of internal stress, more satisfactory role performance, and greater life satisfaction.

Box 13–1
Ego
Psychology

The dynamic use of the functions of the ego in casework practice is illustrated in the treatment of a twenty-four-year-old housewife who sought help from the Family Service of Cincinnati and Hamilton County for her marital problem and her difficulty in managing her three-year-old daughter, who was not yet toilet-trained. Although Mrs. M. focused chiefly on her own problems during the nine months of treatment, she originally sought help following a vacation with her sister, whose children behaved entirely differently from her own.

Mrs. M. was a tall, striking, well-groomed blond woman who looked like a model or show girl. She was the youngest of five children and seven years younger than the next older child. She had been told repeatedly by her mother that she had been conceived only to save her parents' difficult marriage, which finally had culminated in divorce three years before. Her mother, a rigid, controlling person, had constantly complained about her suffering at the hands of her alcoholic husband, a handsome, charming man whose behavior always caused Mrs. M. much shame and embarrassment. Feeling that she had never belonged within her family group, Mrs. M. had participated actively in dramatic programs but felt hurt when her father never attended. After one year of high school and attendance at a special business school, she became a typist in an institution where she lived because of her unpleasant home. This was the happiest time of her life.

She married early in her pregnancy after a stormy three-year courtship during which Mr. M. had constantly belittled and ignored her. She described Mr. M. as pleasant, brilliant, and ambitious in his work in a civil-service position. Although they were well suited sexually, she said she always felt inferior to him and belittled by him as her mother had been by her father. She wondered if she demanded too much from him, compared him to her father, and frequently confused the two. Often referring to her daughter as "it," and as one year older than she actually was, she emphasized her own repugnance to the child's soiling and described, at great length, the stools and the problems around toilet-training. With guilt, she told of frequently sending the "noisy, aggressive, though otherwise normal" child to the paternal great-grandmother who had reared Mr. M. after his own parents' divorce. Mrs. M. found herself yelling at her daughter as her own mother had yelled at her children. She constantly likened her feelings to those of her child's but contrasted her own conforming behavior toward her mother with her daughter's aggressiveness. In the early interviews Mrs. M. emphasized her inadequacies and faults, her desire to be liked, and her constant expectation of being rebuffed, mistreated, and hurt. Her relationships indicated that she continuously set up situations in which she would be depreciated and rejected. She, too, had problems with elimination. She had many rigid patterns of performance, excellent abilities in sewing and designing and in making the most of her appearance. There were indications of good relationships with her siblings and some friends.

After the first thirteen interviews, a psychiatric consultation was utilized to clarify further the clinical, dynamic, and genetic diagnosis as a guide in planning continued treatment. The predominant picture was that of a severe masochistic neurotic character disorder. The unresolved conflicts at both the pregenital and oedipal developmental levels, with resultant lack of personality organization, were similar to those observed frequently in adolescents. The defense mechanisms utilized to handle these various conflicts permeated Mrs. M.'s entire life adjustment. Inasmuch as her behavior patterns and almost all her relationships were determined illogically by previous life experiences, they represented a repetition compulsion. Of genetic significance were Mrs. M.'s early feelings of being unloved and worthless. She felt that she came into existence only to preserve her parents' marriage, that she deserved no basic pleasures for her own sake, and that she had to conform and achieve only for her parents' sake.

In her relationships both with her husband and others, Mrs. M. demonstrated the repetitive pattern of her masochism—her self-depreciation and her need to suffer even to the point of eliciting mistreatment through provocative behavior. Her masochism as well as her conforming behavior represented defenses against the anxiety engendered by her marked hostility toward her parents. The mechanism of identification was also significant in determining her behavior. She was identified with her daughter in expecting and encouraging her to be conforming and much more grown up than she was emotionally ready to be. She also had made a hostile identification with her mother's masochism and attitudes toward children. Her attractiveness and good grooming were overcompensatory and served as a compulsive defense in response to her own soiling tendencies and her concept of women as dirty and inferior. Her interest in dramatics and the meticulous care of her body also served as sublimations for her narcissism and exhibitionism and constituted practically the only channels available to her for counteracting her deep feelings of unworthiness as a person.

In the relationship with the caseworker, Mrs. M. was eager to please but she also tested the worker's acceptance of her through provocative, depreciatory attitudes. Her strengths included a good capacity to relate to others in more positive ways and a real desire for change based on her recognition that life could be different. In adolescence, she had moved away from home to improve her life situation, . . . and she had sought help from the agency after observing her sister's happier family. Early in the contact she indicated a capacity to take responsibility for her own involvement in the family problem.

The casework treatment aimed principally to provide her with a supportive relationship, with some use of the technique of clarification.

The worker helped Mrs. M. acquire more self-regard by pointing out her many strengths and abilities when Mrs. M. emphasized all her deficiencies. The worker did not accept Mrs. M.'s evaluation that events had been as devastating as Mrs. M. had described them. She offered direct suggestions about housekeeping and other feminine activities, and did not accept Mrs. M.'s rigid patterns as desirable for everyone. As a relaxed, accepting, mature woman, the worker provided a healthier pattern of femininity for Mrs. M. and gave her permission to enjoy being a woman and to have more meaningful and enjoyable relationships. Mrs. M. indicated some surprise in finding the worker's attitudes so different from those of other women—her acceptance, her lack of defensiveness, and her encouragement. She showed almost childlike pleasure in gaining approval for something she had done well.

With growing confidence in herself and in the worker, Mrs. M. began to express some hostility by verbalizing her irritation and annoyance about the disheveled appearance of the worker's desk and her casual, "not-too-clean" shoes. In many of Mrs. M.'s comments she expressed a depreciating attitude toward blacks. It seemed especially meaningful to Mrs. M. that the worker, who was black, was not threatened but remained accepting and giving, as she clarified Mrs. M.'s misconception that outward appearances are of major importance. Because Mrs. M. herself was so aware that she tended to confuse her father with her husband, she was further helped to understand that, as two separate persons, they would not necessarily behave toward her in the same way. The worker helped her to see that in some ways she expected belittling behavior from her husband, had elicited it, and at times had had a distorted view of it.

As Mrs. M. gained further security about her own worth and adequacy in the face of her hostile, depreciatory attitudes toward the worker, there was increasing evidence of her improved relationships with her husband and daughter. Her greater relaxation with the child was reflected in her daughter's improved behavior, the absence of soiling, and comfortable acceptance of toilet-training. She was pleasantly surprised when the child expressed her love, and she spoke warmly of how much fun children can be. She showed increasing ability to relate to the positive qualities of her husband, less provocative behavior, and greater capacity to enjoy his companionship. She bought family pictures, expressed happiness at her sister's wedding, and felt more like a member of her original family than ever before. She felt differently about her mother's handling of her father; she no longer thought that her mother bowed down to him, and even began to think that there were two sides to her parents' problems. She spoke humorously of her past upsets over everyday family problems, and compared them to her current relaxed attitudes when similar things occurred. She gradually felt that she had less need for the worker's help as a mutual plan for spacing appointments and eventually terminating treatment was discussed. Approximately one year after termination she was eager to inform the worker about her pleasure in her current pregnancy and about the family's progress, which included her continued improvement, her daughter's good adjustment in kindergarten, and her husband's promotion at work, which would better the family's living conditions.

In this casework treatment, the therapeutic relationship provided the client with a truly corrective experience, through the support of her strengths, and helped to clarify some of her inappropriate defenses. The change in Mrs. M. was effected within the transference relationship but without interpretation or deep insight. It is an example of the effectiveness of casework treatment on the ego-reality level when the principles of ego psychology are utilized.

This case was taken from Othilda Krug, "Part II, Casework Practice, The Dynamic Use of the Ego Functions in Casework," *Social Casework in the Fifties,* pp. 143–147. (New York: Family Service Association of America, 1962). Reprinted with permission.

Problem-Solving Approach

One of the more widely used approaches in social work practice is identified as the "problem-solving approach." This approach, developed by Perlman (1957), emphasizes that successful intervention is based upon the motivation, capacity, and opportunity of the client systems for change. Recognizing that problems often immobilize the client, that the abilities of the client then are neutralized or applied inappropriately, and that opportunities for problem solutions are not engaged, this approach stresses the need to "free up" the client system so that the client can work toward solving the problem. The problem-solving approach requires that the client do more than just identify and talk about problems—although that is necessary. The client must begin to move toward taking action (within his or her capacity to do so) to resolve or alleviate the discomfort produced by those problems. Often this requires that resources (the opportunity structure) be tapped to achieve these goals. Generally, the opportunity resources include those of the agency involved in the helping process, although it may extend to other community resources. Maximal problem solution can only be achieved if the three components—motivation, capacity, and opportunity—are engaged in the process.

Behavior Modification

Social learning theory undergirds behavior modification therapy. Based on the assumption that all behavior (adaptive as well as maladaptive) is learned, behavior modification is an "action" therapy (see Box 13–2). Developmental processes that contribute to the acquisition of positive human responses also are responsible for the development of inappropriate or dysfunctional ones. Since behavior is learned, it is possible to assist the client in discarding faulty behaviors and acquiring new and more appropriate response patterns. Recognizing that external events and internal processing result in specific behaviors, change is effected by modifying one's actions that will result in changing internal thought patterns. Any attempt to change the internal process (i.e., assisting the client to develop insight into the problem apart from directly addressing behavior changes) is considered to be generally ineffective.

Based on these general principles, the practitioner using behavior modification approaches intervention with the following organizing framework:

1. in a social study, only information that is directly related to the current problem is essential for intervention. Antecedent factors are pertinent, such as when the problem began, the circumstances that contribute to the problem behavior, and the client's efforts at problem resolution;

2. intervention must focus upon specific problems, not the entire range of problems, that the client experiences. The practitioner assists clients in resolving each problem in an independent manner rather than treating them in total;

Box 13–2
Behavior
Modification

One case involved a little boy who was unwilling to go to bed alone because he claimed he was afraid of the dark. Many therapists would view such a problem as stemming from underlying dynamic causes, but a careful analysis of the situation indicated that the boy was only afraid of the dark at home. He had no fear when he stayed with his relatives. His parents' attention to the fear seemed to be maintaining it. The clinicians prescribed a simple program in which the parents agreed to play with the child, which they did not ordinarily do, each time the boy went to sleep without crying or fussing. The darkness phobia disappeared within a week.

A more complex case involved a nine-year-old boy who had been very ill in his early years. He was quite demanding and threatened to hold his breath—at times he did so until he actually passed out—if his parents did not give in. Because the parents were so frightened of causing physical damage to the boy, they always gave in to his requests. We were concerned about this physical problem and his parents' apprehension if we advised them to ignore his demands. Hence, we decided to focus on reward for changing behavior rather than extinction. Although we had no control to rule out the effects of novelty or a change in the parents' attitudes, once a point system was set up so that the boy could earn through good behavior the same sorts of things for which he had disrupted the household, the family returned to normal.

Excerpted from Virginia Binder, "Behavior Modification: Operant Approaches to Therapy," Virginia Binder, Arnold Binder, and Bernard Rimland, eds., in *Modern Therapies*. (Englewood Cliffs, N.J.: Prentice-Hall, Inc., 1976). Reprinted with permission.

3. although the client's "feelings" are considered an important factor, the behavioral act is the target not intrapsychic dynamics. The practitioner assists the client in developing specific techniques and learning more appropriate behavioral responses, as opposed to altering thought processes related to the problem and its effect. Thought process are considered to be the results, not causes, of behaviors.

Behavior modification treats the objective, definable dimensions of human response patterns. To facilitate engaging the intervention process, the practitioner and client must agree upon the problem to be addressed, contract to work on that problem, agree upon the responsibility each will assume in the change effort, specify goals and objectives, discuss the techniques to be employed, and commit themselves to the treatment effort. As with other therapies, monitoring and evaluation are important dimensions of the process. As more functional and acceptable behavior evolves, it is reinforced by more adaptive functioning. Dysfunctional responses are discarded as they become less functional and rewarding for the client.

Reality Therapy

This therapeutic approach is based upon the assumption that individuals are responsible for their behavior. Maladaptive behavior is viewed as the product of an identity deficiency. Identity is a basic psychological need of all human beings and is successfully achieved through experiencing love and a sense of self-worth. Individuals who have been deprived of love fail to experience a sense of worth and, as a consequence, develop poor self-concepts. Change is effected by confronting clients with irresponsible behaviors and encouraging them to accept responsibility for their behavior. It is assumed that clients cannot develop a sense of self-worth while engaging in irresponsible behaviors.

Since **self-concept** is an internal reaction to the perception of how others see them, the practitioner's role in establishing a warm, friendly, accepting relationship becomes an important factor in the intervention process. As with the case of behavior modification, the focus of intervention is on the client's actions as opposed to feelings. Confrontation with inappropriate behaviors is emphasized as is the rejection of rationalizations (excuses). Many practitioners elect reality therapy as an intervention framework due to its straightforward application and the more informal, relaxed role of the therapist.

Other Approaches

A number of other treatment theories are used by practitioners. Among the more popular models derived from theory are the "task-centered" approach (Reid & Epstein, 1972), which stresses the selection and the establishment of specific tasks to be worked on in problem solving within a limited time period; "rational emotive therapy," which focuses upon "self-talk" as a target for change, and "role therapy" which examines both descriptive and prescriptive roles played by clients, identifies incongruities in role expectations as well as dysfunctional role behavior, and guides the client toward more functional and appropriate role performance.

THE VARYING ROLES OF THE DIRECT PRACTITIONER

Direct practice is the primary method used by social workers, although contemporary practice generally requires that the worker become involved in group work and community organization methods as well. Competence in the use of all social work methods enhances the effectiveness of the worker in seeking solutions to individual as well as community-related problems. At times, the worker becomes a "generalist" in the problem-solving effort. Many practitioners are employed in highly therapeutic environments, such as psychiatric or family service settings, while others work at agencies, such as a department of human resources, serving people with less specialized problems. Private practice also has increased in recent years, and typically calls for competence in psychotherapeutic and intensive counseling skills. Practitioners continue to develop resources that enable clients to achieve a more satisfactory level of adaptation regardless of the setting in which social work is practiced.

THE BACCALAUREATE SOCIAL WORKER IN DIRECT PRACTICE

As generalist social workers, practitioners at the baccalaureate level typically find employment in social agencies specializing in direct practice. The nature of client problems with which they work is enhanced by a generalist background and focus. Direct practice with individuals does not always demand in-depth psychotherapeutic treatment. Although interviewing and assessment skills always are essential in establishing intervention goals, the BSW worker need not be concerned with those skills required for intensive psychotherapy. It is important to remember that direct practice with individuals extends far beyond psychotherapeutic involvement. The case of Mary, presented at the opening of this chapter, is a good example. The BSW worker could be involved in assisting Mary in identifying needed resources that would reduce the stress she was experiencing. By arranging for food supplies, developing a plan with the school for Carol, and assisting in securing either a job or establishing eligibility for AFDC, the worker would be involved in pulling in an array of resources, thus providing necessary relief for Mary and assisting her in reestablishing a sense of control over her life. The counseling skills of the BSW worker would be useful in providing Mary with an opportunity to "air" her problems and explore alternatives for resolving them. Obviously, if it is subsequently determined that Mary's depression needs psychiatric evaluation and treatment, the worker would assist her in locating the appropriate resources.

The skill of the BSW practitioner in articulating community resources in the problem-solving process must not be underestimated. The knowledge of resources and preparing clients to use those resources is paramount in problem resolution. BSW practitioners are employed in a variety of direct practice settings. Among the many opportunities are agencies such as state departments of human resources (or public welfare), mental health and mental retardation programs, children's service agencies (child welfare and childcare institutions), halfway houses, nursing homes, areawide agencies on aging, agencies serving battered women, rape crisis centers, and day care centers.

SUMMARY

In this chapter, we defined direct practice with individuals and examined the components of the direct practice process, skills essential for effective practice, and theoretical models that serve to structure intervention. Direct practice has been identified as a direct services process that assists individuals and groups through a therapeutic problem-solving process.

KEY TERMS

casework	ego psychology
direct practice	intervention
dysfunctional	self-concept

DISCUSSION QUESTIONS

1. Define direct practice as a social work method. Identify the converging elements of direct practice.
2. Describe the elements of the direct practice process. How is this process enhanced by the direct practice relationship?
3. What types of skills are essential for direct practice? Why?
4. Review and identify the key elements of the various practice theories identified in this chapter. How are they alike? Different?
5. Discuss the role of the BSW social worker in direct practice.

REFERENCES

Biestek, Felix. 1957. *The Casework Relationship.* Chicago: Loyola University Press.

Binder, Virginia, Arnold Binder, and Bernard Rimland, eds. 1976. *Modern Therapies.* Englewood Cliffs, N.J.: Prentice–Hall Inc.

Boehm, Werner. 1959. *The Social Casework Method in Social Work Education,* Curriculum Study, Vol. X, pp. 44–45. New York: Council on Social Work Education.

Bowers, Swithun. 1949. "The Nature and Definition of Social Casework." *Social Casework,* 30 (December): 417.

Brieland, Donald, Lela B. Costin, and Charles R. Atherton. 1985. *Contemporary Social Work.* New York: McGraw–Hill Book Company.

Perlman, Helen Harris. *Social Casework: The Problem Solving Process.* Chicago: University of Chicago Press, 1957.

Reid, William J., and Laura Epstein. 1972. *Task–Centered Casework*. New York: Columbia University Press.

Zastrow, Charles. 1981. *The Practice of Social Work*. Homewood, Ill.: The Dorsey Press.

SELECTED FURTHER READINGS

Germain, Carel B. 1981. "An Ecological Perspective in Casework Practice," *Social Casework,* 6:326.

Hollis, Florence. 1964. *Casework: A Psychosocial Therapy*. New York: Random House.

Pincus, Allen, and Anne Minahan. 1973. *Social Work Practice: Model and Method:* Itasca, Ill.: F. E. Peacock Publishers, Inc.

Reid, William J., and Ann W. Shyne. 1975. *Brief and Extended Casework*. New York: Columbia University Press.

SOCIAL GROUPS: A DEFINITION

Social groups are formed for many purposes. The most common type is the **natural group**, in which members participate as a result of common interests, shared experiences, similar backgrounds and values, and personal satisfactions derived from interaction with other group members. A street gang or neighborhood group of individuals who "hang out" together is a natural group. Such groups are further characterized by face-to-face interactions and an emotional investment in the role of group member. Natural groups are seldom formed purposefully to meet specific objectives. All of us are members of natural groups, and seldom is our membership in those groups the result of a planned effort to become involved. In natural groups, a leader often emerges without premeditation or election by group members but rather because one member possesses behavioral attributes or resources that are highly valued by the other group members. Like all groups, natural groups tend to be transitory in nature, with old members exiting and new ones entering throughout the group's life cycle.

Other groups are formed purposefully for a specific reason. For example, apartment house residents may organize to seek building repairs and better living conditions, or a church or synagogue may organize a softball team. Established agencies, such as the YMCA or YWCA, might organize recreational groups within the city. A common characteristic of each of these groups is that they are developed to achieve a specific purpose.

Regardless of the reasons for which a group is formed, the social group work method may be employed to assist group members in achieving personal growth through the democratic process. Sherif and Sherif (1956, 144) suggest a definition of a **group** derived from empirical observations,

> *a group is a social unit which consists of a number of individuals who stand in (more or less) definite status and role relationships to one another and which possesses a set of values or norms of its own, regulating the behavior of individual members, at least in matters of consequence to the group.*

GROUP FOCUS

Social workers engage in practice with groups to accomplish a variety of tasks. Generally, however, groups may be classified in terms of a specific purpose. Several of the more common types of groups are identified and discussed in Box 14–1.

Recreation Groups

The primary objective of this type of group is to provide for the entertainment, enjoyment, and experience of participants. Activities such as athletic games or table games are typical recreational outlets. Community centers,

YM/YWCAs, and settlement houses routinely provide this type of group activity, as do senior centers for older adults. Participation provides opportunities for shared interaction, interdependence, and social exchange. Group recreational activities also provide constructive outlets for individuals in a monitored environment. Group workers must be sensitive to scheduling arrangements and the development of activities that are of interest to prospective participants.

Recreation–Skill Groups

As differentiated from recreation groups, the purpose of the recreation-skill group is to promote development of a skill within a recreational/enjoyment context. Ordinarily, a resource person with appropriate expertise teaches participants the basic essentials necessary to develop greater competency in a craft, game, or sport. Tasks are emphasized and instruction is provided by the resource person (a coach, for example).

Educational Groups

This type of group is formed for the purpose of transmitting knowledge and enabling participants to acquire more complex skills. Although educational groups may take on a classroom appearance, emphasis is given to group task assignments, and opportunities for interaction and idea exchange buttress didactic presentations. Educational groups vary in purpose, from learning to repair an automobile to learning the most effective techniques in managing an Alzheimer's patient. Group leaders usually are persons with professional expertise in the area of interest for which the group was formed.

Socialization Groups

From a more traditional perspective, these groups typify the purposes and goals of social group work in that they seek to stimulate behavior change, increase social skills and self-confidence, and encourage motivation (Euster 1975, 220). The group focuses on assisting participants to develop socially acceptable behavior and behavioral competency. Personal decision making and self-determinism are emphasized as integral aspects of the group process. Typically, socialization groups may consist of runaway youth, predelinquents, or older adults seeking remotivation groups (Zastrow 1981, 351). Leadership is typically provided by a social worker familiar with group dynamics and knowledgeable of the problem area experienced by the participants.

Self–Help Groups

These groups are composed of individuals with specific personal or social problems. Membership in the group is usually based on voluntary participation, and members often have "given up" on resolving their problem through community agencies or institutions. Members are expected to make a strong personal commitment to the group, its members, and its goals. Mutual aid and interdependence are given high priority. Personal involvement, face-to-face

Box 14–1
Illustrations of
Different
Types of
Groups, Their
Focus and
Membership

Recreation Group: A YWCA organizes and promotes dominos, cards (bridge, etc.), basketball, and volleyball groups for interested community residents of all ages.

Recreation–Skill Groups: The extension division of a local community college offers courses in the manual arts, golf, swimming, volleyball, sewing, and macrame for community residents who wish to develop skill in those areas. Task development is emphasized and mutual interaction is encouraged in the learning process.

Educational Groups: A group of middle-aged adults is offered opportunities to learn more about the aging process and how to cope with problems of their aged parents by a local family service agency. At the same time, the agency sponsors a group for pregnant women and their husbands, who want to learn parenting skills. In both groups, discussion is emphasized and group members are encouraged to identify their specific concerns for group reaction and discussion.

Socialization Groups: A halfway house serving delinquent adolescents develops a weekly group meeting for its residents. Discussion focuses on specific problems experienced by group members. Activities are introduced that require cooperative interaction among group members for successful completion (i.e., yard maintenance, household chores, etc.). Emphasis is given to democratic participation and personal decision making.

Self–Help Groups: An Alcoholics Anonymous group is formed by individuals wanting to overcome an alcohol addiction. The purpose of the group is to provide support and reassurance to group members in dealing with alcohol-related problems, with the goal of helping members "dry up."

Therapeutic Groups: These groups may consist of individuals who have difficulty in dealing with emotional problems associated with divorce, interpersonal loss, alcohol- and drug-related problems, mental health problems, difficulties in parent-child relationships, or other areas in which dysfunctional behavior results. Typically, emotional problems are related significantly to the problems being experienced by group members.

Encounter Groups: A group is organized by a local service agency to help young men and women who lack assertiveness, are self-depreciating, and feel inadequate. Members are encouraged to be self-expressive, learn to risk, to become more insightful into their own and others' feelings, to provide mutual support, and to establish meaningful relationships. A "safe, nonjudgmental" environment is essential for the successful participation of members.

interaction, and a willingness to respond to another member's need are expected.

Self-help groups are formed for different purposes: for recovery and growth, as in the case of Alcoholics Anonymous or Synanon; advocacy, such as Prolife or Women's Liberation; or a combination of personal growth and advocacy such as Parents Without Partners (Zastrow 1981, 348).

Self-help groups do not always seek professional group work leadership. Effective efforts to resolve problems are based upon personal involvement and a willingness to assist fellow members in learning to cope and develop adaptive skills. Since members have experienced the same problem, they may be more empathetic and insightful into the consequences and can provide a more understanding response.

Therapeutic Groups

These groups require skilled professional leadership. Group members typically have intensive personal or emotional problems requiring the expertise of a well-trained professional, such as a master's degree level social worker, a clinical psychologist, or other professional counselor. Monitoring group interaction and its effects upon members is an essential requirement of the group leader. Various therapy approaches may be used to promote therapeutic interaction directed toward behavioral change. Therapeutic groups also may be supplemented by individual treatment in some instances.

Encounter Groups

These groups are oriented toward assisting individuals in developing more insightful self-awareness and interpersonal skills. Such groups are characterized by a secure environment in which members can be openly expressive, develop a sense of trust, receive candid feedback, and develop sensitivity to their own and others' feelings and emotions. Assertiveness and confidence resulting from heightened self-acceptance and awareness promote more genuine relationships and enhance the quality of interpersonal communication. Encounter groups are identified by many different titles: T (training) groups, sensitivity groups, and personal growth groups.

GOALS OF SOCIAL GROUP WORK

Group work is a process and an activity that seeks to stimulate and support more adaptive personal functioning and social skills of individuals through structured group interaction. Euster (1975) and Konopka (1954) emphasize the development of communication competency, adaptive coping skills, and effective problem-solving techniques as goals of the group work experience. Group work techniques can be used more effectively when goals and objectives are related to the needs of group members. Effective group work capitalizes on the dynamics of interaction among members of the group. Members are encouraged to participate in decision making, questioning, sharing, and contributing their efforts toward the achievement of agreed-upon goals and objectives.

EFFECTIVE GROUP DEVELOPMENT

The achievement of desired outcomes of the group process is dependent on several key considerations. *Purposefulness* is an essential characteristic for maximum effectiveness of the group work process. Purposefulness involves the establishment of specific goals and objectives and access to their achievement by the group. Purposefulness provides the direction or intent for each group session and provides a framework for monitoring and evaluating the group's progress.

Leadership is essential in assisting the group maintain its focus and encouraging maximum participation of members. The group worker may play an active or passive role in the group, depending upon the needs of the group as it moves toward the established goals and objectives. The leader must be skilled in group processes and able to perform a variety of roles in supporting the accomplishment of tasks necessary to maintain group integrity and continuing progress. Zastrow (1981, 364) has identified a wide range of role responses that may be required of a group leader, such as "executive, policy maker, planner, expert, external group representative, controller of internal relations, purveyor of rewards and punishments, arbitrator and mediator, exemplar, ideologist, and scapegoat".

Effective leadership is essential to the successful achievement of the group's purposes. The methods which a leader may use to accomplish group goals should be consistent with the values and purposes of social work practice. Wilson and Ryland (1949, 60–99) have identified five leadership styles, four of which are not compatible with social work goals:

1. the *dictatorial* or *authoritarian* method in which the leader orders and the members obey;

2. the *personification* method where members seek to imitate the group worker and attempt to be like him or her, but they do not explore and find their own abilities;

3. the *perceptive* method wherein the worker gives instructions, the group members carry them out and learn skills, but they are not detecting their own resources and capacities;

4. the *manipulative* method where the group worker goes with the group through a phase of planning and decision making. In fact, the group is only accepting a prearranged program of the leader, and is deceived into believing that the group itself came to the decision;

5. the *enabling* method, where the group worker helps the members to participate with full responsibility in the life of the group, in its planning and program, in developing their own ideas, skills, and personal attitudes, and to make their own decisions regarding the purposes and actions of the group.

Only the enabling method fully embraces the principles of democratic process and encourages individual responsibility and risk sharing as products of group interaction and decision making. The success of group process and goal attainment is related to a large extent to effective group leadership. Needless to say, the group leader largely is accountable for group maintenance and the success (or failure) of the group to achieve its purposes.

The selection of group members is an important factor in achieving group cohesion. In composing groups, the group worker must accurately assess the individual's needs, capacity for social functioning, interests, and willingness to assume an active role as a group member. Although diversity of background and experience may enhance alternatives for achieving the group's purposes, homogeneous (common) motives are essential to the formation of the group and identification as a group member. Members with few common interests often have more difficulty in becoming involved in group activities. Age and/or gender may be critical factors, depending upon the purposes of the group and the activities designed to achieve those purposes. Individuals with severe emotional problems or behavior disorders may be disruptive to the group process; thus, careful consideration should be given to including them as group members. Members should have the ability to focus on group tasks. Systematic disruptive behavior is not only disconcerting but may lead to group disintegration. The type of group being formed (i.e., recreational, educational, etc.) will determine the criteria for the selection of members. In all instances, selection should be based upon the "principle of maximum profit" (individuals likely to achieve the greatest benefit). The assessment of individuals for group membership is enhanced by a personal interview prior to inclusion in the group (Klein 1972, 66).

The size of a group is to a large extent determined by its purposes. To determine in advance that four, six, or fifteen members is the "ideal" size of a group has little validity. It is more effective to examine the goals and purposes of the proposed group when determining group size. If, for example, anonymity (or the ability to "lose" oneself) is a desirable end, a larger number of members may be indicated, thus assuring more limited interaction and group fragmentation (i.e., the emergence of subgroups). Smaller groups, by definition, demand more intimate interaction and group pressures typically are intensified. Absenteeism affects group process and task accomplishment more in small groups than large. Small groups may function more informally than larger ones, which usually require a structured format. The role of the group leader also varies with the size of the group. The democratic process can be achieved in both large and small groups, although it is more difficult in the former. The principles and techniques of social group work are effective with large and small groups alike (Klein 1972).

The number of members selected for the group is dependent upon the desired effect upon its individual members, the needs of the members, and their capacity to participate and support group purposes. Generally, a small group may be composed of four to nine members, whereas a large group may consist of ten to twenty members.

THEORY FOR GROUP WORK PRACTICE

Social group work is a direct social work practice method requiring the social worker to be familiar with theories related to group behavior. Group theory

Most social service agencies provide group experiences for clients in order to serve more of them effectively.

provides a framework for promoting guided change through group interaction. The discipline of social psychology has contributed much to our understanding of group formation, roles, norms and values, dynamics, and cohesion. Sherif and Sherif's (1956) contribution to the understanding of group formation, maintenance, and conflict resolution; Lewin's (1951) conceptualization of field theory; and Moreno's (1953) insights into group configurations have been helpful in gaining greater awareness of how groups function. Early social group work pioneers also have contributed valuable experiential and theoretical insights that added to the knowledge base from which an informed approach to working with groups can be employed.

Social group work can be distinguished as a professional social work method by the informed application of theory in assisting groups to achieve their objectives and goals. Since groups vary extensively in their composition, types, and purposes, the worker also must have a broad-based understanding of the life cycle, emotional reactions to stress, and maladaptive behavior. Group workers must have skill in working with the group and sensitivity in assisting the group move toward the achievement of its goals.

GROUP WORK SETTINGS

Traditionally, social group work was practiced in recreational settings, such as the YWCA/YMCA, settlement houses, and community centers. With the growing popularity of group work, along with the redefinition of the scope of social work practice, group work has become a valuable practice method within most direct service agencies. For example, a family service agency might form a group of prospective adoptive parents to orient them to the adoptive process. A treatment center might compose a group of adolescent substance abusers to assist them in learning to identify and manage stress and interpersonal problems. A recreational center might sponsor athletic teams for middle school youth. Older adults living in a nursing home could constitute a "remotivation" group.

Working with groups not only promotes growth and change through the interaction of the members, it also enables the agency and workers to serve a greater number of clients. Although some group members may need the resources of a caseworker in addition to the group experience, in most instances, the group activity is sufficient for personal growth. When direct practice with individuals is not provided by the agency offering the group, referrals are made to an appropriate agency, and a cooperative relationship between the service providers assures the client of maximum assistance with problems.

EVALUATION

Professional practice with individuals and groups must include an evaluative process. Evaluation always is focused upon the extent to which the group is able to achieve its objectives. Evaluation may be both an ongoing process as well as an assessment of the total group process, which comes at the termination of the group. In the former instance, the worker continually "monitors" group behavior, in order to enable the group to focus on its goals. Monitoring also may help the group redefine its purpose and goals, should it become evident that the original ones are unachievable. Monitoring consists of a critical assessment of the group's output.

Evaluation includes an assessment of all activities and behaviors related to the group's performance. Factors such as group leadership, resources, attendance at sessions, changes in group structure, dysfunctional behaviors, and characteristics of group members, group norms, and agency support, among others, all are reviewed in relation to the achievement of personal and group goals and objectives. Evaluation has the potential of providing a basis for answering such questions as: What could have increased group productivity? What were the positive achievements of the group? And, what implications for change are suggested? Efficiency and better quality of service are likely when rigorous evaluative standards are maintained.

GROUP TERMINATION

Groups are terminated when the purposes for which they were established are achieved. Although many groups are initiated with a predetermined expiration period, termination usually is related to meeting group and personal goals of the members. Occasionally, a group is aborted when it becomes obvious that its goals are unattainable or when dysfunctional behavior of one or more group members continually disrupts the group's activities.

The worker must be sensitive to the needs of group members at the time of termination and assist them in phasing out their attachment to the group. Often resistance to termination becomes highly emotional and vocal. Frustration, anger, withdrawal, and grief are among the more common reactions to the loss of the close ties that have developed among members throughout the life of the group. By helping the group to assess its accomplishments and plan alternatives, the worker can assist members in developing a more adaptive transition.

SOCIAL GROUP WORK AS A PRACTICE

As we indicated previously, group work is directed towards the enrichment of an individual's life through a group experience. Coyle (1959, 88–105) observes that group experiences may provide assistance to individuals as

1. a maturing process;
2. a supplement to other relationships;
3. preparation for active citizenship;
4. a corrective for social disorganization;
5. treatment of intrapsychic maladjustment.

Although it is unlikely that group members derive equal benefit from the group experience, all can be expected to experience growth in one or more of these areas. Positive group work is a planned change effort. Change is predicated on benefits derived from group process and interaction. The worker is responsible for assuring that the principles governing social work practice are included in the process. Euster (1975, 232) identifies those principles as follows:

1. *assuring the dignity, worth, uniqueness, and autonomy of all members;*
2. *a clear working agreement between the worker and the group and an articulated understanding of the group's purpose;*
3. *an assessment of the problems and needs of individual group members and special support by the social worker when the need is indicated;*
4. *individualization of the group, which reflects its unique character set of relationships and needs;*
5. *strong communications networks, which permit the expression of feelings and emotions of members;*
6. *relevant program activities, around which constructive interaction, assessment of group process, and the advancement of the group's purpose can be made;*
7. *preparation for termination.*

Each group also has its own life cycle characterized by developmental stages. Stanford and Roark (1974) identify the stages of a group's development as follows:

1. beginning—basic orientation and getting acquainted;
2. norm development—establishing ground rules for operation;
3. conflict phase—members asserting individual ideas;
4. transition—replacing initial conflicts with acceptance of others;
5. production—sharing of leadership, tasks, and trust;
6. affection—appreciation for the group;
7. actualization—flexibility, consensus, and decision making.

An awareness of these stages is helpful in monitoring the progress of the group as it moves toward greater cohesion and effectiveness. Dysfunctional "blocking" at any stage (for example, the conflict phase), once identified, can be addressed and resolved by the group, and the developmental progress continued. Allowed to continue unchecked, the unresolved blockage may result in group dissolution.

Skills in working with groups is an important aspect of social work practice. The efficiency and effectiveness of the group work process has resulted in personal enhancement, skill development, and problem reduction.

THE BACCALAUREATE SOCIAL WORKER AND SOCIAL GROUP WORK

The baccalaureate social worker has developed familiarity with and beginning competency in working with groups as part of the generic educational program. Opportunities to work with groups at the BSW level of practice are commonplace. Most agencies use the group method as part of their practice modalities. Among those agencies are settlement houses, hospitals, youth service organizations, state departments of human resources, nursing homes, family service agencies, correctional centers, and a variety of related human service organizations.

SUMMARY

Group work is a social work practice method that promotes the personal growth of individual members through the group process. Groups may be identified by their purpose: recreational, recreational-skill, educational, socialization, encounter, self-help, and therapy. The formation and selection of group members are important factors in promoting group cohesiveness and purpose. Group goals and objectives are established by group members. Leaders seek to enable the group to move toward the achievement of its goals. The democratic decision-making process is an integral factor in promoting personal growth. Monitoring and evaluating group performance are major activities designed to assist groups in achieving goals and enriching practice methods. Effective group work leads to the enrichment of the lives of individual members.

KEY TERMS

group
group work

natural group
self-help group

DISCUSSION QUESTIONS

1. What is a group? Differentiate between a natural group and groups organized for specific purposes.
2. Identify the role of the social worker in assisting groups to achieve their goals.
3. In what ways do the following groups differ? In what ways are they alike? Socialization groups? Encounter groups? Self-help groups? Recreational groups? Therapy groups?
4. Describe the goals of social group work. How are these goals achieved?
5. Discuss the principles of group work practice. How important are these principles in securing group goals?
6. What consideration should be made in terminating the group? Why are these considerations important to members of the group?

REFERENCES

Coyle, Grace. 1959. "Some Basic Assumptions About Social Group Work," in Marjorie Murphy, ed., *The Social Group Work Method in Social Work Education,* pp. 88–105. New York: Council on Social Work Education.

Euster, Gerald L. 1975. "Services to Groups," in Donald Brieland, Lela B. Costin, and Charles R. Atherton, eds., *Contemporary Social Work,* Chapter 13. New York: McGraw–Hill.

Klein, Alan F. 1972. *Effective Groupwork.* New York: Association Press.

Konopka, Gisela. 1954. *Group Work in the Institution.* New York: Whiteside, Inc.

Lewin, Kurt. 1951. *Field Theory in Social Science: Selected Theoretical Papers,* D. Cartwright, ed. New York: Harper and Row.

Moreno, J. L. 1953. *Who Shall Survive?* rev. ed. New York: Beacon.

Sherif, Muzafer, and Carolyn Sherif. 1956. *An Outline of Social Psychology.* New York: Harper and Row.

Stanford, Gene, and Albert E. Roark. 1974. *Human Interaction in Education.* Boston: Allyn and Bacon.

Wilson, Gertrude, and Gladys Ryland. 1949. *Social Group Work Practice.* Cambridge: Houghton Mifflin Company.

Zastrow, Charles. 1981. *The Practice of Social Work.* Homewood, Ill.: The Dorsey Press.

SELECTED FURTHER READINGS

Boulette, Teresa R. 1985. "Group Therapy with Low Income Mexican Americans," *Social Work,* (September): 403–404.

Hartford, Margaret. 1971. *Groups in Social Work.* New York: Columbia University Press.

Henry, S. 1981. *Group Skills in Social Work: A Four Dimensional Approval.* Itasca, Ill.: F. E. Peacock Press.

Papell, C., and B. Rothman. 1966. "Social Group Work Models—Profession and Heritage," *Journal of Social Work Education* : 66–77.

Roberts, Robert W., and Helen Northen. 1976. *Theories of Social Work with Groups.* New York: Columbia University.

Shulman, L. 1979. *The Skills of Helping Individuals and Groups,* Itasca, Ill.: F. E. Peacock Press.

15 Social Agency Administration

arian Mathis recently was hired as the director of a community mental health agency located in an area of the city with a considerable Hispanic and black population. When she was interviewed for the job, Marian was told by the agency's board of directors and the state mental health agency, which partially funds the program, that the center needed to make a number of changes and that she would be responsible for determining how to make them.

The agency that Marian now directs has been in the community for many years, established when the area was populated largely by poor white immigrants. Although the majority of these families have moved to the suburbs, the agency still serves many of them and other white middle-class families. It has few minority clients and almost none from the immediate neighborhood. None of the staff is black or Hispanic, and the attitude of the agency staff is that there is no need to serve the immediate community, since it would not be receptive to the traditional psychotherapy services they provide.

However, the individuals living in the community surrounding the agency have many needs. Many are elderly, many are young single parents with few economic resources who have difficulty caring for their children, and many are young single adults with no jobs and few job skills. Alcoholism, drug abuse, family violence, juvenile and adult crime, and child neglect frequently are reported as problems in the community.

Marian realizes that she faces a myriad of problems in administrating the agency. However, she has a great deal of experience as an administrator and is especially skilled at getting individuals with different backgrounds and viewpoints to work together to meet common goals. She plans to establish working groups of board members, staff members, and community members to develop ideas about ways to change the agency and to involve them throughout the planning and implementation process. She envisions that, within three years, she will be directing an agency that is run by an enthusiastic multiethnic staff and is responsive to meeting the needs of the immediate community, with positive participation by its members. She is looking forward to this new challenge.

The social work agency is many things to many people. It is a place where people go for help when problems occur and a place society holds responsible for addressing specific problems. It also is a place of employment for some and a setting for voluntary action by others. With the multiple motives of multiple actors, there is no single purpose of the social agency but rather a myriad of purposes. Above all else, the major task of the administrator of a social agency is to bring resources, opportunities, and goals together in such a way that a variety of social missions are accomplished. The focus of this chapter is on the management activities and the administrative processes of the local agency. Management activities are not the sole responsibility of agency executive directors and their assistants. All workers in the agency, the members of the board of directors, and clients play vital roles in the administrative process.

ADMINISTRATIVE STRATEGY

The administrative processes of an agency can be thought of first as a strategic task. **Strategy** is ongoing, dynamic thinking formulated to analyze problems and to establish specific objectives. This process may be described best in terms of a cycle of administrative activity:

1. strategic formulations—comprising analysis of problems and setting of objectives;
2. implementation—comprising specific development of systems and deployment of resources; and
3. control and management—comprising monitoring and directing activities, which are constantly evaluated, establishing a feedback loop back to strategic formulation.

To be effective, the cycle must come full circle, so that the data generated by those working directly with clients lead back to a more precise problem formulation at the highest level of the organization. It is typical to think of strategic formulation as the first phase of the administrative process. However, at any point in time, strategic formulation also is the product of many previous administrative cycles. If one were to design, carte blanche, a new agency to deal with today's problems, most likely it would look very different from the pattern of activities that has evolved within the agency that has existed for some time.

As an example, the Episcopal Community Service Agency of North Fork is "suddenly" expected to devise a strategy to deal with the family break-ups, drug and substance abuse, suicides, crime, and other social manifestations set off by the many farm foreclosures in River Fork County. The agency itself was created fifty years ago to provide social and chaplain services to the residents of the county poor farm. It was established by wealthy farmers, whose own descendants now face the loss of their family farms. How the agency functions today is related to its many decisions of yesterday. For example, the agency provides a food pantry and thrift shop, as well as traditional marriage counseling by a parish priest. Be that as it may, in developing the strategic plan to meet current social problems, the agency must review its traditional role within the community in conjunction with its present environment, such as:

1.   economic forces—What are the most likely sources of funds to address current problems?

2.   government policies—What are state, local, and national governments going to do that will reduce and/or exacerbate the problem?

3.   the current social structure of the agency—Specifically, what are the talents and dispositions of the current staff? This is most often the strongest force in strategic planning.

A key aspect of strategic planning is the recognition that the problems addressed lie far beyond the control of any given agency. As the board, with the assistance of the executive director, contemplates these problems and its response, board members find that opportunities, risks, resources, and responsibilities interact and reverberate along the way.

A systems perspective suggests that an agency's resources and its goals do not exist independent of one another. Clearly, the goals specified influence the capacity to generate resources, just as the manner in which resources are obtained and the nature of those resources affect and change the goals of the agency (Anthony & Herzlinger 1975).

Perlman and Gurin (1972) suggest that there are five types of resources to which the local social agency manager needs to respond (see also Table 15–1):

1.   A supply of *clients,* who expect to receive from the agency some valued product or service. These clients may seek the service/product on their own accord or the service/product may be imposed upon the client, as in the criminal justice system.

2.   *Financial resources,* which are made available to the agency by a system of grants, taxation, fees for service, and/or voluntary contributions.

3.   A *technology,* by which the financial resources are transformed into the service/product sought by its clients. The technology of the social work agency typically is one or more of the social work processes: direct practice, work with groups, etc.

Table 15–1	**Organizing Principles of Social Agencies**	
Resource Base	**Some Examples**	
Clients	Children, delinquents, disabled workers, retired persons	
Fiscal Base	Public, private, voluntary funds	
Technology	Direct practice, group work, advocacy	
Human Resources	Paid staff, volunteer staff, mixed staff	
Mandate	Legislative mandate, United Fund charter, license to practice	

4. The human resources (people) that compose the *agency staff*. These paid or volunteer workers are the ones on the front line, who interact directly with the clients to provide the service/product.

5. *A continuing mandate to operate.* The mandate may be in the form of a license, legislative directive, or charter of some sort.

A specific agency has a set of social programs related to its service/product goals. The fit between the agency's product and its goals is one way in which the agency is judged. An essential administrative task is to achieve an optimal fit between the product and the goal. Similarly, the product and the staff must have some degree of congruence, if the agency is to operate efficiently. The staff members clearly need the training and the competency to deliver the service effectively or to produce the product. Since social agencies tend to be labor-intensive organizations, this fit often is seen as one of the most crucial aspects of the administration of the agency. Since agencies ultimately exist to provide a service to clients, an important aspect of the assessment of the social agency is the degree to which the product/service is valued or needed by its clients.

A social agency is judged by a whole series of pairwise assessments (Figure 15–1). These create very specifically the administrative tasks that must be performed in the successful social agency. Leaving aside the concept of mandates, there are ten essential evaluations or choices to be made. Each choice affects the other choices, so the agency can be understood only as a system. In this chapter we will look at three of these: product-goal (8), staff-agency (7), and client-goal (3).

Goal and Product

An organization provides a product and, while that product is the end stage in the organization's directly visible activities, the product is provided in pursuit of stated, manifest, or latent organizational goals. A retail store sells a particular product presumably in order to make a profit for the owners of the

Figure 15–1
**Ten Pairwise
Choices of a
Social Agency**

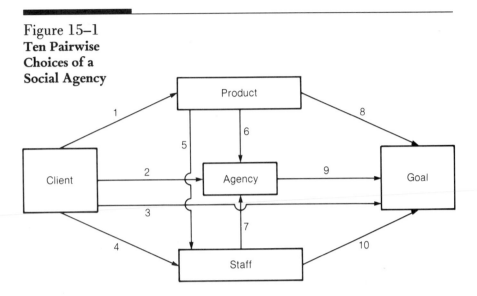

store. It is not the purpose of the bookstore at the local mall to provide employment to its workers or to make first-class literature easily available to potential readers, even though it may serve those ends. For the retail store, the ultimate purpose is profits, and failure to produce profits will cause the enterprise to cease.

For what purpose does the social agency exist? Discerning the intended results of a social agency is not an easy task, for typically there are multiple ends. The stated goals and the manifest goals are not always identical. Etzioni (1975) analyzed nonprofit agencies in terms of the relationship between their products and their goals. He found that, over time, the product itself became the goal of the agency. The National Foundation for Infantile Paralysis at one time was structured as a fund-raising agency (the product) to disseminate information and to collect money for polio-related services and research (the goal). When the Salk and Sabine vaccines were developed, in part due to the success of the foundation's activities, the agency needed to find a new purpose for its very effective fund-raising capabilities. This was seen as a laudable thing to do, since there were other diseases in need of research funds. The National Foundation for Infantile Paralysis became The National Foundation and directed its product toward general health research. Sometimes, however, it appears that organizations shift their intentions to fit their product, simply so that the organization itself can continue to exist. Organizational maintenance becomes an end in itself.

Perhaps, the conclusion just reached is too cynical. In the absence of a profit motive to guide choices, an ambiguity falls on the administration of the social agency. If profit, defined as total revenues minus total costs, is not to be maximized, what should be? Should the intent of administration be to maximize the number of people served, or the quality of service to those who are served, or of some appropriate combination? Attempts to provide answers to these and other queries will force the administrator to begin to think of some of the other pairwise considerations.

Staff and Product

The agency director has to identify staff or position needs, to recruit and retain qualified persons to fill those positions, and to promote an effective, task-centered work environment. An agency requires human resources: paid staff members, professional and technical, as well as volunteers. Board members who help to ensure that the links between the community and the agency are sustained and current also need to be recruited and retained. The care and feeding of staff, volunteers, and board members are sufficiently complex to be the subject of specialized courses for the graduate student of agency administration. However, some general principles are of interest to the student.

It is essential that staff management begin with staffing requirements. The specific objectives of developing staffing standards are:

1. to determine the requirements of the specific task essential to organization maintenance and goal attainment;
2. to determine the qualities, abilities, knowledge, and skills required to perform these tasks successfully;
3. to develop a pattern of task assignments so that staff members are neither underutilized nor expected to accomplish tasks beyond their skill levels.

With a chart of staff needs and staff availability, the agency administrator can set forth position requirements and expectations so that the staff members know what is expected of each of them. This task-oriented staff structure needs to address a number of elements. For example, a pattern of supervisory controls must be specified; that is, the nature, extent, and procedure for reviews of task performance and the means available to correct and respond to substandard performance must be addressed. Also needed are patterns of accountability, review, coordination, and perhaps most important, client satisfaction.

Product and Client

The identification and specification of the problem call for organized intervention and the means selected for that intervention are best seen as a political process rather than a rational, technical one. Some problems, such as crime control, evidence little conflict regarding goals. However, there is considerable controversy regarding the means that various groups within society will see as legitimate social interventions to control crime. In another area, such as childcare for children of working parents, there will be a conflict regarding the desirability of intervention itself. Some see quality childcare as ensuring the quality of care to future generations, while allowing single parents the opportunity to become self-supporting; others, simply a place to watch the "kids" while both parents work. Still other groups in the same society look upon child care as a significant factor in the decline of the American family.

Clearly, the political ideologies that surround the perception of a social problem constitute the core by which the nature and the propriety of social intervention are suggested. There is a social work credo that suggests that the agency needs to be responsive to the clients served. However, the clientele directly served is not the only interest group that affects the resource base of the agency. Who is served by the public housing project? Is it the people who live there, the real estate interests, or the building trade unions and construction companies involved in the building of the facility? Clearly, depending upon the degree of one's cynicism, one can specify a myriad of legitimate interests in the way in which public housing policy, or any other policy, is carried out.

The Choices

Pluralistic politics provide the administrator with no set of substantive rules by which the appropriate product of the agency can be specified. Social service agencies that represent clients with little or no political power have very special problems. Too much concern with the wants and desires of the clients directly served clearly can erode the economic and political support necessary for the very existence of the agency. Too little concern with the wants and needs of the clients in direct contact with an agency will result in the exploitation of those very clients the agency purports to serve. The very fact that the social agency typically is accused of both errors reflects the delicate balance that faces the agency administrator.

This is only a partial list of administrative choices. One very specific problem is who makes what choices? Children, the mentally ill, the mentally retarded, and others may not know what is in their own best interest. The popular phrase, caveat emptor, "let the buyer beware," implies that the customer in the store knows and can best judge his or her own self-interest. It is not expected that the bookstore clerk will help the customer decide between the hardback and the cheaper paperback. Presumably, the ethical responsibilities of the firm are satisfied when the client knows of the availability of both books. The problem becomes more complicated as the choice becomes more complicated. The surgeon is expected to guide the choice of a patient seeking a cure through an operation or chemotherapy when each has different costs and different benefits and, most particularly, different probabilities of being effective. The problem becomes most acute when the client being served directly cannot choose his or her own best interest. The professional social worker in the service agency needs to steer between two dangers. On the one hand, rigid adherence to the rules that benefit the agency or the taxpayers who fund the agency can quickly result in a subtle but debilitating form of tyranny. On the other hand, the agency has a responsibility not to become captives of its clientele or to surrender to its clients the power to determine the structure and nature of the service being offered. When interests are in conflict, there is no one correct way to resolve that conflict. The problem becomes particularly acute in the social agency in which the social worker has to represent the interests of clients incapable of knowing just what their own best interests may be.

Social service administrators must be skilled in many areas and able to work with civic leaders as well as clients.

IMPLEMENTATION

Failure in strategic thought or process can render a social program, however well intended, useless or worse. Even brilliant strategy has to be put into effective operation. **Implementation** involves deciding on the actions and coordinating them. It is a process of turning general thoughts into specific actions, where real people are charged with things they must do within established time frames. Implementation involves selecting the tactics required to carry out the strategy. Further, patterns of communication need to be designed, systems of monitoring and accountability instituted to ensure that activities have been put into place, and the necessary staff recruited and trained.

The key to success in the implementation phase is getting staff and volunteers to understand and support the selected objectives and pattern of attainment. The process is sure to fail if the human aspects of the implementation process are not addressed adequately. The implementation process flows imperceptibly into the specific management activities.

MANAGEMENT ACTIVITIES

The management function, often simply called *administration,* has to do with getting things done on a day-to-day basis. The essence of these administrative tasks has been stated in many ways.

In 1937, Luther Gulick coined an acronym, POSDCORB, in order to describe the activities of the agency executive (Sharkansky 1982, 124). POSDCORB stands for planning, organizing, staffing, directing, coordinating, reporting, and budgeting. Although this acronym has been subjected to three generations of academic criticism—some of it quite savage—it stands up well as a reasonably structured and easily remembered set of tasks to describe the multifaceted activities of agency administration. To place the problem of the management of the agency in perspective, one needs to examine these tasks.

Planning—working out in broad outline the things that need to be done and the methods for doing them to accomplish the purpose set for the enterprise;

Organizing—the establishment of the formal structure of authority through which work subdivisions are arranged, defined and coordinated for the defined objective;

Staffing—the whole personnel function, bringing in and training the staff and maintaining favorable conditions of work;

Directing—the continuous task of making decisions and embodying them in specific and general orders and instructions and serving as the leader of the enterprise;

Coordinating—the all-important duty of interrelating the various parts of the work;

Reporting—keeping those to whom the executive is responsible informed as to what is going on, which includes keeping the entire staff informed through records, research, and inspection;

Budgeting—fiscal planning, accounting, and control.

Planning

Planning is sensing what needs to be done in order to accomplish the purposes of the agency. Agency planning functions can be subdivided into strategy (broad-gauged, overall plans) and **tactics** (day-to-day, specific plans), as well as into short-term and long-term planning. Planning activities should be structured to anticipate future resource needs and delineate specific tasks in an ordered and sequenced pattern in order to accomplish the goals of the agency. Planning receives its most visible form in the development of the agency budget.

Effective planning incorporates the following steps:

1. identification of the precise goals of the agency;
2. ranking those goals in order of their importance;
3. identification of the resources currently available to accomplish the goals;
4. identification of the resources available to meet next week's, next month's, and next year's goals;
5. measurement of resources used and goals accomplished in the past as a guide to goal accomplishment and resource use in the future.

Organizing

Organizing is the establishment of the formal structure of authority through which resources are allocated and transmitted to the goals or targets of the agency. There are alternative ways of organizing an agency, but typically an agency is structured by place, process or purpose, as in Figure 15–2.

Figure 15–2   **Alternate Organizational Forms of a Family
Social Agency**

Agency Organized by Place:

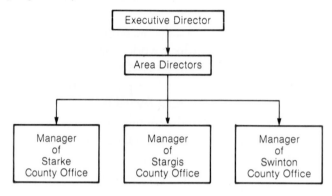

Agency Organized by Process:

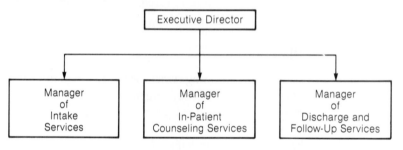

Agency Organized by Program:

The range of organizing patterns is nearly infinite, and most agencies are either in the process of reorganization, planning a reorganization, or have just been reorganized. In the most typical structure, the ongoing director will work out for some particular agency a unique plan for ongoing authority. Social workers in an agency do not just wake up in the morning and go out to "do good" but are required to report on their time and their accomplishments and the ways in which these accomplishments are achieved.

Staffing

Staffing encompasses the entire personnel function: recruiting, training, and retraining the necessary personnel to carry out the tasks of the agency. In a small agency, these functions may be but one of the tasks of the single agency executive, whereas in a very large agency, they very well may be done by an entire subunit of the agency devoting itself entirely to personnel, including staff training.

Directing

Directing is the continuing task of making decisions about client needs and the resources to which clients are entitled. These decisions are allocated to the organized process in a structured way to ensure that all clients are served as nearly identically as possible without regard to the particular social worker that they see. On first blush, this may appear to be highly impersonal but, on reflection, it means that the resources of the agency, in dollars, goods, or staff time, are not dispensed haphazardly but in accordance with an established set of criteria to ensure that all clients receive their due share of the agency's resources. The agency director needs to set forth guidelines for discretion. It is impossible to "dot every i" in the way the social work task is to be performed; social problems are much too complex for that. Nonetheless, the public has the right to be assured that the social worker is not free to act capriciously, tyrannically, or in ways that contravene the socially sanctioned goals of the agency. There are specific problems to be addressed. All clients should be treated alike on the basis of clear rules known to both social worker and client, yet there is a need for responsiveness. The agency director must ensure that in those cases where following the letter of the rule defeats the clear intent of the rule, workers are free and trained to use their intelligence but not to substitute their own personal standards. This is a tricky problem for administrators and directors to solve.

Coordination

Coordination involves the necessary interrelation of the various activities of the agency to achieve the maximum social benefit. This means not only that the left hand of the agency knows what the right hand is doing, but that agency activities are structured and sequenced to achieve the maximum impact on the client. The principal task of coordination within the agency typically refers to the timing of the use of resources to achieve their maximum benefit. For example, the educational and the therapy units of a family service agency need to have their activities structured and attuned to each other, if they are to achieve their best results, because they utilize a common staff and serve a common clientele for a common purpose.

Reporting

The agency director has an ethical, and often a legal, responsibility to inform board members and subordinates about the activities, problems, and accomplishments of the agency. Information about the administration of the agency should flow both from director to the staff and from the staff to director (not just "top down"). The agency director monitors the agency activities through regulations, records, statistical reports, on-the-spot inspections, research, memos, newsletters, and other appropriate reporting devices. Workers, in turn, inform their supervisors through regular reports of their day-to-day use of time, and special reports of unusual activity, as well as informal talks with supervisors.

Budgeting

Budgeting, of course, is the process of specifically allocating dollars to specified purposes. This is the standard budget in which dollars are allocated for specific categories, such as staff salaries, utilities, and mortgage payment. A second budget also needs to be prepared, which has been called the *process budget*. In a process budget, dollars from the agency are allocated not to specific entities but to the function for which they are intended. For example, the proportions of staff salaries, supplies, and fixed costs needed to operate the agency's community education program are calculated and assigned to that function.

SUMMARY

It is not an easy task to find the best pattern of rules and behavior to follow in the administration of the social work agency. In fact, it is probably an impossible task. Ways of doing things are in constant flux due to changes in circumstances. Regulations can appear to be arbitrary and frustrating, yet they reflect judicial and legislative decisions and beliefs about the relative merits of particular goals and actions. Who gets what and why are the key questions in evaluating administrative rules. Ideally, regulations of practice are not the result of good or bad luck, but rather the consequence of the tensions reflected earlier. There is no magic formula that social workers can use or that administrators can apply. The best we can hope for is that clients, social workers, directors, and board members respect one another and assess each situation with sensitivity and care.

KEY TERMS

implementation
planning
strategy
tactics

DISCUSSION QUESTIONS

1. What are some of the factors that need to be considered when developing a strategy for an agency?
2. How might already existing personnel and agency policies shape the direction an agency takes in developing and implementing new programs?
3. Distinguish between strategy and tactics.
4. Give an example of an agency organized around a client resource base.

REFERENCES

Anthony, Robert, and Regina Herzlinger. 1975. *Management Control in Nonprofit Organizations.* Homewood, Ill.: Richard D. Irwin.

Etzioni, Amitai. 1975. Alternative Conceptions of Accountability: The Example of Health Administration. *Public Administration Review* 35, 3 (May–June).

Perlman, Robert and Arnold Gurin. 1972. *Community Organization and Social Planning.* New York: John Wiley.

Sharkansky, Ira. 1982. *Public Administration: Agencies, Policies, and Politics.* San Francisco: W. H. Freeman & Co.

SELECTED FURTHER READINGS

Gates, Bruce L. 1980. *Social Program Administration.* Englewood Cliffs, N.J.: Prentice–Hall.

Lohmann, Roger A. 1980. *Breaking Even.* Philadelphia: Temple University Press.

Schulman, Kary, and Fred Setterberg. 1985. *Beyond Profit.* New York: Harper and Row.

Williams, Walter. 1980. *Government by Agency.* New York: Academic Press.

Williams, Walter. 1980. *The Implementation Prespective: A Guide for Managing Social Service Delivery Programs.* Berkeley: University of California Press.

16 Research and Practice

school social worker at Midtown High School established a group treatment program for boys who were having trouble dealing with anger at school. Twenty boys from similar backgrounds with similar behavior problems were referred to her by teachers. The social worker randomly selected ten boys to participate in the experimental program, which was the largest number she could accept. During a six-month period, she monitored the behavior and grades of all twenty boys referred to her, comparing differences between those in the program and those not in the program. At the end of the period, she found that the boys in her program showed significant improvement in the number of referrals to the office; behavior problems in the classroom, at home, and in the community; school attendance; and grades. During this period, boys not in her program declined in all areas. On the basis of her findings, she was able to persuade school administrators to fund additional group intervention programs, with larger-scale research to document program results, during the next school year.

The social services agency in a southwestern state was considering a policy change that would reduce AFDC payments due to a state budget crisis. A policy analyst from the agency was asked to ascertain the impact of the reductions. In addition to the negative impact on the individual families who would be affected by the budget cuts, the policy analyst determined that instead of saving dollars, the state would actually end up spending more money because it would have to pick up emergency relief and indigent health care costs for families who could not survive without AFDC and Medicaid, both largely federally subsidized programs. Based on this information and other data the researcher provided, the agency increased funding for low-income childcare and employment training to reduce numbers of AFDC recipients but did not reduce the actual payments.

Research, in its most general sense, refers to any disciplined strategy of inquiry. The term sometimes elicits a mental image of a white-coated individual in a sterile laboratory, but this conception is unduly restrictive for our purposes. On the other hand, research is sometimes equated with the mere gathering of facts. For our purposes, this concept is too broad. Research within a profession such as social work has many manifestations, but in this chapter we shall focus on three reasonably specific modes or forms of research: (1) disciplinary research, (2) policy research, and (3) evaluative research.

All three modes are scientific in that all depend upon the scientific method. All three modes are objective in the sense that in all the investigator is required to conform to established canons of logical reasoning and formal rules of evidence; and all three are ethically neutral in the sense that the investigator does not take sides on issues of moral or ethical significance. Each mode seeks to generate a proposition, or set of propositions, capable of falsification. A scientific proposition generated by research must be capable of being confirmed or denied. The modes differ in their intent.

DISCIPLINARY RESEARCH

Disciplinary research is the term used to distinguish investigations designed to expand the body of knowledge of a particular discipline; in the social sciences that means to expand or modify the understanding of social and psychological processes, so that social behavior can be explained. *The intent is explanation for its own sake.* This is sometimes called pure, as opposed to applied, research. Disciplinary research begins with a *paradigm.* This is a perspective (a school of thought) that structures the research, the research goals, and hence the research methods that are seen as appropriate in the analysis of a particular topic. The paradigm directs the investigator as to where and how to look for evidence. Complex social behavior cannot be explained except in terms of a paradigm. The political scientist, the economist, and the social worker each would describe, analyze, and explain identical phenomena in different ways. No one is right and the others wrong; rather, each paradigm generalizes its own special insight into the problem at hand.

The desire to explain how people in a particular social class vote can be used as an illustration. In the 1984 presidential election, if we had counted only the votes of those voters earning less then the median income, Walter Mondale would have been elected. The political scientist in explaining the pattern of voters would focus attention on the differences in various endowments and experiences of lower–income voters, and the ways in which the two parties structured their appeals to voters. An economist would more likely suggest that voters in each class are capable of discerning their own short-term and long-term self-interests, and judge the parties' future performance in terms of their past. The economist may then seek to explain patterns of voting in terms of economic positions taken by each party in past administrations. A sociologist could focus attention on various patterns of information distribution and information assessment through particular institutions; that is, the press, the family, the union hall, etc. Regardless of disciplinary affiliation, a particular investigator is most likely to lend and borrow from each approach in a unique and eclectic way, which he or she believes is best adapted to the question at hand.

The investigator is interested in providing an explanation of why something happened. The first requirement then is to identify a variable and show how it is related to what is to be explained. Careful selection of variables, careful use of both inductive and deductive reasoning, and precise application of the established rules of evidence are required to produce correct inferences about relationships. This is what is meant by a disciplinary explanation. The glue that holds together a disciplinary investigation is theory. Disciplinary investigation is motivated by a desire to produce theoretically relevant explanations (Kuhn 1962). A **theory** is a set of logically related, empirically verifiable generalizations that intend to explain relationships in a parsimonious manner. Since the process of theory building and research is cyclical and constitutes a single feedback loop, we can break into the process at any point.

A formal theory is derived from a set of abstract propositions. One such view within the framework of a formal theory is a Marxist perspective. This view suggests that the state will generate specific institutions designed to perpetuate the existing distribution of wealth. If this were so, the welfare institutions would expand or contract in ways that would reinforce the power of the state. Using critical reason, it is possible to infer how welfare institutions will operate in predictable ways. It is suggested that welfare programs would expand rapidly in times of economic downturn in order to forestall revolutionary behavior and contract rapidly in times of economic expansion in order to preserve the pattern of distribution in place. If this were so, changes in per capita welfare expenditures would be related directly to changes in per capita production. By a process of induction, these generalizations are translated into specific expected observations. This can then be stated in terms of a specific **hypothesis** that identifies specific observation resources for welfare expenditure and production. The hypothesis thus is capable of being accepted or rejected. If confirmed, it becomes the basis for the specification of a yet more precise theory.

Sometimes the process begins with observation. For example Emile Durkheim looked at the crude data on suicides and found that suicide rates were less for Catholics, married persons, and people in rural areas. The common feature of these correlates was a sense of social involvement. This led him to articulate a theory of social integration, anomie (or the sense of being without norms and standards), and suicide. Legions of scholars have deduced various hypotheses from his ground breaking work, which led to a number of empirical generalizations about the social consequences of the condition of anomie. These have been adopted into practice modes to reduce the sense of anomie via specific practice methods. These, in turn, ultimately are utilized to expand, modify, and sharpen Durkheim's original speculation.

It sometimes is suggested that, within the social sciences, there is no established consensus theory, as there is in the biological and physical sciences. It is not the place here to debate that issue. Rather it is sufficient to suggest that much of the research in social work is devoted to the expansion and refinement of disciplinary investigation about the phenomena encountered in the daily practice of social work.

POLICY RESEARCH

Policy planners and policy advocates frequently use specific research methods as they ply their craft. A political decision maker who needs to have a specific uncertainty resolved prior to making a policy choice often will seek the aid of **policy research.** In deciding whether to expand maximum security cells or dormitory type rooms, the individual prison official will want to know more about the effectiveness of various ways of housing prisoners and the reliability of these predictions regarding their post-confinement behavior of prisoners. Using scientific methods to reduce, or at least minimize, uncertainty is part of the social worker's task.

Policy research is a specialized form of inquiry whose purpose is the provision of reliable, valid, and relevant knowledge for public officials, agency managers, and others, in the decision-making processes of government. It is used (or misused) at all levels of government and at all stratas of the bureaucracy and officialdom. Research studies employ techniques that vary from the simple collection and collation of available data to the design of sophisticated econometric models and social experiments.

Scientific research does not guide or control policy choice. History is replete with examples of public officials rejecting the advice of the research community. The rejection of research findings does not inevitably lead to negative results, nor does the acceptance of the recommendations of the research community always yield the intended beneficent results. Deciding upon the contribution to and limits of the research to public decision making is a complex topic that has been treated extensively in other books (Melanson 1978). If welfare benefits are to be raised and if eligibility standards are to be broadened, then there will be certain, obvious consequences. There also will be consequences less obvious and, perhaps, even uncertain before the fact. Identifying, resolving, or at least reducing the policy uncertainty is a central task of policy research. How a society utilizes this knowledge once it is generated is a political issue. The answer clearly depends not on what we know but on how that knowledge is related to the various social conditions and how that information is congruent, or incongruent, with particular ideologies and political belief systems. Knowing, however, as best we can, the precise relationship between welfare benefits on the work efforts of the poor, marital dissolution rates on the welfare population, and so on is an end valued in the American political system, which prides itself on pragmatic rationality.

Today, almost all graduate schools of social work have created policy tracks or concentrations designed to prepare the professional social worker to assist in the formulation and analysis of policy alternatives in specialized areas, such as social work, public health, city management, or education. In addition, a set of graduate schools has claimed policy analysis as a generic professional task. The use of sophisticated research methods to discover and delineate the means available to government to respond to problems is a process as old as government. The specialized education in research procedures, especially structured to policy choice, is a contemporary event.

There are problems encountered in the design, execution, and interpretation of research for specific policy choices that are not encountered in disciplinary research. Policy analysis frequently is expected to produce specific kinds of information in a short time on a limited budget. The problem is not an issue of what is knowable but what can be made knowable by Tuesday at lunch when a specific political event is scheduled. Policy and disciplinary research differ in other ways as well. Both policy research and disciplinary research are disciplined by the canons of scientific methodology. The latter is structured to provide theoretically relevant explanations of social phenomena. The former, however, is structured to provide an identification, assessment, and evaluation of public strategies utilized to produce public ends. As described by Aaron Wildavsky (1979), policy research is an artistic as well as a scientific process, where the solution specifies a desirable relationship between "manipulable means and obtainable ends."

Adequately executed social science research often is an inadequate guide to policy choice, because it often fails to be timely or is structured in a way that is unusable to the public official or agency manager. On the other hand, practitioners in the field often have failed to utilize the most elementary forms of inquiry before instituting a policy action. The connection between scientific demand on inquiry and political demands on action needs to be appraised.

Professionals at all levels in the social welfare system rely on many types of research to help them develop and implement new policies and programs.

EVALUATIVE RESEARCH

Policy evaluation is a specific kind of policy research. The ordinary method used to develop a policy perspective on an anticipated change in a program is to review the literature generally available. When this is done, the social worker typically is confronted with a morass of written documents, all of which are generally relevant but none of which is precisely related. One useful way to begin is with a particularly influential report, such as a study by the federal government or perhaps a study done in a sister state. Then examine all of the principal references and bibliographies for relevant references for the new topic. Few social problems are brand new, and even a cursory examination of how other governments deal with similar problems is a useful way to use existing knowledge to choose among policy options. Sometimes the investigation is very systematic, such as what happens to emergency room use when a particular payment method is introduced. Sometimes it is very general, such as how applications for food stamps fluctuate with shifts in the economy. The social worker who serves as an advisor to policymakers needs to be alert to methods of dealing with such questions.

Evaluation, when competently done, measures the extent to which a program attains its goals. The evaluative process specifies, from the multiplicity of objectives, the specific set of objectives by which the program will be judged; it declares that some observable phenomenon constitutes a presumption of success; it structures an argument to indicate that the favorable outcome, if there is one, is the result of the policy action or program under consideration. **Evaluative research** seeks to use the scientific method as its basic analytic tool in determining the program's impact. Because real world conditions do not have the experimental purity of controlled laboratory conditions, specific research designs are used to maximize the likelihood of determining what were the results of a program. Because of the difficulties inherent in each of the phases of the process, the results are "known" only within a range of certainty. The principal task of the policy evaluator is not only to show success or failure but to indicate the range of certainty with which that judgment is made.

Identification of Goals

The evaluative process begins with an identification of the goals to be evaluated. This seems obvious, but in fact is an inordinately value-laden undertaking. Initially, there is the problem of ranking goals in an effort to indicate which ones are intended, and their order of importance, and which are desirable but unintended consequences of the policy action or program. Second, the evaluator needs to deal with the problem of manifest versus latent goals. If attention is given exclusively to manifest goals, then the real impact of the program that results from the symbiotic relationship of many programs operating together is likely to be lost. Third, the evaluator must frankly and honestly deal with the dysfunctional or undesirable consequences that occur because of the policy action or program. Social science methodology often is overwhelmed by attempts to measure many goals simultaneously, yet the false specification of a program to a too-small set of objectives may mask the good points of a program and expose the bad points. Care in goal identification is a critical first step in a policy-relevant evaluation plan.

Formulation of Operational Definitions of Policy and Program Results

The second critical step is the selection of replicable observations, which are meaningful proxies of selected goal achievements and program dysfunctions. In some very rare cases, these measurable results will be obvious and tangible. In the worst cases, they will be neither obvious nor tangible. If the question under consideration, for example, is the work habits of a particular target population, one has to consider such things as employment rate, wage rate, hours of work, and work habits of relevant others. The evaluator has the responsibility to demonstrate that the "observed" changes are both valid and reliable estimates of the object of the policy action or program. The test of program success must stand up to criticism from the scientific community and the political community. Thus, attention must be paid to the permanency of the impact; the replicability of the observation of success; and the reliability of the observation.

Demonstrating a Causal Connection Between Program and Outcome

It is insufficient to report that a favorable outcome occurred while a program was in place. The evaluator has to demonstrate that the outcome reasonably can be attributed to the policy action or program. The basic argument of causal connection was developed by John Stuart Mill and remains as the foundation feature of social science theories of causation. His method rests on two methods, known as the positive and negative canons. The positive canon, called the *sufficient condition,* states that for a result X to occur, there has been element Y, prior in time. That is to say, whenever Y is observed, X always follows. Y thus is a sufficient condition of X.

Elements of Situation I

A, B, Y   produce- - - - -X

Elements of Situation II

D, E, Y   produce- - - - -X

Elements of Situation N

M, N, Y   produce- - - - -X

To say that Y is a sufficient condition is not to say that it is a *cause.* The negative canon, or necessary condition, states that the absence of Y always is associated with the absence of X.

Elements of Situation III

F, G, non Y   produce- - - - -non X

Elements of Situation IV

H, I, non Y   produce- - - - -non X

Elements of Situation M

M, N, non Y   produce- - - - -non X

Thus, if we were able to observe all theoretically possible connections and found that when Y was present X followed and that whenever Y was absent X did not occur, we could say that Y causes X. Now try to think of an example. Whenever we find a broken optic nerve, we find blindness. Broken optic nerves are a sufficient condition for blindness, but not a cause, since we find blindness occurring as a result of other factors. When there are unbroken optic nerves, we sometimes observe blindness. When we find fire, we find oxygen; when we remove oxygen, we never find fire. Therefore, oxygen is a necessary condition of fire, but not a cause, for we find oxygen and the absence of fire. Social science evaluation uses both the positive and negative canons. This is the classical experimental design and is called the *method of difference*. The inference is then made that Y causes X. This inference is subject to criticism on the grounds that both Y and X could result from some more fundamental but unobserved factor or that Y is associated with X only when some other factor is present. Y and X were observed in the fashion noted, but this was a fortuitous occurrence.

Elements of Situation V

A, B, Y   produce- - - - -X

Elements of Situation VI

A, B, non Y   produce- - - - - non X

To partially blunt the criticism of the classical design, the evaluator uses both theory and probability to increase the likelihood that the observed relationship, in fact, is a causal relationship. Theory is used to select the observations to be made. We observe *A, B,* on through N cases when there are compelling, logical reasons to believe that there is a causal connection. We exclude observations where there is no particular reason for investigations. Theories thus construct observations and thus lead investigators closer to or further away from a realistic understanding of the relationship between observed outcome and the program or policy action, depending on the adequacy of the theory. Second, we trust to the rules of chance. If we note an occurrence, by resorting to various statistical manipulations, we can calculate the probability that the observation would occur by mere random factors. If we give one set of mothers a course in child nutrition and, as far as we know, withhold that information from a second set of mothers, then test the nutritional adequacy of their children's packed lunch both before and after the course on a score of 1–100, we find results such as those in Table 16–1.

We can calculate the experimental impact as $(B - A)$ minus $(D - C)$; $D - C$ being the change expected over time, attributable to nonexperimental factors. Of course, we don't know what in the program caused the change, but

Table 16–1		Nutrition Score Before	Nutrition Score After
Nutrition Scores of Mothers	Mothers given course	A	B
	Mothers not given course	C	D

if $(B - A)$ minus $(D - C)$ is significantly different from what we would expect to occur by any random process, it certainly is reasonable to behave as if nutritional education and nutritional performance are causally connected. If the goal is better nutritional performance, nutritional education is one way of achieving it.

An evaluation that had with distinctiveness identified the most relevant goal, selected the most appropriate units of evaluation, structured the relationship with the most finely tuned of theories, and tested the results with the most sophisticated statistical test still would not show that program Y is the best way of achieving goal X. It would show only that Y is a reasonable way. Social science evaluation can be used to help reject bad policy but cannot help select with certainty the "best policy."

Practice Research

The practitioner-researcher problem-solving process consists of four phases or levels of research activity. Each level of inquiry builds on the levels which precede it, as is illustrated in Table 16–2.

Table 16–2   Forms of Research by Level of Research and Intent of Inquiry

Level of Research	Intent of Inquiry			
	Distinguish Concepts and Identify Significant Variables	Describe and Measure Interaction of Variables	Establish Logically Connected and Verifiable Causal Paths among Variables	Locate and Isolate Manageable Variables to Alter Outcome
	Case Studies			
Level One: Exploratory	X			
		Cross Case Comparisons and Surveys		
Level Two: Descriptive	X	X		
			Field Experiments and Statistical Test	
Level Three: Explanatory	X	X	X	
				Practice Research
Level Four: Perspective	X	X	X	X

Level One   Level One research is undertaken to provide a familiarity with a topic. This may be necessary because the investigator is exploring an old topic for the first time, a new interest for the researcher, or exploratory research may be required because the subject itself is new or unstudied. The purpose of Level One research is to seek out the facts and to provide a structure for thinking about the various aspects of the problem.

As an example let's suppose there is an interest in the topic of family violence. The newly interested student would want to know several things: How is family violence to be defined? How extensive is the problem? Is there an increase in the actual incidences of family violence or is the increase only apparent because of better reporting of incidents? Do any important subcategories of family violence need to be studied separately? The student would want to read the contemporary and classic literature on the topic, check the figures being reported, interview social workers and volunteers working at the crisis centers, and perhaps talk with survivors of incidents of family violence and even perpetrators. In exploratory research the procedures of inquiry are relatively unsystematic. It is a first effort to see what is going on.

After the initial review of the literature, exploratory studies tend to become somewhat more focused. Essentially, the purpose of exploratory study is to focus attention, to learn what are the really important questions. Exploratory studies most typically are done for one of two interrelated purposes: simply to satisfy an initial curiosity or a desire for a better understanding; or as precursor to more careful inquiry at Levels Two, Three or Four.

In this first level of study, an effort is made to define the central concepts of inquiry. Take, for example, the concept intrafamily violence. A researcher would have considerable difficulty utilizing the same conceptual definition for legal, educational, practice, and policy purposes. Various investigators have reported that a lot of emotional energy can be generated into a discussion of whether spanking is appropriate in the concept of family violence. In fact, it is more appropriate to recognize that the inclusion or exclusion of spanking as a category of family violence depends on the conceptual level and the purpose of the specific inquiry.

Level Two   A second basis for knowing is the requirement that the investigator can show the concepts are related structurally one to the other. A complex system of interrelationships among categories is a useful way of establishing a basic framework for social work practice research.

Inquiry at this level seeks to establish the presence or absence of empirical regularities in the problem area. How is socioeconomic class associated with family violence? Are shifts observed in the reported incidence of family violence from one social class to the next? Is the observed change an artifact of reporting incidents or does the actual rate of incidents shift? Our first question is: Does the appearance of an association reflect a real association? Do people who differ from one another on social class lines, differ from one another in regard to the dependent problem; that is, the incidence of violence within the family?

We might find, for example, that low-income families are treated in clinics, whereas other groups are treated by private physicians; and clinic doctors, for whatever reason, are more likely to report suspicious injuries. If such is the case, the relationship is apparent but not real. We might find that class is linked to verbal skills, and verbal skills are inversely linked to family violence. This tells us that the real association between class and violence is only indicative of a more fundamental (yet harder to observe) association.

Level Three   Once a relationship has been established, Level Three research commences. It seeks to show not only an empirical regularity but a causal connection. At this point, a formal logical model is required. A causal connection requires a causal chain of events, such as the association between education and communication skills and family violence. A formal theory is stated that links educational attainment to communication skills and communication skills to family violence. If this were established not only is there an explanation of *why* family and educational levels are connected but also what can change the situation. The practitioner cannot easily change educational level. However, it is possible to provide instruction and information on communication skills and thus break the links between education and family violence.

Level Four   The goal of practice research is the assessment and redirection of practice. Knowledge is gained not for its own sake but for direct use in the day-to-day activities of the social worker. Practice research has been criticized as being too subservient to theory yet insufficiently based in theory. On the one side, there is the assertion that practice models have developed from very highly specialized theoretical frameworks that are of limited use. They are distorted when applied to the range of client problems encountered by the social worker (Muller 1979). There also is the assertion that practice is eclectic and models of intervention are chosen intuitively and thus not sufficiently based in theory to allow broad guidelines for action (Brier 1979). A third critique is that practice models are fixed and closed, unchanged from one generation to the next.

These three very diverse critiques appear to be true simultaneously. This occurs because, until very recently, practice wisdom and social work research developed as separate spheres. The narrow overlap of research and practice was small. In recent years, social workers in practice have begun, particularly with evaluative research, to expand that overlap.

SUMMARY

This chapter introduces the student to the very wide range of activities that constitute social work research. The specific steps in the research process are reviewed and it is shown how each step builds on previous ones. If there is one message of this chapter, it is that research and practice are not separate spheres but interrelated domains each fundamentally dependent upon the other.

KEY TERMS

disciplinary research	policy research
evaluative research	theory
hypothesis	

DISCUSSION QUESTIONS

1. To what extent do you think the practice of social work research gets in the way of the best way to help a client?
2. Can you think of an example where the research process and the practice process actually reinforce one another?

REFERENCES

Brier, S. 1979. "Toward the Integration of Theory and Practice." Paper read at the Conference on Social Work Research, San Antonio.

Kuhn, Thomas S. 1962. *The Structure of Scientific Revolutions.* Chicago: University of Chicago Press.

Melanson, P. H. 1978. *Knowledge, Politics and Public Policy.* Cambridge: Winthrop Press.

Muller, Edward H. 1979. "Evaluating the Empirical Base of Clinical Circles." Paper read at the Conference on Social Work Research, San Antonio.

Wildavsky, Aaron. 1979. *Speaking Truth to Power.* Boston: Little, Brown.

SELECTED FURTHER READINGS

Bailey, Kenneth D. 1986. *Methods of Social Research.* New York: The Free Press.

Cook, Thomas D., and Donald Campbell. 1979. *Quasi–Experimentation: Design and Analysis Issues for Field Settings.* Chicago: Rand McNally.

Festinger, L., and D. Katz. 1953. *Research Methods in the Behavioral Sciences.* New York: Holt Reinhart.

Forcese, Dennis P., and Stephen Richer. 1973. *Social Research Methods.* Englewood Cliffs, N.J.: Prentice–Hall.

IV

Special Issues

This section of the book examines areas of special concern for the field of social work and social welfare. Chapter 17, "Sexism and Racism: Social Inequality," provides an indepth analysis of how racism and sexism disenfranchise women and minority group members. Attention also is given to homosexuality and gender identity issues that result in differential treatment and discrimination. The role of the social·work profession in working toward the elimination of discrimination at the societal level, as well as assisting individuals and groups experiencing adaptive problems, also is addressed.

Chapter 18, "Social Work and the Other Helping Professions," identifies and describes the activities of non-social work professionals who are involved in providing human services. This chapter also seeks to explore the utility of these related professions as resources for problem solving from the social work perspective. This chapter is predicated upon the premise that social work practitioners need to be aware of and skilled at negotiating resources available for clients in the community that will enhance the resolution of problems.

Chapter 19, "The Voluntary Sector," examines the role of the private sector as a critical agent in helping individuals, groups and communities in meeting needs. With recent budgetary reductions at the federal, state, and local levels for social services, the role of nonpublic agencies has been viewed as critical in assuring that resources are available to help public service agencies accomplish their mission. This chapter explores private sector-public sector relationships and examines special issues faced by voluntary social service programs.

Chapter 20, "The Future of Social Work and Social Welfare," reviews the history of changes that characterize the social work profession and the field of social welfare, emphasizing the impact of technological and economic changes on the individual, family, and community. This chapter also attempts to forecast the probable character of the profession and social welfare as they are influenced by future changes at the broader societal level.

As a group, these chapters seek to explicate issues that are both contemporary and central to the profession's continual effort to adapt to social problems and resource development. Social work, as a growing profession, continually must be sensitive to social change and its implications for practice.

17 Sexism and Racism: Social Inequality

 anice Carroll earned a degree in finance with highest honors from a major southern university. Soon after graduation, she was employed by the First National Bank of a large city in the Southwest. Her initial assignment was with the credit department, where her work received the highest praise from her supervisors.

After several years, the position of credit manager was vacated and she applied for it. Her application was supported by references testifying to her competence and skill. After reviewing a number of applications for the position, including Janice's, bank officials hired Tom Ratcliff, an employee of a neighboring bank with less experience than Janice.

When she sought an explanation, she was told that Tom was being groomed for a vice-presidency and needed to gain supervisory experience. After one year with First National, Tom accepted a position with an investment firm. Janice again was passed over for promotion. She protested, citing her many years of excellent work in the credit department and stressing her own knowledge and ability to perform the tasks of credit manager. Her protests were met with the suggestion that she might consider relocating with another bank to further her career goals. Janice Carroll is a thirty-one-year-old single, black woman.

Like Janice, many individuals seek fulfillment and opportunity, only to find that the achievement of these goals is made difficult by social barriers. Janice well may exemplify such a case. All evidence indicates that she was an excellent candidate for the position of credit manager and possessed qualifications that exceeded those of Tom. Why, then, was she passed over for the position? Could it have been that she was a woman? Or that she was black? The limited information provided in the short case history provides little basis for conjecture. If we are confident that Janice was at least as well qualified as other applicants, however, it may be plausible to consider that either her gender or race were determinants in denying her the opportunity for advancement. Even if Janice suspected that gender or race (or both) were factors that resulted in her application being rejected, it would have been difficult to prove.

Unfortunately, Janice represents only one of many millions of Americans who find that social and economic justice is not necessarily achieved through initiative, preparation, and hard work. All too often, social mobility and opportunity are not available equally to all who aspire to achieve the American Dream. Women and minority group members long have been denied opportunities in business and social life that white men have come to expect and take for granted. Under the subtle guise of institutional sexism and racism, the rights to free and full participation in our social and economic institutions are denied to individuals who fail to meet dominant group criteria. In reviewing the case of Janice, it is possible (although not plausible) that the bank officials' justification for not promoting Janice was based on a long tradition of having white men in management positions. Rationalizing their position, bank officials may feel that male credit managers are better supervisors, that women do not like to work for other women, that women are too emotional, that white customers are not comfortable with blacks, or countless other stereotypical arguments. It would probably never occur to the officials that they were behaving in a racist or sexist manner. Whatever their rationale, the result of the decision effectively excludes Janice from opportunities that are available to white men. The likelihood that opportunities for career mobility would ever be extended to her at the First National Bank was made doubtful when officials suggested that her goals might be more achievable at another bank.

In this chapter, we will examine the characteristics of social inequality implicit in racism and sexism in more detail. The effects of social inequality are not always equal between minorities and women. It is somewhat ironic that white women, the targets of gender inequality, often discriminate against minority group members. In order to better understand the differential effects of institutional racism and sexism, each will be reviewed separately. The reader needs to keep in mind that both lead to a life of second-class citizenship in our society. The ways that prejudice and discrimination are directed toward gays and lesbians will also be discussed.

PREJUDICE AND DISCRIMINATION

Social inequality is partly a result of prejudice and discrimination. Prejudice is a value learned through the process of socialization. Prejudices are internalized and become a dimension of an individual's value system. People who are prejudiced generally do not consider themselves so. The objects of prejudice are presumed to possess behavioral characteristics that the holders of prejudice find objectionable, whether real or fictional. Through the process of **stereotyping,** women and minority group members all are assumed to hold behavior traits that justifies their exclusion from free and full participation in the social roles of society. Stereotypes are beliefs that members of certain groups always or generally behave in specific ways. Hence, the belief that women are not as intelligent as men, lack decision-making ability, are prone to be emotional, and are better nurturers; that blacks are lazy and lack initiative; that Mexican–Americans prefer the slower pace of an agrarian life; or that Jews are elitist and money hungry—these are among many of the stereotypes associated with groups. Dominant group members often behave toward members of minorities as though the stereotypes were true. To better illustrate how prejudice effects decision making, consider this illustration paraphrased from the work of Gordon Allport in *The Nature of Prejudice* (1958, 5):

> *Applications for hotel reservations were sent to a number of resort hotels in Canada. The name of Lockwood and Greenwood was affixed to separate letters both sent to the same hotels and mailed separately on the same date. Lockwood received an acknowledgment of his inquiries from over 90 percent of the hotels with most of them confirming his reservation. Less than 10 percent responded to Greenwood's request and only 5 percent offered accommodations.*

Considering that it is highly unlikely that Lockwood's letter was always the first opened and that he was allotted the very last room available, how does one account for this differential outcome? Discrimination, anti-Semitism in this instance, is the only viable answer.

Prejudice is the presumption that certain behaviors are characteristic of all members of a minority group without the benefit of factual information. As a consequence, members of the dominant group may demean minorities by assuming that assigned behaviors in fact are true, and then relate to individual members through the filter of prejudice. In the case of Mr. Lockwood and Mr. Greenwood, it is clear that Greenwood was perceived as Jewish and therefore undesirable as a guest. Lockwood, on the other hand, was presumed to be white Protestant and acceptable. The hotel's decision was made without any specific information or facts about either. The differential treatment afforded Greenwood can only be accounted by the presumption that he was Jewish.

Prejudice is a psychological construct that may result in discrimination. Although it is possible for prejudice to exist without discrimination (and discrimination without prejudice, for that matter), they usually are coexistent (Yinger 1970). Prejudice fuels the fires and provides the justification for discrimination. If it is falsely believed (an axiom for prejudice) that people of different groups are less intelligent, incapable of equal participation, or seriously would challenge traditional practices, differential treatment (an axiom for discrimination) may occur, thereby placing the erroneously feared threat at some distance. Denying women, minorities, the elderly, gays, and other social groups the right to equal social participation limits the opportunity structures through which the desired behavioral characteristics could be acquired. A viscous, self-perpetuating cycle is then set in motion. Discrimination is the action that maintains and supports prejudice. Zastrow (1986, 379) observes that:

> *individuals who are targets of discrimination are excluded from certain types of employment, educational and recreational opportunities, certain residential housing areas, membership in certain religious and social organizations, certain political activities, access to community services, and so on.*

Institutional discrimination with the resultant differential treatment has been codified in administrative rules and regulations and is "intrinsic" to the social mores of society. Discrimination is reinforced through the social practices of dominant group members, who may be oblivious to their discriminatory nature. Institutionalized racism is based upon minority group membership, while institutionalized sexism results in the denial of rights or opportunities for participation based upon gender. In both instances, free and full participation is denied based upon group membership.

In a recently published book, *The Compleat Chauvinist,* Edgar Bergman (1982, 185) raises the question "What would our Neanderthal forefathers have thought of our succumbing to the outrageous myth of sexual equality?" In buttressing his antiegalitarian views, he refers to comments made by Marvin Harris, professor of anthropology at Columbia University, who is quoted as saying:

> *Feminists are wailing in the wind if they think they're (sic) going to abolish sexism by raising consciousness. There is not a shred of evidence—historical or contemporary—to support the existence of a single society in which women controlled the political and economic lives of men.*

Bergman offers a number of illustrations in defense of the position that men are clearly superior to women in decision making. To the detriment of social equality, Bergman's views and arguments are not new. Women have experienced social inequality based on gender throughout recorded history. Invariably, inequality was—and is—justified on the basis of biological superiority of men, in spite of evidence to the contrary. In the social sciences, social inequality is viewed as a product of human interaction and social organization (Perrucci & Knudsen 1983).

WOMEN AND SOCIAL INEQUALITY

In spite of advances made during the past several decades, the treatment of women in our society is characterized by discrimination. Perhaps sex-biased discrimination is more visible in the occupational market and economic areas than in other aspects of social participation. Zastrow (1986, 392) has identified a few of the more salient roles played by women as follows:

> *Women tend to be concentrated in the lower paying, lower status positions of secretaries, child care workers, receptionists, typists, nurses, hairdressers, bank tellers, cashiers, and file clerks. Men tend to be concentrated in higher paying positions: lawyers, judges, engineers, accountants, college teachers, physicians, dentists, and sales managers.*

Although some progress has been made, male-dominated job positions have remained virtually unobtainable to qualified women. Management and administrative positions at the upper levels continue to be held by men.

Income

While it is apparent that the income disparity between men and women largely is attributable to differences in occupational positions, it is noteworthy that little change has occurred during the decade 1970–1980 in the percentage of income earned by women when compared with men (Perrucci & Knudsen, 1983). Income differences are due largely to the fact that men are employed in positions of leadership or in technical fields whereas women are disproportionately employed in lower-paying occupations (see Table 17–1). Even when women hold positions similar to those of men, their income is less. Seniority or related factors do not always account for these differences and employers generally concede that men attract a higher income for equal situations than women.

Notwithstanding traditional notions that incomes produced by women are less essential for family maintenance than those generated by men, the practice of channeling women into lower-level positions with the resultant limited career choices and lower incomes represents an institutionalized policy of sex-biased discrimination. Although efforts recently have been developed to

Table 17–1
Median Income of Males and Females by Occupational Category (in dollars)

	1975			1980		
	Male	Female	Difference	Male	Female	Difference
Total	$12,758	$ 7,394	$ 5,254	$18,612	$11,197	$ 7,415
Percent		58.8			60.2	
Professional, technical and kindred workers	16,133	10,639 65.9	5,494	23,026	15,285 66.4	7,741
Managers and administrators, except farm	16,093	9,125 56.7	6,968	23,558	12,936 54.9	10,622
Sales	14,025	5,460 39.8	8,565	19,910	9,748 49.0	10,162
Clerical and kindred workers	12,152	7,562 62.2	4,590	18,247	10,997 60.3	7,250
Crafts and kindred workers	12,789	7,268 56.8	5,521	18,671	11,701 62.7	6,970
Operatives, including transport workers	11,142	6,251 56.1	4,891	15,702	9,440 60.1	6,262
Laborers, except farm	9,057	6,937 76.6	2,120	13,097	7,892 60.9	5,115
Service workers, except private household	9,488	5,414 57.1	4,074	12,757	9,747 76.4	3,010

Data are for persons 14 years old and over working full time, at longest job during year, 1975, 15 years and older, 1980.
Difference is female income as a percentage of male income.

Source: *Current Population Reports,* Series P–60, No. 105 and No. 127.

provide equal employment opportunities for women, social roles continue to be sex-typed and are passed down from generation to generation through the process of socialization.

Education

Ironically, men hold leadership positions in professions that predominantly employ women, such as public education and social work. In a study of Texas public school school administrators (Shuttlesworth 1978), it was found that

> *Administration and school leadership at all levels are dominated by males. During 1967–1977 less than 1 percent of the superintendents' positions were filled by women. In 1977, the year of the largest number of women appointed to administrative positions, women held only 7 out of 1106 superintendent positions, 607 out of 4471 principalships and 360 out of 2030 assistant principalships.*

These findings suggest that a career-oriented woman entering the educational system would have greater difficulty in securing promotion to an administrative position than a similar man. As a result, women are relegated to the lower-paying, less prestigious position of classroom teacher throughout their careers. Although nondiscrimination policies exist, qualified women educators who seek promotion to administration are confronted with the task of penetrating a sex-biased tradition of assigning men to those roles in the public school system.

When comparing educational attainment, men are awarded degrees in greater numbers than women, particularly at the graduate level. In 1980, men were awarded 23,100 doctoral degrees, compared to only 9,700 awarded to women (see Table 17–2). Although larger numbers of women are now engaged in the educational process at both graduate and undergraduate levels, men continue to dominate the educational degree market (U.S. Bureau of the

Table 17–2 College and Advanced Degrees Awarded	Bachelors		Masters		Doctorate	
	Male	Female	Male	Female	Male	Female
1950	330,000	104,000	41,000	17,000	6,000	600
1960	256,000	139,000	51,000	24,000	8,800	1,000
1970	487,000	346,000	126,000	83,000	25,900	4,000
1980	530,000	480,000	151,000	148,000	23,100	9,700

Source: U.S. Bureau of the Census, *Statistical Abstract of the United States.* (Washington, D.C.: Government Printing Office, 1981).

Census, 1981). Women are less well represented in business administration, engineering, the physical sciences, law, medicine, and dentistry, and are overrepresented in the liberal arts, fine arts, home economics, social work, and nursing, thereby limiting opportunities to achieve educational credentials necessary for entry into the male-dominated occupations and professions.

Social Work

In the field of social work, which long has championed and advocated for equal rights for women, it is ironic that leadership roles are held predominantly by men. In a study on status differentials between men and women in social work, Fanshel (1976) found that men are represented disproportionately in administrative and managerial roles and, as a group, receive higher salaries than women.

Religion

In organized religion where women are more active participants, less than 5 percent are ordained to the clergy (Perrucci & Knudsen 1983). In very few instances do women hold the position of primary leadership in churches, and only exceptionally are they employed in higher levels of administration in religious associations. Many religious groups base their male-biased pastoral leadership roles on the "holy writ," thereby effectively excluding women from appointments to significant leadership responsibilities in those bodies.

Politics

In 1982, only 10 of 435 congressmen and 2 of 100 United States senators were women (Perrucci & Knudsen 1983). Only 2 of the 50 governors were women. These figures reflect the subordinate role that women continue to play in the legislative process. Male bias is everpresent in legislative debates in those areas where laws directly affect women.

INSTITUTIONAL SEXISM

The discussion and illustrations just presented reflect the strong sexual bias in administrative and managerial positions. Women *are* treated differently in the professions and business. Their status as women negatively influences the opportunity to move into those prominent roles *regardless* of their competence or ability. In effect, women are discriminated against at the marketplace solely because they are women. This practice, called **sexism,** is a result of the values and practices embodied in our social institutions. Children are taught by their parents that boys are to be aggressive and dominant and that girls are to be nurturing and submissive. Parents model these attributes in family interaction, where father assumes the roles of rule maker, disciplinarian, and decision maker and mother assumes responsibility for the nurturing roles, caring for the children and homemaking.

Performance differences between men and women invariably reflect societal attitudes and values far more than any inherent physical or psychological variances in maleness or femaleness. In modern society, there are few roles that could not be performed by either men or women, although throughout the life cycle sex-role distinctions are made and differences emphasized. These distinctions become entrenched in societal values, thus creating "barriers" for women in "crossing over" into roles considered masculine. Hence, an aggressive, goal-oriented, intelligent woman may be viewed as masculine and censured for departing from prescribed female role behavior.

Societal values and practices continue to result in a sex-segregated division of labor. Although some progress has been made in identifying roles as "asexual" (neither male nor female), roles in general are sex typed. Women find access to roles identified as appropriate for men only with great difficulty. Sex differentiation also is observed in opportunities to secure credit, purchase homes, negotiate contracts, and obtain credit cards, where men typically have the advantage.

THE ABORTION ISSUE

Perhaps no more emotionally charged issue epitomizes the conflict between feminist and traditional values than abortion. The 1973 Supreme Court (*Roe vs. Wade* decision) maintained that the constitutional right to privacy included the right of a woman to have an abortion. The pro-life (right to life) movement continually has sought to have the decision overturned. It is estimated that over 1.5 million abortions are performed in the United States each year. The accuracy of data is difficult to validate. This conflict may be considered one of moral differences. Efforts to establish that life begins at conception are made by pro-life groups, who view abortion as murder. Pro-choice groups, who argue that life begins at birth, seek to promote the right of a woman to decide whether she wishes to continue her pregnancy or terminate it, a right that is granted by the *Roe vs. Wade* decision.

Additional controversy has erupted regarding the use of public funds to finance abortions for women who lack sufficient resources to pay for the medical procedures. In a recent controversial action, the Supreme Court voted 5–4 to uphold a six-year ban by Congress. This amendment, known as the Hyde Amendment, which prohibits federal funding of abortion, permits states to continue a voluntary practice of reimbursements for abortions. The crux of this issue relates to freedom of choice. Should freedom of choice be supported only for women who can pay for an abortion, while this right is denied to the poor? Public sentiment over this issue is decidedly unclear.

Even proponents of the pro-life movement are not in agreement over whether abortions should be permissible in the cases of a deformed embryo or saving a mother's life. The wide press and media coverage given to this important issue no doubt has shown that arguments for or against abortion are fraught with inconsistencies. In spite of the views held by the pro-life movement, the right to abortion is upheld by the law.

Abortion is not solely a women's problem. However, only women become pregnant and have the legal right to decide whether the pregnancy will be carried to its full term or terminated. Men may exercise influence but not choice regarding the matter. The law remains unusually silent concerning the role of men in matters of conception and pregnancy. Fathers are referred to as "alleged fathers," and have no legal right to affect a woman's decision to abort a pregnancy.

We have included this discussion to further illustrate the problem of differential treatment of women in our society. Women virtually must bear the entire consequences of a pregnancy. Alleged fathers, on the other hand, generally are not legally culpable. Zastrow's position (1986) on the abortion issues is clearly articulated:

> Our premise is that social work as a profession must view abortion as a legal right of every client, should she make this choice, and must therefore sublimate personal beliefs to that end. It is the practitioner's responsibility to facilitate intelligent, rational, and unanimous decision making on the part of the individual client, and to support that decision, whatever it may be.

SOCIAL REFORM: THE FEMINIST MOVEMENT AND SOCIAL ACTION

Women have pursued equal social treatment since this nation's inception. Some of the more noteworthy leaders were Elizabeth Stanton (1815–1902), who petitioned for a property rights law for women in New York (1845); Lucretia Mott (1793–1880), who organized the first women's rights convention in New York: Susan B. Anthony (1820–1906), who helped to form the National Women's Suffrage Association in 1869; and Lucy Stone (1818–1893), who formed the National American Women's Suffrage Association. Carrie Catt (1859–1947), a political activist, founded the International Women's Suffrage Alliance and later, following World War I, the League of Women Voters, an organization that today bears significant political influence. Ms. Catt's efforts were largely responsible for the enactment of the Nineteenth Amendment to the Constitution, which extended voting rights to women in 1920 (Macksey 1976).

In more recent times, the persistent efforts of women's groups to secure equal rights have been intensified. The Civil Rights Act of 1964 addressed the problems of discrimination due to gender as well as race. A major attempt to secure women's rights was embodied in the **Equal Rights Amendment (ERA)**. Bitterly opposed by organized labor, the John Birch Society, the Christian Crusade, and the Moral Majority, and over the protest of Senator Sam Ervin (D–North Carolina) who castigated the proposed amendment, the bill was passed by Congress in 1972 and remanded to the states for ratification. Pro–ERA forces, including the National Organization of Women (NOW), the League of Women Voters and the National Women's Political Caucus lobbied the states to seek ratification for the amendment. Anti–ERA spokespersons lobbied the states against ratification and argued that all women would be sent into combat, subjected to unisex public facilities, and required to secure jobs (Deckard 1983) if the amendment passed. The Carter administration, while favorable to the passage of the ERA, had little affect on influencing all of the states to adopt it. The Reagan administration opposed the measure. The amendment died due to lack of ratification in June 1982.

SOCIAL WORK RIGHTS FOR WOMEN

Although the profession of social work has advocated for the abolition of societal barriers that deny equal treatment of women, it has not been in the forefront in providing leadership for the more significant feminist movements. During the 1960s, however, women's equality was established as a major priority for the profession. Both the National Association of Social Workers (NASW) and the Council on Social Work Education (CSWE) initiated policies geared to commit the profession to actively pursue social and economic equality for women (Zastrow 1986). Social workers were encouraged to function as advocates for women's rights and to actively engage in equal treatment for all their clients. The abolition of sexism within the profession has been vigorously pursued with evidence that sex-biased career opportunities are being eliminated.

GAYS, LESBIANS, AND SOCIAL INEQUALITY

It is a generally accepted fact that 10 percent of the population is homosexual. Within the past decade, considerable attention has been directed to the prejudice and discrimination that characterizes societal response toward homosexual men and women. Although one's sexual persuasion is considered to be a personal and private matter not related to free and full participation in our society, such has not been the case for homosexuals. As Dulaney and Kelly have noted, the intense negative emotional reaction to the homosexual community is a result of "deep-rooted fear and accompanying hatred of homosexual lifestyles and individuals" (1982, 178), a state of psychological conditioning known as **homophobia.** Although it is not known what percentage of the American population is homophobic, Irwin and Thompson (1977, 107–121) found that one-fourth of the respondents to a research inquiry believed that homosexuals should be banned from teaching in colleges and universities. This attitude appears to permeate the business community and carries over to other aspects of social life as well. Acquired Immune Deficiency Syndrome (AIDS) has further promoted the anxiety and fear of homosexual relationships.

While experts appear to lack consensus as to whether sexual orientation is predetermined by genetics or is a product of socialization, this is of little concern to the public, who continue to view homosexuality as a matter of choice. Some gays and lesbians have become more vocal and sought legal redress for discriminatory practices, while others, fearing loss of jobs, intimidation and harassment, have opted to remain "in the closet." In 1973, the American Psychiatric Association removed "functional homosexuality" from its list of behavior disorders and, as a result, mental health professionals no longer view homosexuality as a form of mental illness. One might conclude, however, that the public maintains the perspective that gay and lesbian relationships are a form of perversion and that social contact with homosexuals should be avoided. While some progress has been made in securing legal rights for the gay community, discrimination and prejudice continue to undergird public responses to them.

Unfortunately, in spite of the enlightenment regarding same-sex orientation, many professionals find it difficult to engage homosexual clients in helping relationships free from their own biases and prejudices. Dulaney and Kelly (1982, 178) report that

> social work is most sensitive to contemporary societal pressures because of its sources of funding and orientation to community service. This sensitivity has led to a conflict in the profession regarding sexual issues and gay and lesbian clients that reflects society's dual value system, which consists of one set of values for heterosexuals and another for homosexuals.

De Crescenzo and McGill (1978) found that homophobia was far more prevalent among social workers than among psychologists and psychiatrists. Although there may be a variety of explanations as to why social workers tend to be more homophobic than other professionals, a primary reason may be

> social workers' lack of skill and intense discomfort in dealing with gay and lesbian clients are largely attributable to the fact that social work students receive almost no training regarding homosexuality in their formal education. (Dulaney & Kelly 1982, 179)

Clearly, there is a need for the social work and related professions to address more forcefully the prejudices and biases toward homosexuality as yet pervasive within the professions. In spite of the acknowledged reticence that exists, considerable progress has been made in the preparation of social workers for engaging clients who are gay or lesbian. Accreditation standards for schools of social work require that course content address the needs of divergent populations, including gays and lesbians. Advocacy on behalf of the homosexual population directed towards the enforcement of antidiscrimination legislation has become a priority of the profession.

Unfortunately, until the fear and apprehensions concerning homosexual behavior are dispelled through public enlightenment, prejudice and discrimination will continue to remain a barrier to social and economic justice for the gay and lesbian community.

SOCIAL INEQUALITY AND MINORITY GROUP MEMBERSHIP

What constitutes minority group status? According to Wirth, a minority group "is a category of people distinguished by special physical or cultural traits which are used to single them out for differential and unequal treatment" (Wirth 1938). The assignment to a minority status may be made on the basis of "race, nationality, religion or ethnicity" (Perrucci & Knudsen 1983). Hence, blacks, Mexican–Americans, other Hispanics, Asian–Americans, Moslems, Lithuanians, Iranians, or Vietnamese, among others, are considered by the dominant (majority) group as minorities. The concept of race suggests that strong divergent genetic differences are present. The term, in reality, is a social definition since few genetic differences are found to exist among homo sapiens. Race is commonly used to classify members of groups who have similar physical characteristics such as skin color or facial features. Behavioral traits are attributed to physical differences rather than to socialization experiences. Conversely, ethnic groups tend to be classified by language differences or cultural patterns that vary from the dominant group. Both racial and ethnic groups are viewed as "different" by the dominant group, and prejudice and discrimination are often the result.

PLURALISM

Complete integration of all groups in society would result in the loss of racial or ethnic identity. Many minorities find this prospect objectionable. In recent years, ethnic and racial pride has been given considerable attention by minority group members. Although complete integration (assimilation) theoretically would result in the erosion of racial and ethnic discrimination patterns, it is unlikely that it will occur. There is a strong argument that the contributions of our divergent ethnic and racial groups serve as an enrichment to our culture.

An alternative, **cultural pluralism,** the coexistence of different ethnic groups whose cultural differences are respected as equally valid (Perrucci & Knudsen 1983), is difficult to achieve without some vestige of discrimination. Dominant groups demand adherence to their values. Such a state of affairs is difficult to achieve within the matrix of prejudice, discrimination, and cultural differences. Recent attempts to create cultural pride have been emphasized by minorities, yet less than equal coexistence continues to characterize their relationship with the dominant group.

Members of minority groups invariably suffer the results of prejudice and discrimination. It is ironic that these conditions persist and are institutionalized by members of a society that values its Judeo–Christian heritage and provides equal constitutional rights and privileges to all. Progress has been made in opening avenues for social and economic participation; however, members of minorities still must cope with differential treatment and limited opportunities. The following discussion identifies issues and problems that confront minority groups and examines antidiscrimination efforts designed to neutralize racial and ethnic prejudices.

Afro–Americans

Although discrimination in varying degrees has been experienced by all minority groups, nowhere has it been more visible than with the black population. During the "Jim Crow" era in the deep South, blacks were not permitted to dine at public restaurants used by whites, could use only specially marked public restrooms and drinking fountains, were forced to ride in the rear of public conveyances, attended segregated schools, were expected to behave in a subservient manner in the presence of whites, and were relegated to lower-paying domestic or manual labor jobs. Few were able to achieve justice before the law or to gain acceptance as equals to even the lowest-class white. Although the prescribed behaviors that characterized Jim Crowism represented an extreme manifestation of discrimination, all minority groups have experienced social inequality in its more subtle form.

Today, blacks represent about 11 percent of our population and are our largest racial minority group. They are victimized by the effects of past and present discrimination. Although 80 percent of the black population lives in cities, they earn only 60 percent as much income as whites. Unemployment is particularly high among young black adults (30 percent), and black families are three times more likely to have incomes below the poverty line as whites. Numerically, more whites receive public assistance benefits; however, blacks are proportionately overrepresented on welfare rolls. Educationally, whites tend to complete high school in greater proportions than blacks. In the professions of law, medicine, and dentistry, blacks are underrepresented,

Major tenets of the social work profession accept the uniqueness of each individual and the diversity of groups of people in an effort to overcome injustice and inequality.

whereas they are overrepresented in the occupations that require hard manual labor.

Mexican–American and Other Hispanic Populations

People of Mexican descent constitute the second largest minority population in the United States. While most live in major urban areas of the West and Southwest, many continue to reside in rural areas. The Mexican–American population is a diverse group. The urban population tends to be better educated, and the effects of acculturation are more visible among them. Those living in rural areas are less acculturated, continue to use Spanish as a primary language, and work in lower-paying jobs related to harvesting of farm crops. This population group is rapidly growing as "aliens" continue to flow across the border into the southwestern states and California. Cultural pride is greatly emphasized and is best reflected in the retention of Spanish as a first language. Bilingual education programs have been designed to enable Mexican–American children to progress in public school systems, although dropout rates continue to be much higher than for the dominant group population. In general, people of Mexican ancestry have experienced the consequences of discrimination in that they hold lower-paying jobs and are underrepresented in politics, live in de facto segregated neighborhoods, and are viewed as being "different" by the dominant group. Upward mobility has been painfully slow in coming, although some progress has been made. Ethnic organizations such as "La Raza" and LULAC (League of United Latin American Citizens) have sought to unite the Spanish-speaking population to promote favorable social change and to provide greater visibility to the issues and problems that impede the achievement of social equality.

Puerto Ricans and Cubans constitute the largest other Hispanic populations. Approximately two-thirds of the Puerto Rican population reside in the New York City area, while the Cuban population has settled primarily in Florida. The social and economic progress of these groups is similar to that of the Mexican–American group. Housing is often inferior, jobs tend to be menial and lower paying, the school dropout rate is high, and access to services and support systems is difficult. Social progress has been considerably greater for the Cuban population due, in part, to its higher educational level. Recently, a Cuban immigrant was elected mayor of Miami, Florida. As has been the case with newly migrated Mexicans, other Hispanics came to the United States with the hopes of being able to achieve a higher quality life, only to find that prejudice and discrimination presented barriers to achieving that dream. Cultural and language barriers continue to make them "different" and more visible targets for differential treatment.

Asian Americans

The Japanese, Chinese, Vietnamese, and other Asian immigrants have divergent cultural traits and physical characteristics that separate them from the dominant group. They represent less than 2 percent of the United States population. The immigration of the Chinese dates back to the mid-nineteenth century, the Japanese to around the turn of the twentieth century, and the

Vietnamese to the 1960s and 1970s. All have experienced differential treatment; however, their cultural heritage inspires incentive and hard work and, as a consequence, many have been able to achieve a relatively high standard of living in spite of the social barriers. The Chinese have been noted for their in-group living patterns; "Chinatowns" in San Francisco, Los Angeles, New York, and other larger cities encourage the preservation of their cultural heritage. Prejudice and discrimination continue to be among the more significant obstacles for Asian Americans in achieving social and economic progress. The Vietnamese have been the most recent target for discrimination and have found difficulty locating adequate housing, employment opportunities and acceptance in American communities. Language barriers have intensified "differences" and resulted in closing avenues for social and economic participation.

Native Americans

Native Americans numerically are our smallest minority group and have long experienced the consequences associated with minority status. As American citizens, they have seldom been able to experience free and full involvement in society. Large numbers continue to live on reservations, which serves to segregate them from interaction with the dominant group and thwarts opportunities for equal participation. Discrimination against Native Americans has been purposefully institutionalized by governmental policy. Barriers to social participation remain and are difficult to overcome.

EFFORTS TO PRODUCE SOCIAL EQUALITY FOR MINORITY GROUPS

Bringing an end to institutional racism and discrimination is not an easy task. Prejudices have lingered over a number of generations and are difficult to extinguish, in spite of efforts to enlighten the public of the consequences of maintaining false beliefs and practices. Little progress was made in dismantling segregation until the government initiated action to do so. Until President Truman ordered the cessation of segregation in the Armed Forces (1948), most government agencies supported separation of the races (Perrucci & Knudsen 1983). The catalyst for ending separate public school education was embodied in the Supreme Court decision *Brown vs. Board of Education* (1954), which mandated an end to segregation in public schools. Ruling that "separate was not equal"; the Court ordered public school facilities integrated and opened to children of all races and ethnic groups. De facto housing patterns result in minorities living in common neighborhoods and their children attending neighborhood schools. In order to implement the court's decision, busing became necessary, which resulted in strong resistance by the white population. White citizens' councils emerged in the South and Midwest to resist school integration. Many state governments questioned the constitutionality of the Court's decision and resisted taking appropriate action to hasten the integration process. "Evidence" was sought to support the position that integration of school facilities would have catastrophic effects on the educational achievements of children of all races. In a 1962 report *The Biology of The Race Problem* by Wisley C. George, a biologist, and commissioned by the governor of Alabama, an attempt was made to offer scientific evidence that blacks innately were inferior to whites and would not be capable of competing with whites in the educational process. Other racist, white supremacist groups, such as the Ku Klux Klan, joined in efforts to prevent school integration. In spite of all organized resistance, school busing became commonplace and school integration a technical reality. Since 1980, a movement to return to the neighborhood school concept has attained favorable sentiment by the Reagan Administration. Although policies to eliminate busing have not been forthcoming, fear that such action will ensue has been resisted by minority and equal rights organizations.

During the 1960s, significant progress was made in eliminating segregationist policies and controlling the effects of discrimination. President Johnson's Great Society programs sought to eradicate segregation entirely and to make discrimination an offense punishable under the law. In 1964, the **Civil Rights Act** was passed. This act, amended in 1965, sought to ban discrimination based on race, religion, color, or ethnicity in public facilities, governmentally operated programs, or employment. A similar act, passed in 1968, made the practice of discrimination in advertising and the purchase or rental of residential property or its financing illegal.

Under the new legal sanctions for desegregation, a groundswell of support mounted among disenfranchised minorities and sympathetic dominant group members. The Rev. Martin Luther King and organized freedom marchers sought to raise the consciousness of society regarding the obscenities of segregationist policies. King's nonviolent movement provided great visibility to the injustices of discrimination and served to stimulate and influence policies for change. Other significant minority organizations, such as the Southern Christian Leadership Conference, the National Urban League, and the National Association for the Advancement of Colored People (NAACP), La Raza, and The League of United Latin American Countries, were actively pursuing social and economic justice for minorities during this period. As the new civil rights legislation was implemented, an air of hope prevailed that discrimination would soon become a matter of history. School busing facilitated public school integration, public facilities were opened to minorities, and the employment market became more accepting of minority applicants. Further advances were made under the influence of the Economic Opportunities Act of 1964. Neighborhoods were organized and their members registered to vote. This movement was furthered by the Voting Rights Act of 1965, which prohibited the imposition of voting qualifications upon citizens based on race, color, age, or minority status. The impact of the civil rights movement was far-reaching in securing a toehold in the struggle for full and equal participation by minorities in the social and economic area of our society.

The rapid pact of the change effort was short lived. By the late 1970s, racial polarization had increased with a new wave of conservatism. Whites were much more prone to attribute the "lack of progress" among the black population to the blacks themselves, rather than to discrimination, thus supporting the position that discrimination was no longer a problem for "motivated" blacks. By the late 1970s, it was clear that racial and minority issues were not among the top priorities for the white majority. Instead,

> *national defense, energy supplies, and inflation have readily replaced minority concerns as priority issues during the last decade, and that shift in attention has been accompanied by a shift of resources away from minorities. Fostered by this contraction of resources the most intense overt conflicts over resources now occur not between the majority and minority groups, but among minority groups. (Walters 1982, 26)*

Although efforts to achieve minority equality are still intact, the strong, active, government commitment has waned. Affirmative action programs, which once mandated the selection of qualified minority group members for publicly operated business, appear to have been downgraded. Affirmative action efforts were directed at breaking institutional discrimination in employment. Challenged as creating a **reverse discrimination** employment market, conservatives have "cooled down" efforts to vigorously pursue opportunities for minorities through this program. The Federal Civil Rights Commission has become noticeably silent and inactive since 1981. The gains achieved in the quest for social equality during the 1960s and 1970s gradually are being eroded by apathetic leadership in the 1980s.

Social Work and the Civil Rights Movement

Inherent in social work's identity is its commitment to social action directed toward the elimination of barriers that deny equal rights and full participation

to all members of society. Since the early days, when social workers assisted in assimilating new immigrants into our culture and sought to improve social conditions for them, the profession has engaged the citizenry in working toward social equality and an equal opportunity structure. The National Association of Social Workers, as well as the Council on Social Work Education, has given high priority to incorporating minority interests into professional social work practice and social work education. Social work practitioners strive to be mindful of the consequences of minority status and familiar with the racial-cultural backgrounds of their clients when assisting them in achieving solutions to problems. Through social action, efforts are made to change community attitudes, policies, and practices that disadvantage minorities. As advocates, social workers seek to modify rules and regulations that deny equal treatment to those assigned to a minority status. As organizers, they work with minority leadership in identifying priorities, gaining community support, and facilitating change through the democratic process.

Social workers are active in organized public efforts to abolish discriminatory practices. As citizens (as well as professionals), they support political candidates who are openly committed to working for social equality. They are involved in public education designed to dispel prejudice and to promote productive interaction among divergent races and ethnic groups. In a public climate where the pursuit of social and economic equality has lessened, social workers have the responsibility to maintain a vigilant pursuit of equality for minorities.

SUMMARY

Few observers would deny that the United States has experienced a major sexual revolution during the past few decades. As part of the human rights movement, many advances have been made in reducing sexism in our society. Opportunities for economic and social participation of women are greater now than they have been throughout the history of this country. Although there have been "reversals," such as the failure to ratify the ERA, societal pressures continue to be underway to assure equal treatment and opportunities for women. Although resistances from both men's and women's groups are everpresent, the continued efforts of groups committed to the achievement of equal rights should result in significant gains during the coming years.

Social inequality also has characterized the treatment of racial and ethnic minorities and homosexuals in the United States. Although some progress has been made in achieving more favorable treatment, full participation rights have not yet been achieved. Discrimination and differential treatment of women, minority group members, and homosexuals continue to impose restrictions in their achievement of social and economic progress. Although legislation has served as a catalyst for removing long-standing practices that denied equal rights, in recent years, the conservative movement has lowered the priorities for attaining social equality for women and minorities. Even less attention has been given to social equality for homosexuals. Social work has a long tradition of promoting social equality, and the commitment of the profession to continue pressing for this will be greater as the societal thrust to do so declines. Prejudice and discrimination are the products of social interaction. As social constructs, they can be replaced by values that respect the dignity and worth of all human beings and result in a society that promotes equal treatment for all.

KEY TERMS

Civil Rights Act   reverse discrimination
cultural pluralism   sexism
Equal Rights Amendment   social inequality
    (ERA)   stereotyping
homophobia

DISCUSSION QUESTIONS

1. What is prejudice? Discrimination? Institutional sexism? Racism?
2. What impact has the feminist movement had on producing social equity for women?
3. Why is homophobia more prevalent among social workers than psychologists and psychiatrists?
4. Compare and contrast *cultural pluralism* with *coexistence* and different ethnic and racial groups. Identify problems inherent in each.
5. What efforts have been made to produce social equality for minority groups? How successful have they been? What suggestions would you make to alleviate the problems of prejudice and discrimination?
6. Identify the role of social work in the civil rights movement.

REFERENCES

Allport, Gordon. 1954. *The Nature of Prejudice*. Reading, Mass.: Addison–Wesley.

Bergman, Edgar. 1982. *The Complete Chauvinist*. New York: Macmillan.

De Crescenzo, Teresa, and Christine McGill. 1978. "Homophobia: A Study of the Attitudes of Mental Health Professionals Toward Homosexuality." Unpublished master's thesis, University of Southern California, School of Social Work.

Deckard, Barbara S. 1983. *The Women's Movement: Political and Psychological Issues*. New York: Harper and Row.

Dulaney, Diane D., and James Kelly. 1982. "Improving Services to Gay and Lesbian Clients." *Social Work* 27, no. 2 (March): 178–83.

Fanshel, David. 1976. "Status Differentials: Men and Women in Social Work." *Social Work* 21, no. 6 (November): 448–53.

George, Wesley C. 1962. *The Biology of the Race Problem.* Report prepared by Commission of the Governor of Alabama.

Irwin, Patrick, and Norman C. Thompson. 1977. "Acceptance of the Rights of Homosexuals: A Social Profile." *Journal of Homosexuality* 3 (Winter): 107–21.

Macksey, Joan. 1976. *The Book of Women's Achievements.* New York: Stein and Day.

Perrucci, Robert, and Dean D. Knudsen. 1983. *Sociology.* New York: West Publishing Company.

Shuttlesworth, Verla. "Women in Administration in Public Schools of Texas." Unpublished doctoral dissertation, Baylor University, 1978.

U.S. Bureau of the Census. 1981. *Statistical Abstracts of the United States.* Washington, D.C.: Government Printing Office.

Walters, Ronald W. 1982. "Race, Resources, Conflict." *Social Work* 27, no. 1 (January): 24–29.

Wirth, Louis. 1938. "Urbanism as a Way of Life." *American Journal of Sociology* 44 (July): 3–24.

Yinger, J. Milton. 1970. *The Scientific Study of Religion.* New York: Macmillan.

Zastrow, Charles. 1986. *Introduction of Social Welfare Institutions.* 3d ed. Homewood, Ill.: The Dorsey Press.

SELECTED FURTHER READINGS

Berger, Raymond. 1983. "What is a Homosexual: A Definitional Model." *Social Work* 28, no. 2: 312–316.

Brown, Caree R., and Marilyn L. Hellinger. 1975. "Therapists's Attitudes Toward Women." *Social Work* 20 (July): 266.

Cass, Bettina, and Cora V. Baldock. 1983. *Women, Social Welfare and the State.* Winchester, Mass.: Allyn and Bacon.

Davis, Angela. 1983. *Women, Race and Class.* New York: Vintage Books.

Feagin, R. 1984. *Racial and Ethnic Relations.* 2d ed. Englewood Cliffs, N.J.: Prentice–Hall.

Goodman, James, ed. 1973. *The Dynamics of Racism in Social Work.* Washington, D.C.: National Association of Social Work.

Szymanski, Albert. 1976. "Racial Discrimination and White Gain." *American Sociological Review* 41 (June): 403–14.

Weinberg, Martin S., and Colin J. Williams. 1976. *Male Homosexuals: Their Problems and Adaptations.* New York: Penguin.

18 Social Work and the Other Helping Professions

C harles and Sarah have been married for fifteen years. They have two children, Oscar, age fourteen, and Cheree, age eight. Sarah is two months pregnant. Neither Charles nor Sarah desired to have additional children. Charles has been urging Sarah to have an abortion, yet she has refused steadfastly. Sarah is a devout Catholic and feels that an abortion would be a grave sin. Charles argues that they can not afford to have another child since Cheree has chronic health problems and Oscar has become a behavior problem in school. They suspect that he is using drugs but have not been able to prove that he has.

Both Charles and Sarah have difficulty in facing problems head-on and hope that the problems will go away with the passing of time. The marital relationship between Charles and Sarah has become tense and the conflict between them has intensified. Charles has resorted to staying out later after work and is away from home more frequently during the evening. Sarah has accused Charles of losing his love for her, but he denies that he has. Sarah is experiencing headaches regularly, feels faint often, and has difficulty in handling her chores.

Sarah and Charles have not been willing to seek outside assistance with their problems, primarily because Charles feels that a man should be able to take care of his family's problems, and Sarah is reluctant to seek counseling without him. Recently, their discussions have centered around separation, which both say they do not want. Both Charles and Sarah want to be happy again but find that their situation continues to deteriorate. Sarah has finally convinced Charles that they should see a counselor to help them sort out their problems and work towards improving their relationship.

Assume that you are a friend of Charles and Sarah and they turn to you for assistance in finding a specialist to help with their problems. To whom would you refer them? A psychiatrist? A family counselor? A social worker? A pastoral counselor? A clinical psychologist? The school guidance counselor? Helping Charles and Sarah locate the appropriate professional help is not always an easy task, since there are many professionals who work within the human helping services. Most are trained to assist people with a variety of problems. Unfortunately, there also are individuals who lack the essential professional education to engage in human problem solving. In this chapter, we will describe briefly those professional helping disciplines that are the most likely to be found in the human services network. Social workers often find that the unique skills of other professionals are helpful in resolving problems that are less appropriate for the social work approach. At the conclusion of the chapter, we will attempt to identify which of the professional helping fields might be appropriate to assist Charles and Sarah with their problems.

PSYCHIATRY

Psychiatry is a specialized field of medical practice that focuses upon mental and emotional dysfunctioning. While psychiatrists typically treat patients experiencing some form of psychopathology, many engage in other problems of social dysfunctioning and interpersonal relationships. For example, a psychiatrist may counsel with couples experiencing marital discord, assist adolescents with problems in adaptation, engage children whose social development has been retarded in play therapy, counsel with individuals and couples who experience sexual dysfunctions, and so on. Unlike other professionals who assist with psychological and emotional problems as well as those of social dysfunctioning, psychiatrists are able to provide medications where physiological symptoms indicate the need for them. Because psychiatrists are physicians (with an M.D. degree), they have at their disposal a wide array of medical interventions as well as their expertise in treating problems of a mental and emotional nature.

Psychiatrists practice in a variety of settings. Hospitals established for the treatment of the mentally ill constitute the most frequent employment sites. Many psychiatrists establish private practices in major metropolitan areas. Others are either employed full-time or serve as treatment consultants in residential treatment centers, children's agencies, centers designed for the treatment of specialized problems, such as alcohol or substance abuse, family violence, suicide prevention centers, or assist other agencies that provide specialized services to the emotionally disturbed.

Like other helping professionals, psychiatrists are educated in various programs that emphasize different theoretical and methodological approaches to problem solving. Some embrace Freudian psychology, others Adlerian or Jungian, while still others incorporate Sullivanian theories into their practice, all of which are "insight therapies." In recent times, many psychiatrists have adopted learning theory approaches (behavior modification) as well as reality therapy, rational emotive therapy, transactional analysis, and related approaches. Psychiatrists typically are well educated for their speciality and constitute a significant and important resource for treating problems of the mentally ill and emotionally disturbed.

PSYCHOLOGY

Coon (1982) has identified thirty-four subspecialities in the field of **psychology**. The majority of these specialities do not involve special preparation in counseling or psychotherapy. According to Coon, over one-half of all psychologists are employed by educational institutions, another 15 percent work in hospitals or clinics, 10 percent are in government service or research, 7 percent are in private practice, and 6 percent are employed by public or private schools. In terms of the focus of their employment, 29 percent engage in clinical practice; 10 percent are experimental psychologists; 19 percent are educational or school psychologists; 9 percent are developmental, social, and personality psychologists; 8 percent are general, engineering, and other industrial specialists; 3 percent are involved in testing as a subspeciality; and 1 percent are environmental psychologists (Coon 1982, 18).

Without some awareness of the differences in speciality areas, one might find it difficult to identify the appropriate resource for problem solving! Unlike psychiatrists, professional psychologists are not physicians. Those who engage in practice designed to assist with psychological and emotional problems generally are referred to as *clinical* or *counseling* psychologists. Like psychiatrists, psychologists are educated in universities and professional schools that emphasize a wide variety of theoretical and methodological approaches to practice. Again, like psychiatrists, many have developed skills in psychotherapy and psychoanalysis. Others prefer methodological approaches that reflect a behavior modification, cognitive therapy, Gestalt therapy, or related practice modality. Psychologists treat clients with deep-rooted emotional conflict, faulty personality development, interpersonal problems represented in marriage and family conflict, substance abuse, and various psychological and behavioral disorders. Psychologists typically use various forms of **psychometric instruments** (testing) in arriving at a problem diagnosis. These instruments are designed to provide information about clients and their functioning that often is not readily observable during the interview. Tests also may be used as a basis for establishing a personality profile for clients. Tests can be useful in providing insights into the clients' abilities to handle stress and areas where the client is vulnerable. Tests, however, are only one of many sources of evidence needed to assess clients' problems.

Many psychologists are skilled in group therapy as well as individualized practice. In recent years group psychotherapy and group treatment have emerged as significant treatment techniques in helping clients with similar problems resolve those problems through the use of group dynamics and the skilful intervention of the group therapist.

Psychologists engaging in psychometry are often called upon as consultants to test clients in social service agencies and educational institutions. This service is often very helpful in gaining better insights into clients and establishing appropriate treatment and intervention plans.

SOCIOLOGY

Sociologists are experts in the study of society, its organization, and the phenomena arising out of the group relations of human beings. As such, professionals in this area contribute much to our awareness of human interaction including the establishment of norms, values, social organization, patterns of behavior, and social institutions. Sociologists are skilled in research techniques and methodologies. Like other professionals, they may focus upon a subspeciality area such as the family, deviancy, industrial sociology, symbolic interaction, bureaucracy and related forms of social organization, and the sociology of knowledge and social problems, to name a few.

The majority of sociologists are employed at institutions of higher education and related educational institutions, although a growing number are entering the field of clinical or applied sociology. Professionals engaging in clinical or applied sociology seek to apply the knowledge and principles gleaned from sociological theory to identify or enrich the understanding of organizational or interactional relationships with the goal of resolving problems. Sociologists utilizing this approach may function as family counselors, group therapists, industrial consultants, problem analysts, or program planners. The contribution of sociology to the understanding of the impact of environment and group membership on behavior has proven immeasurable.

PASTORAL COUNSELORS

Perhaps no other single source of contact by persons experiencing problems is sought out more than that of religious leaders. Priests, pastors, ministers, rabbis, and other persons in positions of spiritual leadership are called upon readily by their parishioners and others in trouble. Religious leaders are placed in a unique and valued position by the laity. As spiritual leaders they are presumed to have an extraordinary understanding of human frailty, as well as possessing superhuman communication with supernatural powers. Just as congregations vary in size and sophistication, so do the educational background, experience, and education of religious leaders as problem solvers. Many receive extensive theological education coupled with a subspeciality in counseling. Others become counselors by demand, with little academic and supervised practical instruction to do so. Still others are relatively uneducated and hold their positions by what they perceive as a unique calling from God. In most instances, they are committed to assist their parishioners with finding solutions to problems within the context of a religious belief system.

Professional **pastoral counselors** are most often educated at schools of theology offering specializations in counseling. Typically, these programs offer classroom theory and a practicum which utilizes various psychological approaches to intervention and problem solving. Many religious leaders complete their theological education and enter graduate schools in clinical or counseling psychology, social work, or guidance and counseling programs. It is not uncommon for larger congregations to employ pastoral counselors to supplement the overall pastoral ministry.

Pastoral counselors may assist parishioners with marriage and family problems, developmental problems, social problems, difficulties with interpersonal relationships, and a myriad of other problems. Individuals experiencing inner conflict with respect to spiritual problems are frequently given assistance and support by the pastoral counselor. Skilled practitioners also may form groups to work on specific problems. Pastoral counselors also are engaged in various educational activities with the congregation, designed to enrich the awareness and understanding of members or as a preventive effort. Like other human service professionals, pastoral counselors must develop an awareness of the limits of their professional skills and make referrals, where necessary, to assure that the best interests of the client are served.

GUIDANCE COUNSELORS

Guidance counselors typically are educated in public school–teacher educational programs and certified by state educational agencies. Most are required to have classroom teaching experience prior to the time that they are eligible for certification as guidance counselors. Guidance counselors specialize in assisting students with educationally related problems and in locating educational resources best suited to meet their individual interests. It is not uncommon for students with problems in behavioral as well as those in academic progression to be referred to the guidance counselor for assistance. While the guidance counselor's focus is upon academically related concerns, it is not uncommon for them to become engaged in a therapeutic relationship with students who are experiencing adaptive or emotionally related problems. Guidance counselors also may assist the school psychologist in administering tests to students and, in smaller school systems, may assume primary responsibility for the testing program. They are called upon to provide essential information to classroom teachers about the performance of students and, in collaboration with them, to develop an educational plan for students experiencing difficulty with their academic progression. Guidance counselors occasionally find themselves in the role of **ombudsman** as they seek to assist students and teachers or administrators in resolving conflicts in their interaction. They may work with the school social worker where truancy or family-related problems are related significantly to the student's academic performance. The guidance counselor's specialized awareness of educational process and resource alternatives can be of value to students needing information or an awareness of options available to them.

Guidance counselors usually are required to have an advanced degree as well as specialization coursework. In general, required coursework does not prepare the counselor for psychotherapy or long-term counseling.

EMPLOYMENT COUNSELORS

Professionals who focus their effort upon assisting clients in locating employment, assessing their skill levels, and enrolling in educational courses designed to prepare them for skill development and ultimate employment often are employed as "employment counselors." Their specialized knowledge of the employment market and unique skills in matching clients needing work with the needs of employers are designed to improve the probabilities of securing satisfaction with a job as well as competence in performance on the job. Employment counselors are skilled at interpreting various tests used to determine a client's aptitude for various positions. Not only do employment counselors assist persons needing a position or those maladapted in the positions they hold to find employment of the most suitable nature, they also are available to assist them with locating the essential supports to maintain involvement on the job. For example, transportation or childcare could represent barriers for an individual who otherwise needs work. Locating and referring the client to an appropriate resource may resolve those problems and produce a more favorable arrangement for meeting the demands of the job.

Employment counselors work with the business community in identifying employment needs and the skill requirements that will be necessary to provide optimum benefit for the business as well as the worker. Feedback and monitoring systems may be established as mechanisms for "fine-tuning" the job referral process.

Vocational education programs abound in the United States and provide instruction in a variety of areas: cosmetology, aircraft maintenance, welding, carpentry, computer technology, auto mechanics, heavy machine operations, office management, hotel administration, and many, many other speciality areas. Workers who are dissatisfied in their current employment or whose jobs have disappeared in the changing technology, persons reentering the job market, or new workers entering employment often find vocational education beneficial in learning a skill that will lead to employment. Handicapped persons also find vocational education an invaluable resource in adapting their abilities to skills that are salable on the job market. Employment counselors typically are influential in assisting clients in utilizing vocational educational programs, when it is perceived as a viable resource in assisting them with the development of job-related skills.

ATTORNEY–AT–LAW

Lawyers are professionals who engage in both criminal and civil matters to assist individuals in securing their rights under the law. Most communities, large or small, have practicing attorneys. Law, like other professional areas, has many subspecialities. Many lawyers are employed by large corporations and deal with contracts and their interpretation, assessing legal specifications relative to business practices and providing the legal expertise essential for corporate ventures. Others are in private practice, some handling primarily civil matters such as lawsuits, divorces, property settlements, deeds, estate management, wills, and similar civil matters. Lawyers are educated in graduate schools of law throughout the country. As professionals, they encounter a myriad of problems that have legal consequences. In some cases, such as that of divorce or child custody, the lawyer often becomes involved in a counseling role. Although many lack the appropriate educational background and expertise, clients often seek assistance with emotional as well as legal problems.

Lawyers seek to make referrals to appropriate agencies or other professionals when indicated.

Many of the larger communities have established legal aid clinics, which specialize in offering legal counsel to the poor or near poor. The poor, as well as the nonpoor, encounter many problems that need the attention of a legal expert, such as divorce, child custody, property settlements, and adequate defense in a court of law. Legal aid clinics are an invaluable resource for the poor. Many lawyers are employed as full-time legal counselors at the clinics, while others work part-time or volunteer time at the clinic. Legal aid clinics seek to promote justice for the poor as well as for those in better financial circumstances. Typically, law firms assign a portion of their staff time to pro bono (for the public good) efforts, often representing indigent clients.

Lawyers constitute a valuable resource to the problem-solving process. Matters that need legal attention often are a source of stress and are responsive to the skillful intervention of the legal profession.

Although the brief discussion of selected professions is by no means complete, it does encompass the primary disciplinary areas in the human service field. Social workers and others in the helping professions need to develop an awareness of the expertise available in their practice arena. Many problems require the attention of experts from diverse areas of practice in order to move toward resolution. It also is requisite that all professionals develop an awareness of their limitations as well as strengths, if clients are to receive the maximum benefit in the problem-solving effort.

In our complex, highly technological society, the emergence of a variety of specialists is a necessity. With the explosion of knowledge and our understanding of human need, it would not be possible for any one person to master it all! Just as our society is complex, so, we have learned, are human beings.

Social workers and other helping professionals often work as a team in assisting clients. Here, a social worker and a physician make a home visit to a client.

Socialization has produced many likenesses as well as differences in the population. Values vary, as do the many diverse groups with whom we hold an identity. Speciality areas have emerged in response to both such diverse needs and the understanding of the theoretical explanations of behavior. Life is a problem-solving process and our ability to respond appropriately to those problems involves not only our personality make-up but knowledge, awareness, resources and sensitivities as well. Invariably, all of us will at times encounter problems for which there appear no ready solutions. Often, the friendly advice of a neighbor, spouse, or confidant is sufficient in providing the perspective that will lead to an acceptable solution. At other times, professional assistance is essential in achieving a satisfactory resolution of the problem.

A question often raised relates to the likenesses and differences among the professions. What, for example, does a psychiatrist do with clients that is different than what a psychologist would do? Or a social worker? Or a pastoral counselor? And so on. All, for example, might engage in marital counseling, or provide assistance to a family struggling with the behavioral problems of an adolescent. To an uninformed observer, the professional response to those problems may appear to be approximately the same. Clients see the professional for an hour or so per week, the content of the interaction consists primarily of verbal interaction, and generally the client is given specific tasks to work on until the next visit. The professionals may contact other social systems related to the client's functioning, such as the school system or employment system. What, then, constitutes the difference? In part, although not exclusively, the differences may lie in the theoretical perspective that the professional brings to bear on the problem. The specialized emphasis on individual psychodynamics as reflected in psychiatry and psychology often varies with social work's emphasis on the relationship between the person and the environment within which the person functions. Also, social work's mastery of and emphasis on utilizing community resources are distinctively different from the typical approaches used in psychiatry and psychology.

Social work emphasizes the problem-solving approach. Recognizing that stress may be generated by the lack of resources as well as intrapsychic conflict, concrete resources, such as locating a job, adequate housing, health care services, childcare, or other needed services are part of the professional armament of the social worker. The various roles that the social worker plays, such as advocate, broker, enabler, case manager, and intervener often are essential to creating an environment in which clients may move toward problem solution.

The cooperative relationship and respect that exist among the helping professions are necessary if the optimum helping environment is to be attained. Social workers have clients who need psychiatric treatment, or the special services provided by a clinical or counseling psychologist or pastoral counselor. Many clients are assisted by referrals to the employment counselor, and students experiencing difficulty in school adaptation benefit by referrals to the school guidance counselor. Positive interaction and collaboration among these professionals enrich the service systems and increase the probabilities of securing a better quality of intervention for clients in need. Each profession has its own distinct professional culture, and an awareness of these varying cultures should promote more appropriate referrals.

A CASE REVISITED

Let us return now to the case with which we opened this chapter. It might prove of value for the reader to review the problems of Charles, Sarah, and their children. Assume that you are a friend of the family and are aware of the family. Charles and Sarah turn to you for assistance. Where would you refer them? To a psychiatrist? A clinical psychologist? A social worker? To a pastoral counselor? The school guidance counselor? All of these professions might provide some assistance with the problems. Because of the multiple problems that are evidenced in this family, a social worker might serve as a case manager in assuring that appropriate resources are secured. The social worker might engage Charles and Sarah in marriage counseling, refer Oscar to the school guidance counselor, secure medical attention for Cheree and Sarah, and coordinate the efforts of professionals providing assistance to the family. The nature of the problems at this stage of development does not appear to call for psychiatric attention. Oscar's behavioral problems may indicate a need for psychological testing, which could be performed by a clinical psychologist and made available to the guidance counselor, social worker, pastoral counselor, and others involved in the intervention process. Because of the nature of the family's problems, it is doubtful if only one professional discipline could manage the variety of problems indicated. Sarah's guilt over the abortion issue may be addressed by a pastoral counselor sensitive to the spiritual issues involved. Alternatives may be indicated, and if so, both Charles and Sarah must commit themselves to whatever option appears to be mutually agreeable for them. Families similar to that of Charles and Sarah are commonplace throughout our society. They merit the best professional effort that we can supply in assisting them toward life satisfaction.

THE BACCALAUREATE SOCIAL WORKER AMID OTHER PROFESSIONS

The baccalaureate social worker (BSW) typically functions as a generalist practitioner and holds a unique position in the professional community. The great variety of human problems that are objects of their intervention activity calls upon their skills as counselors, resource finders, case managers, evaluators, advocates, brokers, enablers, and problem solvers. The BSW's awareness of community resources and the ability to use them skillfully in the problem-solving process are particularly valuable in securing the needed assistance for distressed clients. BSWs work in varied social service agencies and community settings.

SUMMARY

In this chapter, we have identified some of the more prominent human service professionals who engage in assisting clients with problems of adaptation. An attempt also was made to identify similarities and differences among the professional areas. The need for interprofessional collaboration was examined in relation to obtaining the greatest expertise for clients in the intervention process.

KEY TERMS

ombudsman   psychology
pastoral counselor   psychometric instruments
psychiatry

DISCUSSION QUESTIONS

1. Identify the similarities and differences among the professions discussed in this chapter.
2. Describe the differences in the social work approach to problem solving and those used by other helping professions.
3. After reviewing the case of Charles and Sarah, how would you approach the case? To whom would you make referrals? Why?
4. What is the baccalaureate social worker's role in working with other professions in the problem solving process?

REFERENCES

Coon, Dennis. 1982. *Essentials of Psychology,* 2d ed. New York: West Publishing Company.

SELECTED FURTHER READINGS

Health. 1984. Career Information Center, No. 7. Irving, Calif.: Glencoe/Macmillan, 1984.

Norback, Craig. 1980. *Careers Encyclopedia.* Homewood, Ill.: Dow Jones–Irwin.

19 The Voluntary Sector

Carl Elders is a social worker for Lutheran Social Services of Minnesota, a voluntary social services agency funded primarily by the Lutheran Church. Carl works at an outreach center in a rural community, providing a variety of services to individuals and families who live in the surrounding area. Although many of Carl's clients are not Lutherans, he works closely with church congregations in the area, providing information about his agency's services and educational programs on topics such as dealing with stress and teen-age pregnancy.

Carl sees clients for a number of reasons. Some need marriage counseling, some are having difficulty with children or teen-agers, and some have serious emotional problems and have been in and out of the local state hospital. Carl also leads several groups of individuals with alcohol and drug problems and a group of families of senior citizens coping with the aging process. He counsels pregnant teens and refers those interested in adoption to his agency's extensive adoption program. He is working with a community task force to develop a special program for teens who choose to keep their babies rather than to release them for adoption.

Carl enjoys working for a voluntary agency, particularly the opportunities for involvement with many programs and age groups and to work closely with the church and the community. Many church members in the area volunteer their time to work with the agency, and the agency also plays an active role in the community, helping to address needs as they arise.

From its earliest days, responsibility for the provision of social welfare services within the United States has been split between government and the private sector. The government was not expected, indeed not able, to deal with the diversity of circumstances that generated human need. As suggested in Chapter 2, the Poor Laws inherited from England provided that the government supply a meager help of last resort. But as Daniel Boorstin notes, in the new nation "communities existed before governments were there to care for public needs" (1985, 121). The responsibility fell to ad hoc spontaneous forms of assistance and the organized efforts of the churches.

We previously have treated in detail the history of American social welfare institutions. An overview at the turn of the century would have revealed a neat compartmentalization of social welfare and social service responsibilities (see Table 19–1). The **public sector** accepted responsibility for long-term or chronic dependency in its poor houses, which were funded and administered at the local level. The government, typically the state government, also accepted responsibility for those social services that intrinsically required the use of sovereign authority, such as child welfare programs, the criminal justice system, and the confinement of mentally ill persons. Such institutions would be in violation of civil liberties were it not for the courts granting to the states the "right" to treat children, the insane, and the criminal as dependent persons. Sometimes that state overstepped this line as it treated the aged and the widowed as if they, too, had somehow lost their civil rights.

Private sector agencies largely were administered at the local level and often by sectarian groups. They provided the more intensely personal social services, such as orphanages, nursing homes, adoptions, and family counseling. The churches very jealously protected their right to provide these personal social services, and the social work profession as an entity vigorously defended the notion that the government should stay out of the private social service sector. The division of responsibilities is indicated in Table 19–1. In the twentieth century, this neat compartmentalization of responsibilities disappeared.

The historical summary of the relationship between voluntary and public welfare shows that the single constant is that the two exist in a kind of dynamic tension. A good part of voluntary welfare was an organized effort to

Table 19–1 Welfare Responsibilities Circa 1900	Public	Private
	State Chronically mentally ill Prisoners Child Welfare Aged	Sectarian Moral supervision
	Local Outdoor relief to widows and half orphans	Nonsectarian Orphan homes Advocacy Settlement houses

force governments to act. Sometimes public and private agencies have been rivals, sometimes unwilling partners. The historical constant is that the shape and structure of one at any point in time cannot be understood without reference to the other. The primacy of the voluntary effort in the nineteenth century was challenged by the social reform movement of the progressive era (1890–1920). The reform effort was split irrevocably following the Wilson administration. State responsibility was for cash aid to the deserving poor, and the provision of social services was the responsibility of voluntary efforts. A significant strain of thought in the first third of this century held that cash public aid was less risky and less humiliating than dependence on private charity. Following the Depression, public assistance and social insurance programs performed the cash aid function. The **voluntary sector** jealously guarded its independence from government.

The spirit of earlier cooperation resumed on a small scale in the 1950s, when voluntary agencies began to accept grants and contracts to deliver highly specific child welfare services. This relationship mushroomed in the mid 1960s, when Great Society programs funded "old" social work agencies to provide many of their "new" activities. Not so gradually, public funds began to play the dominant role in the budget. Some social workers in the private sector raised questions about whether the heavy reliance on public dollars would affect the autonomy and integrity of the private agency. Paradoxically, this period (1965–1980) witnessed the growth of advocacy organizations engaged in monitoring the performance of public actions and working to influence the quantity and quality of publicly funded social service expenditures by direct lobbying, grassroots organizing, electioneering, and particularly litigation. No doubt, these activities contributed to the significant rise in public spending for social services.

The tables have now turned nearly 180 degrees: There is debate over the proper function of the voluntary sector. The Reagan administration has eliminated federal support for legal aid and organizing activities and is encouraging returning direct social service functions to private charity. It is argued by the Reagan administration that private charity can and should meet the needs for service assistance that are being created by the curtailment of publicly funded social programs.

CONTEMPORARY STRUCTURE

Today, organized social service activities clearly are not limited to those provided directly by governments or sectarian agencies. A significant share of social service expenditures (a precise estimate is dependent upon the assumptions made) comes from and/or is spent by the little-understood nonprofit private social agency. The nonprofit private sector of the social service system employs a majority of the social workers engaged in direct practice to individuals, groups, neighborhoods, and communities. The **nonprofit private agency** is private in charter and organization but public in function. Neither the economic model of the private firm nor the public finance constructs of the public enterprises quite catches the essence of its operations. The nonprofit social service agencies are a diverse lot of 40,000 entities, which employ 675,000 persons and collectively spend $15 billion to accomplish rather imprecise goals. The nonprofit agencies provide a host of services ranging from prenatal to postdeath. The services are offered without a profit "intent" to individuals, groups, neighborhoods, and communities. They also serve as an organizing entity and conduit for charitable funds and voluntary efforts, with tax dollars comingled and channeled to specific projects.

The social service portion of the nonprofit agencies can be seen as made up of three interdependent parts. A specific agency can accomplish one or all three functions. These parts are:

1. agencies that serve public and charitable purposes, but serve principally for fund raising and planning, such as the United Fund agencies;

2. advocacy organizations, which bring together a group of like-minded persons who seek to generate government funding or more specific public understanding and support of a specific social problem area or a specific class of persons deemed to be in need, such as retarded persons, aged persons, or disabled persons. Advocacy organizations are in essence political interest groups that attempt to promote support for the their causes including public spending;

3. finally, there are the direct service agencies that deal with particular clients with specific or multiple problems of social functioning.

Despite the importance, relevance, and resources of the private sector social agency, there is no satisfactory explanation for its very existence, much less an explanation of its vitality and durability. There are three explanations that place emphasis on historical, administrative, and economic perspectives of private sector social agencies.

Historical

The first of these three explanations stresses simple historical antecedents. This theme is most completely developed by John Leiby. The American society, particularly on the frontier, developed in a context of almost nonexistent government. Lacking public institutions to address the problems of collective needs, the frontier society turned to formal and informal voluntary associations, which took roots and maintained their own integrity once governments were vibrant. This explanation often is garnished with various ideological assertions about individuals living on the American frontier and their healthy distrust of government. Alexis De Tocqueville found this tendency of Americans to form nonprofit, nongovernment associations to accomplish public tasks to be a characteristic of the new nation.

> *Americans of all ages, all stations of life, and all types of disposition are forever forming associations . . . to give fetes, found seminaries, build churches, distribute books and send missionaries to the Antipodes. . . . In every case, at the head of any new undertaking, where in France you would find the government or in England some territorial magnate, in the United States you are sure to find a voluntary association. (Alexis De Tocqueville,* Democracy in America *as quoted in Palmer & Sawhill,* Reagan Record, *1978, 263)*

Administrative

The second explanation is considerably more prosaic, though it builds on the first with a contemporary focus. The argument is made that during periods of expansion, public officials can more quickly provide a newly mandated service by contracting with private vendors then than they could if they had to put into place a full-scale public program. Equally important in the mind of public officials is that a service highly sought today may be seen as an incumbrance or luxury tomorrow. It is far easier administratively and politically to cancel a contract with a vendor than it is to dismantle a fully operative program. Thus, during periods of expansion and contraction of social service spending, public officials have an incentive to utilize purchase of service contracts with nonpublic entities. The private nonprofit agencies, in turn, find their fund raising and maintenance requirements more easily met by offering to contract to provide a particular social service.

An Economic Model

The third explanation focuses attention on the interaction between economic and political factors in the social service marketplace. This can be visualized by assuming an oversimplified world. Suppose that only three groups competed for public funds. One group wanted to spend $6 billion, another $8 billion, and the third $10 billion on a particular social service. The $8 billion group, by threatening to form a coalition with either of the other groups, can get the remaining group to agree to its preference. The $8 billion dollar amount is between the two extremes. Where the compromise actually is reached depends on many factors; the critical point is that the group that wants the most certainly will be dissatisfied. If the public institutions spend only $8 billion on, say, AIDS research and a group wants society to spend $10 billion, money for that program can be collected from the marketplace—donated voluntarily.

Increased needs and depleted public funds have placed a greater emphasis on voluntary social services agencies as well as their strong partnership with the public sector. Here, staff from a voluntary agency operate a 24-hour hotline.

This happens all the time. Just as Col. Oliver North was able to convince concerned citizens who agreed with him to give money to aid the Contras in Central America, so too do social workers convince concerned citizens to give money to do that which the government ought to do but isn't doing. The voluntary sector is a kind of private voluntary government.

Basic Characteristics of Voluntary Agencies

First, voluntary agencies are the manifestations of special interest groups. They express a special concern of particular groups of persons with reference to fairly specific problems. This is expressed in (1) a commitment to deliver a specialized service to a client-constituent group, (2) a commitment to try to influence public policy on behalf of that specialized client population, and (3) a desire to educate a nonattentive public about the service needs, potential, and special attributes of the group of clients to be served.

Second, voluntary agencies have a considerable degree of discretion in their allocation of agency resources, since, unlike a public entity, they do not have narrow legislative mandates nor do their clients have specific legal claims on agency resources. As a consequence, the voluntary agencies have the freedom to choose who they will serve and how they will be served. This provides maximum freedom to the professional social worker. The social worker often sees employment in the voluntary agency as a way to escape the constraints of bureaucracy. However, over time serving a particular group in a particular way becomes institutionalized. Over time, the voluntary agency acquires traditions and obligations that limit its freedom. This often leads to splinter agencies spinning off from the older agencies, which can become as ossified as public ones.

Third, because of their small size, unique history, discretionary power, and freedom (in the short run) from bureaucratic and legal constraints, voluntary agencies are more than usually dependent on the quality of their executive leadership. We discussed this theme earlier in the chapter on administration.

The voluntary agency plays a special role in the three-sector social service economy; it is bounded on both sides: on the one side by the private profit-oriented approach of the free market, and on the other side, by a politically driven public sector. Neither governed by marketplace or voting booth, the voluntary agency can be creative and innovative. However, it also is vulnerable to the expansionary drive of both profit and public enterprises. Voluntary agencies also are vulnerable to their own excesses. Because of all of this, any agency may not exist for a long period of time. Much like business firms, there are the few—very few—old venerables, a small number of agencies in their middle years, and a whole rash of new agencies. A survey conducted in 1976 found that only 40 percent of the agencies in place that year were in place ten years earlier.

There is a great deal of romantic fantasy about the voluntary way. Candidate Ronald Reagan in 1980 pledged to "restore in our time the American spirit of voluntary service, of cooperation of private and community initiative." Candidate Reagan caught the spirit of the free and vigorous voluntary way, where communities out of love rebuilt the barn and cared for the victims of disaster in a warm, heartfelt, caring way. Conservatives listened to his message and feared the loss of a world that never was. Liberals listened to his message and recognized it for what it was—a historical inaccuracy. We cannot return to a voluntary way, not only because today the world is more complex, but principally because the voluntary spirit, then as now, responded only to a small section of the total problem.

The volunteer agency, in fact, has expanded as the public sector has expanded. Today, only a small part of our social welfare problems are responded to by the voluntary sector. Firms historically have given about 1 percent of their pretax profits to all of the voluntary sector agencies. Families have contributed about 2 percent of their pretax income to "churches and charities." Between 1969 and 1979, private family giving as a share of the GNP dropped from 2.1 percent to 1.8 percent. Tax law changes may accelerate this decline. An increasing share of the voluntary budget now comes from grants, contracts, and purchase of service agreements from the public sector.

Social services agencies with voluntary charters spent an estimated $13.2 billion in 1980. Of this, it is estimated that $7.3 billion came from the federal government, with an additional $2.5 billion from state and local public budgets. One estimate of the flow of funds to an "average" nonprofit service agency is given in the Table 19–2.

The Social Agency as Interest Group

Interest groups are not synonymous with self-interest. The interest need not be selfish. The mother of a handicapped child hopes that government will structure educational and health agencies in such a way that the life chances of her child are improved. A physical therapist with special skills in developmental

Table 19–2   **Changes in Revenue for the Average Nonprofit Agency, 1981–1982, by Source (1981 dollars)**

Source	Income in Fiscal Year 1981	Change in Income 1981–1982	
		Amount	Percentage
Government	295,665	−18,530	−6.3
Corporations	21,639	+261	+5.8
Foundations	24,253	+1,262	+5.2
United Way	38,165	+712	+1.9
Religious and other federated funders	19,317	+703	+3.6
Direct individual giving	42,747	+3,387	+7.9
Fees, charges	200,001	+13,251	+6.6
Endowment, investments	32,097	+1,323	+4.1
Other	40,134	+891	+2.2
Unallocated	3,595	−599	NA
Total	717,613	+3,661	+0.5

disabilities will want help in educational institutions structured so that children in need can benefit from his or her skills. A health, welfare, and education planner in state government wants to utilize his or her skills so that scarce educational dollars can be utilized more effectively to aid all medically impaired children. Soon an association is born to effectuate their joint aims.

The care and the maintenance of the new association become central. There is soon a mosaic of organizations that the mother of the handicapped child seeks to shape health and welfare policy. Each is committed to the public good, but each has a limited span of attention. As a public choice is made, we can think of the evolving associations, both formal and informal, as having two forms: One form is within and the other outside of government. Those within government are called *agencies, bureaus, divisions,* in that formal sense. However, there also is an informal association of paid professionals who have a common set of goals. Social workers typically are employed in such public bureaucracies and have an association in such informal groups. These associations outside of government are called **interest groups.** They may be formal or informal. These interest groups typically are loose confederations of individually oriented policy associations. Such associations often have paid staff, but they also have a membership of dues-paying persons. These members may be either potential clients or professional providers. Together, the agency and the interest group form two parts of a political community. The third part of the political community is the staff members of the relevant congressional or legislative subcommittees who write the legislation and initiate the authorization of public funding for the mission at hand. Policy making in a particular substantive area is thus a function of the close cooperation, conflicts and interactions of these triads of power. Government becomes a mere holding corporation for hundreds of such "subgovernments." The subgovernments repeat themselves at each level: local, state, and national.

SUMMARY

While the responsibilities and cooperative efforts between the public and voluntary sectors differ markedly among the states, there is an extent to which there is a common perception of the role of the voluntary sector within the social service system. The voluntary agencies are expected to be innovative, flexible, and the vanguard of social service technology and delivery patterns. This perception is not well researched, and there are many instances where the public sector is the vanguard. Essentially, however, the position is that because the voluntary sector agencies have had to react in response to highly idiosyncratic historical reasons, the presence or absence of a sector at a particular time explains a great deal. These agencies also often are forced to adapt quickly to changes in what the public agencies do or fail to do.

A number of hypotheses have been advanced concerning the origins, growth and functions of voluntary agencies. They have been studied intensely by social psychologists, sociologists, economists, and political scientists. In fact, all of the explanations about the voluntary sector are flawed in one way or another, and more research needs to be done.

KEY TERMS

interest group   public sector
nonprofit private agency   voluntary sector
private sector

DISCUSSION QUESTIONS

1. Discuss the public social agencies in your community and the voluntary
    social agencies. How many agencies are there that you do not know
    whether they are public or voluntary?

2. Which of these agencies do you think *ought* to be voluntary or *ought* to
    be public?

3. What principle of separation into public and voluntary would you use as
    an ideal? What principle of separation appears to operate in practice?

REFERENCES

Boorstin, D. J. 1985. *The Americans: The National Experience*. New York:
    Random House.

Leiby, John. 1978. *A History of Social Welfare and Social Work in the United
    States*. New York: Columbia University Press.

Palmer, John, and Isabel Sawhill. 1984. *The Reagan Record*. Cambridge:
    Ballinger.

SELECTED FURTHER READINGS

Gates, Bruce L. 1980. *Social Program Administration*. Englewood Cliffs, N.J.:
    Prentice–Hall.

Lohmann, Roger A. 1980. *Breaking Even*. Philadelphia: Temple University
    Press.

Salamon, Lester M., and M.F. Gutowski. 1986. *The Invisible Sector*. Washing-
    ton, D.C.: Urban Institute.

Waddilove, Lewis E. 1983. *Private Philanthropy and Public Welfare*. London:
    Allen–Urwin.

Williams, Walter. 1980. *Government By Agency*. New York: Academic Press.

Williams, Walter. 1980. *The Implementation Perspective: A Guide for Managing
    Social Service Delivery Programs*. Berkeley: University of California Press.

20 The Future of Social Work and Social Welfare

Lou Bennett recently retired after forty-five years as a social worker in a variety of settings. His first job was as a case worker in a settlement house, where he earned a yearly salary of $2000. An active member of the state and local chapters of the National Association of Social Workers, Lou has been involved in many changes in the social work profession over the years. "In those early years, we did everything for our clients, since there were very few social service agencies," Lou stated in a recent interview. "In my first job, I led groups of teen-agers, ran programs for senior citizens, set up a daycare center, set up a rat control program in the neighborhood, transported people's belongings when they moved, and took kids into my house when they had nowhere else to go. When I retired as the director of a family services agency, there were 47 other social service agencies in the community, and most of my time and my staff's time were spent coordinating and linking resources for our clients with those other agencies."

"Today," Lou continued, "services are much more specialized—and we are more aware of human problems. I'm sure, for example, when I look back, that lots of kids I worked with when I was younger were sexually abused, but social workers in those days were relatively unaware of how extensive a problem that was."

Lou is especially excited because his grandaughter Jeanine is a senior in the Bachelor of Social Work program at the state university and will graduate as a social worker this year. Jeanine is completing her field internship at the local battered women's center and hopes to work for the state human services agency as a child protective services worker when she

graduates. Both grandfather and grandaughter agree
that social work has grown as a profession and that
many challenging opportunities are ahead for
Jeanine.

Any attempt to forecast future trends, of necessity, requires some degree of
reservation. Technological and social change does not always progress at an
even rate nor is the direction of change always predictable. Nevertheless, there
do appear to be indicators of trends that enable us to suggest what factors will
have an impact on the profession of social work and the field of social welfare
within the next decade. This chapter will identify briefly the probable
directions that social work will take in relation to the trends that presently affect social welfare and social services.

THE RELATIONSHIP BETWEEN PAST AND PRESENT

In order for us to comprehend the difficulty of predicting the effects of social
change upon social work and social welfare, it is helpful to review the earlier
chapters of this book. The history of the profession is related integrally to the
unpredictable nature of the world in which we live, particularly as social
change alters the economic base of society, as well as other basic social
institutions, such as the family, education, religion, and political and related
social organizations. The rapid growth and development of the social work
profession in the latter part of the nineteenth century were related directly to
the emergence of large urban communities and the accompanying problems associated with increased numbers of displaced persons, detachment from means
of production, high rates of employment, migration, slums, the rise of a sub-
culture of poverty, increasing health-related problems, and other conditions
associated with urban blight. The need for societal response to remediate or
eliminate the sources of these problems and to provide support for these displaced persons and their families necessitated that "trained" helpers become an
integral part of the solution. Hence, the profession of social work was born
from the need to assure that a cadre of professionals armed with an understanding of human behavior, awareness of how social organizations function,
and sensitivity to the effects of the environment as a determinant of options
would emerge as society's first line of remediation.

As the technological and industrial revolution erupted, the disintegration of
the stability inherent in a primarily agrarian society began to undergo rapid
metamorphosis. The structure and function of the family, once stable and secure, were affected by the stresses and tensions produced by the economic marketplace, which called for greater mobility, division of labor outside of the
home, and consequently, a restructuring of family priorities. As a result,
families have become less stable, the divorce rate has increased dramatically,
multiple marriages are more common, and child abuse, spouse battering, and
various forms of neglect have emerged as more visible problems.

As the economy has become more unpredictable, financial security, a long
sought-after goal, has become more difficult to achieve. The poor have continued to be victimized by the lack of opportunity and often blamed for their

condition. As our population has grown older, greater numbers of older adults have become detached from means of production and often lack sufficient supports to provide for their maintenance and health-related needs. In addition, crime, delinquency, substance abuse, and a variety of related problems have become a constant source of societal concern.

The organization of social welfare services is far different today from that of the Poor Law days. Gone are the almshouses, the poor houses, and "indoor" relief as a solution of first choice. The field of social welfare has expanded dramatically to meet the proliferation and magnitude of new needs, thus requiring substantial societal resources to maintain. The social services have responded with diversification in order to meet a variety of needs expressed by individuals for whom personal resources are incapable of providing an adequate level of social functioning and life satisfaction.

This diversification has emerged as essential in the delivery of social services (Box 20–1). Today, social workers are skilled in working with the displaced, the poor, substance abusers, single parents, criminal offenders, and persons experiencing marital conflict, family violence, mental illness, problems associated with late life, and a myriad of other related personal and social problems. In addition, the role of social workers as advocates for disenfranchised populations—the poor, women and minorities, gays and lesbians, and related groups—has become important, as society increasingly becomes more complex and tends to overlook these groups. As new problems have emerged, the capacity of the social work profession to incorporate the knowledge and skills essential to providing assistance always has been forthcoming.

CURRENT ISSUES IN SOCIAL WORK PRACTICE

The positions members of society take toward social problems and the resolution of those problems invariably relate to the resources available. Unfortunately, members of society do not always take an unequivocably progressive stance. For example, currently fiscal concerns are paramount in society. Federal indebtedness has resulted in massive reductions in funds available for solving social problems. As a result, monies for the social services have been reduced significantly and populations at risk have not received the assistance essential for even the most minimal level of functioning. In response to the reduction of public monies for the social services, considerable emphasis has been directed to encouraging the private sector to "take up the slack" and provide both funds and extend assistance through volunteerism. While a noble gesture, the magnitude of the need is such that private efforts have fallen far short of success. As indicated earlier, a society inevitably must take a position relative to its commitment to its members in need. The expression of the position it takes is influenced by values, morality, and the availability of resources. In a materialistically oriented society, such as ours, it is paradoxical that the definition of *need* is invariably related to the "amount" of resources that society is willing to allocate. Hence, in times of monetary scarcity or when demands will be made upon individuals to share (through the taxing process) more of their earned incomes, the tendency to redefine need levels is inevitable. This redefinition, of course, does not always address the "real" need that is apparent. Today, as a society, we stand at the crossroads of either continuing to reduce allocations for the resolution of problems for our members at risk or to reorganize our priorities to assure that all of our members are guaranteed access to the best of our problem-solving abilities and hope that at least their minimal needs will be met.

Related challenges facing future social work professionals include determining which of the myriad of societal and individual problems fall within the domain of the social welfare system. While a traditional view of the social welfare institution is that its services should be residual—incorporating those areas that cannot be served by other societal institutions—increasingly, the social welfare system is seen as a panacea to address all needs not being met by other systems or, in other words, a system that is looked to to be all things to all people. There is a need to define and to limit the boundaries that encompass the social welfare system so that its services can be effective and retained with available resources. At the same time, however, social workers are faced with serious value conflicts over not addressing human needs that fall beyond social welfare boundaries when no one else is meeting them and they are critical for individual and societal survival.

With scarce resources, ethical decisions about types of services to be provided and who should get them increasingly fall to the social worker. How do you say no to a woman with four children under age six with no housing, no food, and a temporary part-time job, who makes five dollars more each month than the income eligibility guidelines for receiving AFDC allow? How do

The future of social welfare programs remains uncertain as funds diminish and needs grow.

you determine whether limited funding should be allocated to the elderly, to children, or to the disabled? How do you decide who should have first priority for heart and other organ transplants, whether limited dollars should be spent on neonatology care for premature infants who may live only a limited time, or at what point resources should no longer be provided to families with little potential to be rehabilitated and the children placed in foster care or adoption? If limited resources do not allow for a full range of preventive and remedial/rehabilitative services, how do you prevent problems such as child maltreatment, knowing that this may limit your resources for those already abused in the short run but prevent more abuse in the long run? Or, instead, do you help those in immediate crisis, knowing the lack of preventive services will mean even more crises for families in the future? One social welfare advocate told his state governor and legislature that social workers were being asked to take positions similar to the one exemplified in the popular novel *Sophie's Choice,* where a mother in occupied Poland under Hitler's regime was forced to decide which of her two children would be spared the gas chamber and which would be sent to death.

Limited resources, rapid social change, and the influx of additional social problems such as AIDS, the increase in an underclass of ethnic minorities and women, the health care crisis, and the shift to a technocratic society, however, suggest new opportunities for social work professionals willing to accept these challenges. The social work profession and the issues it faces are challenging at all levels of society—whether one works with individuals, families, groups, the community, or at the state or national level. Social work practitioners need to increase their involvement at the legislative and policy levels and become more involved in the political arena where key social welfare decisions are made. At whatever level they practice, social workers as professionals will continue to expand both in scope and in numbers as society becomes increasingly complex.

TRENDS IN SOCIAL WORK CAREERS

As this text has indicated, social workers function in a variety of job settings and fields of practice and hold degrees at the undergraduate (BSW), masters (MSW), and doctoral (PhD or DSW) level. From 1958, when MSW programs were first accredited by the **Council on Social Work Education,** to 1984, 250,339 social work degrees were granted by CSWE–accredited institutions. From 1974, when BSW programs were first accredited by CSWE, to 1984, 86,751 BSW degrees were awarded, or 46 percent of the social work degrees awarded by CSWE–accredited schools during that time period (Hardcastle 1987).

A valid question asked by social work students is whether the supply of social workers exceeds the demand, particularly during fiscal cutbacks. A 1982 survey of social work practitioners found that 83 percent were employed in social work jobs, 4 percent were employed in non-social work jobs, 6 percent were retired, and 8 percent were unemployed, with over half of those unemployed at their own choosing (they were in school, raising families, etc.).

Box 20–1
Professional
Levels of
Practice

The National Association of Social Workers has developed a hierarchy which delineates four levels of professional social work practice and their respective job responsibilities. The hierarchy also identifies the knowledge, skills and values that social workers are expected to demonstrate at each level:

Basic Professional Level represents practice requiring professional practice skills, theoretical knowledge, and values that are not normally obtainable in day to day work experience but that are obtainable through formal professional social work education. Formal social work education is distinguished from experiential learning by being based on conceptual and theoretical knowledge of personal and social interaction and by training in the disciplined use of self in relationship with clients.

Specialized (Expert) Professional Level represents the specific and demonstrated mastery of therapeutic technique in at least one knowledge and skill method, as well as a general knowledge of human personality as influenced by social factors, and the disciplined use of self in treatment relationships with individuals or groups, or a broad conceptual knowledge of research, administration, or planning methods and social problems.

Independent Professional Level represents achievement by the practitioner of practice, based on the appropriate special training, developed and demonstrated under professional supervision, which is sufficient to ensure the dependable, regular use of professional skills in independent or autonomous practice. A minimum of two years is required for this experiential learning and demonstration period following the master of social work program.

This level applies both to solo or autonomous practice as an independent practitioner or consultant and to practice within an organization where the social worker has primary responsibility for representing the profession or for the training or administration of professional staff.

Advanced Professional Level represents practice in which the practitioner carries major social or organizational responsibility for professional development, analysis, research, or policy implementation, or that is achieved by personal professional growth demonstrated through advanced conceptual contributions to professional knowledge.

The educational standards for the four levels of Social Work Practice are:

Basic Professional Level: Requires a bachelor's degree (BSW) from a social work program accredited by the Council on Social Work Education (CSWE).

Specialized (Expert) Professional Level: Requires a master's degree (MSW) from a social work program accredited by the CSWE.

Independent Professional Level: Requires an accredited MSW and at least two years of postmaster's experience under appropriate professional supervision.

Advanced Professional Level: Requires proficiency in special theoretical, practice, administration or policy or the ability to conduct advanced research studies in social welfare; usually demonstrated through a doctoral degree in social work or a closely related social science discipline.

Source: National Association of Social Workers, *NASW Standards for the Classification of Social Work Practice.* (Silver Springs, Md.: NASW, 1981), p. 9.

Even with funding cutbacks, funding for social welfare programs has increased: from 1960–1979, public expenditures in social welfare rose from 10.5 percent of the U.S. gross national product to 18.5 percent, and private philanthropy in social welfare increased 214 percent during that same time period (Hardcastle 1987).

While social workers are employed in a variety of settings, most work for government or voluntary agencies (88 percent), with approximately 12 percent working for private proprietary organizations. With the privatization of health care, however, large numbers of for-profit hospitals, alcohol and drug treatment programs, psychiatric residential treatment programs, and gerontology facilities are being developed and are hiring social workers. Also, as states pass licensing requirements for social workers and insurance companies include social workers under third-party reimbursement agreements, an increasing number of social workers are establishing private practices, seeing clients for psychotherapy, marriage and family counseling, and other types of clinical services. An increase in the numbers of social workers in private or proprietary settings is expected during the coming years. At the same time, new attention is being given to the need to encourage social workers to seek jobs in public social service settings, particularly state social service agencies. NASW and other organizations such as the American Public Welfare Association are working together to increase awareness about the challenges of public social services and the commitment that social work as a profession has to the indigent, who are most likely to come to the attention of a public agency.

Social workers are employed primarily in social agencies, hospitals, and outpatient facilities. A recent study indicates that 57 percent of all social workers, and 63 percent of all BSW social workers, are employed in these types of settings (see Table 20–1). When the study focused on the field of practice in which social workers were employed, it was determined that most were in mental health, which has been a trend for over a decade. When looking at BSW graduates only, the largest numbers were working with children and youth, followed by mental health. Sixty percent of all social workers, no matter what degree they had, were employed in the fields of mental health, health, or children and youth services (see Table 20–2).

The study also found that the profession is expanding in alcohol and drug programs, occupational/industrial social work, developmental disabilities programs, school social work, and gerontology/health programs (Hardcastle 1987). The U.S. Bureau of Labor Statistics forecasts for the next several years

Table 20–1   **Employment Setting of Primary Employment for Social Work Labor Force by Degree Level (1982)**

Employment Setting	Percentage				
	BSW	MSW	Doctorate	All	Rank
Social Service Agency/Organization	34.2	27.7	10.8	27.2	1
Private Practice/Self–Employed or Solo	3.7	7.2	9.9	7.1	6
Private Practice/Partnership	1.9	3.1	2.4	2.9	7
Membership Organization	1.4	0.9	0.7	0.9	13
Hospital	17.9	19.6	9.6	19.0	2
Institution (non-hospital)	4.2	3.1	1.5	3.1	8
Outpatient Facility (Clinic, Health, Mental Health Center)	10.8	16.7	7.8	15.9	3
Group Home/Residence	4.8	2.3	0.5	2.3	10
Nursing Home/Hospice	6.4	1.7	0.5	1.8	10
Court/Criminal Justice System	1.8	1.4	0.7	1.4	12
College/University	5.7	6.5	49.1	8.5	4
Elementary/Secondary School System	4.9	8.2	3.8	7.7	5
Non–Social Serv. Employment	1.8	1.6	2.0	1.5	10

Source: David Hardcastle, *The Social Work Labor Force.* (Austin: University of Texas at Austin School of Social Work, 1987), p. 16.

include 16,000 new social services positions annually (Statistical Abstract of the United States 1983). Several popular magazines recently have cited social work in health care and gerontology as rapidly growing fields that those seeking careers should consider. Whatever the field of practice or the setting, social workers today and in the future face may challenges—and many opportunities for professional and personal growth.

SUMMARY

This book has addressed the current state of the art in social work and social welfare. As the reader reviews each chapter, the effects of problems upon various segments of our population have been identified and the societal responses through the social welfare structure have been described. The significant and dramatic modifications in both the social welfare institution and the social work profession since the early days of organized helping efforts are apparent. Armed with the knowledge and understanding of human behavior, complex organizations, and bringing a systems/ecological perspective to bear, the contemporary professional social worker has never been more capable of skillful intervention in the resolution of problems.

Table 20–2   **Practice Area of Primary Employment of Labor Force by Degree Level (1982)**

Practice Area of Primary Employment	BSW	MSW	Doctorate	Total	Rank
Children and Youth	15.8	15.8	10.5	15.6	2.5
Community Organization/Planning	2.2	1.6	3.4	1.7	11.5
Family Services	8.4	11.9	7.5	11.5	4.0
Corrections/Criminal Justice	1.7	1.6	1.9	1.6	11.5
Group Services	0.5	0.4	0.5	0.3	16.0
Medical/Health Care	18.4	15.8	9.3	15.7	2.5
Mental Health	16.3	28.9	26.5	28.1	1.0
Public Assistance/Welfare	2.2	0.8	1.0	0.8	13.0
School Social Work	2.8	3.4	2.5	3.3	9.0
Services to Aged	11.0	4.2	4.2	4.5	5.5
Alcohol/Drug and Substance Abuse	2.6	3.2	2.9	3.1	9.0
Developmental Disabilities	5.8	3.2	2.0	3.3	9.0
Other Disabilities	0.4	0.5	0.5	0.5	14.0
Occupational	0.5	0.4	0.7	0.4	15.0
Combined Areas	6.0	4.4	11.7	4.7	5.5
Other	5.0	3.8	14.2	4.1	7.0

(Percentage)

Source: David Hardcastle, *The Social Work Labor Force.* (Austin: University of Texas at Austin School of Social Work, 1987), p. 17.

KEY TERMS

Basic professional level of social work practice
Specialized (Expert) professional level of social work practice
Independent professional level of social work practice

Advanced professional level of social work practice
Council on Social Work Education
National Association of Social Workers

DISCUSSION QUESTIONS

1. Identify at least three societal trends that have an impact on the future of social welfare and social work. Show how these trends will shape social welfare as an institution and social work as a profession.

2. Briefly describe at least three issues that current and future social workers must address as practicing professionals. What suggestions do you have in dealing with these issues?

3. Identify the four levels of social work practice and describe each briefly.

4. In which settings are social workers employed most often? In which fields of practice are social workers employed most often? Where are most BSW social workers employed?

5. Discuss some of the future employment opportunities for social work professionals. In which career areas are you most interested and why?

REFERENCES

Hardcastle, D. 1987. *The Social Work Labor Force.* Austin: School of Social Work, University of Texas at Austin.

National Association of Social Workers. 1981. *NASW Standards for the Classification of Social Work Practice: Policy Statement 4.* Silver Spring, Md.: NASW Task Force on Sector Force Classification.

U.S. Bureau of the Census. 1983. *Statistical Abstract of the United States: 1982–83.* 103rd ed. Washington, D.C.: Government Printing Office.

SELECTED FURTHER READINGS

Atkinson, Z., and E. Glassberg. 1983. "After Graduation, What? Employment and Educational Experience of BSW Programs." *Journal of Education for Social Work* 19, no. 1, (Winter 1983): 5–13.

Bell, Daniel. 1974. *The Coming of the Post-Industrial Society.* New York: Basic Books.

Krager, H. J. 1983. Reclassification: Is There a Future in Public Welfare for the Trained Social Workers? *Social Work* 28, no. 6 (November–December 1983): 427–33.

Minahan, A. 1981. Social Workers and the Future. *Social Work* 5, no. 26 (September 1981): 363–64.

Professional Social Work Practice in Public Child Welfare: An Agenda for Action. 1987. Portland: University of Southern Maine Center for Research and Advanced Study.

Theobold, R. 1968. *An Alternative Future for America II.* Chicago: Swallow Press.

Theobold, R. 1972. *Futures Conditional.* Indianapolis: Bobbs–Merrill.

Appendix A
Code of Ethics,
National
Association of
Social
Workers

PREAMBLE

This code is intended to serve as a guide to the everyday conduct of members of the social work profession and as a basis for the adjudication of issues in ethics when the conduct of social workers is alleged to deviate from the standards expressed or implied in this code. It represents standards of ethical behavior for social workers in professional relationships with those served, with colleagues, with employers, with other individuals and professions, and with the community and society as a whole. It also embodies standards of ethical behavior governing individual conduct to the extent that such conduct is associated with an individual's status and identity as a social worker.

This code is based on the fundamental values of the social work profession that include the worth, dignity, and uniqueness of all persons as well as their rights and opportunities. It is also based on the nature of social work, which fosters conditions that promote these values.

In subscribing to and abiding by this code, the social worker is expected to view ethical responsibility in as inclusive a context as each situation demands and within which ethical judgement is required. The social worker is expected to take into consideration all the principles in this code that have a bearing upon any situation in which ethical judgement is to be exercised and professional intervention or conduct is planned. The course of action that the social worker chooses is expected to be consistent with the spirit as well as the letter of this code.

In itself, this code does not represent a set of rules that will prescribe all the behaviors of social workers in all the complexities of professional life. Rather, it offers general principles to guide conduct, and the judicious appraisal of conduct, in situations that have ethical implications. It provides the basis for making judgements about ethical actions before and after they occur. Frequently, the particular situation determines the ethical principles that apply and the manner of their application. In such cases, not only the particular ethical principles are taken into immediate consideration, but also the entire code and its spirit. Specific applications of ethical principles must be judged within the context in which they are being considered. Ethical behavior in a given situation must satisfy not only the judgement of the individual social worker, but also the judgement of an unbiased jury of professional peers.

This code should not be used as an instrument to deprive any social worker of the opportunity or freedom to practice with complete professional integrity; nor should any disciplinary action be taken on the basis of this code without maximum provision for safeguarding the rights of the social worker affected.

The ethical behavior of social workers results not from edict, but from a personal commitment of the individual. This code is offered to affirm the will and zeal of all social workers to be ethical and to act ethically in all that they do as social workers.

The following codified ethical principles should guide social workers in the various roles and relationships and at the various levels of responsibility in which they function professionally. These principles also serve as a basis for the adjudication by the National Association of Social Workers of issues in ethics.

In subscribing to this code, social workers are required to cooperate in its implementation and abide by any disciplinary rulings based on it. They should also take adequate measures to discourage, prevent, expose, and correct the unethical conduct of colleagues. Finally, social workers should be equally ready to defend and assist colleagues unjustly charged with unethical conduct.

SUMMARY OF MAJOR PRINCIPLES

I. The Social Worker's Conduct and Comportment as a Social Worker

Propriety. The social worker should maintain high standards of personal conduct in the capacity or identity as social worker.

Competence and Professional Development. The social worker should strive to become and remain proficient in professional practice and the performance of professional functions.

Service. The social worker should regard as primary the service obligation of the social work profession.

Integrity. The social worker should act in accordance with the highest standards of professional integrity.

Scholarship and Research. The social worker engaged in study and research should be guided by the conventions of scholarly inquiry.

II. The Social Worker's Ethical Responsibility to Clients

Primacy of Clients' Interests. The social worker's primary responsibility is to clients.

Rights and Prerogatives of Clients. The social worker should make every effort to foster maximum self-determination on the part of clients.

Confidentiality and Privacy. The social worker should respect the privacy of clients and hold in confidence all information obtained in the course of professional service.

Fees. When setting fees, the social worker should ensure that they are fair, reasonable, considerate, and commensurate with the service performed and with due regard for the clients' ability to pay.

III. The Social Worker's Ethical Responsibility to Colleagues

Respect, Fairness, and Courtesy. The social worker should treat colleagues with respect, courtesy, fairness, and good faith.

Dealing with Colleagues' Clients. The social worker has the responsibility to relate to the clients of colleagues with full professional consideration.

IV. The Social Worker's Ethical Responsibility to Employers and Employing Organizations

Commitments to Employing Organizations. The social worker should adhere to commitments made to the employing organizations.

V. The Social Worker's Ethical Responsibility to the Social Work Profession

Maintaining the Integrity of the Profession. The social worker should uphold and advance the values, ethics, knowledge, and mission of the profession.

Community Service. The social worker should assist the profession in making social services available to the general public.

Development of Knowledge. The social worker should take responsibility for identifying, developing, and fully utilizing knowledge for professional practice.

VI. The Social Worker's Ethical Responsibility to Society

Promoting the General Welfare. The social worker should promote the general welfare of society.

Source: Preamble and Summary of the NASW Code of Ethics, Revised Edition, approved by 1979 Delegate Assembly; from *NASW NEWS,* Vol. 25, No. 1 (January 1980), pp. 25–26. By permission of the National Association of Social Workers, Inc.

Glossary

Adoption Process by which a child whose birth parents choose not to or cannot care for is provided with a permanent home and parents who are able to provide for the child; legal adoptions can take place only when the court terminates the parental rights of the birth parents, but many adoptions, particularly in minority communities, are informal and do not involve the court.

Advanced professional level of social work practice Level of practice in which the practitioner carries major social or organizational responsibility for professional development, analysis, research, or policy implementation; usually requires a doctoral degree in social work or a closely-related discipline.

Ageism Discrimination against the elderly because of their age.

Aging The process of growing old.

Acquired Immunodeficiency Syndrome (AIDS) Fatal disease that attacks the body's natural immune system.

Aid to Families with Dependent Children (AFDC) Public assistance program which provides cash assistance to families with children in need because of the loss of financial support as a result of death, disability, or the continued absence of a parent from the home.

Aid to Families with Dependent Children—Unemployed (AFDC–U) A supplemental AFDC program for two-parent families where financial need is due to specific unemployment conditions.

Apathy-futility syndrome Term used to describe a set of behaviors exhibited by a neglecting parent who is severely depressed and apathetic toward his/her immediate environment, including his/her children.

Association A relationship between two or more factors that occur together but are not necessarily causative, e.g., alcoholism and child abuse.

Basic professional level of social work practice Level of practice representing professional practice skills, theoretical knowledge, and values; requires a bachelor's degree (BSW) from a social work program accredited by the Council on Social Work Education.

Battered child syndrome Medical term used to describe a child in various stages of healing, indicating the child has been physically abused on a number of occasions.

Best interests of child Standard of decision-making used by courts and child welfare agencies which places emphasis on what is best for a specific child as opposed to what is best for other family members or persons.

Blended family Family formed by marriage or long-term relationship between partners where at least one partner or both brings children from a previous relationship into the new family system.

Boundary The limit or extent of a system; the point where one system ends and another begins.

Casework Services provided to individuals, groups, and families to strengthen social functioning, based on assessment of client situation, identification of problem areas, determination of appropriate interventions to address problem areas, and monitoring and evaluation of the process to ensure that outcomes address problems identified.

Catastrophic illness Chronic and severely debilitating illness that results in high medical costs and long-term dependence on the health care system.

Categorial assistance Cash assistance programs given to individuals and families under the provision of the Social Security Act, which established specific categories of persons in need of cash assistance, including the aged, blind and permanently disabled (Supplemental Security Income) and children (Aid to Families with Dependent Children).

Cause/effect relationship A relationship between factors where one or more factors can be shown to directly cause a change in an additional factor or set of factors.

Charity Organization Society (COS) First relief organization in the U.S. that developed a systematic program to help the needy, promoting "scientific philanthropy" which incorporated individual assessment and development of coordinated service plans prior to providing services.

Child neglect Condition in which a caretaker responsible for a child either deliberately or by extraordinary inattentiveness fails to meet a child's basic needs, including failure to provide adequate food, clothing, shelter, medical assistance, education, and/or to supervise a child appropriately.

Child protective services Mandated services provided by state social services agencies to families who abuse or neglect their children, for the purpose of protecting children whose safety is seriously endangered by the actions or inactions of their caretakers.

Child welfare delivery system Network of agencies and programs that provide social services to children, youth, and families.

Child Welfare League of America (CWLA) National organization consisting of agencies, professionals, and citizens interested in the well-being of children and families which promotes standards for services, advocates child welfare policies and programs, conducts research, and provides publications related to child welfare issues.

Child welfare services Social services which supplement or substitute for parental care and supervision when parents are unable to fulfill parental responsibilities and which improve conditions for children and their families.

Civil Rights Act Federal legislation passed in 1964 and amended in 1965 which prohibits discrimination based on race, religion, color, or ethnicity in public facilities, government programs or those operated or funded by the federal government, and employment.

Client system Individuals, families, groups, organizations or communities at whom intervention is directed in order to enhance social functioning.

Clinical social worker Person whose major focus is the provision of clinical social work services, usually individual, group or family counseling, often in a psychiatric, hospital, residential treatment, or mental health facility. An MSW is usually required (also termed "psychiatric social worker" in some settings).

Closed system A system with a boundary that is difficult to permeate; such systems are usually unreceptive to outsiders.

Community organization A method of social work practice which involves the development of community resources to meet human needs.

Competencies Skills that are essential to perform certain functions; social workers must have competencies in a number of areas to be effective professionals.

Council on Social Work Education (CSWE) The national organization of schools of social work that focuses on social work education and serves as the accrediting body for professional social work undergraduate (BSW) and masters (MSW) programs.

Crisis intervention Intervention provided when a crisis exists to the extent that one's usual coping resources threaten individual or family functioning.

Cultural pluralism The existence of two or more diverse cultures within a given society where each maintains its own traditions and special interests within the confines of the total society.

Custody   Legal charge given to a person requiring him/her to provide certain types of care and to exercise certain controls in regard to another individual, as in parent-child custody.

Deinstitutionalization   Philosophy which advocates care of individuals with mental health problems and developmental disabilities in local community out-patient programs, whenever appropriate to the client's needs, as opposed to hospitalization in an institution.

Developmental disability   Severe, chronic disabilities resulting from physical or mental impairment, usually prior to age 21, which results in substantial limitations of the individual's social, emotional, intellectual, and/or physical functioning; 75 percent of those with developmental disabilities are mentally retarded.

Diagnostic and Statistical Manual of Mental Disorders (DSM)   Classification system of types of mental disorders, which incorporates both organic and environmental factors, developed by the American Psychiatric Association for assessment and intervention purposes.

Direct practice   A method of social work involving face-to-face contact with individuals, groups, or families and actual provision of services by the social worker for the purpose of resolving problems; also referred to as casework or social casework.

Disciplinary research   Research designed to expand the body of knowledge of a particular discipline; also called pure or basic research.

Diversion   Process where persons coming to the attention of the criminal justice system are diverted to other programs such as social services, community services, or educational (defensive driving) programs, rather than going through the court process.

Dual-career family   Family where both spouses have careers outside of the family.

Dysfunctional   Impaired or abnormal functioning.

Ego psychology   Theoretical perspective which emphasizes ego growth and development.

Emotional abuse   Acting out against a person emotionally, such as verbally belittling or attacking a person constantly.

Emotional neglect   Failure to meet emotional needs through acts of omission, such as not providing love, attention, and/or emotional support to persons.

Employee Assistance Program (EAP)   Workplace-sponsored program providing mental health and social services to employees and their families; services may be provided directly at the workplace, or through a contractual arrangement, by a social services agency.

Enabler   Person whose behavior facilitates another person's behavior to continue; term is used most often to describe situations in families where alcoholism is a problem and other family members enable the alcoholism to continue by their reinforcing behaviors.

Entropy   Unavailable energy in a closed system which creates dysfunction within that system and eventually results in the system's inability to function.

Equal Rights Amendment (ERA)   Proposed amendment to the U.S. Constitution to assure the complete and equal rights of all citizens without regard to race, color, creed, or gender; the amendment has not been ratified by the number of states necessary for its adoption and its future remains uncertain.

Etiology of crime   Theories relating to the origins or causes of crime, including physiological, psychological, and sociological perspectives.

Evaluative research   Research undertaken to show how a program achieves (or fails to achieve) its goals.

Exosystem level   The level of social environment that incorporates community factors in which an individual does not participate directly, but that affects the individual's functioning, such as school board and city council actions.

Family   Group of individuals bonded together through marriage, kinship, adoption, or mutual agreement.

Family violence   Use of force, or threatened use of force, by one family member against another, usually by a family member who is more powerful against a member who is less powerful.

Feminization of poverty   Term used to describe the result of the increasing numbers of single-parent women being classified as poor.

Food Stamps   In kind assistance program funded by the U.S. Department of Agriculture designed to supplement the food-purchasing power of eligible low-income households in order to allow families to maintain nutritious diets and to expand the market for agricultural goods.

Gender   Classification by sex, e.g., male or female.

General assistance   Public assistance programs that provide financial aid to persons who are in need but do not qualify for federally-authorized programs; such programs are usually administered by county and local governments and are also referred to as "relief" programs.

General deterrent   Deterrent toward committing inappropriate/illegal acts targeted at the total population by specifically punishing those who commit such acts; imprisoning persons who commit crimes deters others from committing the same crimes.

Generalist practitioner   A social worker who applies intervention methods within a systems/ecological framework to assist client systems with problem-solving.

Generalizable   The ability of a theory to use what happens in one situation to explain what happens in other situations.

Gerontology   The study of aging and the aging process.

Great Society   A social reform program proposed by the Johnson administration in the 1960s to improve the quality of life for all Americans, with emphasis on the poor and disenfranchised; the War on Poverty was one of the major Great Society programs.

Health and welfare services   Programs providing services that facilitate individual health and welfare, such as maternal health and child care, public health, family planning, and child welfare services.

Health maintenance organization (HMO)   Pre-paid medical group practice where individuals pay monthly fees and receive specific types of health care at no cost or minimum costs per visit.

Health risk factors   Factors that affect a person's health and place him/her at risk for serious health problems, e.g. smoking.

Home health care   Health care provided in a person's home as opposed to a hospital or other institutional health care setting; made available through outreach visits by social workers, nurses, physicians, and other health practitioners.

Homeostasis/steady state   The constant adjustment of a system moving toward its goal while maintaining order and stability within.

Homophobia   A fear of homosexuals and homosexuality.

Hospice   Programs for terminally-ill individuals and their families that enable them to die with dignity and support often away from a hospital setting.

Hypothesis   A tentative assumption derived from theory that is capable of empirical verification.

Implementation   Carrying out the steps required to put a program or plan into practice.

Impulse-ridden behavior   Behavior exhibited by a neglecting parent with low impulse control, including inconsistency, leaving a child alone or in an unsafe situation without realizing the consequences to the child, or because a new activity is given a higher priority.

Inclusive   The ability of a theory to consistently explain events in the same way each time they occur.

Incest   Sexual abuse between family members.

Independent professional level of social work practice   Level of practice based on academic training and professional supervision which ensures the regular use of professional skills in independent or autonomous practice; requires a masters degree from an accredited social work program and at least two years of post-master's experience under appropriate professional supervision.

Indoor relief   Assistance given to the poor and the needy through placement in institutions, such as poorhouses, orphanages, and prisons.

Industrial social work   Social work services provided through the workplace; also termed occupational social work. Such services allow for focus on the relationships between work stresses and other systems within which the individual functions.

Infant mortality rate   The number of infants who die at birth or before they reach a certain age or, compared to the total number of infants, both living and not living, within that age range, within a specified geographic location.

Institutional programs   Traditional, first-line efforts designed to meet the expected needs of individuals and families, such as the family or retirement programs.

Interest group   Group of individuals organized to focus on a special interest, e.g., the homeless, the mentally ill, usually for the purpose of advocacy within the political system.

Intervention   Planned activities that are designed to improve the social functioning of a client or client system.

Job-sharing   The sharing of one full-time job by two or more individuals; this practice is increasingly being allowed by employers and is advantageous to women with young children who do not want to work outside the home on a full-time basis.

Laissez faire   An economic theory developed by Adam Smith which places emphasis on persons taking care of themselves and limits government intervention.

Least detrimental alternative   Decision-making premise that places priority on making decisions regarding children based on which decision will be least damaging or upsetting to the child.

Life-span model   A framework that focuses on relationships between individuals and their environments with major emphasis on where persons are developmentally and what transitional life processes they are experiencing (e.g., marriage, retirement).

Long-term care facility   Program that provides long-term care to individuals, including the elderly and the disabled; state and federal regulations have established specific requirements facilities must meet to be classified as long-term care facilities.

Macrosystem level   The level of social environment that incorporates societal factors that affect an individual, including cultural ideologies, assumptions, and social policies that define and organize a given society.

Mediation   Intervention between a divorcing or divorced couple to promote settlement of child custody and property issues in order to reconcile differences and reach compromises; mediation teams usually include an attorney and a social worker.

Medicaid   Federal grant-in-aid program to states to allow them to provide comprehensive medical care to low-income individuals and families.

Medicare   Federal health insurance program for the elderly.

Mental retardation   A type of developmental disability attributable to mental or physical impairment which results in sub-average intellectual functioning.

Mesosystem level   The level of social environment that incorporates interactions and interrelations among those persons, groups, and settings which comprise an individual's microsystem.

Microsystem level   The level of social environment that includes the individual, including intrapsychic characteristics and past life experiences, and all the persons and groups in his/her day-to-day environment.

Moral treatment   Philosophy among professionals and advocates working with the mentally ill in the late 1700s and early 1800s that advocated a caring, humane approach, as opposed to a punitive, repressive environment.

National Association of Mental Health   A national association of professionals and organizations concerned about mental health issues and care of persons with mental health problems; provides education, advocacy, and research.

National Association of Social Workers (NASW)   The major national professional organization for social workers which promotes ethics and quality in social work practice; stimulates political participation and social action; and maintains eligibility standards for membership.

National Institute of Mental Health   Federal agency created by Congress in 1949 to address mental health concerns; now a part of the U.S. Department of Health and Human Services.

Natural support system   Resources available within a person's immediate environment to provide support without the person having to rely on formal community support systems; natural support systems include family members, neighbors, friends, and co-workers, as opposed to community agencies and programs.

Non-organic failure to thrive   Medical condition that results when a child is three percentiles or more below the normal range for height and weight and no organic reason can be determined; placing a child in a hospital and providing an adequate diet and nurturing will cause the child to gain height and weight, suggesting parental deprivation as the cause.

Nonprofit agency   Agency that spends all of its funding to meet the goals of the agency with no financial profit earned for agency owners, directors, or employees.

Official poverty   Way of measuring poverty that provides a set of income thresholds adjusted for household size, age of household head, and number of children under 18 years old.

Ombudsman   Public or private official whose function is to assist citizens in dealing with a bureaucracy.

Open system   A system in which the boundaries are permeated easily.

Outdoor relief   Cash or in kind assistance given to persons in need, allowing them to remain in their own homes; public assistance payments for food and fuel, for example.

Outsourcing   The practice by U.S. businesses of having portions or all of their production carried out outside of the U.S. and its territories.

Own-home services   Services provided to children and families within their own homes as opposed to placement of children in out-of-home care; e.g., homemaker services, child care, and counseling.

Parole   Condition given to an imprisoned person to serve the remainder of the sentence outside of the detention facility, in a supervised situation, monitored by a parole officer.

Pastoral counselor   Provides counseling services under the auspices of a religious organization, which usually includes an emphasis on spiritual well-being; usually members of the clergy.

Pedophile   Person who is physically and sexually attracted to children as opposed to persons of his/her own age.

Permanency planning   Concept which states that all child welfare services provided should be centered around a plan directed toward a permanent, nurturing home for that child.

Physical child abuse   Physical act of harm or threatened harm against a child by a caretaker which results in physical or mental injury to a child, including beating, hitting, slapping, burning, shaking, or throwing.

Planning   Outline of a design which incorporates the strategic use of resources in problem-solving.

Policy research   Research that focuses upon evaluating the effects of proposed or existing social policy on constituent populations.

Poor Law   Legislation passed in England in 1601 which established categories of the poor, including the deserving poor (orphans, widows, etc.) and the nondeserving poor (ablebodied males) and the treatment they were to receive from national and local governments. This law established precedents for policies toward the poor in the United States.

Primary prevention   Targeted at the total population to prevent a problem from occurring.

Primary setting   Setting where the types of services a professional provides match the primary goals of the setting; e.g., a hospital is a primary setting for a nurse but a secondary setting for a social worker.

Private insurance   Insurance programs available to individuals and families through the workplace or through purchase of policies with private insurance companies.

Private sector   Includes programs and agencies funded and operated by non-public entities; e.g., voluntary and proprietary agencies, and private businesses.

Probation   Official correctional option in which the offender has an opportunity to remain free from detention, or have a fine held in abeyance, if he/she follows the conditions of probation set by the court which are monitored by a probation officer.

Psychiatrist   Person with a degree in medicine (MD) with additional training in psychiatry, the study of mental disorders.

Psychoanalysis   Method of dealing with emotional problems which focuses on intra-psychic functioning (internal conflicts within the individual).

Psychological parent   Person viewed by a child as being his/her parental figure from a psychological or emotional standpoint as opposed to a birth relationship; if a boy were being raised by his grandparents and rarely sees his mother, they would be his psychological parents. Many court decisions are being made based on the concept of psychological as opposed to biological parent.

Psychometric instruments   Tests used to measure psychological functioning.

Psychotropic drugs   Used in the treatment of severe mental health problems, including depression and psychoses, which have resulted in major reductions in numbers of individuals with emotional problems needing long-term hospitalization.

Public assistance   Programs that provide income, medical care, and social services to individuals and families based on economic need, paid from state and local taxes, to provide a socially established minimum standard usually set by the state; Aid to Families with Dependent Children (AFDC) and Medicaid are public assistance programs.

Public insurance   Insurance programs provided by the public sector to those in need who are not covered by private insurance programs and meet eligibility requirements, such as Medicaid.

Public sector   Includes programs and agencies funded and operated by government entities, including public schools, agencies, and hospitals.

Relative poverty   A less stringent definition of poverty than official poverty, which suggests that classifying a person or family as poor should take into consideration factors in addition to cash income and family size and should allow for comparison of that person's or family's well-being relative to others in similar circumstances, such as age, family size, and possessions such as home ownership.

Residential treatment center   Facility that provides 24-hour care with a treatment component for persons with mental health problems or developmental disabilities such as alcoholism; such programs are usually considered to be less restrictive than psychiatric hospitals.

Residual programs Temporary programs established when first-line institutions fail to meet the expected needs of individuals and families; e.g., federal relief programs established during the Depression.

Reverse discrimination Acts that result in unequal treatment of majority group members.

Secondary prevention Targeted at subpopulations determined to be "at risk," or more likely to experience a specific problem, to prevent the problem from occurring.

Secondary setting Setting in which the types of services a professional provides differ from the primary focus of the setting; e.g. a social worker in a hospital works in a secondary setting while a social worker in a social services agency works in a primary setting.

Self-concept The image that one has of one's self in relation to appearance, ability, skills, motivation, and capacity to react to the environment; derived primarily from feedback from others.

Self-help group Group of individuals with similar problems that meets for the purpose of providing support and information to each other and for mutual problem-solving; Parents Anonymous and Alcoholics Anonymous are examples of self-help groups.

Senior Citizens luncheon programs Publicly-sponsored programs that provide nutritious meals for senior citizens either by delivery to persons in their own homes or by providing meals in a community center, often with special socialization activities also provided.

Sexism Discrimination against an individual because of gender.

Sexual abuse The use of a child by an adult for sexual or emotional gratification in a sexual way, such as fondling, exposure, sexual intercourse, and exploitation, including child pornography.

Single-parent family Family headed by one parent, usually a female.

Social agencies Organizations whose primary focus is to address social problems.

Social casework A social work method involving face-to-face contact with individuals, families, or groups where the social worker provides services directly to clients for the purpose of resolving problems, also referred to as direct practice.

Social groupwork A social work method involving intervention with groups of individuals that uses structured interaction to promote individual and group functioning and well-being.

Social insurance Financial assistance for those whose income has been curtailed due to retirement, death or long-term disability of the family breadwinner; paid to former working persons or their dependents through a tax on earned income.

Social Security Act Major social welfare legislation passed by Congress in 1935 which established social insurance programs based on taxes paid by working persons; public assistance programs to provide for those who do not qualify for social insurance programs and cannot provide for themselves or their families financially; and health and welfare services for children, families, the disabled, and the aged such as child welfare services, maternal and child health services, and services for the disabled.

Social welfare Efforts organized by societies to facilitate the well-being of their members, usually focused on activities that seek to prevent, alleviate, or contribute to the solution of a selected set of social problems.

Social work The major profession that implements planned change activities prescribed by social welfare institutions through intervention with individuals, families and groups or at community, organizational, and societal levels to enhance or restore social functioning.

Social worker A member of the social work profession who works with individuals, families, groups, organizations, communities, or societies to improve social functioning.

Socialization The process of learning to become a social being; the acquisition of knowledge, values, abilities, and skills that are essential to function as a member of the society within which the individual lives.

Specialized (expert) professional level of social work practice Level of practice which includes mastery in at least one knowledge and skill area (e.g., child and family or aging) as well as general social work knowledge; requires a MSW degree from an accredited social work program.

Special needs child Child who is available for adoption but is considered difficult to place because of special needs; special needs children are older, members of minority groups, members of large sibling groups, and/or have physical and emotional disabilities.

Specific deterrent Program or sentence targeted at an individual to discourage him/her from repeating inappropriate/illegal behavior.

Spillover effect Occurs when feelings, attitudes and behaviors from one domain in a person's life have a positive or a negative impact on other domains; e.g., from the workplace to the family.

Strategy Broad, long-range plan for implementing a program or policy.

Substitute care Out-of-home care provided for children when parents are unwilling or unable to provide care in their own homes; types of substitute care include foster care, group home care, and residential treatment, and are determined based on the needs of the child.

Supplemental Security Income (SSI) Program administered in conjunction with the Social Security Program to provide cash assistance to needy aged, blind, and/or permanently and totally disabled persons who meet certain eligibility standards established by state and federal regulations.

Synergy The combined energy of smaller parts of a larger system that is greater than the sum of the energy of those parts.

Systems/ecological framework Major framework used to understand individual, family, community, organizational, and societal events and behaviors which emphasizes the interactions and interdependence between individuals and their environments.

Tactics Specific, often day-to-day, plan for implementing a program or policy.

Tertiary prevention Efforts targeted at individuals who have already experienced a specific problem to prevent that problem from re-occurring.

Testable The ability of a theory to be measured accurately and validly.

Theory A way of organizing facts or sets of facts to describe, explain or predict events.

U.S. Children's Bureau The first federal department established by the federal government (1912) to address the needs of children and families; programs addressing problems of child abuse and neglect, runaway youth, adoption and foster care, and other child welfare services are currently operated by the Children's Bureau, which is part of the U.S. Department of Health and Human Services.

U.S. Department of Agriculture Federal department that oversees the food stamp program and houses the Agricultural Extension Service, which provides services targeted to rural areas.

U.S. Department of Health and Human Services Federal department that oversees the implementation of legislation relating to health and human services, including public assistance programs, child welfare services, and services for the elderly.

Values Assumptions, convictions, or beliefs about the manner in which people should behave and the principles that should govern behavior.

Voluntary sector Third sector of society, along with the public and for-profit proprietary sectors; the voluntary sector includes private, nonprofit social agencies.

Index